D1462357

Economic Planning,
East and West

Economic Planning, East and West

Edited and with an introduction by
Morris Bornstein

76BTD830X

HD
82
,E2873

Ballinger Publishing Company ● **Cambridge, Mass.**
A Subsidiary of J.B. Lippincott Company

This book is printed on recycled paper.

Copyright © 1975 by Ballinger Publishing Company. All rights reserved. No part of this publication may be reproduced, stored in a retrieval system, or transmitted in any form or by any means, electronic mechanical photocopy, recording or otherwise, without the prior written consent of the publisher.

International Standard Book Number: 0-88410-283-1

Library of Congress Catalog Card Number: 75-20470

Printed in the United States of America

Library of Congress Cataloging in Publication Data
Main entry under title:

Economic planning, east and west.

Revised papers from a conference conducted by the comparative economics program at the University of Michigan; held in Oct. 1973 at the Rockefeller Foundation Study and Conference Center, Bellagio, Italy.
  Includes index.
  1. Economic policy—Congresses. 2. Comparative economics—Congresses.
I. Bornstein, Morris, 1927-   II. Michigan University.
HD82.E2873   330.9   75-20470
ISBN 0-88410-283-1

Table of Contents

List of Tables

Preface

Economic planning is a complex social process affecting many aspects of welfare, including the level and composition of output, the rate and pattern of economic growth, economic freedoms, economic security, the distribution of income and wealth, and the state of the environment. The nature, extent, and success of economic planning are therefore among the most prominent topics in the comparison of nations and economic systems, particularly of the predominantly "centrally planned" economies of the East and the chiefly "market-oriented" economies of the West.

This book examines and compares national economic planning in East and West from both theoretical and empirical standpoints, in the belief that neither approach alone is adequate for an understanding of the potentialities, problems, achievements, and lessons of economic planning. Chapter 1 provides an introduction to the nature of economic planning and major current issues discussed in this volume. Chapters 2–5 analyze selected problems of economic planning, including its social and political bases, intertemporal aspects, methods of dealing with the uncertain future, and the application of advanced mathematical techniques. Chapters 6–9 then consider these and other features of economic planning in comprehensive and systematic case studies of selected Western and Eastern economies—France, Japan, Poland, and Hungary. Each chapter is supplemented by discussants' comments.

For this project the Comparative Economics Program at the University of Michigan assembled a team of specialists in economic planning from nine countries. Draft versions of the papers were discussed intensively at a four-day working conference in October 1973 at the Rockefeller Foundation Study and Conference Center, Bellagio, Italy. In light of the discussion at the conference, the papers were subsequently revised for publication in this volume.

We are grateful to the Ford Foundation for financial support of the Comparative Economics Program, and to the Rockefeller Foundation and the

Joint Committee on Eastern Europe of the American Council of Learned Societies and the Social Science Research Council for their support of the Bellagio Conference. Thanks are also due to Mrs. Phyllis J. Romo for expert assistance in arrangements for the conference and in the preparation of the manuscript for this book.

This volume is the third in a series resulting from research conferences conducted by the Comparative Economics Program at the University of Michigan. The earlier volumes are *Comparison of Economic Systems: Theoretical and Methodological Approaches,* ed. Alexander Eckstein (Berkeley and Los Angeles: University of California Press, 1971), and *Plan and Market: Economic Reform in Eastern Europe,* ed. Morris Bornstein (New Haven and London: Yale University Press, 1973).

Economic Planning,
East and West

Chapter One

Introduction

Morris Bornstein

National economic planning is a broad, complex, and varied phenomenon reflecting not only the respective sociopolitical system but also the size, structure, and level of economic development of the particular country. As a result, planning has many facets, and a comparison of national experience requires some general framework. The first section of this chapter provides such a framework by examining the concepts, structure, and process of national economic planning.

In the light of this framework, the second section then considers how national economic planning in East and West deals with selected major current issues which are the focus of this book. They include the relationship of economic planning to the social system, the nature and coordination of plans of different time horizons, the handling of uncertainty inherent in planning for the future, and the use of advanced mathematical techniques. This section explains and compares how these issues are analyzed from the theoretical and the empirical standpoints in the chapters which follow.

THE NATURE OF ECONOMIC PLANNING

The nature of economic planning may be analyzed in terms of its essence, differences from related activities, and its various dimensions or facets.

The Concept of Planning

"Planning" (and "economic planning") is one of many terms—like "socialism" and "capitalism"—used by different people (economists, political scientists, politicians, businessmen, trade union officials) with rather different meanings.[1] "Planning" may refer to central control or intervention in some vague sense, to programs of public expenditure (such as annual budgets or the Planning-Programming-Budgeting System attempted in the United States), to detailed target-setting for some or many state-owned enterprises, or to goals or projections characteristic of "indicative" planning. Furthermore, the connotation intended by "planning" may be neutral, laudatory, or pejorative. To some, "planning" conveys order, logic, rationality; to others, it means regulation, control, loss of freedom.[2]

A concise—and ideologically neutral—definition of planning is therefore desirable. A simple but very useful definition is that a "plan" is a program for future action. "Planning" is then the process of preparing such programs, and "national economic planning" refers to such national programs covering economic activities. Thus the three main characteristics of a plan are: (1) that it must involve the future, (2) that it must involve action, and (3) that some agency must be responsible for causing the future action. (Although the plan may not, in fact, be carried out, in whole or in part, nonetheless it is *intended* that it be implemented.)

Planning may be distinguished from several related concepts and activities.[3]

Plans vs. decisions. A "decision" refers to a choice among conflicting (mutually exclusive) alternatives. But it need not involve either the future or action, if it is not accompanied by a program to obtain the preferred alternative in the future. Thus, a plan goes beyond a decision by seeking to implement choices. For instance, a cabinet minister may decide that a 5 percent rate of growth of national product is preferable to the current 4 percent rate but planning does not occur until a program is elaborated to raise the growth rate.

Plans vs. forecasts. "Forecasts" are predictions of future events, which need not involve any action to make them occur or prevent them from occurring. The classic example is a weather forecast. However, forecasting is commonly used in planning. Planners attempt to predict what is likely to happen in the absence of plannned intervention, to decide what they would like to have happen, and to estimate how far the planning organization can go toward achieving what is desired.[4]

Plans vs. policies. A "policy" may be considered a standing plan, i.e., a general guide to future decisionmaking intended to shape those decisions, for example that per capita consumption should grow by 4–6 percent per year. It is, however, possible to have a plan without a policy, when decisions are made about specific situations without any understanding or agreement that future situations will be dealt with in the same way.

Planning vs. intervention. Government intervention in the economy can, and does, occur outside the framework of an integrated, more or less comprehensive plan. For example, as Komiya and Dernberger point out in Chapter 7, the Japanese government has intervened (through tax exemptions, subsidies, tariffs, and low-interest credit) in various branches of industry, often successfully, but not in a coordinated consistent way. Hence, Japanese "planning" must be considered largely "cosmetic," with targets which are intentionally over-optimistic forecasts, are too aggregative to be operational, and are not considered binding on economic policymakers. Similarly in France, as Seibel explains in Chapter 6, many important economic policy decisions are made outside the framework of the national plan, and plans have been abandoned or altered for stabilization reasons. Also, as Höök notes in Chapter 3, the entire area of structural measures to reduce market imperfections is commonly omitted from medium-term plans in Western Europe.

Dimensions of Planning

In order to analyze and compare national plans and planning processes, it is useful to distinguish a number of dimensions or facets of economic planning. These include the sphere, geographical area, comprehensiveness, objectives, significance, intensity, complexity, completeness, flexibility, time span, frequency, degree of decentralization, cost, and methods of implementation of planning.[5]

Sphere. Planning may be conducted by or (although done by some other agency) cover individuals, firms, or governments. Virtually all of the following dimensions apply to each of these spheres.

Geographical area. A plan, whether for a firm or a government, may have regional, national, or international coverage. This aspect is closely related to the question of decentralization in planning discussed below.

Comprehensiveness. The scope of a plan, or the breadth of its influence, depends on the range of activities covered and the number of organizations involved. A common distinction is between the partial planning of capitalist regulated market economies and the more extensive planning of socialist centrally planned economies. In Chapter 2 Lindblom analyzes this question in detail in regard to the differences between "strategic" and "conventional" planning and their relationship to the nature of the society.

Objectives. Among the aims of national economic planning are growth, structural change, stabilization (of output, employment, and the price level), military power, redistribution of income and wealth, and so forth.

Significance. Plans may vary in the significance of the objectives to be achieved. Naturally, this involves a value judgment on which people may disagree, but it is necessary to decide the relative significance of different plans and planning activities in order to determine priorities in the allocation of limited planning resources among, for example, urban renewal, regional development, and export promotion. One measure of significance is the results to be obtained. For example, a regional development plan may reduce unemployment by 15 percent, and an export promotion plan by only 10 percent. Another measure is the strategic nature of a plan or subplan. In a national plan there are various components, some of which are more important than others for the success of the plan as a whole. For instance, fulfillment of the plan for steel production may be more critical than achievement of the plan for housing construction. The changing relative significance of objectives in national plans in France, Japan, Poland, and Hungary is examined in Chapters 6–9.

Intensity. A plan (or component of a plan) may be elaborated in greater or lesser detail. For example, plans may be more aggregative in nature, dealing with sectors or branches, but not individual products or firms, as in Western Europe; or more detailed, covering quantity and assortment of output, authorized inputs, prices, and so forth, for individual enterprises, as in Eastern Europe.[6] In the latter, the specificity of planning increases as plans move down the administrative hierarchy from central planning agencies, through ministries and associations of firms, to the producing units. However, in both East and West, the intensity of planning must depend on the relationship between the resources allocated to planning and the comprehensiveness of plans, that is, between the effort and the task to be done. Thus, although Eastern economies devote considerable resources to central planning, the scope of their planning is so large that the intensity of planning for subject matters of relatively low significance (i.e., priority) may in fact be less than the intensity of planning in Western economies where the resources allocated to planning are concentrated on fewer activities. The appropriate intensity of planning is analyzed by Lindblom in Chapter 2, and changes in intensity resulting from economic reform in Hungary are examined by Morva in Chapter 9.

Complexity. A number of factors affect the complexity of a plan (and the planning process). (1) The more comprehensive the plan, the greater the number of logically distinct parts which must be coordinated. (2) Some components of the plan may be related, and thus coordinated, in relatively straightforward ways (such as estimation of average wage bills from the size and composition of the labor force and wage rates). Other relationships may be much more complex, with successive effects on other sectors and feedback effects. (3) The larger the number of alternatives to be considered within a particular component of a plan, the more complex the overall planning process becomes. For instance, in the early stages of an industrialization drive, a relatively small set of industries may be regarded as major claimants for investment funds, whereas in later stages more industries compete for available resources.

(4) Complexity also depends on the number of variables or factors to be taken into account in choosing among alternatives for each decision. Thus, planning is less complex if investment decisions are based only on the rate of return (or recoupment period), rather than (also) on location preferences, use of particular scarce materials, and other considerations.[a] (5) Finally, complexity is affected by the extent to which (a component of) a plan involves specialized technical information. Thus, planning the assortment of instrument production is more complex than planning the distribution of the labor force to make it. In Chapter 5, Augustinovics compares how the traditional and the newer mathematical methods attempt to cope with various aspects of complexity in planning.

Completeness. A "complete" plan includes all the components and information necessary for a sound decision on whether it should be adopted or rejected, and for subsequent successful implementation. What constitutes completeness clearly depends on such other dimensions as comprehensiveness, intensity, complexity, and time. Plans may be incomplete for various reasons. (1) The original plan directives may suffer from ambiguity, which is subsequently exposed by the delivery of a plan formulated according to them. (2) The plan may be prepared by unqualified personnel. (3) Inadequate funds or specialized resources (e.g., computation facilities) may be allotted to the planning agency. (4) Insufficient time may be allowed for the preparation of the plan. (5) Some relevant information may be unattainable, either because it does not exist (e.g., consumer demand schedules fifteen years hence) or because the cost and time required are prohibitive (e.g., a much more disaggregated input-output table). The completeness attainable by different methods of planning is examined by Augustinovics in Chapter 5, while Radner analyzes different strategies for handling uncertainty about the future in Chapter 4.

Flexibility. It is desirable to be able to modify plans to take advantage of addtional information obtained either after the plan is drawn up but before it is implemented, or during the period of implementation. This information may include changes in objectives, the availability of resources, and exogenous elements (such as the effect of the weather on the harvest), as well as an uneven pattern of plan fulfillment. Flexibility in planning depends on several factors. (1) The greater the significance of a particular target, the less readily it will be altered. (2) The more nearly homogeneous or mobile a resource, the more easily it can be transferred to another use. For this purpose the standardization of parts or models may be preferable to specialization, with some sacrifice of performance characteristics in return for a gain in flexibility. Examples include

[a]The number of choices in (3) or variables in (4) depends on the number and content of the objectives of the plan and also on the existence and coverage of policies which provide standing criteria for choice.

the production of multipurpose rather than specialized trucks, and the broader rather than more specialized training of engineers. (3) Flexibility is greater if different parts of a plan are relatively independent in time or subject matter. In regard to time, flexibility exists if two phases of a project are more or less separate and a future decision not to undertake the second phase does not jeopardize the first. For example, a project may include two rail lines to be built at different times, but if the second line is not constructed this will not hamper the operation of the first. Similarly, independence of subject matter makes it possible to alter or even terminate one part of a plan without adversely affecting another, because the latter is not closely linked, e.g., when curtailment of steel output has little effect on shoe production (or vice versa).

(4) Flexibility is gained by provision in plans for alternate courses of action. Alternate plans ("variants") may actually be formulated, with the choice among them deferred for a decision in the future in light of conditions prevailing then, or resources (the more nearly homogeneous the better) may be left uncommitted, as "reserves" to be used where future circumstances dictate. (5) Finally, flexibility depends also on the rigidity of the planning process itself—on how quickly and successfully it can modify plans to meet new conditions. This in turn is a function of the organizational structure, personnel, and techniques of the planning agency. Theoretical literature on flexibility in planning is examined by Radner in Chapter 4, while Polish experience with "open" plans is discussed by Porwit in Chapter 8.

Time. The time dimension has two aspects: (1) the length of the period covered by a plan, and (2) the amount of time to prepare and implement a plan.

It is conventional to distinguish among three planning periods: short-term, a year or less; medium-term, four–five years; and long-term (or "perspective"), ten–fifteen or even twenty years. On the one hand, longer-term plans provide a framework within which shorter-term plans should be elaborated; on the other, longer-term plans represent the desired cumulative result of shorter-term plans. These issues are discussed further in the second section, below.

Planning involves a number of time-consuming steps: decisions on objectives, data collection, analysis of data and decisions on the content of the plan, coordination of these decisions with other agencies, approval of the plan by the authorizing organization, communication of the plan to implementing agencies, and implementation of the plan. The amount of time needed to prepare a plan depends on such dimensions as its comprehensiveness, intensity, complexity, and completeness. The implementation of some plans may begin as soon as they are approved (or indeed in anticipation of approval). Other plans may be approved for contingent implementation if circumstances warrant in the future. In this case, additional time is involved because of several types of "response lags": the lag between the need for action and recognition of it, the lag between recognition and taking action, and the lag between action and its effects.

Methods and problems of plan preparation and plan implementation are discussed in the case studies of Eastern and Western planning experience in Chapters 6–9.

Frequency. A closely related dimension is frequency, i.e., the number of times a plan is prepared. A plan for the construction of an individual factory will ordinarily be prepared only once. Some plans, such as for production, will be prepared periodically—monthly, annually, or every five years. Other plans will be drawn up more than once but irregularly, as relevant circumstances change, for example, when a large increase in the price of imported oil leads to a new plan for domestic energy production.

Planning may be regarded as a "continuous" process in either of two senses. First, the planning agency will always be working on *some* plan, whether on the execution and revision of the current plan or on the preparation of the plan for the next period. Second, the planning agency may prepare "sliding" or "rolling" plans. For instance, a new five-year plan might be drawn up each year covering the next five years: in 1971 for 1972–76; in 1972, for 1973–77; and so forth. The appropriate frequencies of plans and the feasibility of "sliding" plans are discussed further in the second section, below.

Decentralization. This dimension refers to the sharing of responsibility for planning among different levels of a hierarchical organization. There are various possible degrees of decentralization in relation both to the number of levels involved and to the distribution of authority and responsibility among them.

The arguments for decentralization in planning are essentially the same as those for decentralization in administration and operations.[7] (1) Decentralization reduces delay and inaccuracy in the transmission of information from the point of collection to the point of decisionmaking. (2) It also decreases the volume and cost of information processing, (3) It permits faster and sounder adaption to changing conditions of demand, resources, or technology. (4) It leads to the resolution of conflicts at lower levels (and perhaps more on economic than political grounds). (5) It frees central planners from details they are not qualified to handle and enables them to concentrate instead on critical major decisions which they alone can make. (6) Although errors in planning will occur under a more centralized or a more decentralized system, the possibility for very large mistakes may be smaller under a more decentralized scheme. If many agents (regional governmental units, enterprises, households) make decisions, they partly neutralize each other, so that incorrect decisions by some are offset by correct decisions by others.[8]

On the other hand, decentralization of planning may be limited for several reasons. (1) It may be feared that decentralized planning will yield different results from more centralized planning, because of problems involved in communicating the objectives and preferences of higher authorities to lower levels, and motivating the latter to accept, identify with, and strive for those objectives. (2) In addition, centralization of planning may concentrate scarce personnel and resources (including data processing equipment) where they are needed most, although the higher levels still depend on lower levels for information required in the planning process.

The extent of decentralization will be affected by other dimensions of planning, including the geographic area, significance, intensity, and complexity. The bigger the geographic area, the more likely that the problems to be handled by planning will vary spatially (e.g., labor supply), and some decentralization may therefore be considered desirable. Components of plans which are not considered so important are more likely to be entrusted to lower levels of the hierarchy (e.g., the production of clothing vs. the output of aircraft). The more detailed the plan, the greater the need for decentralization (e.g., the assortment of women's clothing). Finally, planning responsibility is less likely to be decentralized for those parts of a plan which are closely tied to other parts which the central authorities wish to plan (e.g., steel production, because of its connection with machine building).

The distribution of planning responsibilities among different levels of government is examined in each of the case studies in Chapters 6–9.

Cost. The cost of planning may be expressed in various ways, including the money bill for the operation of the planning apparatus; the use of scarce human, material, computational, and foreign exchange resources; the burden on the economy from the disincentive and distorting effects of taxes to finance planning activities; and the cost to other organizations and enterprises of supplying information to the planning agency. The cost of planning will depend on such other dimensions of planning as comprehensiveness, intensity, frequency, and the time allowed for the preparation of plans (it may be more expensive to draw up a given plan more quickly).

As in the case of other economic activities, the cost of planning should be evaluated in relation to the benefits—i.e., the extent to which desired objectives (for example, regarding the rate of growth of national product) are accomplished, compared to what would have occurred in the absence of planning. In this respect, planning may show decreasing returns, if the gains attributable to planning do not rise in proportion to the additional effort devoted to increasing the comprehensiveness or intensity of planning.[9] Further intervention through more planning may hurt the economy, for example when central planners make decisions on such detailed questions as product mix and product characteristics which are not as sound as the decisions which enterprises, if permitted, would make in response to market forces. These considerations have limited the extent of planning in Western economies, as the case studies of France and Japan in Chapters 6 and 7 show, and have led to the changes in the scope of central planning in Poland and Hungary explained in Chapters 8 and 9.

Methods of implementation. Several approaches to the implementation of plans may be distinguished. (1) The "information" approach of "indicative" planning expects that plans will, at least in part, be "self-realizing" because they contain the best forecast of what is likely to happen and therefore profit-seeking autonomous firms will adjust their decentralized decisions about production and investment accordingly. (2) The "steering" approach attempts to induce decentralized economic agents (firms and households) to fulfill a plan by altering the market conditions they face in their independent decisions about production, investment, employment, and consumption. It uses 'indirect" or "aggregative" fiscal and monetary measures (taxes, government expenditures, regulation of interest rates and the supply of money and credit) to affect demand, supply, and prices. (3) Under the "administrative" approach, government agencies issue orders to subordinate organizations, enterprises, and households authorizing or commanding maximum or minimum behavior. They use such "direct" instruments as production quotas; allocation of materials, equipment, labor, and foreign exchange; rationing of consumer goods; and fixing of prices and wage rates.

All three approaches are found in contemporary economies, and their relative importance differs according to the nature of the economic and social system, as Lindblom shows in Chapter 2. The "information" approach is sometimes thought to play a significant role in French planning, but, as Seibel explains in Chapter 6, little reliance is in fact placed upon it in France. The "steering" approach is dominant in Western market economies, and its active use is illustrated in Komiya's discussion of Japanese experience in Chapter 7. The "administrative" approach is associated with the centrally planned economies of Eastern Europe, although they also make considerable use of the "steering" approach. The different, and changing, combinations of these two approaches in Poland and Hungary are analyzed by Porwit and Morva in Chapters 8 and 9, respectively.

ISSUES IN ECONOMIC PLANNING

With this comprehensive view of the nature and main features of national economic planning, we now turn to an examination of a number of issues discussed from various standpoints in the following chapters. These include the social bases of planning, appropriate time horizons, the treatment of uncertainty, the technology of planning, and emerging trends in East and West.

Economic Planning and Social System

To what extent are the nature and ambitions of economic planning a function of the social system? In Chapter 2, Lindblom compares two fundamentally different approaches to planning and identifies the social frameworks with which they might be associated. The case studies of two Western and two Eastern planning experiences in Chapters 6–9 then provide a test of these relationships.

According to Lindblom, one approach to planning intensively analyzes social objectives and resources available to meet them and then works out a detailed program of resource allocation to achieve those objectives to the maximum extent possible. He labels this approach "conventional" planning because most of the literature on economic planning deals with it. In contrast, "strategic" planning eschews such detail and instead concentrates on formulating a process to cope with any one of a large variety of possible situations which may appear in the future. This approach is concerned with planning "not directly the solution to a problem but instead the development of a capacity to invent a solution tailored to the particular form in which the problem eventually appears." Thus, for example, the "strategic" approach involves planning market structure, enterprise size, the rules of competition, and the distribution of income and wealth, rather than the allocation of resources directly.

Lindblom suggests that an analogous contrast exists between the "intellectually guided" society and the "preference guided" society. In the former, an intellectually superior elite—endowed with wisdom and vision, possessing a monopoly of political power, and believing in the existence of inherent harmony among the needs and wants of the citizenry—undertakes to achieve what is best for society, through comprehensive direction of economic and social life. In the latter, harmony is considered not only undiscoverable but nonexistent, and conflict among preferences is assumed. Institutions and policies emerge in the political sphere as a result of bargaining among interest groups, and in the economic sphere through the interplay of market forces. This social interaction is regarded as an essential problem-solving device, and therefore procedures for interaction are highly valued in themselves.

The "conventional" approach to planning is thus more logical in the "intellectually guided" society, and the "strategic" approach in the "preference guided" society.[10] It may also be tempting to associate the former pair with Eastern socialist centrally planned economies and the latter with Western capitalist regulated market economies. For example, Eastern socialist regimes consider comprehensive and detailed national economic planning the appropriate vehicle for economic and social development, as the discussions of Polish and Hungarian planning in Chapters 8 and 9 show. In contrast, in Western economies, the scope and ambitions of planning are more modest, and it is not expected that the entire society will accept and cooperate in the national plan, as Chapters 6 and 7 explain in regard to France and Japan.

However, it would be a gross oversimplification to think of Eastern socialist economies as engaged only in "conventional" planning, and Western market economies practicing only "strategic" planning. Instead, both approaches to planning, as well as elements of both the "intellectually guided" and the "preference guided" society, are found in all countries. Lindblom's paradigm is thus intended as an analytical framework to study different economies, rather than as a classification of them. On the one hand, there is a considerable amount of "strategic" planning and bargaining among interest groups in Eastern socialist economies (as Chapters 5, 8, and 9 show). On the other, much "conventional" planning is conducted both by national governments (sometimes under the label of "industrial policy," as Chapters 6 and 7 explain for France and Japan) and by large corporations.

Indeed, one aspect of "strategic" planning is the decentralization of responsibility for some "conventional" planning, from the national government either to regional governments or to enterprises themselves.

In the case of regional planning, a major issue is whether planning should be "from the bottom up" or "from the top down," as Höök explains in Chapter 3. The former method starts with regional plans and proceeds to national plans. It is usually rejected as impractical because of the lack of sufficient data on a regional basis for consumption, production, investment, exports, and imports. The latter method, which disaggregates the national plan into regional components, is therefore more commonly used in both East and West. However, it also faces some serious problems. First, uncertainty increases very sharply when national aggregates are broken down for small units, aggravating the problems discussed by Radner in Chapter 4. Second, a commitment to regional goals may represent a constraint on the achievement of a national goal. For instance, it may be harder to meet a national (un)employment target if restrictions are also imposed on regional employment levels or their dispersion from the national average. Regional planning is still in its early stages and success has been limited in both France and Japan, as Chapters 6 and 7 explain. In Poland and Hungary (see Chapters 8 and 9), the administrative implementation of detailed plans has required some regional disaggregation, but explicity regional development planning—for example, covering land use patterns, urban growth, and the like—is less advanced than national planning.[11]

In Western market economies, national governments tend to concentrate on "strategic" planning, and large private enterprises on "conventional" planning, although governments and firms in fact do both kinds.[12] However, corporate planning is done in the light of government planning and intervention. Thus, the aim of "indicative" planning is for national economic plans to provide a projection of economic activity which will guide enterprises in the formulation of their own plans. But the influence of such an "indicative" plan depends both on the nature and extent of enterprise planning (as Seibel notes in Chapter 6 on France) and on the credibility of government plans (as Komiya discusses in Chapter 7 on Japan).

In Eastern Europe, economic reforms in the last decade have sought greater flexibility and efficiency in resource allocation, through two different types of decentralization. In Poland, as Porwit explains in Chapter 8, the emphasis has been on administrative decentralization designed to improve the functioning of central planning. In Hungary, as Morva shows in Chapter 9, the approach was greater "marketization" intended to reduce the scope and role of central planning and to increase the sphere of enterprise decision making in response to market forces. Yet, as Thornton's comments stress, both the Polish and the Hungarian systems are compromises: Poland's adminstratively decentralized planning scheme has many market elements (especially in relation to foreign trade and agriculture), whereas in Hungary considerable central direction operates through the regulation of investment, taxes and subsidies, and price control.

Time Horizons

How long a period should a plan cover? The basic theoretical principle is to include in a plan for a particular period those variables which can and should be affected by economic policy measures during that span of time, and to exclude what cannot be effectively altered during the period. Thus, the greater the extent to which a plan is a genuine action program for a government, the shorter its period will tend to be. In contrast, if the main aim of the plan is a political declaration, the "planning period" will tend to be much longer and the specification of promised concrete actions much vaguer (as Komiya shows in his discussion of Japanese planning in Chapter 7).

Short-term plans. These plans commonly have a period of one year, connected with the annual government budget cycle (and also in some countries with the agricultural harvest). Traditionally in Eastern centrally planned economies, annual planning was supposed to set forth a detailed program of directives intended to accomplish that year's part of a medium-term (five-year) plan. However, in both Poland and Hungary (as Chapters 8 and 9 explain) the emphasis in annual planning has shifted in recent years toward the analysis of fluctuations, disequilibria, and tensions in the economy—of domestic or foreign origin—and the formulation of corrective tax, credit, price, and foreign trade and exchange measures. Thus, to some extent, "current" planning in these countries has become more like the monetary and fiscal policy making of Western market economies, although the latter eschew "annual plans" on the ground that they imply a closer control over the private sector that is compatible with their economic systems.

Medium-term plans. These plans usually cover four or five years, to take into account the average length of the business cycle (from trough to trough or peak to peak) and the gestation period of major investment projects (from conception to entry into production). The aim of medium-term plans, whether in Poland and Hungary or in France and Norway, is to accomplish structural changes, chiefly by affecting investment. As Höök notes in Chapter 3, there is less uncertainty in the medium term than in either the short term or the long term. On the one hand, short-term plans are vulnerable to cyclical fluctuations or movements in the balance of payments. On the other, it is difficult to estimate long-term changes in the labor force, the capital stock, production techniques, and so forth. Similarly, in Chapter 9 Morva argues that five years should be the basic planning period because it is short enough to permit a sensible assessment of economic conditions and prospects and to formulate reasonable targets, and long enough to carry out the necessary implementing measures.

Long-term plans. These plans for 15 or more years—such as those described for Poland in Chapter 8 and for Hungary in Chapters 5 and 9—must inevitably be less comprehensive and detailed, as well as more qualitative and less quantitative, than medium-term or annual plans. Long-term plans may be drawn up but not formally adopted by the government in the same way as shorter-term plans. For these reasons, Höök suggests in Chapter 3, "perspective studies" may be a more appropriate name for these documents.[13]

When plans of different time horizons are drawn up, an effort must be made to link them. The Hungarian practice, explained by Morva in Chapter 9, is to extend the time horizon of the plan beyond its nominal limit. Thus, short-term plans covering a year are in fact prepared with a perspective of two—three years, five-year plans involve calculations for up to ten years for some aspects, and long-term plans for fifteen—twenty years include projections in some fields for twenty-five—thirty years.

However, as Porwit points out in Chapter 8, plans with longer time horizons cannot be viewed simply as the sum of interlinked plans for shorter periods. Because they differ in nature and tasks, their methodologies also differ. Polish planners have found no easy or straightforward ways of linking and reconciling short-term (static) and longer-term (dynamic) criteria of efficiency. They do not expect that a series of short-term optimizations will necessarily lead to the desired path of development, nor that it is possible to determine detailed time schedules extending far into the future and to subordinate short-term actions to them.

In addition to these methodological problems, common to East and West, the problem of linking shorter- and longer-term planning is complicated in Western Europe by the division of responsibility among government agencies. Typically, short-term planning is done by the Ministry of Finance, which has major responsibility for stabilization of output, employment, and the price level through taxes and public expenditures. Medium-term planning may be performed by a separate agency, as in France or Japan, or not at all. Usually, no agency has responsibility for long-term planning, although "perspective studies" may be done by government and private research organizations.

Handling Uncertainty

The uncertainty inherent in the future limits the capability of planning to shape the development of the economy. Two types of uncertainty are involved:

uncertainty about the "environment" (resource supplies, technology, and so forth), and uncertainty about behavior of agents in the eonomic system (enterprise managers, workers, consumers). Although these two classes of uncertainty may be distinguished conceptually, in practice they are closely linked. For example, a major task in the construction (and revision) of plans is the generation and exchange of information among levels in the administrative hierarchy. For bargaining reasons, some units (e.g., firms) may distort information, understating resources and overstating costs. Thus, any plausible theory of planning must be one of "bounded rationality" which recognizes constraints on the capacity of planners to acquire and to process information, as Radner points out in Chapter 4.

The theory of national planning under uncertainty is still in its infancy and can at most give only some insights into general features of planning problems. The literature, summarized and evaluated by Radner in Chapter 4, deals with the characterization of optimal paths, optimal decision rules, and procedures for calculating optimal allocations, such as dynamic programming. The specific models and solution procedures require highly restrictive assumptions, a multitude of sophisticated data, and very complex calculations. Radner concludes that optimal planning under uncertainty calls for "rolling" or "sliding" plans—i.e., sequential planning strategies which involve updating plans as new information about the environment and the economic system becomes available.[14] As a reasonable approximation to an optimal strategy, Radner proposes that planners follow a "certainty-equivalent" approach, by making decisions for each new period on the basis of expected values of random variables, and to that extent ignoring their stochastic character.

However, the frequency, comprehensiveness, and accuracy of such sequential updating must depend on the information involved, the extent of change in it, and costs of information collection and processing. In Western market economies subject to business cycle fluctuations, it may be unwise to adjust medium-term plans annually, because of the difficutly of distinguishing between cyclical movements and actual trend changes. As Morva explains in Chapter 9, Hungarian planners have concluded that, although it is useful to extend long-term plans for another five years after each five-year plan is completed, it is not feasible or desirable to "roll" the medium-term plan annually. First, preparation of a new five-year plan takes two to three years. Second, annual revision of the five-year plan would interfere with the objective of providing a stable framework for application of "economic regulators" and for the preparation by enterprises of their own plans. Therefore, Hungarian planners prefer to deal with new information bearing upon the five-year plan, not by revising it annually, but by reviewing fulfillment and problems at the mid-point (i.e., during the third year) of the plan period. The results of this review affect both the annual plans for the last two years of that five-year plan period and the preparation of the new plan for the next five-year period. A similar commitment to revision, as appropriate, underlies the Polish concept of "open" plans discussed by Porwit in Chapter 8.

One way to gain flexibility to deal with the uncertain future is to prepare multiple plan variants involving different assumptions about constraints in the economic environment, so that the chosen variant can be replaced by another if new conditions dictate. Another approach is to adopt more cautious plans which provide reserves (for example, uncommitted stocks or flows of commodities and foreign exchange), so random shocks do not create bottlenecks whose effects, spreading through the economy, may far exceed the size of the initial disturbance, as Portes explains in his comments on Chapter 4.

Given the constraints on the quantity, speed, and accuracy of information reaching the central planners about the economic environment and plan fulfillment, another source of flexibility is to adapt the process of plan construction and plan implementation. The government may move more toward "strategic" planning, by allowing lower units to make decentralized decisions as new information becomes available to them, although under constraints and rules prescribed by the central authorities. This is consistent with the emphasis, in the theoretical literature on planning under uncertainty, on formulating optimal policies and decision rules.[15] Such an approach recognizes that informational decentralization leads to de facto, and logically also de jure, decentralization of authority. These problems are discussed from a theoretical standpoint by Radner and Portes in Chapter 4, while Porwit explains recent Polish experience in Chapter 8.

In contrast, the theory of "indicative" planning rests on the principle that the central authorities should provide information, in the form of a comprehensive forecast of the future economic environment, to guide decentralized decision-makers. In the purest version of this theory, planners attempt to make forecasts of prices and quantities such that, if the various economic decisionmakers believe these forecasts, they will behave in such a way as to fulfill them.[16]

However, various case studies indicate that this approach is of limited success in practice. In Chapter 6, Seibel concludes that in France the effect of indicative planning on the private sector has been weak and that it is not appropriate to speak of a "self-validating" forecast. In Japan, Komiya finds in Chapter 7, the national economic plan should be regarded as "a long-term forecast with some flavor of wishful thinking of plan makers as far as its quantitative aspects are concerned" and similar to a long-range weather forecast. Thus it is not surprising that the Japanese plan is often disregarded not only by the private sector but also by the major government agencies making economic policy, such as the Ministry of International Trade and Industry and the Ministry of Finance. Nor has British experience been encouraging.[17]

As Morva explains in Chapter 9, under a system of comprehensive and detailed administrative control of the economy, it is not useful to distinguish between planning and forecasting. In Hungary, forecasts as estimates of future economic trends acquired significance only after the 1968 reform stressed medium-term over annual plans and introduced greater autonomy for enterprises to decide their input, output, and investment programs in a market setting influenced by "economic regulators" (rather than following detailed instructions from their administrative superiors). Under the reform, central planning agencies are obliged to inform enterprises at regular intervals of economic trends, results and problems in the fulfillment of the national plan, and future plans—as a basis for the enterprises' own planning. However, in practice the role of forecasts remains limited, and they are not a regular tool of planning. In Poland too, forecasting is in its early stages, as Porwit discusses in Chapter 8.

The Technology of Planning

The choice of planning methods not only is a technical question for specialists but also has wide political implications in regard to the distribution of power among planning agencies, industry and sector groups, and regional interests. The issues may be seen by considering "traditional" versus "mathematical" methods of planning and the problems involved in integrating them.

As Augustinovics explains in Chapter 5, the "traditional" approach (to what Lindblom calls "conventional" planning) involves the preparation of detailed plans for many important types of economic activity and the coordination of the major direct relations among these plans by "balancing" techniques, such as material balances. This coordination is carried out largely by a man-man (as opposed to a man-machine) system, in which people act on behalf of larger or smaller units (which in turn represent sectoral, branch, or regional constituencies). The procedure is iterative in nature, with iterations between provisional plans for parts and for the economy as a whole, between past and future, between what is "given" and what is still open for decisions, between "physical" and "synthetic" (value) consistency, and so forth. In this process, the main stream of quantitative information is always upwards from lower levels in the hierarchy, while information flowing downwards is mainly qualitative.

This approach has several disadvantages. (1) It proceeds from a larger to a smaller group of proposals step by step, without a uniform criterion for assessing proposals. What is from one viewpoint an inferior proposal compared to another and is thus omitted from later consideration, could in fact be judged a better one if *all* alternatives could be evaluated at the same time with the same criterion of efficiency. (2) This approach does not yield a simultaneous comprehensive solution. Rather it is devoted mainly to overcoming inconsistencies and producing a complete plan proposal which satisfies constraints and economic policy aims withing reasonable limits and in an acceptable combination. As Morva notes in Chapter 9, this task usually takes all of the time available for preparing the national economic plan. (3) Thus, there is little or no opportunity for planners to present to decisionmaking bodies a number of alternatives for comparison and choice, because most of the primary alternatives have not been worked out, checked for consistency, and evaluated. In short, the "traditional" approach cannot supply alternative, consistent plan-variants covering the economy as a whole.

In contrast, mathematical methods of planning strive to grasp what Augustinovics calls the "total process." They seek to incorporate and systematically combine large numbers of variables and to evaluate alternatives by explicit rigorous criteria. Thus, Augustinovics asserts, the major contribution of linear programming to economic analysis and planning is its ability to generate alternative solutions (for different objective functions and constraints) which reveal the sensitivity of the system to various preferences and conditions.[18]

Mathematical models thus have several advantages. (1) They trace the entire network of indirect interdependencies. (2) They yield a complete simultaneous solution, so that decisions need not be made separately and hierarchically about parts of the plan. (3) They thereby supply the downward flow of quantitative information often lacking under the traditional approach. (4) Planners can produce a number of consistent variants for the entire system for the consideration of decisionmakers, with whom they can conduct a dialogue about the implications of objectives and constraints.

However, Augustinovics explains, the application of mathematical methods also involves various problems. (1) They appear to demand much new data. Although this information exists in the economy, or perhaps even in the statistical system, it is not available in the particular classification or disaggregation needed for the model. Model builders will also want some data which the planner responsible for a particular segment of the economy considers unnecessary, and they will disregard some information which he deems important. (2) Use of mathematical models thus requires more effort and time than expected to prepare and process the data, proving to be disappointingly labor-intensive and time-consuming. (3) The man-machine methods used to generate consistent comprehensive plans lack some of the personal contact of the man-man methods of plan coordination under the traditional approach. Loss of this contact may, on the one hand, create resistance to the introduction of more sophisticated methods, and, on the other, hamper the reconciliation of interests and priorities necessary to reach agreement on the plan variant which is socially and politically as well as economically most advisable.

Yet integration of the mathematical with the traditional approach is necessary. According the Augustinovics, the first step is to persuade planners to experiment with the new methods, by pointing out their advantages. Next a plan for a particular time period prepared by traditional methods is compared with what the more sophisticated model would produce: better in some respects but inferior in others. Then the use of mathematical models is officially incorporated into the planning process but in an auxiliary capacity. The models supply additional results for the analysis of the past and the future, but plan coordination continues in the traditional way. During this "parallel" phase, the information requirements of the models affect the data collection process of the statistical system. However, progress is slow, because new types of models must be constructed, and new links created between different models, with consequent new demands for information. Furthermore, the new, unified set of statistics must reach far enough back into the past and must be arranged in a data bank accessible by flexible and easy-to-use computer programs.

For these reasons, the introduction of mathematical methods of planning has been slow, as the case studies in Chapters 6–9 explain. In France, input-output tables have been used since the Second Plan (1954–57) and a table of financial consistency since the Fourth Plan (1961–65), but formal model-building did not begin until the FIFI model used in preparing the Sixth Plan (1971–75). In work for the Seventh Plan (1976–80), this model is being developed further, along with models to link national and regional development, and short-and medium-term projections. Japanese planners use econometric models to simulate alternative plan variants with different targets or instruments, but they wish to avoid explicit specification of objectives, preferring simply to choose the plan variant they like best. Although input-output, linear programming, and, to a lesser extent, econometric models have been developed in Poland and Hungary, they still play a supplementary rather than a primary role in planning in those countries. However, the process of integrating mathematical with traditional methods is proceeding as additional trained personnel and computational facilities become available.[19]

Trends in East and West

Economic planning differs substantially in Eastern and Western countries because of important differences in the nature of the socioeconomic system, which are reflected in the conception of economic planning, the role of short- vs. medium-term plans, the methods of plan implementation, and other dimensions of planning. In Eastern planned economies, as Chapters 8 and 9 on Poland and Hungary show, planning is viewed as the overall framework for government guidance of production, investment, and distribution. Planning is detailed and continuous, and planners monitor fulfillment of plans and revise them as necessary. In contrast, in capitalist market economies, national economic planning is less comprehensive and detailed, and much government economic policy is made and executed outside the framework of a national plan, as Chapters 6 and 7 on France and Japan illustrate.

Yet the differences between Eastern and Western economic planning are less than sometimes supposed, and emerging trends may reduce them further. In both East and West, plan-making is a social process of consultation and coordination of sectoral, regional, and occupational interests. In Eastern economies, there is much less "conventional" planning in practice than theoretical models of "planned" economies suggest. At the same time, the extent of their "strategic" planning is greater than often appreciated in the West.

On the other hand, in Western countries, there is considerable "conventional" planning by government agencies in the conduct of public expenditure programs and the regulation of the private sector, as well as by large corporations preparing their own production, investment, and marketing programs.

Furthermore, the relative importance of "strategic" planning appears to be increasing in the East, and that of "conventional" planning growing in the West.

In Eastern Europe, an economic reform movement in the 1960s sought to reduce the comprehensiveness and intensity of central planning, by giving enterprises more responsiblity for output, input, and investment decisions in response to market forces. Both reform blueprints and their subsequent implementation varied from one country to another.[20] The evolution of Polish and Hungarian theory and practice is discussed in Chapters 8 and 9, respectively. In Poland, it was recognized that the practical possibilities for central control were limited, and that many kinds of choices could not in fact be made by the central authorities—i.e., that assertion of central control over these questions would be "illusory." Hence, the Polish government decided that central planning should concentrate on far-reaching structural changes, large investment projects, and income distribution, including the availability of health, education, and other social services. Lower levels of the administrative hierarchy—ministries, associations, and enterprises—should be concerned with what Porwit calls the "microstructure": current decisions on output and input mixes, the introduction of new or improved products or technologies, and other aspects of "X-efficiency." In Hungary, the 1968 reform conceived of the "planned economy" as a combination of central planning and management of the economy as a whole, on the one hand, and market relations among enterprises and between enterprises and households, on the other. The coordination of the two elements—central planning and market relations—is the task of the system of "economic regulators," as Morva explains.

In contrast, the problems of inflation and recession have led to more extensive and detailed government intervention in Western economies in the early 1970s. The measures taken include administrative allocation of scarce supplies, price controls, incomes policies, and public employment programs—all characteristic of "conventional" rather than "strategic" planning. Various Western countries are now involved in short- and medium-term planning, of national and international scope, concerning oil and food supplies and other problems. In addition, the speed and extent of recent changes in international economic relations have stimulated planners and policymakers, in both East and West, to search for better methods of handling uncertainty in preparing plans and adjusting them as circumstances change.

Also common to Eastern and Western planning, as the case studies in Chapters 6–9 show, is new attention to social questions—including the relationship of man to nature (problems of pollution, exhaustion of natural resources, food shortages), the relationship of people to their work (the length of the work week, job satisfaction, retirement age), and the relationship of people to each other (social, cultural, income, and wealth inequalities). Higher priority for social objectives in national economic planning involves not only policy issues ("growth—to what ends and in whose interests?," as Trzeciakowski puts it in his comments on Chapters 6 and 7), but also methodological problems, such as the elaboration of "social indicators" and the formulation of more comprehensive models incorporating these aspects of economic planning.

Thus, the conception, objectives, and techniques of national economic planning are changing in both East and West as countries seek to adapt their planning systems to meet new domestic and international conditions.

NOTES

1. This discussion draws on several basic studies, including Carl Landauer, *Theory of National Economic Planning* (Berkeley: University of California Press; 1st ed., 1944; 2d ed., 1947); John E. Elliott, "Economic Planning Reconsidered," *Quarterly Journal of Economics* 72, 1 (February 1958): 55–76; Preston P. Le Breton and Dale A. Henning, *Planning Theory* (Englewood Cliffs, N.J.: Prentice-Hall, Inc., 1961); Jan Tinbergen, *Central Planning* (New Haven and London: Yale University Press, 1964); and Herbert S. Levine, "On Comparing Planned Economies," in *Comparison of Economic Systems: Theoretical and Methodological Approaches,* ed. Alexander Eckstein (Berkeley and Los Angeles: University of California Press, 1971), pp. 137–60.

2. A classic statement of the latter view is Friedrich A. Hayek, *The Road to Serfdom* (Chicago: University of Chicago Press, 1944).

3. Le Breton and Henning, *Planning Theory,* pp. 7–10.

4. These three types of forecasts have been labeled, respectively, the "reference,""wishful," and "planning" projections by Russell L. Ackoff, *A Concept of Corporate Planning* (New York: John Wiley and Sons, Inc., 1970), pp. 40–41.

5. See Le Breton and Henning, *Planning Theory,* Ch. 2, and Yehezel Dror, *Ventures in Policy Sciences: Concepts and Applications* (New York: American Elsevier Publishing Co., Inc., 1971), pp. 108–17.

6. Thus, Dror, *Ventures in Policy Sciences,* p. 110, calls this dimension the "degree of penetration"—how far planning tries to go into its subject matter.

7. See Gregory Grossman, "Notes for a Theory of the Command Economy," *Soviet Studies* 15, 2 (October 1963): 112–14.

8. Theodore Morgan, "The Theory of Error in Centrally-Directed Economic Systems," *Quarterly Journal of Economics* 78, 3 (August 1964): 400–404.

9. Tinbergen, *Central Planning,* p. 50, and James C. Emery, *Organizational Planning and Control Systems: Theory and Technology* (New York: The Macmillan Co., 1969), p. 149.

10. The "intellectually guided" society would strive much harder for the unattainable "perfect" planning described in Zygmunt Bauman, "The Limitations of 'Perfect Planning,' " *Co-existence* 3, 2 (July 1966): 146–48.

11. On regional planning, see also *Issues in Regional Planning,* ed. D.M. Dunham and I.G.M. Hilhorst (The Hague: Mouton, 1971), and Kevin Allen and Malcolm MacLennan, *Regional Problems and Policies in Italy and France* (London: Allen & Unwin, 1970).

12. On corporate planning, see, for example, Ackoff, *Concept of Corporate Planning;* George A. Steiner, *Top Management Planning* (New York: Macmillan, 1969); and John Snow Schwendiman, *Strategic and Long-Range Planning for the Multinational Corporation* (New York; Praeger Publishers, 1973).

13. See also "The Rationale and Nature of Long-Term Studies and Plans in Europe," *Journal of Development Planning* (United Nations), No. 3 (1971), pp. 1–16; United Nations, Economic Commission for Europe, *Long-Term Planning* (New York: United Nations, 1971); and United Nations, Economic Commission for Europe, *Long-Term Aspects of Plans and Programmes* (New York: United Nations, 1973).

14. For a theoretical exposition of such plans, see Jaroslav Habr, "A Contribution to the Theory of Sliding Plans," in *Problems of Economic Dynamics: Essays in Honour of Michal Kalecki* (Oxford: Pergamon Press; Warsaw: PWN–Polish Scientific Publishers, 1966), pp. 157–68.

15. Administrative procedures to deal with uncertainty are discussed in Ruth P. Mack, *Planning on Uncertainty: Decision Making in Business and Government Administration* (New York: John Wiley and Sons, Inc., 1971).

16. See J.E. Meade, *The Theory of Indicative Planning* (Manchester, Eng.: Manchester University Press; New York: Humanities Press, 1970); Peter S. Albin, "Uncertainty, Information Exchange, and the Theory of Indicative Planning," *Economic Journal* 81, 321 (March 1971): 61–90; and Roy Radner, "Existence of Equilibrium of Plans, Prices, and Price Expectations in a Sequence of Markets," *Econometrica* 40, 2 (March 1972): 289–304.

17. See, for example, Richard Lecomber, "Government Planning, With and Without the Cooperation of Industry: Reflections on British Experience," *Economics of Planning* 10, 1–2 (1970): 53–87; and M.J.C. Surrey, "The National Plan in Retrospect," *Bulletin of the Oxford University Institute of Economics and Statistics* 34, 3 (August 1972): 249–68.

18. For a recent survey of mathematical planning models, see G.M. Heal, *The Theory of Economic Planning* (Amsterdam and London: North-Holland Publishing Co.; New York: American Elsevier Publishing Co., Inc., 1973).

19. On Soviet experience, see *Mathematics and Computers in Soviet Economic Planning,* ed. John P. Hardt and others (New Haven and London: Yale University Press, 1967); and Michael Ellman, *Planning Problems in the USSR: The Contribution of Mathematical Economics to Their Solution, 1960-1971* (Cambridge, Eng.; Cambridge University Press, 1973).

20. See, for example, *Plan and Market: Economic Reform in Eastern Europe,* ed. Morris Bornstein (New Haven and London: Yale University Press, 1973), and J. Wilczynski, *Socialist Economic Development and Reforms* (New York: Praeger Publishers, 1972).

Chapter Two

The Sociology of Planning: Thought and Social Interaction

Charles E. Lindblom

Whatever planning is—and the term means different things to different people—it is an aspect of, perhaps a kind of, problem solving. In the face of problems, we sometimes plan. Planning is sometimes a way of attempting to solve simultaneously a group of related problems. Sometimes also it is a way of anticipating problems, of coping with certain problems in the future by solving certain problems now. The simple statement, "I plan to have my hair cut within the next few days," reveals an attempt to head off imminent small problems by commitment today to a line of action.

When institutions attempt to solve problems, we often speak of the activity as policymaking, especially when the institution is government. The two terms "problem solving" and "policymaking" are not synonymous, not even in the case of governmental problem solving or policymaking. Yet we often use the term "policymaking" to refer to activities in which government officials and other political actives identify social problems or goals to be achieved, examine them, examine and discuss alternative possibilities for solving the problem of approximating the goals, and reach a choice.[a]

Governmental and other institutional planning is consequently an aspect of, perhaps a kind of, policymaking, as well as an aspect or kind of institutional problem solving.

In the study and practice of institutional problem solving and policymaking, a cleavage is apparent. Some scholars and practitioners go far toward believing that policymaking can be highly rational in conventional ways. They tend toward believing that even complex social problems can be more or less definitively analyzed, that the necessary information can be had, that the information can be

My thanks to J.M. Montias, David Braybrooke, and members of the Conference for helpful comments on an earlier draft of this chapter.

[a]These processes are not necessarily as rational as words like "identify," "examine," "discuss," and "choose" imply. Policymaking also requires authority, often requires coercion; policymakers are often ignorant, intransigent, and thoughtless.

processed, that all important alternatives open to the policymakers can be canvassed, that the consequences of each potential policy can be explored, that criteria of choice can be formulated, and that all these can be done within the limits of time, money, and personnel within which governments and other institutions have to work.

In contrast, other scholars and practitioners believe that at best policymaking cannot even approximate the above description of it. They do not believe that for complex problems we do or can know enough to reach analytically well grounded solutions. Moreover, they believe that for sufficiently complex problems enough information is always too much. Either one does not know enough, or he cannot process all the information available to him. They also believe that limits of time, personnel, and money preclude the canvassing of all important alternatives, as well as the investigation of the consequences of each potential choice. Nor can serviceable criteria for choice be found. They consequently endorse methods of policymaking different from those endorsed by those who believe policymaking can be conventionally rational.[1]

Among scholars who would identify themselves as students of policymaking processes or of collective problem solving, it is now almost unanimously agreed that for complex problems information is indeed to some degree inadequate, that enough information at least sometimes causes an informational overload, and that time, personnel, and resource constraints preclude the kind of complete analysis envisaged above as conventionally rational. The cleavage remains, however. Among these scholars there is wide disagreement on how far policymaking must depart from conventional rationality.

Since planning is an aspect of problem solving and policymaking, scholars and practitioners of planning must attend carefully to this cleavage. If institutional problem solving can approximate conventional rationality, then planning can be conventionally rational. If, however, institutional problem solving cannot approximate conventional rationality and must instead cope in inventive ways with the obstacles posed in the second view of it, then perhaps planning can only be successful if unconventional. Planning may require methods heretofore unappreciated.

The opposing views about rationality in policymaking are symptomatic, we suggest, of a more fundamental or deeper opposition—an opposing set of views on the maximum role of reason, thought, analysis, or intellect (for our purposes the terms are synonymous) in social organization and social change. In order to consider the implications of the opposing views about policymaking for planning, we want therefore first to go back or down to this underlying fundamental cleavage. We shall therefore first examine two alternative views on the possibilities of organizing and changing society by studying it, thinking about it, analyzing it. Pari passu, then, we shall also be examining two alternative views on the degree to which social organization and change are inevitably the product of social forces other than man's intellectually calculated and deliberate attempts to organize or change society. Only thereafter will we examine the implications of each alternative view for methods of planning. Our task, it ought to be noted, is not to debate the merits of alternative views but to clarify each of them so that their consequences for methods of planning are illuminated. How to plan cannot be well understood except in the light of these alternative views on what the intellect can accomplish in social organization and social change.

The two views on the role of intellect in social organization and social change can be developed by comparing its role in two visions, models or pictures of a well-ordered society, to each of which we can subsequently associate an appropriate method of planning.

Why must the model, picture, or vision be of a well-ordered society? Because we are not interested in methods of planning suitable to social orders that none of us would defend. We mean by a model, picture, or vision of a well-ordered society a construct that at least some significant number of informed, thoughtful minds will espouse as a norm for intelligent social organization. Only from such a norm can one infer appropriate methods of planning.

The two models to be discussed are both "democratic" in the specific sense that the society is seen as pursuing the welfare of the great mass of inhabitants.[b] Both are egalitarian in significant ways. Because most informed, thoughtful minds in our time espouse democracy in at least one of its forms, we simplify the analysis by ignoring possible models or visions of nondemocratic societies and, subsequently, of nondemocratic planning.

It will quickly be apparent that the two visions or models correspond in certain of their attributes to idealized liberal democracy and to idealized communism respectively. But only in some attributes. Moreover, they do not correspond to actual liberal democratic and communist societies.[c] Such tempting associations are to be avoided. Moreover, at a later stage of the analysis, certain critical disassociations will be discussed.

TWO VISIONS OF
WELL-ORDERED SOCIETIES

Some readers will be curious about why I do not soften the contrast between the two starkly opposed models or visions by substituting for the first model, with its unqualified faith in reason, a model of society organized intellectually but by

[b]Not only liberal democratic. Our usage embraces "democratic" as the term is used in Eastern Europe and the USSR.

[c]I use the term "Communist" both to refer to an idealized system that Marxists call Communist and to refer to existing real world systems that Marxists denote as Socialist on the ground that they have not yet reached full communism. Modifiers and context will make clear which I intend in any given passage. The point here, in any case, is that neither of the two models of the well ordered society corresponds to existing real world Communist systems (which Marxists call socialist), nor does either correspond except at certain points to idealized full blown communist systems.

imperfect or limited intellect. I might have taken, for example, H.A. Simon's concept of "bounded rationality" as the key concept of how the intellect organizes and changes society.[2] Or I might have introduced such a model as a third alternative, located between my two, though of course much nearer to the first model than the second.

Clearly, confidence in, or at least hope for, enlarging the role of intellect in guiding social organization and social change rests, among thoughtful people, more in the idea of a bounded rationality than in the idea of omniscient intellect. Moreover, the idea of a limited or bounded rationality points to some methods of policymaking and of planning that differ from those appropriate to a wholly competent intellect.

I want, however, in this chapter to explore the difference between the intellectual or analytic method of policymaking and planning, on one hand, and the social-interactive, on the other, as the title of the chapter indicates, and thus to explore methods of planning appropriate to the social-interactive. Given my purpose, the two rather starkly drawn visions or models are useful as limiting cases, illuminating because they possess the simplicity of limiting cases. If I were to introduce a bounded rationality model, the principal point I would want to make about it is that when the intellect cannot handle a problem, some method of social interaction must substitute for it. And that principal point I can make with the present two models, without the complication of another.

The Efficacy of Thought in Organizing Society

Intellectual competence. The outstanding feature of the first vision or model is there are men in the society wise and informed enought to ameliorate its problems and guide social change with a high degree of success. An outstanding feature of the second vision or model is that no individual or group in the society can achieve a high degree of competence. All men are fallible in crippling and dangerous ways in dealing with society's problems and in guiding social change. One vision assumes a match between man's intellectual capacities and the difficulty of understanding and controlling the social world; the other argues that a gross mismatch exists.

Theory. As a consequence, in the first vision or model the intellectual leaders of the society are envisioned as having been able to produce a comprehensive theory of social change that serves to guide the society, especially its policymakers. In the second, no such synoptic theory exists, not even in embryo. Scholars produce scattered partial theories—about money and prices, for example, or on the causes of juvenile delinquency, or on voting patterns; but the theories all taken together do not add up to a comprehensive or overarching set of guidelines. They are also tentative, inadequately tested, consequently dubious sources of guidance in practical affairs even within their limited domains.

The correct versus the preferred. In the first vision, since men *know* how to organize society, the test of an institution or policy is that it is correct.[d] Since, in the second, men are not competent to know what is correct, men fall back on their own felt preferences as a test.[e] In the first, men justify their society because it is the right one; in the second, because they prefer it.

In the second, preferences are not taken as the test because it is believed that men correctly or truly know their own preferences, for it is assumed that they only imperfectly know them. They are taken as a test for lack of any better test.

Criterion for correctness. Logically, it is not possible to say that one has the correct answer to a problem, a correct policy, or a correct set of social institutions unless one has a criterion for correctness. Only in the first model is it assumed that there always exists such a criterion. It is the correspondence of an institution or policy to man's true needs—needs not limited to subsistence, but including all the requirements of the good life—which can be known. In the second model, many of man's needs can be known only imperfectly and inconclusively.

Ultimately both visions appeal to man's needs as, in principle, the test of institutions and policies, if those needs could be known. But, since in the second model many cannot be known, or known with sufficient confidence, the correctness of institutions and policies cannot always be tested by reference to them.

If men in fact preferred and chose what they truly needed, in both models a correct and a preferred institution or policy would be the same. But because of false consciousness and for other reasons, most men for a long time to come will not understand their own true needs very well, will not necessarily express preferences for what they truly need, and will in fact even be confused about their preferences, often interchanging what they think they prefer with what they actually prefer.

The elite. Although most men are generally misled by false consciousness and other defects of insight into their own needs, in the first model some among them are capable of surmounting these obstacles to correct insight. Some men, it is clear from what we have already said, are envisioned as superior analysts by reason of innate capacity, education, practice, or environmental influence. It is their knowledge rather than popular preference that guides the society. Consequently, there is, pending a distant future when all men will understand themselves fully, an intellectual elite that is simultaneously a political elite. In the second vision, there is no such elite.

[d]The 1969 Constitution of the Chinese Communist party declares that the Party is "great, glorious, and correct." Consider also the wish of extreme enthusiasts of systems analysis to substitute correct policies for policies chosen through "politics."

[e]Preferences revealed by the actual choices that men make.

A digression on the liberal democratic faith in reason.   Since the Enlightenment, one great tradition in liberal democratic thought has identified liberal democracy with government by reason rather than by authority. It has been saluted as "government by discussion."[3] Its defenders have pointed to free speech, for example, as evidence of liberal democracy's dependence on fact and analysis; and in parties and factions they have found instruments, however imperfect, for testing and challenging, thus uncovering the truth. A now parallel younger Western tradition identifies communism with force, authority, the suppression of debate, and tight constraints on gathering and transmitting information. If we look for points of correspondence between our two models and idealized communism and idealized democracy, our description of them revises the traditional identification of liberal democracy with reason and of communism with unreasoned authority. For we are suggesting that the model that would be seen as approximating idealized communism practices reason more than the model that would be associated with idealized liberal democracy.

If actual Communist societies constrain debate and the flow of information among those believed by the elite to be incapable of making good social use of debate and information, it is nevertheless true that Communist thought displays a faith in man's best intellectual capacities that goes far beyond the troubled concern with man's fallibility in actual liberal democratic society. It seems clear that Marxian thought plays a guiding role in institution building and policy-making that is not matched by a unified or comprehensive social theory in the liberal democracies. Liberal democracy's faith in reason was historically impressive only in contrast to earlier traditionalism and authoritarianism in science, religion, and politics. Compared to the Marxian and Communist faith in reason, it is puny.

As will be noted below, having faith in the powers of the intellect is not the same as valuing those powers. Here the point is that the first model postulates that intellectual competence is sufficient for tasks of social organization and change. Later will see that the confidence leads such a society to prize intellectual competence less than in the second model of society, in which intellectual competence is always in short supply.

Marx's scientific socialism was meant to be scientific; the term is not just a slogan. Liberal democrats make no similar claim that their societies are scientifically designed, although the contributions of science and social science to them are conspicuous at particular points.

Discussion, debate, and intellectual conflict are indeed protected in liberal democratic societies, but perhaps more to permit dissent from a misguided course of action than to set new courses, more to criticize institutions and policies than to design them. The civil liberties are everywhere alleged to protect the right to dissent, not to encourage a science of society but to expose error.[4]

The intellectually guided society and the preference guided society.   In any case idealized communism and liberal democracy cannot, as already noted, be simply associated with the two models. To avoid identifying the two models with the Communist and liberal partial versions of them, let us give each a name and continue with their identification. We shall call the one the intellectually guided society. The name is not a perfect fit, but it will do to emphasize the role of knowledge, intellectual competence, and social theory in tasks of social organization and change. The other will be called the preference guided society.

Harmony. Implicit in what has already been said about the model of the intellectually guided society is that it postulates an underlying harmony of men's needs that can be known to the guiding elite. In the preference guided society, it is assumed that harmony of needs is not only undiscoverable but nonexistent. Conflict among men in the pursuit of their preferences is assumed to be ineradicable, although it can be reduced by the uncovering of many harmonious needs.

The assumption of harmony in the intellectually guided society is necessary, given the assumption of a criterion for testing correct solutions to problems of social organization and change. If the criterion is, as already noted, man's needs—if, that is to say, an institution or policy is correct if it serves man's needs and incorrect if it does not—the criterion can be applied only if an institution or policy that serves one man's needs does not obstruct meeting the needs of other men. If the guiding elite had to choose between meeting the needs of one segment of the population or another but not both simultaneously, it would be without a criterion for an intellectual resolution of its problem. A wholly reasoned or analyzed solution would be impossible.

Ideology. In the preference guided society, in which men do not know enough to identify correct institutions or policies, participants in political life have to be constrained by authoritative rules in order to limit overt conflict arising out of conflicting preferences. Rules are also required in the intellectually guided society. The knowledgeable elite in that society has the competence, however, to educate the rest of the population in correct theory and practice on social organization, government, policy, and political participation. Insofar as they do that, they dampen conflict and encourage social cooperation with less reliance on authoritative rules than in the preference guided society.

The content of their teaching we shall call ideology. Ideology is not, in this model, anti- or non-scientific; it is a body of teachings derived from scientific knowledge about society and adapted to a larger audience than can digest that knowledge in full detail and precision.

Centralism. In the intellectually guided society, authority and other power are more centralized than in the preference guided society. To claim that at least some few men have the intellectual capacity to design correct institutions and policies is to claim that they are able to achieve a comprehensive central overview of the problems of social organization and change. They understand the interrelatedness of parts; they can consequently manage the interrelatedness of parts; and unified centralized control is required for coordination. In the preference guided society in which no one can claim to have achieved a competent overview of all aspects of society, partial views and partial solutions are the responsibility of a variety of policymakers to whom authority and other power are decentralized. Moreover, institutions and policies emerge less by deliberate decision than as resultants of the interplay of conflicting authorities and other powers widely distributed throughtout the society, as in political bargaining and maneuvering among interest groups or as in market system determination of resource allocation. Decentralization is therefore characteristic of preference guided societies.

Social Interaction as an Alternative to Thought

It is indeed a major and fundamental feature of the preference guided society that institutions and policies are formed by social interaction rather than, as in the intellectually guided society, designed by thought. In the contrasting roles of interaction and thought, in this one point of difference alone, we can capture much of the most fundamental difference between the two visions of a well-ordered society. It is this distinction that answers a question left unanswered since we first asserted that conspicuous faith in thought marks the scientific society. If analysis is inadequate for the design of institutions and policies, as is the case in the preference guided society, how then are institutions and policies to be designed? The answer is that they are not to be wholly designed but instead established by social interactions[f] or acts that substitute for analysis. Analysis does not disappear, but its role is reduced.

The difference between thought (or intellect, analysis) and social interaction is illustrated in the contrast between conclusive analysis of the best way to curb air pollution, on one hand, and choosing an antipollution policy by majority vote of citizens or their representatives, on the other. Each citizen or representative does some analysis; but the final resolutions is by acts (voting and counting votes), not by analysis. It is also illustrated in the contrast between research on whether a person has broken the law, on one hand, or determination of that fact by an adversary procedure in a courtroom, on the other. It is of course illustrated in every market transaction. Through the effects of market interactions, resources are allocated, income shares are distributed, and production is divided between that which is consumed and that which is plowed back into further growth of productive capacity. If a market system exists, no one faces up to the resource allocation problem, the income distribution problem, or the consumption-investment problem as an analytical problem. No one has to try to understand it, solve it, or make any explicit decision on it; it is finally "solved" through acts not thoughts.

[f]Strictly speaking, social interaction other than purely intellectual interaction among a group searching for correct policies, for that too is a form of social interaction.

Some of the other interactions that take the place of analysis are: opinion polling, delegation of decisionmaking to authoritative decisionmakers (who are not, it should be noted, assumed to undertake conclusive analysis), bargaining, and elaborate schemes for the division of labor among policymakers so that policies can be set only if various participants can cooperate, as in the American constitutional separation of powers and system of checks and balances. Specific instruments for interaction include elections, representative assemblies, political parties, cabinets, conference committees to reconcile decisions reached by two independent houses in bicameral legislative systems, committee systems in legislatures, and tripartite boards for wage and price control.[g]

An approxmation to the contrast between thought and interaction is captured in the proposition that there is no politics in the intellectually guided society. (Remember that this is a model to which no real-world society corresponds closely.) Marxian theory makes (or once made) the point in the doctrine of the withering away of the state.[5] Politics abounds in the preference ordered society.

Close and distant interaction. Interaction runs the whole range from close and recognized (by the participants) to distant and unrecognized. One familiar kind is explicit negotiation or bargaining, in which the participants are known to each other, addressed by each other, deliberately influenced by each other, and in which they finally come to some explicit settlement. At the other extreme is the interaction between a Brazilian coffee farmer and an Icelandic coffee drinker. They, along with coffee broker, shipper, retailer, and many others, are linked only in distant impersonal interaction of which they are only in small part aware. Between the two extremes are countless cases that mix close recognized with distant unrecognized interaction, as in the interactions among taxing authorities in the United States.

Obviously interractions like these are to be found in all actual societies. The difference between the two models or visions is that in the intellectually guided society interactions are assumed to be disorganizing, trouble-making, or, at best, neutral with respect to problems. In the preference guided society, it would have to be admitted that interactions are often disturbances, often cause problems instead of solving them. But some interactions are problem solving, it would be held. Some interactions constitute alternatives to intellectual resolution of a social problem.

If in the intellectually guided society it is conceded that an interaction is occasionally an alternative to intellectual problem solving in that it will produce

[g]All these are here presented as methods of policymaking. Some of them are also instruments for implementation of policy. Although we are not concerned with implementation in this chapter, it could be noted that some implementation procedures in the preference guided society are among the interactions that make policy, as is not the case in the intellectually guided society.

a "solution" of sorts, it would immediately be argued that interaction is even in those cases an inferior alternative.

In the preference guided model, it is of course not assumed that interaction produces perfect solutions to problems, only that often they will be superior to the solutions attempted directly and deliberately by the intellect. Looking at the "solution" to the problem of what should be the distribution of income in the United States (its distribution being a product of interaction rather than deliberate intellectual design), proponents of a preference guided society would have to admit that in some people's eyes the "problem" has not yet been solved. But, they would believe, it is "solved," however badly, better than it would be solved through a frontal intellectual attack on it.

Interaction seen as problem solving rather than as democratic. In most references to them in the literature, many of these forms of interaction are presented as methods for popular control in democratic government. Many of them are indeed methods of popular control in government, but that is too narrow a view of them. The model of the preference guided society emphasizes their role as problem solvers, as alternatives to intellectual design of institutions and policies. In that perspective, their liberal democratic significance for popular control is only secondary.

Their problem-solving capacities and their popular control characteristics are, however, intertwined. For the defense of any interactive problem-solving process in the preference guided model is that the interaction serves ultimately to subordinate social organization and social change to the preferences of the population. Basically, interaction is required to form institutions and policies because without them the intellect is incapable of doing so. But which of various possible forms of interaction is desirable (if that secondary issue is raised as a question that can be answered) is determined by reference to the efficacy with which equally weighed preferences achieve a control over institutions and policies.

Hence in a preference guided model, interaction patterns will be marked by frequent and easy participation on the part of as wide a set of participants as can be imagined to have any interest in the outcome, with as much equality as possible in the influence of an individual's preference as against any others.[h] Of course, the final test of any such interaction pattern is not always that it can be conclusively analyzed to demonstrate that it permits easy, broad, and equal expression of preference, for whether it does or not may not be within man's intellectual competence to know. The final test of a pattern of interaction for effecting their preferences is that people prefer it.

[h]Remember again that we describe a model to which no existing society closely corresponds.

Epiphenomenal "solutions."[i] Hypothetically, we have seen a society can reach a policy decision through analysis. It can also do so through interaction processes, like voting or bargaining, in which a resolution of a given recognized problem is achieved. But, it is now to be added that it can, through interaction processes, achieve resolutions of unrecognized problems not on the agenda of any participant in the interaction.

Just as the problem of income distributions is "solved," not deliberately and thoughtfully but as a by-product of countless market transactions, so also the design of a city will be left to emerge as a by-product—that is, epiphenomenally—from individual decisions on land use.[j] In the preference guided society, many people will sometimes actually shrink from proposals to solve certain problems through deliberate thoughtful or intellectually guided choice; they might prefer a by-product method of solution. Sex distribution of newborn infants is an example; people might want that "decision" to emerge only epiphenomenally. They might also shrink from analyzing directly a policy on euthanasia, preferring that death be decided as a by-product or epiphenomenon of customary medical practices.

The special case of the market aside, the more typical cases of epiphenomenal formation of institutions and policies are those in which a diffusion of authority and other power sets in motion a political interaction among individuals and groups in which no person or group analyzes the problem and arrives at a solution but in which a "solution" nevertheless emerges from the interaction. For example, the important question in the United States of what share of each person's income should be turned over to public purposes is decided by interaction among a large number of taxing authorities in national, state, and local governments. Each governmental unit faces a problem of what taxes it ought to collect. Its problems are specific: how to raise enough revenue to finance its activities or, in some cases, how to use taxation as a weapon to induce or constrain certain responses, as in the case of tax concessions to induce business investment. Each governmental unit has to pay some attention to what the others are doing, since two units cannot legally claim the same income from a citizen. But no unit has to analyze and find a solution for the question of how personal incomes should be divided between private and public use; that policy is set epiphenomenally through their interactions.

One more example. A major institutional development in the United States and certain other nations has been the giant, multiproduct, often multinational corporation, that takes on, in addition to its production tasks, political,

[i]I mean by an epiphenomenon a by-product. In the philosophy of mind, the term has a special meaning: a phenomenon without causal efficacy. That meaning is not intended here.

[j]I take these as good examples of epiphenomenal "solutions" because they are not such unambiguous examples of excellence in policymaking as to beg the question of the usefulness of epiphenomena.

educational, and other philanthropic responsibilities. This one complex institutional development can be argued to be as important to the structure of these societies as any other that can be mentioned. It is a by-product or epiphenomenon, not any person's, committee's or government's analyzed and deliberate design. That is not to say that the development has been uncontrolled. Insofar as developments raised specific problems, they have been analyzed, debated, deliberately acted upon. But, these specific problems aside, the societies in which this development has occurred have permitted the major features of this important new institution to emerge as a by-product of a variety of specific interacting activities. Advocates of preference guided societies will, of course, argue that such a path of development for the corporation, monitored by explicit attention to specific attendant problems, is as well-ordered as a path set by a necessarily incompetent attempt to analyze and directly control the entire development.

In both models of society epiphenomena exist. The difference between the two is that they are seen as trouble-making or neutral with respect to problem solving in the intellectually guided society. In the preference guided society, however, some are seen as problem solving.

Ordinary and academic language might be argued to be biased against preference guided systems. For it is cumbersome to denote epiphenomenal outcomes except through the use of words that strongly suggest irrationality or disorder. If we refer to the many important institutional and policy determinations made in a preference ordered society as mere resultants of interaction rather as "policies" or "decisions," we immediately put them under a cloud. Yet it is a fact of fundamental importance that they are not policies or decisions; they are results systematically achieved by another route in which explicit decisions are not made on certain issues. Nor, strictly speaking, are epiphenomenal outcomes or resultants to be identified as "solutions" to problems, for although they emerge from interaction among persons intent on solving their own particular problems, it is a characteristic of the epiphenomenal "solution" that no one recognizes on his agenda the "problem" that is in effect "solved." Some terminological distinction, however unidiomatic, is needed: perhaps between "interacted effects" and "intellectually designed effects." Any such distinction is, however, clumsy, given our language habits.

Whether to classify the interacted effects of close and recognized interaction as epiphenomenal is disputable; terminological tastes will differ. If explicit negotiation between officials of the British and American governments in World War II finally settled the question of where the allied invasion of Europe would be attempted, one would probably wish to say that the decision was an intellectually designed deliberate decision, not an epiphenomenon. But suppose employer and union representatives negotiate a wage settlement. They are not joined to settle a common problem of right wages. The employer's problem is making profits. The employee's problem is getting higher wages. Neither may feel any responsibility for wage policy.[k] Under these circumstances, it makes some sense to say that wage determination is an epiphenomenal interacted result of two groups of persons each intent on solving its own problem.

To be sure, the two groups can be viewed as sharing a common problem of finding an agreement, a bargain profitable to both groups. But if that, not the establishment of wage policy, is their common problem, then it is not unreasonable to say that wage "policy" is an interacted effect that grows epiphenomenally out of the solution to the problem of finding a working agreement between employer and employees. The terminological uncertainty is not important. What is important to understand is that neither employer nor union representatives need face such a question as "What is a desirable wage policy?" for the industry or for the economy as a whole. If they simply face the question, "How can we agree on a wage rate that serves our respective interests?," their interaction may make it unnecessary—and in historical fact in many societies has made it unnecessary—for any person, official, or group to answer the first question. It is "answered" as a by-product of answering the second.

Procedures highly valued. A major aspect of a society which depends heavily on social interaction rather than intellect for problem solving is that it will highly value—as though ends in themselves—certain key interaction patterns. Certain processes or procedures will come to be more highly valued than any one end or goal. For example, that a decision be made by majority rule will be more important than that it be correct or in any other way defensible. A fair trial will come to be valued more than that the true facts of guilt or innocence be established. Or it will come to be accepted that a good defense for what is criticized as a bad policy is that it was the resultant of a process in which everyone was heard.

In traditional liberal democratic theory, the emphasis on procedures expresses a concern for personal liberty.[6] Our view adds—it does not contradict the traditional view—that the emphasis on procedures in the preference guided society reflects instead a concern for problem solving. Seen in this light, constitutionalism is a major feature of problem solving in the preference guided society quite aside from its contribution to the protection of individual liberties.

Consider the venerable question of whether the ends justify the means. That in the intellectually guided society they do is not an indication of corrupt values. In the intellectually guided society, leaders are competent to choose ends suitable to man's known needs and wants. Given that the ends are correct, it can be argued that they are a sufficient criterion for the choice of means. All values that competent leaders weigh positively are presumably among the ends sought by them. Hence the established ends preclude a choice of means that fails to respect those values.

[k]In Sweden, however, they do. In the United States in some circumstances, they do not.

In the preference guided society, the ends do not justify the means. Some procedures themselves are valued, they are not merely instrumental to ends. Moreover, the value placed on means is not necessarily derived from an estimate of their efficacy in reaching ends. Some procedures or patterns of interaction are to be endorsed, others rejected, not because the practice of them can be related to certain ends but because, given man's incompetence to know the correct ends, he has to evaluate and form preferences about procedures in substantial ignorance of the ends toward which they tend.

His justification of these procedures is not wholly independent of his guesses about ends; but it is independent of the procedures' usefulness to reach a particular end at a particular time; and it is not always even based on a probabilistic calculation that in general the procedures will serve desired ends. Men will often defend procedures because they can directly grasp aspects of them pertinent to their preferences. Moreover, the defense of certain procedures may turn solely on consequences of using them other than for the achievement of the ends toward which they are or come to be deliberately directed—on the consequences, for example, of majority rule for the strength of social bonds rather than on its probable suitability for democratic, or rational, or otherwise efficient policymaking.[1]

Safeguarding interactions. The preference guided society is full of social mechanisms designed to protect society from its errors in institution building and policymaking. The proliferation of such mechanisms is understandable in the light of man's limited competence to solve his social problems, in the light of his conspicuous fallibility. The right to criticize is one of these safeguards; and, as we already noted, the civil liberties are prized less to permit men to use their minds to design—positively and creatively—improved institutions and policies than to permit them to dissent, to question, to criticize. Another mechanism, the rationale for which is erected into an ethical principle, is limited grants of authority. Another is the governmental device known as the separation of powers, which is a method of allocating limited grants of authority in such a way as to make cooperation among those in authority prerequisite to action by any one of them. Governmental checks and balances are a more extreme form of safeguard. More generally, widespread diffusion both of authority and of other powers, as in voting and other forms of participation in politics, including interest activity groups, are safeguards because they make policymaking contingent on the cooperation of large numbers of participants. By contrast,

[1]If there is one "end" to which, it would appear, man in the preference guided society must inescapably tie the defense of means, it would appear to be the satisfaction of his needs. But he is driven to that "end," we have noted, not so much because satisfying preferences is a worthy end but because in the absence of competence to specify correct institutions and policies, he has to fall back on some determinant. That being so, it is actually possible for him to attach greater value to a procedure, for reasons other than its efficacy in satisfying his preferences, than to satisfying his preferences.

none of these mechanisms are necessary in the intellectually guided society in which policymakers know correct policies.

Conflict interaction. The interactions that characterize a preference guided society are not all cooperative. Voting may be thought of as a cooperative ritual for choosing leaders, but even voting is a conflict, or at least simulated conflict. Many of the other common interactions are conflict ridden or are expressly designed to cope with conflict: separation of powers, tripartite boards, parliamentary removal of prime minister, and the like.

Conflict is not simply regretted in the preference guided society as it is in intellectually guided society in which harmonious needs are postulated; it is positively exploited (rather than suppressed, as in the intellectually guided society). It is exploited to bring scrutiny to bear on possibly mistaken institutions and policies. It is also exploited to stimulate an always inadequate supply and quality of analysis, specifically to stimulate intellectual controversy, and through that new insights, new findings of fact, new hypotheses.

Intellectual conflict is prized in the rarified worlds of science and academe, and it is prized as well in discussion among political leaders and among the public at large. Conflict of policy position, conflict among interacting participants in political affairs, is prized too, although men recognize that it can easily go too far. For it stimulates innovation in policy and institutions, especially in situations in which participants are motivated, in order to resolve a conflict over old policy positions, to find new positions on which they can agree. Where conflict thus leads not to mere compromise but to invention, to a new "integration," it is especially valued.[7]

Mass versus group and individual interaction. In the intellectually guided society in which an elite is competent to design institutions and policies to meet human needs and wants, the elite discovers and responds to the common needs and wants of all men. The intellectually guided society recognizes, of course, difference among individuals in age, sex, intelligence, strength, and certain special skills. Beyond that, it holds that racial, religious, ethnic, and other individual differences among men are only happenstances of cultural and personality variation in a past in which societies varied greatly because they were not intellectually guided. Institutions and policies are adapted to what is universal in mankind; group and individual differences tend to disappear. A "new man" appears.[8]

In the preference guided society, preferences differ from one group to another, and from one individual to another, and, although the spread of a common technology erodes cultural and personality differences, they persist with the help of institutions and policies that perpetuate differences among groups and individuals. Group and individual diversity is positively valued. For if men are incompetent to design the correct society, cultural and personality diversity turns out to be a method of experimentation, of exploring alternative institutions and policies, of keeping alive a variety of them, among which some may over time prove to have great merit, and of maintaining a lively discussion of alternative policies and institutions. In a preference guided society, individual and group differences are of course acknowledged to be divisive in some circumstances.

There is some recognition in the preference guided society that differences among individuals and groups are equally essential to social order. It is recognized that people are bound together by Durkheim's organic solidarity, by differences that make them dependent on one another.[9] A society of alikes is hardly imaginable. If all Frenchmen were alike, they would all want to live in Paris, or none of them would; would want to be engineers or none of them would; would all want to vacation in Honfleur or none of them would. In a preference ordered society, differences in preferences make it possible for men to stay out of each other's way and also facilitate a division of labor.

The political process and political skills. As noted above in the intellectually guided society, since men know correct answers to questions about social organization and social change, the political system is simple and is not much more than an administrative organization. In the preference guided society, the political system is a major, central, critical set of institutions and processes, composed as it is of many of the interaction processes through which policies and institutions are formed in the absence of intellectual capacity to design them. This is an enormously important point of difference between the two models.

One of its major implications is for the character of political leadership. In the intellectually guided society, the political leader looks something much like Plato's philosopher-king or is a cooperating group of elitists. Leaders are members of the elite that is competent to find correct policies and institutions. Their only "political" problem arises from the possibility that, pending the emergence of the "new man," their subjects protest correct policies and institutions because they do not know what is good for themselves. If so, leaders require some skill in maintaining authority.

In the preference guided society leaders need special skills for that same purpose. Their problem of maintaining authority is exacerbated because the preference guided society, we have seen, is committed to certain procedures and outlaws others. Leaders must, consequently, be especially skillful in exploiting those limited possibilities that remain open. If, for example, they cannot terrorize their subjects, they must develop other appeals for consent to authority.

Its inability to find correct solutions for social problems further alters and complicates the skills required of leadership in the preference guided society. The preference guided society needs politicians; the intellectually guided society does not. To call a political leader a politician is in some contexts to demean him. In other contexts, it is to acknowledge that political leaders in a preference guided society have to develop specialized political skills to maneuver within continuing interactions and to redesign those interactions, in addition to their skills in mastering the substantive problems of policymaking and institution building. A politician is a political leader who is skilled in the interaction processes that characterize preference guided systems.

An illustrative and fundamental problem faced by the politician is that of moving diverse preferences toward each other so that politics and institutions can be found that will satisfy more rather than fewer preferences. What talented politicians do is find new unifying issues and new unifying policies that wean citizens away from older divisive ones. The most talented politicians are those who have found the skill to find or invent what we have labeled integrated rather than compromised solutions.

The principal skill requirements for the leader of the intellectually guided society are that he understand those problems of his society that would exist if there were no political system and that he know how to solve them. The principal skill requirements for a leader of a preference guided society are that he understand the political system, composed as it is of the interaction processes through which social problems are attacked, and that he know how to use it.

Role of Thought in Interaction Processes

Adaptation of thought to interaction. It should be apparent that thought, analysis, and even sophisticated scientific inquiry are engaged in by participants in social interaction. An employer negotiating wages may spend heavily on staff studies, consultant services, or specialized analysis like operations research. An individual consumer may very thoughtfully decide on his purchases, even systematically reading to inform himself about major complex products. An interest group may finance a large staff to advise it on how best to achieve its purposes. A congressional committee may call on a variety of research studies before reporting a bill out.

Simplification of intellectual tasks. In interaction processes the intellect is typically given, however, simpler problems than those that confront institution and policy designers in an intellectually guided society. Where the elite in such a society has to face up to the staggering question: "What is best for society?," participants in interactive processes ask the simpler questions: "How can I get ahead?" "How can I most effectively influence others whose cooperation I need?" "How can I reconcile a difference that separates me from potential allies?" Often the question is nothing more than "What will I buy? What shall I sell? How shall I vote?"

Sometimes questions are posed about the interests or welfare of the entire society. But they are then typically restricted to a particular aspect of society:

for example, urban congestion, health, or conservation of resources. They do not pose massive integrated problems of social organization and change such as are attacked in the guiding theory of a scientific society. Moreover, the largest questions raised for analysis in a preference guided society produce answers that, because they are dubious and tentative, are not permitted to exercise much direct influence on policy and institution design. Political and other practical decisions feed on the modest questions whose answers can be more easily and safely digested. Where in the preference guided society the answers to the grand questions are left for the edification of those who are curious about them, there is a major systematic effort in the intellectually guided society to make them effective as a guide to institution and policy design and to the construction of a guiding ideology.

New and altered intellectual tasks. It follows from the above that thought or analysis is given certain specific direction or assignment in the preference guided society. First, it will often be directed, as already noted, not at the substantive ostensible questions of policy, but instead at the design of a participant's strategy for playing his part in interaction, as when a businessman hires market researchers or a politician hires public opinion surveys. Second, it is often directed to an understanding of the motives, probable behavior, and possibilities of influencing behavior of others in the interaction process. Third, it is often directed to the design of interaction processes themselves.[10]

In addition some kinds of analysis become, as academic disciplines, specialized in the study of interaction processes and their consequences for outcomes. Economics, with its interest in the market system, and political science, with its interest in legislative and other policymaking interaction, represent specialized disciplines such as would not be necessary in an intellectually guided society in which such interaction processes were absent. Social science is largely concerned with alternatives to scientific methods of social organization.

The value of thought. In many ways, the preference guided society values thought, intellect or analysis more than does the intellectually guided society. In the former, it is recognized that analysis is difficult, in short supply, and of an inadequate level of competence. If, on the one hand, the recognition undercuts a faith that men can solve major social problems by the intellectual design of institutions and policies, the same recognition, on the other hand, leads men to prize highly what capacities for analysis they possess. A man in a desert expects to be hot, but he will prize the shade of any single tree he finds.

Confident of the adequacy of basic guiding theory, confident that there are no major obstacles to knowledge of correct institutions and policies, the intellectually guided society does not protect scientific research, inquiry, and public discussion through guarantees of freedom to pursue them, as does the preference guided society. In the preference guided society personal liberties of many kinds are not viewed as nuisances to public authority, as they often are in the intellectually guided society, but are valued as aids to making the most out of society's ability, always inadequate, to apply intelligence to tasks of social organization and change. Personal liberty is valued, not simply for its own sake or on humanitarian grounds, but for its function in stretching society's meager resources of intellect in solving its social problems.

TWO PLANNING METHODS

The implications for planning of each of the two models of society are apparent. The great and fundamental distinction in planning methods is between those that confidently plunge the intellect directly into its tasks in the style of the intellectually guided society, and those that, mindful of the intellect's fallibility, employ the planner's intellect selectively and in subordination to social interactions. The contrast between two different roles of thought in the two models of society gives us our two methods of planning. Because all real world societies are only approximations to the models and are composed of differing mixtures of elements from each, every real world society can, within limits, choose a mix of elements of the two planning methods.

The theory and practice of planning are both in their infancies. Theory is overwhelmingly concerned with planning of the first type, planning that is confident of possibilities of intellectual mastery. And practice of the second type, though more common, is distorted or crippled by the deference of planners to an inappropriate theory. In the case of planning of the second type, in which the limitations of intellect are the central difficulty, theory and practice are amateurish in the extreme; and many planners have not yet even recognized the possibility of that kind of planning. Let us examine it further.

In the absence of a developed theory or systematic description of planning of the second type, it has to be characterized by some of its main features. It is a method that treats the competence to plan as a scarce resource that must be husbanded, carefully allocated, not overcommitted. Because planning is both costly and limited in what it can accomplish, planners are seen as needing a strategy for guiding their planning. The second method of planning consists of planning regulated by such a strategy, which means planning that picks its assignments with discrimination, that employs a variety of devices to simplify its intellectual demands, that makes much of interaction and adapts analysis to interaction as a substitute for an analysis, and that departs from logical and scientific canons because they are rules for achieving a level of intellectual mastery that planners cannot achieve when faced with actual complex social phenomena.

For convenience, although again our terms will be far from ideal, we call the first kind of planning conventional planning, since it has no distinguishing characteristics more conspicuous than that most planners and students of planning take it for granted as *the* model of planning. We call the second method strategic planning, thus emphasizing that it requires discrimination or selection among tasks to which the intellect is to be assigned, as well as a calculated interplay between thought and social interaction.

Consider some examples of the difference between the two, examples drawn from a variety of situations, simple to complex. The conventional way to plan the evacuation of a burning ship is to calculate and provide for the required number of lifeboats, then plan escape routes from the various areas of the ship to their nearest lifeboat stations, and post directing signs and/or rehearse each shipload of passengers on using the escape routes.

Strategic planning might, let us say, again begin with lifeboats. Strategic planners also take account of the fact that passengers panic in case of serious fire, do not read or quickly grasp signs. They further note that at different times of the day and night the passengers are distributed over the ship in different patterns and, consequently, cannot be taught standard escape routes unless they can all be persuaded, wherever they are in case of fire, to return to their staterooms and begin a rehearsed escape route from there. But that is a foolish expectation (thought it is in actual fact the operative plan on many ships).

Instead of planning escape routes, strategic planners might therefore ask themselves such a question as whether they can plan to make use of any social process already operating on ships or possible to design to organize the evacuation. They might then recognize the possibility of training the crew to organize evacuation, thus set themselves the task of planning crew direction of evacuation rather than designing escape routes directly. They might plan to train the crew to cope with a representative variety of fires in different locations and with different distributions of passengers throughout the ship. In this example, the planners would not then plan either an evacuation or the management of an evacuation but would plan instead a multipurpose interaction process that might successfully cope with any one of an infinite variety of possible required evacuations. They do not directly plan the solution to a problem but instead they plan the development of a capacity to invent a solution tailored to the particular form in which the problem eventually appears.

At an extreme, strategic planners might conclude that escape routes, which are the core of a conventional plan, will inevitably be uncontrollable in case of actual fire, passengers choosing escape routes for themselves as they please. They may turn their planning efforts entirely toward such a specialized objective as controlling hysteria, including training the crew to calm the passengers, as airline stewardesses are taught to do for their passengers. In any case, they do not take it for granted that the original problem, which is evacuation, is the one that calls for a plan. Discrimination or selection among problems may lead them to any one of several other related problems for which they then plan a solution as their contribution to solving the evacuation problem.

The Controlled Materials Plan of U.S. World Way II economic mobilization is another example of strategic planning. Unable to plan allocations for a large variety of industrial resources for war, planners decided to concentrate their planning on steel, copper, and aluminum. They believed that a plant could use other resources only if it had supplies of steel, copper, or aluminum, and that if they planned an allocation of the three the allocation of many other resources would follow without their being planned.[11]

To illustrate how far at an extreme strategic planning can depart from conventional planning, consider planning to curb environmental pollution in the United States. Conventional planning would attack the problem directly; strategic planning might instead develop plans for altering the interaction processes through which environmental policy is determined. Thus planning for reform of congressional procedures, or for a reconstruction of interest-group activities, or for party realignment—although such strategies are strange to us as methods of dealing with a specific problem like environmental degradation— might be substituted for a frontal attack on the original problem. One sometimes suspects, given the American political system, that any significant long-term planning on any specific major policy problem must take such a roundabout route if it is ever to succeed. It is an indication of the amateurishness of planning that the roundabout route is not seriously considered by most planners.

A closely parallel example will be immediately more persuasive. If a society wants to improve the efficiency of resource allocation, it can do so through conventional planning, as attempted in the USSR, in which major questions about best resource use are subjected to explicit study and followed by planned allocations. Or it can do so through strategic planning. Among several possible types, one obvious one would be the planning of improvements in the way in which the market operates to allocate resources, thus concentrating analysis on a pattern of interaction rather than simply substituting thought for social interaction. No nation has ever employed the market with any great skill; planning to do so is a significant alternative to planning that replaces the market. It calls for planning such factors as market structure, size of enterprise, rules for competition, and income and wealth distribution, rather than planning resource allocations directly.

As a final example, consider two methods of planning a twenty-year program of vastly expanded highway building. Conventional planners require that all the proposed highways be seen as part of an integrated grid and that no one highway be justified except in relation to the others. Such an overview is possible on the assumption in conventional planning that men are competent to know what they need to know. Strategic planners, operating on the assumptions that they cannot look twenty years ahead with much confidence in their predictions and that their minds are incapable of grasping all the interconnections of traffic that make the case for one route dependent on the design of other routes, will plan to build some of the required highways, then examine the results before scheduling others. They may also schedule the sequence of construction in such a way as to maximize feedback.

The systematic features of strategic planning follow fairly directly from the features of the model of the preference guided society.

1. Because of man's limited intellect, an analytical resolution of some complex issues in social order and change is simply not attempted. The issue is left to be decided by some such interaction as majority rule or bargaining, or the market, or some such process as rule-of-thumb policymaking or emergency decision under the pressure of events. A conventional planner would be willing directly to tackle the task of resource allocation for an entire economy; a strategic planner would not.

2. For any problem faced, the first task is analysis of the always limited possibilities of intellectual resolution of the problem. The planner asks: what aspects of the problem are within our competence? How can limited analytical competence best be mobilized and allocated? What important aspects have to be ignored? What devices are available for simplifying the analysis? Insofar as analysis will be inconclusive, what interactive policymaking method will take its place? How can the analysis best be fitted to that method of policymaking? Will other planners and other policymakers have an impact on the decisions we plan or on policies that will impact on ours? How should our planning be adapted to that fact?

3. Strategic planning is then systematically adapted in several specific strategic ways to interaction processes that take the place of analytical settlements of problems of organization and change.

4. Specifically, strategic planning plans the participation of the planners (or of the government for which they plan) in interaction processes, rather than replacing the processes. It plans, for example, interest-rate manipulation in order to stimulate investment, rather than plan investment directly to supersede the market. Or it plans a government intervention into wage-price negotiations rather than displace the negotiations. Or it plans to influence the curriculum of the public schools by specific interventions into state and local curriculum design rather than by transforming the entire administrative machinery of public education.

It generally plans in ways systematically adapted to the political process and to the particular needs of the political leaders for whom it plans. More than conventional planning, it directs its attention to the political process through which the problem is eventually to be ameliorated or solved, rather than to the substantive social problem considered largely in isolation from the political process. Thus French indicative planning is sensitive to the political system, to the possibilities of winning agreement among important participants in it, to the special problems of French political leadership. It does not develop in a technocratic sense a set of targets derived exclusively from calculations of resources and demands.[12]

5. Strategic planning plans systematic alterations in the interaction patterns in addition to specific participation in interactions, as, for example, when it designs a system of industrywide wage bargaining to replace bargaining between single enterprises and their unions or as when it plans a United Nations or new authority for the U.S. Budget Bureau.

Planning of improved procedures is a major standing task of strategic planning, and the values accorded preferred procedures operate as constraining side conditions on all nonprocedural planning. Thus, on the one hand, planning of improved judicial procedures is a major planning task; and, on the other hand, planning the suppression of crime is constrained by respect for highly valued legal procedures on search, wiretapping, right to counsel, and the like.

6. Strategic planning tries to make systematic use of the intelligence with which individuals and groups in the society pursue their own preferences by molding their pursuit, rather than substituting the planners' intelligence wholly for the individual's or the group's. Thus, for example, it is respectful of the degree to which market systems offer participants in the economy possibilities for informed choice and rational calculation and, on this count, will plan improvements in the market rather than its displacement. Similarly, it will plan to mold rather than replace interest-group maneuvering when it appears that interest group conflict stimulates fact-finding, preference clarification, and the possibility of achieving a Pareto optimum.

7. Strategic planning attempts to develop, and plan in the light of, a rationale for deciding which effects are to be achieved through decision and which only as epiphenomena. For example, important as the distribution of income is in every society, it may be deliberately left to develop epiphenomenally as a result of plans on such specifics as old-age security, income subsidies to farmers, unemployment compensation, and the like.

8. Strategic planning rejects certain conventional guidelines to intellectual problem solving derived—inappropriately, a strategic planner would say—from logic and science, and puts others in their place. Conventionally one does not say that he has an intellectually defensible solution to a complex social problem until he can claim to have canvassed all the important alternative methods of solving the problem and examined the implications of each. For until he has done that, simple logic tells him that he may have overlooked a solution better than any under examination. Moreover, scientific conventions demand that empirical evaluative aspects of an analysis be separated so that the latter do not corrupt the former. Hence conventional planning requires a specification of goals and other relevant values independently of and logically prior to the empirical examination of the consequences of alternative possible policies for attaining the desired goals or values.[13]

By contrast, strategic planning proceeds in the belief that for complex social policy problems, these canons cannot possibly be either followed or approximated. For complex social problems, all analysis is grossly incomplete;

important considerations are inevitably left out of the analysis. Hence guidelines are required specifying not that nothing must be left out but indicating what must be left out. Similarly, guidelines are needed not to keep evaluative and empirical aspects of analysis in isolation from each other but to make each, by skillful mixture with the other, fruitful to the other. One might add that in their departures from conventional canons of analysis, these strategic guidelines are disturbing to conventional planners.

Conventional logico-scientific norms that prescribe, for example, analysis in all possible depth and in all possible breadth are internally contradictory in real world application, for depth can only be had at the expense of breadth and vice versa. One needs norms that indicate when breadth is worth sacrificing for depth and vice versa. For another example, since no analyst can exhaustively pursue all the important possible adverse consequences of any one possible solution to a problem, he needs guidelines that tell him not to pursue them all but how to decide which of the important ones can be neglected. Such guidelines will take account of the possibility that some adverse consequences are reversible if they actually appear (inventory declines, for example), while others are not (a crop shortfall, for example); that some can be dealt with by policies subsequently designed to cope with them if they appear (traffic congestion near new factories), while others cannot (end of life on planet by nuclear explosions); and that some of them are in the domain of other planners and policymakers who can be assumed to stand ready to cope with them (health officers to cope with effects of insecticides), while others are not (in some systems no one stands ready to cope with environmental adversities). A strategic planner will design his planning tasks in the light of such considerations

For lack of attention to strategic planning in the theoretical literature of planning, norms or guidelines for strategic planning are not well articulated. even if it is clear that strategic planning abandons the conventional logico-scientific norms. They can be illustrated, however, by a sample from one set of them that I have elsewhere presented in detail. The set prescribes a method I have called disjointed incrementalism.[14]

1. *Limitation of analysis to alternative policies only incrementally different from prevailing policies.* Such a tactic simplifies analysis in several ways:
    a. reduces the total number of alternatives to be examined,
    b. focuses analysis on policies of some familiarity, and on which empirical evidence is available,
    c. permits the isolation of variables for analysis since incremental policies differ from prevailing and other incremental policies in only a few ways,
    d. eliminates the need for a comprehensive guiding theory.
2. *Conversion of "the problem" into a sequence of problems.* Such a tactic simplifies analysis in several ways:

a. reduces the complexity of each problem analyzed,

b. makes the most of feedback and correction, thus both safeguarding against error and positively improving policy design,

c. permits reconsiderations of both ends and means through examination of feedback.

3. *Examination of goals or values in close connection with, rather than prior to, empirical investigation of policy alternatives and their respective possible consequences.* Such a tactic has the advantages of:

a. shortcutting interminable free-floating inconclusive abstract, non-operational debate on values,

b. converting abstract value questions into specific questions about value trade-offs implicit in each alternative policy under consideration,

c. sensitizing the analysis to value considerations the relevance of which appears only when empirical consequences of alternative possible policies come to be discovered,

d. thus responds to the impossibility that all relevant values can be "given" to the planners as parameters.

THE TWO METHODS OF PLANNING
IN LIBERAL DEMOCRATIC SOCIETIES

The two methods of planning become clearer if we now examine them in liberal democratic societies. Although we derived the model of strategic planning from a model of a society with many liberal democratic characteristics, both kinds of planning are attempted in the liberal democracies, just as both are attempted in socialist or Communist societies.

In the liberal democratic systems, paradoxically, it is conventional rather than strategic planning that enjoys the highest esteem; and, although policymakers and their advisors actually employ strategic rather than conventional analysis, the "theory" of planning is almost wholly about conventional planning. Studies of the planning process do not appreciate the difference between the two kinds of analysis and planning. For example, Charles Schultze, economist and one-time U.S. Budget Director, sets conventional notions of planning embodied in the U.S. governmental PPB (Planning-Programming-Budgeting), which is a method of combining systems analysis and program budgeting, against disjointed incrementalism, which I have just identified as one form that strategic planning can take. Defending conventional planning, he sees strategic planning as no more than a substitution of bargaining or of "politics" for analysis. He wholly misses the distinction between two forms of analysis, two forms of planning; the one conventional, the other strategic; the one confident, comprehensive, ambitious; the other selective, discriminating, economical of analytical talent.[15]

In the liberal democracies, planning theory has developed as a form of applied social science and applied mathematics. Theory has been written for the most part by scholars—usually those with conventional scientific, engineering, economics, or mathematics training—who have taken it for granted that planning is intellectual or analytic. To many of them planning is attractive because they see it as a way to substitute human intelligence for the crudities of politics.[16] Many of them well understand that politics is inescapable, but they want to minimize it while maximizing analysis as a determinant of policy. In their preoccupation with what they see as a rivalry between politics and analysis, they miss seeing the possibility that analysis can be made most effective not as an outright alternative to politics but in skillful adaptation to inevitable interactive processes. Especially striking is the failure of economists to understand that the need to economize on planning, because it can never accomplish all that is asked of it, argues for an elaborate strategy of planning in interactive processes rather than for an endorsement of conventional planning whenever it can be advanced at the expense of politics.

The most methodologically accomplished planners in these societies are many mid-sized to large corporations.[m] In their systematic gathering and organizing of data and their use of techniques like budgeting, operations research, systems analysis, and mathematical programming, they plan with a sophistication rarely found in any government and perhaps never characteristic of any attempts at economy-wide economic planning in Communist systems.[17] Corporate planning methods are on many points conventional rather than strategic. But on some critical points they are thoroughtly strategic.

They do not attempt such an overview of the whole economy of which the corporation is a part, as central planners attempt; they disregard consequences and values other than a restricted set for which they take responsibility, even if the disregarded consequences and values result in important adversities elsewhere in the system; and their planning is instead adapted to a narrow corporate role in an interaction process, the market. The corporation plans its participation in the market system, does not plan the whole process of resource allocation and production.

We all quickly recognize that corporate planning is—has to be—strategic as just described because market systems are based on specialization of entrepreneurial function and motivation. It is the function of the corporation to make profits. A similar argument holds for governmental planning.

To a degree, governmental organizations have a broad option open to them. On the one hand, to some degree they can attempt a comprehensive analysis of and responsibility for all consequences and all values on which their plans impinge. Yet, on the other hand, they must disregard broad goals and plan an adaptation to a political interaction—in some respects very much like a corporation in a market—leaving to other agencies responsibilities for consequences and values they themselves ignore.

[m]Not necessarily the most efficient or socially useful planners, however.

A few political scientists have lately suggested that democratic politics is market-like. Exchange, they believe, is the core phenomenon in both the familiar market and the political market, in which political favors are exchanged. They make much of the role of bargaining and of debts in both arenas.[18] I believe they overstate the similarities, and the argument here rests on no such parellel. All we are claiming is that, just as the corporation or other business enterprises operates within an interaction process to which its planning can better adapt it, so does a governmental official or organization—in all real world societies.

The corporation might be thought of as a limiting case of strategic planning in which planning is wholly subordinated to an interaction process. The opposite extreme is one single central planning authority for the whole of society, combining economic, political, and social control into one integrated planning process that makes interaction unnecessary. But no such authority exists in any liberal democratic society. All actual government planning in liberal democratic systems falls between. Consequently, for all government planning in such systems there is a choice to be made as to degree and character of adaptation to interaction.

We have been led to an important conclusion worth repeating: in liberal democratic societies governmental planning is a process for helping government officials and organizations play their respective roles in a vast interaction process that is unplanned. All actual planning is subordinated at some point—either badly or well—to interaction processes. Planning of different kinds differs in the degree to which analysis is substituted for or adapted to interaction and in the skill of the adaptor. No planning ever wholly replaces interaction with analysis.

Government agencies, even broad-assignment agencies like the Indian Planning Commission or the French Commissariat du Plan, can succeed only if they pursue greatly restricted purposes. Their purposes may be, of course, broader, larger or more complex than those of a single corporation; but they cannot ever rise wholly above participation in a specific role in an interaction process. That is to say, they cannot, in a liberal democratic society modeled at least roughly on our vision of a preference guided society, claim the broadest policymaking function that is discharged by interaction processes rather than by any participant in them.

Failure of theory and practice to recognize this fact goes far to account for the poor record at the hands of governmental agencies in the liberal democracies of many of the planning techniques successfully employed by corporations. Despite some scattered successes in military planning and a few other uses, attempts both to generalize the techniques within the military and to extend their use throughout the U.S. federal government have failed. President Johnson's effort to tie systems analysis to program budgeting in the PPB formula was thwarted by the incapacity of government planners and budgeters to perform the operations called for by PPB and is now in disrepute.

Sometimes the failures of formal, sophisticated techniques of planning are attributable to the cynicism with which they are embraced, as when the Army Corps of Engineers employs spurious or distorted cost-benefit analysis simply to justify projects already decided on for other reasons. Their failures have also been explained by an excess of ambition in their use. The techniques, complex as they appear to be, are not complex enough for any but the smallest problems of public policy. As was pointed out years ago by Charles Hitch, a distinguished advocate and practitioner of the techniques:

> I would make the empirical generalization from my experience at RAND and elsewhere that operations research is the art of sub-optimizing, i.e., of solving some lower-level problems, and that difficulties increase and our special competence diminishes by an order of magnitude with every level of decisionmaking we attempt to ascend. The sort of simple explicit model which operations researchers are so proficient in using can certainly reflect most of the significant factors influencing traffic control on the George Washington Bridge, but the proportion of relevant reality which we can represent by any such model or models in studying, say, a major foreign-policy decision, appears to be almost trivial.[19]

The use of techniques of this kind in government has been especially plagued by criteria problems. It is sometimes suggested that corporations can employ the techniques successfully because corporate objectives, hence corporate criteria, are few. In government a multiplicity of objectives renders any sufficiently simple payoff function, welfare function, or set of solution criteria unacceptable.[20]

These difficulties—general complexity and, specifically, criteria difficulties—only partly explain the failures of the techniques in government for, as Hitch would argue, they permit a successful use of the techniques for problems of suboptimization in which complexity can be greatly reduced and specialized criteria made acceptable. The additional and fundamental obstacle to the successful use of these techniques, even for suboptimization problems, is the other side of the coin of corporate success. Corporations tailor their use of the techniques to the organization's role in interaction. Government agencies do not yet know how to do so.

In the case of the corporation, narrowness of purpose and disregard of most aspects of the public interests are challenged only marginally by advocates of the soulful corporation. On the whole, everyone pretty well understands that the system works, not well, but tolerably, through corporation preoccupation with profit-making (or sales promotion, or capital growth) rather than with a larger view of the welfare of society; and corporate planning is without difficulty adapted to helping the corporation plan successfully its assigned role in a complex interaction process in which more is accomplished for the society than the corporation itself intends. But a great deal of liberal democratic and scientific and academic rhetoric asks government agencies to discharge just those broad responsibilities that, by our argument, they cannot and should not. Hence government officials and especially planners and other policy analysts are constantly pulled in two directions to a degree the corporation is not; and, not having yet achieved a reconciliation of the two forces pulling on them, they are not competently using forms of analysis adapted to the organization's role in an interaction process.

It might be argued that, even if each government official and organization has a specialized role in interaction processes, each ought to pursue on a comprehensive view of the whole society its vision of what is best for society. Insofar as they plan, then, each should plan in the conventional style rather than strategically plan a specialized role in interaction processes. But almost everyone in liberal democratic societies knows that a fire chief or inspector of weights and measures is not competent to say what is best for society and should not be encouraged to try to decide. The fire chief should try to control fires and should plan accordingly, leaving to others and to interaction processes the determination both of other goals and of other policies, including policies to cope with possible excesses or deficiencies of the fire chief's policies. Most thoughtful people in liberal democratic societies have similarly come to understand that judges and courts are not competent to decide what is just, for that is a question that runs beyond the competence of any government official and answers to which would in any case be distorted by the professional biases of judges. Judges in liberal democratic societies are consequently given the more limited assignment of interpreting and enforcing the law, which is only one of many alternative ways of achieving justice. Similarly, we now need a fuller understanding in liberal democratic societies that regulatory agencies, municipal planning authorities, state development commissions, congressional committees, budget bureaus, and even the chief executive are each incompetent and not to be trusted to achieve a synoptic view of the whole society and its many interests and must each play a specific role. Appropriately, their planners must adapt their work to those roles.

The Indian Planning Commission provides an example. The Commission accepts a generalized responsibility for guiding Indian economic development, a responsibility that calls for an omniscience that it knows it does not possess. The Ministry of Finance also claims such a responsibility for itself, to be discharged not through scheduling and coordination of investment outlays, which is a major task of the Commission, but through coordinating financial controls. For at least one short period in 1964, the Ministry of Agriculture also claimed such a responsibility, believing, as the minister said, that the key to Indian development was agricultural policy. The prime minister similarly claims general responsibility for guiding development policy; possibly the cabinet also claims it; possibly also the Working Committee of the Congress Party; and there may be other claimants too.

Under these circumstances, the beginning of wisdom for the Commission is to acknowledge to itself that it will interact with several other powerful claimants to a coordinating role. It cannot expect all the others to yield to it; nor could it make a good case that all ought to. To play its most useful role, the Commission must then ask itself how its role might differ from the others and how, in view of its interactions with the others, it might best shape its role. Its guiding objectives should be suited to its role and should be in any case, something less and more precise than the vast amorphous task of guiding Indian economic development. Finally, then, its planning should pursue those limited objectives. Correspondingly, the highest level participants in the interaction—prime minister and cabinet—should guide, through authoritative assignment if required, the Commission into an appropriate role, to a concern with limited objectives and to planning activities adapted to role objectives. This is only to say that, for any governmental organization, the refined specification of its role, objectives, and planning task is not to be left wholly to itself.

The difficulties that government officials and organizations face in adapting their roles and their planning to interaction processes suggest that in addition to a great amount of hardheaded sophistication on the part of participants in government, we need an improved theory of liberal democratic government to help governmental organizations find their way. Specifically, we need a democratic theory that will tell us, as economic theory tells us for business enterprises, the circumstances in which the pursuit of limited manageable objectives by specific organizations will, through interaction processes, accomplish social purposes that policy analysis and planning are incapable of pursuing directly. All this will be slow in coming.

Innovations in planning theory are still largely preoccupied with achieving a comprehensive or synoptic mastery of the problem whose solution is to be planned. Thus electronic computation is hailed for greatly extending the amount of data that can be processed and the number of calculations that can be incorporated into a solution. Both electronic calculation and formal designs for problem solution, like those of operations research and systems analysis, are argued to have the merit of advancing analysis toward completion, of organizing the consideration of all important variables into the discovery of a problem's solution. Fundamentally, the defense of these innovations is that they permit analysts to incorporate what they formerly had to omit and that they permit, through quantification, a systematic aggregation of large numbers of variables earlier only roughly, often intuitively, related to each other in the design of a solution.[n]

[n]In the last half of her chapter in this volume, Mária Augustinovics offers a number of important fresh insights into the use of mathematical models and methods in economic planning. But she assumes that the case for these methods is that they facilitate a greater degree of comprehensiveness and completeness of analysis. Economic planning is to plan the "total process." The problem is: "How can the total process be grasped?" She would see the possibilities of strategic planning and of skillfully employing mathematical methods in strategic planning only by believing that the total process cannot be grasped.

In short, none of these promising innovations in planning methods are designed in the style of strategic planning, in which completeness or synopsis is acknowledged to be impossible and in which, consequently, improvement in planning skill must come largely from better designed selectivity and discrimination—better designed shortcuts and omissions. Possibly the major innovations in planning design that acknowledge the need for selectivity rather than completion are those, paradoxically, that have come to be only reluctantly conceded as necessary, as analysts find that even the most powerful of computers cannot complete complex analyses that must instead be given shortened heuristic procedures if they are to reach solutions. But insight into the shortcuts needed by the computers has not been generalized to enrich the theory of planning.

Presumably there are important advances to be made in planning methods along both lines: by some movement toward completion of analyses (even if completion is impossible) and by more skillful selectivity in inevitably incomplete analysis. In the liberal democracies today intellectual fashion endorses the former; the latter, however, is suggested by the model of the preference guided society.

PLANNING IN COMMUNIST SYSTEMS

Because conventional planning is adapted to the needs of the intellectually guided society, after which on some points Communist or socialist systems are modeled, it is striking how little of conventional planning is to be found in Communist systems. It has long been observed of Soviet economic planning, for example, that for the most part it consists of incremental alterations of the production scheduled for the last previous period. It is remedial, sequential, and incremental in just those ways characterized above for disjointed incrementalism. Moreover, actual productions schedules and input allocations are endlessly reconsidered and altered in a variety of interactions: among enterprises, between enterprises and planning authorities, and among planning authorities at various levels. Some of these interactions are those of grey, if not black, markets, as in transactions among enterprises not provided in the formal plans. Some are what some of us would call political bargains, negotiations, exchanges of threats, promises of mutual benefits between enterprise and planning authority.[21]

In its formal techniques, Communist economic planning is not comprehensive, as conventional planning requires. Formal planning is pursued through such methods as materials balances, input-output analysis, and iterative procedures. For our purposes, the most significant feature of such methods is that they aim at no more than balance or consistency in economic plans; they do not even attempt optimality. Communist systems do not systematically practice any planning method designed to achieve optimality. At least to that extent all their methods recognize the impossibility of intellectual mastery of the planning problem; all make do with a limited assignment for the planners.

Consistency rather than optimality planning is stronger evidence for the impossibility of conventional planning in Communist societies than it is for the existence of strategic planning. For, given the impossibility of conventional planning, Communist planners have simply reduced their tasks in obvious ways, as in materials balances, and have not, any more than their Western colleagues, imaginatively addressed themselves to the design of strategies, tactics, shortcuts, dodges, strategems, or new designs necessary for what we have called strategic planning. Possibly, however, on a sympathetic view of what they are doing, we ought to regard consistency planning, in input-output analysis and the like, as a strategy or as elements in strategic planning, thought not well developed.

Communist debate in recent years on how to make more effective use of the market system is another indication of limitations of conventional planning. In the debate, it is perceived that the increasing technological complexity of the economy is one of several reasons for methods of planning adapted to elements of a market system—which is to say strategic planning—rather than methods not adapted—which is to say conventional planning.[22]

Another way to look at Communist economic planning is to see it as the planned adaptation of secondary decisions to unplanned primary decisions. Since the unplanned primary decisions are the product of interaction in large part, Communist planning is to that degree strategic rather than conventional, that is to say, adapted to interactions rather than substituted for them. All over the world, economic planning tends to take this form in fact. Key decisions—for example, to give a big push to heavy industry, or specifically to electric power facilities, or to stress armament, or to increase the supply of consumer goods—are too important to be left to the ostensible planners. These key issues are resolved at the higheset level in the governmental system, and less through analysis than through interactions among political leaders each of whom takes a position from practical judgment rather than from an analytical input consequential enough to deserve the name of planning. Once the key decisions are made, it is the planners' job to reconcile all other resource allocation and production decisions with them.

For all these reasons, we can generalize the important conclusion reached about planning in the liberal democracies to planning in Communist systems—for that matter, to all systems: all governmental planning is—and has to be—adapted to interaction process, which it can not wholly displace. And it follows that planning theory in Communist or socialist systems needs to accommodate this fact no less so than in the liberal democracies.

We may also take note that there is less planning at the enterprise level, conventional or strategic, in Communist systems than in liberal democratic. In part, it is because computer technology and knowledge of specialized planning techniques are more available in the liberal democracies. It may also, however, be attributable to the fact that the relative autonomy of the corporate enterprise in the liberal democracies makes clear to each corporation that it faces important policy questions to which sophisticated planning techniques offer an answer. By contrast, the subordination of enterprises to authoritative direction in Communist systems discourages serious analysis of enterprise policy. And the incentive systems and success indicators used in Communist systems reduce enterprise policy making to bargaining and other similar forms of interaction between enterprise and higher authority, with a minimum of analytical input on the side of the enterprise.

For questions of economic policy even more complex than production planning, Communist systems have made almost no attempt at planning of any kind: conventional or strategic. And they reveal, in the methods by which they make policy on the most complex problems, that they are, after all, similar in major respects to the preference guided rather than to the intellectually guided society. For the most complex problems, they are able to make no greater claims to use analysis, or to use theory, than do the liberal democratic systems; and they are heavily dependent on interaction processes to accomplish what analysis cannot. The governing elite is neither stable nor homogeneous in its beliefs as to what constitutes a correct solution to these complex problems. Hence it has to substitute for analysis and theory a whole range of interactions, ranging from voting or bargaining within a Politburo, through negotiation among the Party leadership, the military, and the high levels of the civil service, to adaptation of Party-made policy to meet the challenges of mass unrest, or at least the challenge of dissent from the intelligentsia. Having accepted the substitution of interaction for complete analysis for these complex problems, Communist leadership has fallen back, as has leadership in the liberal democracies, more on what might be called unplanned policymaking than on a careful adaptation of analysis to the interactions, as in the model of strategic planning. And, of course, who the leaders or governing elite are to be is not analytically determined but is a consequence of interaction.

Thus since the Liberation of 1949, China has intended to eliminate small-scale private agriculture in favor of collectives. In the first years of communism, the leaders concluded that, whatever plans they might have, expedience required that private family agriculture be left largely intact. From 1953 to 1955, however, they moved to organize peasants into "lower level" agricultural producers' cooperatives, in which land was pooled and unified management practiced, although leaving supplementary private plots of limited size at the disposal of each peasant. In 1956–57, they organized the peasants into "advanced" cooperatives in which payment to each peasant for his pooled land was abolished. Supplementary private plots were still allowed. In 1955, however, they had in effect closed down free markets in which peasants could sell produce from their private plots, as well as some of the collective product.

A year later, in 1956, the free markets were again permitted, and private plots were enlarged. In 1958, the cooperatives, averaging about 160 households, were combined into communes of almost 5,000 households each, and free markets were curbed. The private plots were legally eliminated, although the intent to eliminate them may not have been effectively implemented. Communal dining and free supply of basic commodities were instituted with the communes. By 1959, one year later, free supply and communal dining were already on their way out, by decision of top leadership. Free markets and private plots were reintroduced in 1959. Later in the same year, private plots were again eliminated. But they were again reintroduced in 1960.

Subsequently, communes were reduced, on the average, to less than half their former size, and they were divested of their earlier responsibilities as the major economic organization for agriculture and local industry. Responsibility for agricultural production was moved back to organizations the size of the earlier "advanced" cooperatives and to even smaller production teams.[23]

A similar record is displayed in industrial planning. And for formal planning, the Chinese Five-Year Plan for 1954 to 1957 was not in fact approved until 1955; it was then revised in 1956; and it was perhaps abandoned during 1957.[24]

Policymaking of this kind is not irrational. What is significant is that policies are changed from year to year, even month to month, are tailored quickly to expediency, are advanced when politics makes it possible to advance, constrained when politics calls for constraint. In these respects, Communist policymaking looks like policymaking in the United States. In this record, it is difficult to find any distinctive qualities of analysis that deserve the name of planning.

Similarly, the USSR experimented with worker control of production and the elimination of money in the period of War Communism; recoiled in 1921 from its disastrous effects on production into the partial restoration of "capitalism" in the period of the New Economic Policy until 1927; then began a sequence of five-year plans for industry and agriculture that persisted with remarkable stability until the death of Stalin in 1953, since which time policy has moved, at varying speed and with reversals, toward an enlarged use of the market system and a reduction of the physical controls of the Stalin period. But the Stalinist period of conspicuous steadfastness in policy is not now seen either by the Soviets or by foreign observers as an illustration of planned policymaking but as a period of rigidity in policy, which, despite its successes, gradually sapped the Soviet Union of its growth capacities, and the persistence of which is attributable less to its analytical underpinnings than to the unbending tyranny that Stalin exercised over major policy. Again, therefore, Communist policymaking is not to be identified with planning.

As for the scope of formal economic planning, it is not comprehensive. It does not specify the relation of the economy to the rest of society, nor even all the major features of the economy and their desired relations with each other. Formal plans are usually economic growth plans of restricted scope. They are not plans for "educating" a population in Mao's sense, or educating in the liberal-democratic sense. Nor are they plans for comprehensively attacking ecological problems, or political reform, or income distribution, or peace, or for enlarging the amenities of life. A plan is largely no more than a first approximation to a resource deployment schedule, thereafter endlessly altered through interaction, coupled with a financial plan to balance money income and outgo.

For our purposes, what distinguishes Communist systems from others is less that they plan the methods and sequences by which they intend to achieve their great goals than that they have great goals and act boldly to reach them. Mao and Castro, even more than other Communist leaders, are intent on making a "new man." This is bold, and so are also their massive attempts at indoctrination to make the new man. Stalin, Mao, and Castro all set out to collectivize agriculture, which is, again, a bold ambition; and they were bold in pursuing it. They decided upon these goals, not in any planning process different from the processes that decisionmakers who do not plan employ, but in all the rough and tumble of politics, emboldened no doubt by their extraordinary power over the populace and guided perhaps by a more definitive ideology than those that guide leaders in the market-oriented democracies. Boldness, however, is not planning.

OTHER MODELS OF PLANNING?

It is just possible that China is in the process of discovering or inventing a new concept of planning that breaks out of our two models. Fundamentally, the Maoists appear to aspire to reach the intellectually guided society, as do European Communists. An innovation, however, may be revealed in Mao's concept of democracy which is somehow connected with the idea of a vast outpouring of the energies of the masses.[25] His attempt to "educate" the masses, to form a new Communist man, an attempt that goes beyond any similar attempts in the Soviet Union, appears to seek to mobilize energies, to stimulate resourcefulness, to make every individual citizen a decentralized force for economic development.[26] His stress on energy is impressive. It appears again in his hostility toward bureaucracy and his hope that a repeated renewal of revolutionary fervor, as in the Cultural Revolution, can repeatedly roll away bureaucratic obstacles—even hostility—to the release of the energy of the masses.

Mao is offering energy as an alternative to coordination of specialized functions as the key to production and growth. Ever since Adam Smith's analysis of the division of labor in pin making, good economic organization has been identified with good coordination of parts. In liberal democratic societies, economics is the study of resource allocation and combination, a way of looking at economics that puts coordination at the center of attention; and in conventional Communist societies, the chief ambition of planning has been coordinated production and input allocation schedules, as through materials balances. To many scholars and practitioners, alike, planning *is* coordination.

What Mao seems to be arguing is that individual energies are at some point a good substitute for an increasingly fine articulation of parts of a complex organization, that too nicely calculated coordination stultifies, and that the release of energies requires a looser connection of parts that allows room for individual autonomy, resourcefulness, and energy at suitably low levels in the social or political hierarchy.

If there is anything valid in his thought, it calls for a recognition of two propositions about planning. The first is that central planning should move in the direction of planning a release of energies and not merely for coordination. The second is that planning, defined again as the attempt to raise the role of thought and analysis in policymaking, needs to be pushed greatly in the direction of drastic decentralization, so that many opportunities to plan appropriate policies are thrown into the hands of masses of people with appropriate energy and resourcefulness. That this is indeed what Maoist thought intends is indicated by Mao's repeated expressions of confidence in the problem-solving capacity of the masses and in the merits of the generalist over the specialist.[27] In his attack on the specialist, Mao is turning against both Adam Smith's specialized pin makers and the Soviet Union's highly specialized Stakhanovites. If we reply that at low levels in the hierarchy, even energetic and intelligent individuals do not know what to do, I take it that the Maoist argument is that their mistakes in what they choose to do are less serious than the stultification of their energies in both liberal democratic and conventional Communist systems.

In these respects Mao is part of a worldwide current of thought in which motivation is being stressed at the expense of design. Some straws in the wind are—and see what an interesting heterogeneous collection it is—youth movements in the United States and Western Europe for participatory democracy, new forms of industrial engineering in which the assembly line is abandoned in favor of less specialized work assignments, and, among economic theorists far removed from Maoist thought, a new interest in efficiencies other than allocative, illustrated by Leibenstein's seminal article on X efficiency.[28]

One can persuasively argue that planning a drastically decentralized release of energies has to be done, if at all, either through conventional or through strategic planning and that Mao's third way, however important it may turn out to be, is not inconsistent with our attempt to divide planning into two major types, each related to a model of a well ordered society. On the other hand, it is also possible that a fuller development of the implications of planning for a drastically decentralized release of energy will reveal in the background a third model of the well-ordered society, neither simply intellectually guided or preference guided but guided instead by a new combination of elite competence, ubiquitous social interaction among decentralized individual and small-group policymakers, and heretofore unappreciated analytical competence at the level of individual citizen and small organization.

Finally, suppose that participation in interaction processes turns out to be, as some liberal democrats have always believed, a valuable form of human activity for its own sake, its ends aside. If so, then the intellectually guided society will discover the value of interaction for its own sake and will have to plan opportunities for it. But in that case, the distinction between the intellectually guided society and the preference guided society largely disappears. In short, there is a possibility that the model of the intellectually guided society is internally inconsistent in its assumption that correct solutions to social problems require analysis to the exclusion of interaction. If so, then even by the standards of the intellectually guided society, the only defensible planning method is planning adapted to interaction processes too valuable for their own sake to be eliminated even if it were possible to do so. In short, even the intellectually guided society would have to practice strategic planning.

NOTES

1. Perhaps the best known and most influential single statement of such a line of thought is Herbert A. Simon, *Models of Man* (New York: John Wiley & Sons, Inc., 1957). See also Charles E. Lindblom, "The Science of Muddling Through," *Public Administration Review* 19, 2 (Spring 1959):79–88.

2. Simon, *Models of Man*, pp. 196 ff.

3. Frank Knight, *Freedom and Reform* (New York: Harper and Brothers, 1947), p. 190. Ernest Barker, *Reflections on Government* (London: Oxford University Press, 1942), p. 40.

4. See, for example, the stress on fallibility in John Stuart Mill, *On Liberty* (1859).

5. See also the argument that knowledge displaces politics in Robert E. Lane, "The Decline of Politics and Ideology in a Knowledgeable Society," *American Sociological Review* 31, 5 (October 1966):649–62.

6. As in Mill, *On Liberty*.

7. See Mary Parker Follett on integrated versus compromised solutions to problems and the role of conflict in motivating the search for integration, in *Dynamic Administration*, ed. H.M. Metcalf and L Urwick (New York: Harper and Brothers, 1942), pp. 239ff. See also Lewis Coser, *The Function of Social Conflict* (New York: Free Press, 1956).

8. As envisioned by some behavioralists. See, for example, B.F. Skinner, *Beyond Freedom and Dignity* (New York: Knopf, 1971). See also Raymond Bauer, *The New Man in Soviet Psychology* (Cambridge: Harvard University Press, 1952); E.L. Wheelwright and Bruce McFarlane, *The Chinese Road to Socialism* (New York: Monthly Review Press, 1970), p. 147; and Richard R. Fagan, *The Transformation of Political Culture in Cuba* (Stanford: Stanford University Press, 1969), p. 14.

9. Emile Durkheim, *The Division of Labor in Society* (1893).

10. For examples of the third, see any items in the literature on governmental reform, as well as theoretical studies like Kenneth J. Arrow, *Social

Choice and Individual Values (New York: John Wiley and Sons, Inc., 1951), or Douglas Rae, *The Political Consequence of Electoral Laws* (New Haven: Yale University Press, 1971).

11. David Novick, Melven Anshen, and W.C. Truppner, *Wartime Production Controls* (New York: Columbia University Press, 1949), Ch. 8.

12. See two chapters in which French planning is discussed in Everett E. Hagen and Stephanie F.T. White, *Great Britain: Quiet Revolution in Planning* (Syracuse: Syracuse University Press, 1966), Chs. 9 and 10. See also Stephen S. Cohen, "From Causation to Decision: Planning as Politics," *American Economic Review* 60, 2 (May 1970): 180–85.

13. See, for example, Jan Tinbergen, *Economic Policy* (Amsterdam: North-Holland Publishing Co., 1956).

14. C.E. Lindblom, "The Science of Muddling Through"; David Braybrooke and C.E. Lindblom, *A Strategy of Decision* (New York: Free Press, 1963); and C.E. Lindblom, *The Intelligence of Democracy* (New York: Free Press, 1965).

15. Charles L. Schultze, *The Politics and Economics of Public Spending* (Washington: Brookings Institution, 1968).

16. For an example of the distinction in the literature between analytical and political policymaking (but without advocacy of one or the other), see James G. March and Herbert A. Simon, *Organizations* (New York: John Wiley and Sons, Inc., 1958), pp. 129 ff.

17. Neil W. Chamberlain, *Private and Public Planning* (New York: McGraw-Hill, 1965), Ch. 1.

18. For example, R.L. Curry and L.L. Wade, *A Theory of Political Exchange* (Englewood Cliffs, N.J.: Prentice-Hall, 1968); Warren Ilchman and N.T. Uphoff, *Political Economy of Change* (Berkeley: University of California Press, 1969).

19. Charles Hitch, "Operations Research and National Planning—A Dissent," *Operations Research* 5, 5 (October 1957):718.

20. On criteria difficulties, see Roland N. McKean, *Efficiency in Government Through Systems Analysis* (New York: John Wiley and Sons, Inc., 1958), Ch. 2.

21. Raymond P. Powell, "Plan Execution and the Workability of Soviet Planning," Yale University, Department of Economics Discussion Paper No. 20, mimeo, Sept. 1972.

22. Gregory Grossman, "Economic Reforms: A Balance Sheet," *Problems of Communism* 15, 6 (November-December 1966):43-55.

23. Details on these changes in policy, and on others related to them, are in Jan Prybyla, *The Political Economy of Communist China* (Scranton, Pa.: International Textbook Company, 1970), pp. 148–350, esp. 148 ff, 233 ff, 283–89, 298, and 350.

24. Prybyla, *Political Economy of Communist China*, p. 110.

25. Franz Schurmann, *Ideology and Organization in Communist China* (revised edition; Berkeley: University of California Press, 1971), pp. 54 and 88.

26. See John G. Gurley, "Capitalism and Maoist Economic Development," *Bulletin of Concerned Asian Scholars* 2, 3 (April-July 1970):39.

27. Schurmann, *Ideology and Organization in Communist China*, pp. 100 and 233.

28. Harvey Leibenstein, "Allocative Efficiency *vs.* X-Efficiency," *American Economic Review* 56, 3 (June 1966):392–415.

Comments on Charles E. Lindblom's Chapter

Andrzej Korbonski

Professor Lindblom refrains from suggesting a "narrow" definition of planning, which he sees simply as "an aspect of, perhaps a kind of, policymaking, as well as an aspect or kind of institutional problem solving." This was a wise decision for more than one reason. First, there has been a proliferation of such definitions in the literature and any additional entry would most likely compound the existing confusion.[1] Second, there is the problem of comparability of approaches to, and methods of, planning in different political, economic and social systems—which favors the kind of broad conceptualization put forward by Lindblom. The validity and usefulness of his definition become abundantly clear in the course of considering planning methods in such disparate societies as France, Hungary, and Japan.

It can, of course, be argued, that the identification of "planning" with "policymaking" and "institutional problem solving" represents, in Sartori's words, "conceptual stretching" resulting in a certain loss of precision.[2] This would have been true if Lindblom intended to engage in an empirical investigation of planning techniques in different systems. Such, however, is not his purpose. Instead he is interested in analyzing the "cleavage"—with regard to the role and function of rationality in policymaking—which derives from an "opposing set of views on the maximum role of reason, thought, analysis or intellect in social organization and social change." Thus, the broad concept of planning appears eminently suitable for this particular purpose.

In his effort to throw new or additional light on certain features of planning, Lindblom introduces what he calls "two visions, models or pictures of a well-ordered society," corresponding respectively in limited ways to idealized liberal democracy and idealized communism. He then proceeds to construct a checklist which is intended to serve as a yardstick with the aid of which the two models can be compared.

Because the usage of the word "model" has been frequently abused in the literature, especially in recent years, my own predilection would be for an "ideal type," which as a methodological device for making comparisons is probably preferable to a "model." If we define "ideal types" as "theoretical constructs such that no concrete examples of these constructs can be found in reality,"[3] then it can be argued that they rather than "models" provide a better description of the two types of societies suggested above, in addition to having a considerable heuristic value.

My difficulty with the features of Lindblom's two "visions" is not that I do not understand them; I do indeed. What I find hard to accept is his postulated dichotomy between these features as they manifest themselves in the respective idealized societies. For example, just as I cannot possibly imagine a society in which "there is no politics" but which is ruled by an intellectually superior elite endowed with wisdom and vision, capable of producing a comprehensive blueprint for change, believing in the existence of an inherent harmony and concord among its citizens, and possessed of a monopoly of political power—so I find it also next to impossible to visualize a polity governed by an elite totally deprived of these attributes. And even if I could visualize such a polity, I am not at all certain that as a result I would be in a better position to understand more fully the functioning of that society, or the essence of planning.

Continuing his comparison, Lindblom applies the terms "intellectually guided" and "preference guided" to denote the two "models," and postulates an axiom which, he claims, embodies much of the basic difference between the two societal visions. Thus while in preference guided societies institutions and policies are mainly the outcomes of· "social interaction," in intellectually guided societies they are the result of specific design and analysis.

Methodologically we can think of the above "ideal types" as the two extremes on a continuum showing the relative mix of "design" and "interaction." Alternatively, I suggest, we could postulate a single model describing a "mixed" system containing both elements, which for lack of a better term we could call a "post-industrial society."[4] Thus, if we are interested in comparing different societies with respect to their planning procedures or policies, we could do so with reference to one or two "visions" or "models." The advantage of the single-point approach seems again to be its greater realism and plausibility.[5]

Moreover, to cite Sartori again, "as long as we pursue the either-or mode of analysis, we are in trouble; but if concepts are understood as a matter of more-or-less, as pointing to differences in *degree,* then our difficulties can be solved by measurement."[6] As Lindblom is the first to agree, every society is a "mixed" society representing a synthesis of "thought" and "interaction." According to Tinbergen, it is also the "mixed" system which maximizes welfare, which is presumably also the goal of a "well-ordered society."[7]

We are thus presented with a methodological choice. In drawing a clear line between two societal visions, Lindblom's approach has the great merit of forcing us to face the issue squarely and to differentiate, albiet at a high level of abstraction, between two diametrically opposed models of political, economic, and social systems. The other approach, although possibly somewhat less rigorous, has one major virtue—that of greater realism. In the final analysis the choice is likely to be dictated by one's strategy and goals. If one is interested in finding out "how the system works," the more "realistic" approach may well be the one to adopt.

In the "cleavage" mentioned earlier, Lindblom sees important implications for planning methods. The "great and fundamental" distinction is between methods "that confidently plunge the intellect directly into its tasks in the style of the intellectually guided society, and those that, mindful of the intellect's fallibility, employ the planner's intellect selectively and in subordination to social interactions." The "systematic features" of the types of planning are said to follow fairly directly from the features of the respective models of "intellectually" and "preference" guided societies. In real life, each society is free to adopt a planning system that includes elements of both methods—the former labeled "conventional" and the latter "strategic."

This leads one to ask whether there is a necessary "fit" between planning methods and the nature of the political system; and if there is such a congruence, how it can be empirically tested. Must a democratic society necessarily give birth to democratic planning practices? Are nondemocratic planning processes inevitably an offspring of authoritarian systems? What is the connection between the two? Many scholars have busied themselves with this problem and have postulated several hypotheses linking, for example, the level of economic development with democracy and economic planning with mobilization regimes.[8] All of them took it for granted that there was some kind of mutual dependence between the political and economic milieus.[a]

Lindblom's discussion of the differences between strategic and conventional planning and their respective functions in liberal democratic societies is most illuminating. For me at least, it is the high point of his chapter, even though, now and then, I felt sympathetic to the views of those who saw "strategic planning as no more than a substitution of bargaining or of 'politics' for analysis." I can easily see the great need for planned and unplanned social interaction, I can appreciate the great value of "disjointed incrementalism" as a planning method, and I suspect that there is no government in the world today, Communist or non-Communist, which is not aware of the importance of both. However, I am not sure that I share Lindblom's confidence in the efficacy of

[a] An interesting recent confirmation of this tendency occurred in Czechoslovakia in the mid-sixties, according to what I was told in a personal interview in Prague in the spring of 1967. It appears that when the top political elite gave the green light for the implementation of far-reaching economic reforms in that country, it firmly believed in its ability to maintain the separation between the political and economic spheres. In other words, it assumed that while the economy would gradually undergo liberalization, there would be no spillover into the political arena. Just to make sure, the leadership appointed a special blue-ribbon commission to investigate the possible political effects of the economic reforms, but, as stated by one of its members, the commission met once or twice and then adjourned. The rest is history.

interaction as a problem-solving device, and his optimism regarding the planners' ability to "mold" the behavior of groups and individuals in a "strategic" fashion. Similarly, I have some doubts about the assured advantages of "epiphenomenal" solutions. I would argue that for every positive epiphenomenal solution of a problem, there emerges an epiphenomenal problem itself requiring solution. The repercussions of the recent meat and petroleum shortages in the United States are cases in point. Altogether, the argument strikes me as uncomfortably close to a restatement of the venerable doctrine of "the invisible hand."

A word about corporate planning. Here again I am not nearly as convinced as Lindblom that "the most methodologically accomplished planners in [liberal democratic] societies are many mid-sized to large corporations." Once could, of course, cite the example of the Edsel, RCA computer, Litton and Lockheed fiascos, but it would be too easy. However, I would venture the hypothesis that if in the United States, for example, many corporations are indeed sophisticated planners, it is largely because they operate in an environment established, maintained, and protected by the government, which, with the aid of regulatory agencies and other instruments, creates a suitable climate for corporate planning. Moreover, a sizable part of industry depends heavily on government orders and guarantees. Even in these favorable circumstances, the record of many of these corporations has not been impressive—as manifested in cost-overruns, government handouts, and corruption. Thus, while I am willing to accept the proposition that, at least in the United States, the private rather than the public sector may have proved more adept at planning (however defined), I am not really persuaded that "on the whole ... the system works, not well, but tolerably, through corporation preoccupation with profit making ... rather than with a larger view of the welfare of society." The recently announced high profits made by the petroleum industry can hardly be said to be related to the "tolerable" working of the American economy.

In his discussion of Communist societies, Lindblom finds two things particularly striking: first, "how little of conventional planning is to be found in Communist systems," and second, that the planning methods employed there "aim at not more than balance or consistency in economic plans; they do not even attempt optimality."

I would argue that there is really nothing striking about this. That in reality Communist systems have not, now or ever, come close to the model of an "intellectually guided" society is a well established fact which needs no elaboration. If for a relatively brief period a significant share of the Soviet and East European economies was subject to fairly tight central planning "from above," it was still a far cry from the ideal type of "conventional" planning suggested by Lindblom. Similarly, the absence of optimal planning should not surprise anyone, since it was impossible by definition so long as the conventional yardsticks used for the purpose of achieving optimal solutions remained irrational. What is surprising perhaps, especially in the Soviet case, is the rather strange coexistence of irrational and rational theories and ideas affecting planning.[9]

The conclusion which emerges from the discussion of Communist planning practices is that they are really not so much different form those in liberal democratic societies. Both of them represent a mix of conventional and strategic planning characterized by disjointed incrementalism, and in both cases the key decisions at the highest level are the outcome of interactions among the top elites rather than the result of careful analysis conducted by planners.[10]

One may assume that the post-World War II introduction of central planning in Eastern Europe was seen by many as the only panacea to a multitude of problems faced by nearly all countries in the area: wartime destruction, urban and rural unemployment, uneven regional development, lack of capital, and last but not least, the shortage of managerial know-how. In the circumstances, planning was perceived as perhaps the sole instrument capable of breaking through the "vicious circle of poverty" so characteristic of the East European environment.

The institutionalization of planning, even when initially mistrusted, was eventually accepted and even welcomed by certain important groups. Apart from the opportunistic elements always present in every mass political organization such as the Party, large segments of the government bureaucracy, managerial class, and nonagricultural labor force looked at central planning as a device guaranteeing them light work, security of employment, and relatively decent income. No wonder then that it was those groups which appeared either lukewarm or openly hostile to the economic reforms of the 1960s aimed at reducing the extent of central planning in the various countries.[11]

This last phenomenon is a testimony to the pernicious influence of central planning on East European society which cannot be easily documented or tested but which nevertheless seems to permeate just about every corner of social, political, and economic life. It can be described as a kind of mass demoralization or malaise stemming from living under the protective umbrella of the central planning commission. The literature is full of examples of the unholy alliance between bureaucrats and enterprise managers, and between managers and workers, which tended to make a mockery of the planning process. As a result, administrative skills, entrepreneurship, and high labor productivity fell into disrepute as representing a threat to the established order, which put such a high premium on mediocrity.

In fairness, it must be admitted that a similar situation existed (and exists today) also with respect to large segments of the American economy, especially those heavily dependent on government contracts. Thus there is considerable evidence of subpar performance and of the existence of cabals involving management and government and military officials aimed at restricting the scope of competition.

In time, the planning process in Eastern Europe became transformed into what Lindblom so aptly calls "unplanned policymaking." Whereas in the initial stages there was some semblance of interaction between government planners and managers, eventually it ceased completely and the economic plans were prepared at the center on the basis of past and incomplete information which was periodically updated in a more or less arbitrary fashion. This meant that as time went on the enterprises began to operate largely on their own. To be sure, they received directives from above. However, the targets were not really the outcome of thorough planning or analysis but simply represented enterprise production schedules adjusted so as to make "plan" fulfillment relatively easy.

The problem of information was, of course, crucial. However, it was not so much the quantity as the quality of information available to the East European planners that left much to be desired. False reporting became an established procedure which, although occasionally risky, carried with it considerable rewards.

Thus, the notion of "the plan" became a fiction, albeit a useful one since it kept everybody relatively satisfied. The plan targets were set up to make Party officials, managers, and workers collect bonuses for overfulfillment. In the relatively rare cases of underfulfillment, next year's targets were simply lowered so that nobody would suffer. Once an enterprise's output or investment schedule "got into the plan" (i.e., was approved by the center), the firm's problems were largely over: it did not have to worry too much about obtaining supplies or disposing of its output. Everything was planned, there was no risk involved, and no one carried any responsibility. Here again the parallel with major segments of American industry appears quite striking. Also in those circumstances it is to some extent surprising that the system of planning in Eastern Europe did not become self-perpetuating and that at some point it came under strong criticism which culminated in the series of economic reforms throughtout the area.

NOTES

1. See, for example, Rudolf Bićanić, *Problems of Planning, East and West* (The Hague: Mouton & Co., 1957), p. 12; Neil W. Chamberlain, *Private and Public Planning* (New York: McGraw-Hill, 1965), p. 4; Carl Landauer, *Theory of National Economic Planning* (Berkeley and Los Angeles: University of California Press, 1947), p. 13; Herbert S. Levine, "On Comparing Planned Economies: A Methodological Inquiry," in *Comparison of Economic Systems: Theoretical and Methodological Approacnes,* ed. Alexander Eckstein (Berkeley and Los Angeles: University of California Press, 1971), p. 140; Gerald Sirkin, *The Visible Hand: The Fundamentals of Economic Planning* (New York: McGraw-Hill, 1968), pp. 45–46.

2. Giovanni Sartori, "Concept Misformation in Comparative Politics," *American Political Science Review* 64, 4 (December 1970): 1034.

3. Frederick J. Fleron, Jr., "Soviet Area Studies and the Social Sciences: Some Methodological Problems in Communist Studies," in *Communist Studies*

and the Social Sciences, ed. Frederic J. Fleron, Jr. (Chicago: Rand McNally, 1969), p. 21.

4. For an interesting discussion of the concept, see Daniel Bell, "The Post-Industrial Society: The Evolution of an Idea," *Survey, 17, 2* (Spring 1971): 102–68.

5. For an interesting discussion of methodological problems connected with the comparison of planned economies, see Levine, "On Comparing Planned Economies," pp. 138–40.

6. Sartori, "Concept Misformation," p. 1036.

7. "If a question is asked what economic order—that is, what set of institutions—will maximize welfare under the constraints imposed upon us by nature—that is the laws of technology and psychology— the answer is a mixed order." Jan Tinbergen, "Planning, Economic: I. Western Europe," in *International Encyclopedia of the Social Sciences,* Vol 12 (New York: Macmillan Company and Free Press, 1968), p. 103.

8. Perhaps the best known one can be found in Seymour Martin Lipset, "Some Social Requisites of Democracy: Economic Development and Political Legitimacy," *American Political Science Review* 52, 1 (March 1959): 69–105.

9. See Robert W. Campbell, "Marx, Kantorovich, and Novozhilov: *Stoimost* versus Reality," *Slavic Review* 20, 3 (October 1961): 402–18.

10. For an interesting discussion of the behavior of Soviet and American elites, see Zbigniew Brzezinski and Samuel P. Huntington, *Political Power: USA/USSR* (New York: Viking Press, 1965), Ch. 3.

11. Andrzej Korbonski, "Bureaucracy and Interest Groups in Communist Societies: The Case of Czechoslovakia," *Studies in Comparative Communism* 4, 1 (January 1971): 57–79.

Chapter Three

Long-Term and Medium-Term Planning and the Current Management of the Economy

Erik Höök

INTRODUCTION[a]

Varieties of long-term or medium-term planning have been used for a very long time as an important feature of the economic policy of different countries. Long-term structural assessments have played a significant part in the shaping of measures which have affected the conditions of development for many industries. Going back to the early period of industrialization, or to the era of railroad construction, to the debates on free trade in the nineteenth century, etc., one will find many instances of long-term planning. Examples are not fewer in other fields where the government has been more directly responsible for supplying services, such as education, prophylactic health care, social security, not to mention defense. Planning, in these cases, was mainly limited and isolated to one sector or to one principal problem. On the other hand, the analysis of the planning questions of the sector concerned could go deeper and more in detail.

I have recalled these matters as an introduction to this chapter to emphasize a view of the relations between different planning problems and planning horizons which will dominate my presentation. According to this view, the sectoral planning problems which I have just hinted at and the way of attacking them

[a]In discussing different planning problems—relationships between medium- and long-term planning, conflicts of goals, etc.—this chapter reflects a personal interpretation based on experiences from Swedish planning and discussions in international organizations concerning planning in different countries. Specific references to sources will therefore seldom be given. In a comparison of the planning systems in different West European countries, the natural thing is to look upon the situation primarily in those countries where work in this field has gone on for a longer time—France, the Netherlands, Norway, and Sweden. No references in footnotes will be made to the published plans or surveys of these or other countries. Detailed documentations on medium-term plans and programs have been published from time to time by the United Nations Economic Commission for Europe. The most recent is United Nations, Economic Commission for Europe, *Long-Term Aspects of Plans and Programmes* (Papers presented to the Ninth Session of Senior Economic Advisers to ECE Governments) (New York, 1973).

have not changed very much through the planning activity concerning the development of the economy as a whole and usually for a five-year period which has come into existence in the European market economies after World War II. This general planning covering the whole economy and considering the interdependences and interrelations between different sectors has provided a frame of reference and allowed a test of consistency and a discussion of priorities for sectoral development problems. As far as Sweden is concerned and, to judge from a general impression, also most other countries, the work of analysis and planning at the sectoral level has taken place without much contact with total planning and been built up and developed from an older basis.

In this chapter, long-term planning (the planning horizons can be of ten to twenty to twenty-five years) is related to and covers the sectoral planning problems. The position of long-term planning will primarily be discussed in its relation to medium-term planning (the perspective there can be three–six years but is usually a five-year period). As with all planning activities, the aim of the studies of development and problems over the longer term must be to give a better basis for the decisions to be taken in the current management of the economy. There are, however, reasons for not linking the results of long-term planning directly to short-run decisions, e.g., the one-year budget. It will be argued here that the step from long-term studies to budgetary appropriations can best be achieved via a consistent overall medium-term plan, which in that context can be used as an instrument for checking and reevaluation of long-term political goals and ambitions. The reason for passing through such an intermediate link is that studies of long-term development problems can hardly be carried out as quantified, consistent development pictures of the economy but will be limited to specific sectors and problems.

SOME BASIC PRECONDITIONS FOR PLANNING IN WEST EUROPEAN MARKET ECONOMIES

The Role and Meaning of Uncertainty

Planning under uncertainty is characteristic of the planning activity of the European market economies. Quantified, consistent development pictures of big aggregates which are contained in the five-year plans are possible, thanks to a relatively greater stability in the economic conditions treated. But when the economy is broken down into smaller and smaller sectors or when the time perspective for the total economy is lengthened, uncertainty increases very sharply. Then planning becomes a problem mainly of securing flexibility and adaptability.

It follows that the view of the nature of the planning problems and their internal relationships is strongly dependent on how uncertainty and its various manifestations will be presented here. However, one side of the problem—where the conditions for planning in the Eastern and Western countries deviate from each other—should be observed in this context. The extent of uncertainty and how it is handled in economic planning are partly conditioned by the fundamental principles on which the political authorities base their economic actions. It is true that certain differences in these respects exist among the West European market economies, but on the whole there are a few recurring characteristics which also form the basis of the "indicative" planning which is a common feature of these countries.

Among the fundamental principles for the management of the West European economy which we have in mind here are liberty of choice for the consumer, liberty of choice of profession, freedom of establishment of business and, on the whole, a liberal trade and tariff policy. Some basic conditions under which economic policy operates should also be recalled in this connection. Private business works largely under free market conditions, and there are a considerable number of enterprises, which make production and investment decisions independently. Within the entire private sector there is a strong reliance on market forces as instruments of allocation. This is necessary also because a considerable share of production is not directly related to domestic consumption: exports account for a considerable part of the total production. Quite large variations in this respect are, however, found from one country to another, as table 3–1 shows.

Yet in the public sector, the government is directly responsible for production and has to act in the same way as an entrepreneur. And also for parts of the private sector, governments have the same kind of responsibility, as a consequence of widespread subsidization which requires detailed regulations, for instance in agriculture and housing. Naturally, the planning system will reflect this responsibility in different ways. Depending on the degree of direct control assumed over different sectors, the character of indicative planning will vary from one country to another. An indication of the differences between countries

Table 3-1. Share of Exports and Public Consumption[a] in GDP(percentage of GDP)

	Exports, 1971	*Public consumption, average 1967-69*
France	16.8	12.4
West Germany	21.6	15.8
Netherlands	47.9	15.8
Norway	40.2	17.8
Sweden	24.7	20.8
United Kingdom	22.5	18.0

Sources: Exports: IMF, *International Financial Statistics,* April 1973. Public consumption: OECD statistics.

Note:
[a]Public consumption includes expenditures for defense and civil purposes financed through central and local government budgets.

is given in table 3–1, which shows the relative size of the public sector in some of the West European countries.

Target Setting and the Need for Flexibility

In view of these fundamental principles and basic conditions under which economic policy operates, planning in the market economies clearly cannot mean setting up specific and rigid targets for the larger part of production and utilization of resources. This will be done mainly in areas where government has a direct entrepreneurial responsibility. And even in those sectors a large degree of flexibility may be needed due to the requirements of stabilization policy. For the economy as a whole, the goals will have a more general formulation—a favorable development of efficiency or productivity, prices, employment, working conditions, etc. The main approach to achieve such a desired development must be to use rather general policy measures in the fields of fiscal, monetary, trade and industrial policy. Under the principles of liberty of choice for the consumer and of free competition nationally and internationally, the measures must be general in the sense that they do not discriminate against certain activities or certain products. Under a decentralized decisionmaking system, the measures must furthermore be general in the sense of not leading to detailed interference in the operation of firms but must rather aim at creating or modifying the external conditions in which firms operate. General policy must, however, be complemented in different cases by measures of a selective nature. This applies, for instance, in regional policy or in employment policy for handicapped and similar groups where the needs are quite specific.

One aim of economic policy, upon which planning activities have been focused to a high degree in most countries, is to create favorable conditions for overall economic development. It is obvious that the ways of implementing such a policy vary and that countries use different approaches to ensure that market forces are transformed and utilized in an effective way in relation to present goals of economic policy. However, this policy commonly aims to create a more adequate price system by encouraging competition, to adapt productive resources to structural changes—particularly in industry—chiefly by stimulating the mobility and flexibility of labor, and to apply a research policy that promotes a balanced expansion of research and technological development.

The growth aspect of policy must be coordinated with other aims of the general economic policy, especially those of full employment, balance in external payments, a proper income distribution, "fair" regional development, and reasonable price stability. It is quite obvious that the setting up of a number of rather ambitious goals for economic policy easily leads to open or more or less potential conflicts between them. Some aspects of these conflicts will be examined later in this chapter.

Let us now consider the problem of target setting further. In the spectrum of planning systems of Western countries, one would perhaps find that the French contains the largest elements of normative planning. The earlier French plans certainly aimed at setting quite specific targets for the development of different sectors. Efforts were also made to design measures—mostly of a financial nature—to carry out the plans. Subsequent plans have gradually put less emphasis on drawing up such targets and have shifted over more to a discussion of possible development trends. This change can surely be seen in relation to the quite different economic situation confronting the First and the Sixth French Plans. After the damage during World War II, the task of rebuilding the French economy had to be in the forefront of economic policy and planning, and selecting and formulating priorities was a natural and indispensable basis for a working policy in such a situation. As the production potential was gradually reconstructed and could allow for an ordinary exchange of goods with other countries, and as the free choice of the consumer was reestablished, the setting of rigid sectoral targets lost its relevance. The Sixth French Plan thus has little resemblance to the First Plan in this respect.

As to the public sector, where the government in the capacity of entrepreneur has a special responsibility for production planning, Norwegian planning provides an interesting example. A four-year budget for government expenditure has been in use for many years. It covers public consumption areas—defense, education, health, social services, and so forth. The development of the different public areas is calculated in constant prices. The figures given reflect not only the consequences of decisions already taken but also the intentions of the government concerning future expenditure policy, reforms, and the like. The four-year budget thus serves as a basis for the *annual* budget decision. This long-term budget has also been incorporated in the overall long-term plans, and in this way a target is set for this—but only for this—special sector of the economy. The reasons for doing so are mainly that the government ought to put its priorities before the electorate and that revealing the government's political intentions makes it easier for other sectors to plan their own activities. It can, however, be pointed out that, up to the latest plan covering 1973–77, Norwegian governments have been quite reluctant to spell out in current prices the financial and tax consequences of the planned expansion of the public sector.

Norwegian attitudes can be compared with those held by the Swedish government. In Sweden too a long-term budget (with a five-year time span) has been used since the beginning of the sixties. It highlights the consequences—mainly of a financial nature—for the next four years of decisions that have already been taken. Its purpose is simply to indicate the size of the resources required for the realization of current goals. But it does not attempt to foresee which decision will be made during the period under review. The five-year medium-term "surveys" go a bit further in this respect, as they also try to estimate the possible future development of the public sector, starting from plans collected from government agencies, municipalities, etc. The resource requirements and especially the implications for taxation are clearly stated. When submitting its proposals for the implementation of policy questions emerging from the medium-term survey, the government does not, however, commit itself to any quantitative goals for the public sector or for different subareas of it. Rather, the government restricts itself to a more general discussion of the demand for public services and of the weights which ought to be given to different items in a priority list.

The motives for such a restrictive attitude towards quantitative target-setting are intimately connected with a general conception about the best way to counterbalance cyclical movements. It is true that the big size of the Swedish public sector calls for elaborate production plans which are made known to the public. But as this sector is so big, it cannot escape taking its full share in stabilization policy. That cannot be done with rigid targets. On the contrary, development plans must be flexible. With this way of reasoning, it could be claimed that the public sector has to be treated in the same manner as the other sectors of the economy and that planning under uncertainty about business cycle changes must—as in the case of private enterprises in a market economy—be applied also to these areas.

The indicative planning systems in the West European countries have certain differences as far as target-setting is concerned. It seems, however, that there has been a tendency for such differences to become smaller. Among the three countries discussed here, the largest element of fixed target-setting was to be found (earlier) in France, comparatively little of it characterized Swedish planning, and Norway was somewhere in between. With growing international integration and interdependence, the setting of sectoral targets in individual countries has become less relevant, and this development has manifested itself especially in France.

INTERRELATIONS BETWEEN SHORT-, MEDIUM- AND LONG-TERM PLANNING

The Relationship of Medium-Term Plans and Annual Budgets

The problems discussed above lead us to the question of the relationship of medium-term plans and the annual budgets. Comparing the medium-term plans, surveys or studies worked out in different countries, one will find a striking resemblance in regard to the problems dealt with, the areas covered by the studies, and the methods used. However, there are major differences in the organization of the work and the status of the published documents. For example, in France and Norway political deliberations occur at an early stage of the work and the published reports are documents committing the governments politically. In contrast, the Dutch and Swedish surveys are examples of the entire study being carried out at an "expert" level. The government then gives its comments on the published reports and restricts its opinions and commitments to the main political issues.

The implications of these differences have been particularly obvious when cyclical disturbances have brought to the foreground the question of the likelihood of achieving the figures of the five-year plan or forecast. In France, both the Third and Fourth Plans were abandoned when cyclical developments over the first years of the planning period had been such that the plan figures were not considered likely to be reached. A revised plan, in one case, and a special stabilization program, in the other, replaced the original plans. Afterwards it was found in both cases that the actual development over the period proved to agree more with the assessments of the original plans than with the revisions carried out during the planning periods!

The situation in Sweden was a similar one during the period 1965–70. The stagnation years 1966 and 1967 brought a fairly general conviction that the development of the economy forecast in the medium-term survey would not be realized. As the government had not taken a very precise stand on the original report and had not committed itself to any fixed targets, the situation did not call for a new official position. In the general political and economic debate, however, the medium-term survey was considered to be obsolete and no longer appropriate as a basis for the shaping of policy. After the upswing in the economy which took place in 1968–70, it was seen at the end of the period, however, that the average rate of increase in GDP over the five years in question and the general development trend did not deviate very much from the original forecasts.

Regardless of the differences in the formal treatment of the medium-term plans, the same real problems occurred in the cases mentioned. Medium-term planning mostly starts from trend studies and ends in average yearly development figures for a (five-year) period, where cyclical swings are, or are presumed to be, evened out.[b] Naturally, considerable methodological difficulties are inherent in such a manner of proceeding. An example is the possible difference between actual and potential output in the starting year and how this will be reflected in the various growth rates for the period.

Problems for economic policy are inevitably raised by the interpretation and application of these trend assessments. In different countries five-year plan figures are used in political and economic discussions to evaluate the development of each particular year. The firm statements, found in most five-year reports, that it has been impossible to consider cyclical development over the period ought to eliminate such uses. But at the same time, it is obvious that those responsible for the plans have in many cases themselves contributed to this practice. It is not unusual to run across a view of the relationship between

---

[b]This is not always the case. Another method is used, for instance, in the Netherlands, where the model reflects business cycle changes during the five-year period.

the annual budgets and the five-year perspective which implies that the latter should be the basis of and determine the shape of the one-year budgets.

It is rather evident, however, that it is impossible to tie the components so closely to each other. Cyclical changes take place all the time and cannot be pinned down in advance for a five-year period. In these circumstances, figures for the medium-term perspective can only indicate the general direction but not the actual cruising course of an annual budget. That course must be chosen with due regard to the economic climate prevailing at the particular time. The interplay which can be established between the two planning horizons must therefore be of a more general and flexible character. The five-year assessment could be regarded as a strategy. It must not lace one-year action too tightly but should be a basis for testing and observation so that short-term measures as far as possible promote, and in any case do not counteract, a desired development in the long run. Sailing to windward and the problems of setting sails, the length of the legs, etc., is an appropriate and clarifying metaphor.

Medium-Term and Long-Term Planning

When it comes to the position of the five-year plans in relation to long-term planning, the stand in this chapter coincides very closely with one that has been presented by two Swedish economists.[1] In long-term or perspective planning there has been a natural inclination to go on using the same methods that have proved so successful in the short run. And the aim is often stated in terms of analyzing and solving global imbalances. This approach they believe to be a fallacy:

> First, we do not think it is possible or that it has any meaning to try to analyse and solve the "Treasuries" task of balancing the economy in the 1990s. It is not possible because some background determinants, e.g. public consumption and parts of public expenditure, have short "lead-times" and adapt to short-run influences. The meaning of the efforts is all the more doubtful since these balancing problems always have to be solved with regard to short-term variations and the political evaluation at the time.
>
> Secondly, we think that in focusing attention on the global aggregates in monetary terms, one easily overlooks those possible changes in technological, economic and social structures in and between the sectors which the present-day decision-makers might want to aim at, or to hedge against. The procedure could, even in this sense, be said to introduce a certain bias—in favor of *status quo* restrictions and relations. To put it another way, the procedure could easily make one forget that the main reason for perspective planning or "perspective studies"—as it should perhaps be called to avoid misunderstandings—is to try to take advantage of the fact that in the long-term perspective most of today's restrictions are changeable, while one can still to a certain extent shape or adapt to new restrictions.

A conclusion drawn from this discussion is that perspective studies should be used mainly as guidelines for successive adaptation of executive decisions and research and development work, rather than for final selection of the available forecasting information and unnecessary advance decisions. Furthermore, perspective studies should be restricted to those strategic sectors where decisions commit the economy more or less irrevocably for a long time ahead. The aim of perspective studies for such a sector would then be to recommend modifications in present decisions on new alternative project-designs in order to minimize the cost of necessary future adaptive measures. The basis for such recommendations would be an analysis of the possible future changes of the relevant economic and technological structures—which in short- and medium-term studies usually are supposed to be unchangeable—and the means of influencing them.

Coordination of perspective studies for several such sectors would make explicit the future interdependence between sectors, would "pool" the necessary common information and, when possible, would devise interrelated strategies for future decisions. Consistency in the usual economic sense of the word should not, and cannot, be sought since there are no one-valued sector projections to make consistent and since one of the main objectives of perspective studies is to make the sector decisions adaptive and thus "consistent" with several future decisions.

If this view is accepted, the planning technique used in the five-year perspective would be less relevant for a study of development problems in the long run. This implies that one cannot assume that there is or should be an exact linking between medium-term and long-term planning. It also follows that the presentation of a total picture with exact and balanced figures applied in the five-year plans does not appear to be a working method which can very well be used also for long-term planning problems. The reason is that the five-year perspective appears to be a particularly favored one as to uncertainty. In this time horizon, influences from different factors of uncertainty taken together can indeed be very significant, but nevertheless less troublesome than in shorter *or* longer perspectives. A period of four to five years is fairly well adapted to the length of the cycles observed in West European countries. A planning horizon of at least this distance is therefore required for studies which aim at assessing and indicating trends in the development of the economy. On the other hand, if one tries to extend the planning horizon much beyond the five years, other important elements of uncertainty will enter the picture. The manifold restraints determining short- and medium-run economic life—the physical infrastructure as well as the structure of economic and social organization—make for a certain inertia and continuity in economic behavior. Only rarely do political measures and reforms, which influence more deeply the manner in which the economy acts, have time to be carried out and gain effect over a five-year period. The same applies also to changes in production techniques, which by themselves are more far-reaching, and to the volume of investment. With the size of the capital stock in the European industrial countries, drastic shifts in investment are required during the first years of the planning period for a noticeable change, for instance in the growth rate of GDP, to be attained in the course of a five-year period.

These conditions have helped to make medium-term forecasting and planning rather successful. At the same time, they delimit the problems and questions that can be efficiently handled in this planning horizon by means of the analytical methods described. Some of the factors that make for a certain inertia and continuity in economic behavior which were mentioned above are connected with problems which are very difficult to analyze in a five-year perspective. Intertemporal priority and allocation problems connected with investment policy are an important example. It has not been possible to treat satisfactorily the question of determining the optimal investment ratio in a medium-term perspective. Economic theory has not yet been able to provide much help in solving these problems. In welfare economics models, capital formation essentially plays the role of transforming consumption opportunities between generations. This theory in itself is rather abstract and its application involves numerical specification of parameters whose values are very difficult to estimate. Furthermore, it seems to be more relevant in a much longer time perspective.

CONFLICTING GOALS IN PLANNING
AND ECONOMIC POLICY

The various goals for economic development established by the government form an important part of the basis for economic planning since they limit the alternatives available with respect to development in the future. A complication facing medium-term studies is that these goals and their mutual priorities are not specified in detail. One reason is, of course, that the government cannot specify *in advance* how it will balance the various features of economic development since actual development continuously raises new problems in this respect. A medium-term study therefore cannot be undertaken as a technical calculation based on conditions that are already given for the whole range of political goals.

The way of handling problems of conflicting goals varies between countries but in most cases a procedure of singling out and concentrating on central or primary goals has been chosen. Such primary goals very often include full employment, a high rate of growth, balance in foreign payments, a proper income distribution, "fair" regional development, and reasonable price stability. Most other goals are treated as subordinate or secondary, though some of them may at times be accorded high priority and given special attention. In this context, the discussion will deal only with the "primary" goals and some of the conflicts between them. But, before we turn to these problems something should perhaps be said about measuring economic growth.

Use of National Accounts in Formulating Goals

In medium-term plans or studies the development of production as a rule is measured in terms of GDP, which occupies a central position in the analysis. The concept of GDP has been discussed extensively in recent years and its relevance as a measure of economic progress has often been questioned. The discussion of these problems has a long history in the economic literature, and the deficiences of GDP in covering aspects of economic development have been quite well known for a long time. Yet the concept of GDP has been and can still be looked upon as quite adequate for analyzing productive capacity—and hence the resources available for future consumption and capital formation, the scope for aid to developing countries, goals for current payments, etc.

When it comes to welfare and other qualitative aspects of economic and social development it is clear that the national accounting omits a number of factors of great importance. To the extent that they cost money, qualitative elements are included in the concept of GDP, but much more is involved.

The national accounts were not, and do not claim to have been, designed to measure the development of welfare in the widest sense. A quick review of political debates, the arguments for reforms in parliamentary bills, the programs of political parties, etc., in Sweden indeed gives the impression that the concept of GDP is not in fact interpreted in this way in serious political contexts. Qualitative as well as quantitative effects have been considered explicitly in the discussions on shorter working hours, day nurseries, national supplementary pensions, environmental conservation, new power stations, and so on. But the problem has been that intuitive methods have had to be used for adding and balancing the various items without the help that can be derived from quantifying their importance. It should be noted, however, that national accounts have in most cases served as a starting point and frame of reference for considerations about these matters.

Even though there is—contrary to what has been argued in many popular debates—reason to believe that the politicians have not been misled in their decisions by the concept of GDP, it is relevant and necessary to arrive at a more systematic and comprehensive calculation of human welfare. Different courses of action have been discussed for a long time and measures have also been taken in many countries for developing instruments. An example is the work on social indicators going on in a number of quarters. From the point of view of the problems facing ministries and government agencies, this approach does not seem especially promising as long as it is directed at constructing a global measure of welfare. Also, when it focuses on sectoral problems, the concept of social indicators is very often discussed by itself without close reference to the production and policy problems of the area concerned. To do their job, the indicators must be demarcated and framed directly in relation to the demand and production problems in a certain field. In other words, they must be closely integrated with the planning and budget questions which arise when policy is defined regarding health care, social security, education, etc.

In such fields, social indicators are by no means a novelty. Considerable work has been devoted to creating a basis for, and illustrating, different quantitative and qualitative relationships which must be considered in shaping policy. It is obvious, however, that these studies need to be extended and made more systematic. This should not necessarily meet with too great difficulties. Experience shows, on the contrary, that the decisive problems are found in evaluating and translating the indicators into political action. In the process, interest is immediately shifted towards other instruments and methods of work, where intensified efforts are going on in many countries. I refer, for instance, to program budgeting, shadow-pricing, price-policy for public services, studies of the possibilities for revealing preferences for public goods, research concerning the problems of externalities, cost-benefit studies, etc.

More and more work has been devoted to development of methods in these areas as the service sectors, and particularly the public sector, have increased their shares in the West European economies. The much stronger attention to environmental problems which has appeared in the last few years has also worked in the same direction. In the process, most of the basic problems concerning externalities and public goods have become concrete, and have been brought to the foreground in a way which has vitalized research and discussion. Somewhat opposing attitudes toward the system of national accounts have been brought forth in the debate on the environment. Rather often it has been claimed that the economic conceptions which have found an expression in the concept of GNP have caused and complicated many of the environmental problems. At the same time, we find that the solutions and the arsenal of instruments in environmental policy are on the whole based precisely on traditional economic theory. The fundamental principle of "polluter pays" which the OECD countries have agreed on is designed to use the adjustment mechanisms of market systems to fight pollution problems by "internalizing" the environmental costs.

Goal Conflicts in the Short Run

In medium-term and long-term planning, the focus is naturally mainly on growth and structural problems in the economy. Therefore, it is not very surprising that one rarely finds, in the plans of different countries, any thorough discussion of matters of stabilization policy or goal conflicts which are chiefly connected with cyclical policy. This is true for instance of the relation, much discussed both in economic theory and in practical economic policy, between the rate of inflation and level of employment, and this example is probably valid for a wide range of problems.

These circumstances give a reason for us to avoid treating goal conflicts of this nature here. Quite a different reason is found in the difficulties of defining more sharply the nature and importance of the conflict which may be presumed to be found between, for instance, a goal of stabilization policy and one of growth. A long-term trend may be regarded as the sum of events over a series of short periods, and disturbances during some of these periods may be expected to have long-run effects. There is, however, an interdependence between periods of recession and expansion which becomes apparent in the fact that the excess capacity which arises in a recession and then gives low growth figures generates a compensating increase in the upswing. How complete this compensation becomes is extremely difficult to measure or judge. For Sweden, a relatively steep increase in productivity was recorded in 1960–65. A possible explanation may be that development during those years was relatively stable without major cyclical disturbances. But other elements weaken this hypothesis. The years 1960–65 may be said to have shown a relatively strong growth in the capital stock as a result of great investment increases at the end of the 1950s and in the early years of the 1960s.

Other circumstances which hamper an interpretation of the underlying relationships could also be mentioned. The productivity increase, very high for a recession, which was recorded in 1966–67 in Swedish manufacturing industry and which can in part be related to an increased closing-down of less efficient production units, illustrates a question which is pertinent in this context but difficult to answer. The size and speed of the transformation of the economy are determined by the interplay between introducing new techniques and capital equipment and discarding obsolete techniques and equipment. There seems to be no basis for a more exact assessment of how the net result of that interplay is affected by different cyclical sequences.

The concern of political decisionmakers about instability relates primarily to the rate of growth and to prices. In an article on disturbances in the growth process from a Swedish viewpoint, a comparison was made of growth rates and degrees of instability in different countries, through 1962.[2] Table 3–2 shows figures representing the instability in both these respects, with data added also for the period 1963–70. The observations show a very irregular pattern, and it is clear that one cannot find, by such a simple comparison, any relations between stability and growth. For a better assessment, one would have to study the prevailing demand conditions, the cyclical policy pursued, and other external circumstances which may have influenced the course of events.

Goal Conflicts in the Longer Run
The role of the price system. As was emphasized earlier, growth questions are in the focus of medium- and long-run planning. One would then expect that problems which are essential for the shaping of policy in different areas of development would be analyzed more closely in the plans. In the West European economies the allocation of resources between different sectors and for different purposes is made through market mechanisms. In such a system, the efficiency of the markets determines the extent to which a growth process can continue undisturbed and the extent to which inertia and institutional obstacles impede

Table 3-2.   Growth Rate and Degree of Instability, 1950-70 (percentage)

	Rate of growth				Average annual price increases	
	1952-62		*1962-70*		*1950-62*	*1961-70*
	averages	*mean deviation*	*averages*	*mean deviation*		
Belgium	3.1	1.6	4.8	1.4	2.0	3.5
Canada	4.3	2.9	5.2	1.4	3.0	3.2
Denmark	4.1	2.4	4.6	2.6	3.9	5.9
France	5.0	1.5	5.7	1.0	6.5	4.1
West Germany	7.2	1.8	4.8	2.5	3.6	2.7
Italy	6.2	1.3	5.3	1.3	2.7	4.0
Japan	9.8	3.5	11.1	2.9	4.8	5.7
Netherlands	4.5	2.3	5.5	1.8	3.7	4.8
Norway	3.8	1.4	4.8	0.7	4.4	4.6
Sweden	3.8	1.3	4.4	1.1	4.5	4.2
Switzerland	4.9	2.1	3.9	1.3	2.3	3.4
United Kingdom	2.6	1.4	2.9	1.3	3.8	4.1
United States	3.8	2.8	4.0	2.2	2.3	3.2

Source: OECD statistics.

adjustments in production areas and commodity markets. From such a starting point it would be rather natural to devote special attention to possible imperfections in the market, for instance to the prospects of setting right, through policy measures, shortcomings in the functioning of the price system in different parts of the economy, obstacles to the occupational and geographic mobility of the labor force, restrictive trade practices, inertia in introducing and disseminating innovations, imperfections in the money and capital markets, etc.

Generally speaking, it is fair to say that plans give rather little space to the analysis of such problems. The reason does not seem to be, however, that the planners are not aware of the importance of these questions. It is probably rather an effect of how the planning work is organized. Medium-term plans are designed to give a total and consistent general view of the development trends in the economy. This work may reveal and illustrate different problems and adjustment difficulties which may crop up. Such a task is already in itself so big that it is impossible to carry out a detailed study of different special problems within the same framework. Naturally, there are variations. In France, where planning work is relatively strongly centralized and an important central group is assigned to it, a larger problem area can be covered in the actual plan, while in most other countries the field is more limited. Analysis and discussions of problems of the types just mentioned take place more or less independently of the planning work and are carried out by bodies which are responsible for policy in the field in question.

Problems related to regional planning.   The area of regional planning is one where it is particularly difficult to see any distinct patterns as regards the integration with medium-term planning or coordination with other planning agencies. Studies and discussions of policy often take place outside and independently of the work on medium-term planning even if the plans rather regularly include an account and analysis of regional questions.

In off-the-record discussions among planners from different countries, questions have often been raised about the technique for coordinating a national plan with regional studies. In most cases, it has been found that planners are faced with proposals to build up the national studies on the basis of regional data. Nearly as often, it is found that those who have been working with the national plans have rejected such a "from the bottom up" method. For practical reasons, such a method has been found impossible, without any necessity for theoretical deliberations about how consistency problems and similar questions should be solved. Sufficient data on consumption, production, investment in the regions, regional export and import figures, etc., are rarely available. The method applied is instead to break down a national plan into larger or smaller regional units. There are, naturally, considerable technical and theoretical difficulties involved also in such a method. One aspect concerns the problem of uncertainty in planning.

The assessments made in the national plans about larger demand and production sectors have rather wide margins of uncertainty. It is easy to prove that the uncertainty increases very sharply when these aggregates are broken down into smaller units. When it comes to regional studies, this problem increases because of differences among regions in production structure, natural resources, the competitive situation of the existing firms, etc. For a certain branch, a reliable projection can perhaps be made for total demand and total production. But, when the plan is broken down by regional units, it can easily happen that every such region has only a few firms operating in this special market. Which of the individual firms has possibilities to expand and which one is going to lose part of its market share? The possibilities for reasonable and meaningful regional disaggregation are rather limited. It is obvious that this restriction presents more inconvenience in small countries such as the Netherlands, Norway, and Sweden, due to the more limited size of production and number of firms, then, for instance, in France and the United Kingdom.

This set of problems can then be combined with the question of regional goals. These goals can on the whole be said to consist of a wider application of general national goals through introducing a regional dimension. An example is the evening-out of employment and income conditions among regions which regional policy commonly seeks. Such a "regionalization" of political goals means that certain adjustment mechanisms will no longer be available— mechanisms which could otherwise have been used to meet cyclical or long-term disturbances in the economy. The conflict that might then arise is perhaps not a conflict between goals as much as a matter of possibilities of realizing a particular goal. For instance, the difficulties of keeping unemployment below a certain average level for the country as a whole may prove to be greater if certain restrictions are introduced on allowed deviations from the average. In such a case, "regionalization" very often means that the political parties commit themselves to keep the employment in a region at a certain level. But that means at the same time a restriction on the use of measures to promote mobility in the labor force and a narrow limitation, in demand and allocation policies, to those activities that exist or can be developed in a specific region. The same is true for a goal of income distribution. In economies which are strongly dependent upon other countries, tensions in the distribution of income can reasonably be expected to be accentuated through commitments to regional goals. In some cases such tensions may have helped to give rise to neo-protectionist tendencies.

Problems related to income distribution questions. As regards income distribution goals, questions are often raised in general political debate about the extent to which a strong evening-out of income may weaken incentives to work, to risk-taking, and to new initiatives. Especially in modern welfare states with an extensive social security system, such a latent conflict with growth goals is evident. It is very difficult to illustrate and answer these questions by means of unequivocal data. Under the security systems of different countries, the citizens can be sure of a reasonable standard of living in unemployment, sickness, old age, etc. No doubt the details of this system may have their faults with respect to their influence on incentives to work and innovate. But generally the social security program should also have great advantages from the point of view of progress. Because individuals are reasonably sure about a certain standard of living, they can afford to accept the risks which keen competition, rationalization, structural changes, etc., may force them to take when it comes to changing occupation or place to live. It is likely that the results which may appear when advantages and drawbacks are balanced will depend to a considerable degree exactly on how attitudes to mobility and adjustment are affected and on how the trade union organizations shape their views toward rationalization measures. Superficial international comparison will not reveal that countries with an extensive security system have in any way shown less favorable results than others.

To some extent more important than the conflicts which may exist between goals of income distribution and of growth is how the prerequisites for better and more even income conditions are shaped. In stabilization policy there is a strong argument for keeping down unemployment as far as possible. Experience shows how differences in income grow strongly in periods of falling employment. Using common methods for measuring differences in income distribution, one could thus find in Sweden that the distribution became more uneven during the recessions in the years 1966–67 and 1971–72. When it comes to long-term development and the attitude of the relation between growth and income distribution, the picture may not be so clear. There are both negative and positive opinions of the significance of growth in this context. As far as Sweden is concerned, economic policy is on the whole characterized by a positive attitude toward this interplay. In a Swedish contribution to the United Nations Economic Commission for Europe an attempt is made to illustrate this in a general and concise way.[3]

The hypothesis in this contribution is that a continuous growth of production is not only favorable but essential for the redistribution of income. This becomes increasingly clear as the level of income in a country rises. Hence, over time growth becomes more, not less, important as a vehicle for redistribution of material welfare. There is a very simple mechanism behind this way of reasoning. Changes in the *vertical* income distribution can be achieved either by redistributing a constant sum of income or by increasing this sum and giving more of the increase to the lower income groups. An increase in the sum of wage income can be achieved either by changes in the *functional* income distribution (the distribution between wage and nonwage income) or by growth of total production. As the wage share of production increases, it becomes more difficult than before to change the functional distribution. This tends to place more relative importance on growth. Furthermore, with a progressive tax system in force, it gradually becomes more difficult to raise additional revenue for redistribution purposes by increasing tax rates. But when total income is growing, such revenue will be created also at constant tax rates.

Some figures illustrating the problems discussed can be reproduced here. Table 3–3 gives data for sixteen countries concerning the level of GDP per capita and of the wage share of GDP. It can be seen that there is a strong correlation between the level of income per capita and the level of the overall wage share. (Tentative calculations suggest that the relation will look different but the correlation will be as strong when corrections for wage-income of the self-employed are introduced.)

As regards the relative wage relation and the result that could arise from a change in this relation, a calculation was made on the basis of the Swedish wage situation in 1968. It was estimated that the amount needed to raise below-average hourly wages up to the average, while those above it would remain constant, would be some seven billions of kronor. Such an amount is made available—at a constant wage share of value added—by approximately a 10 percent growth in GNP, i.e., about 2.5 years' normal growth. On the other hand, it also corresponds to the amount made available by the actual increase in the wage share during the last ten years (and this was a period of an extremely fast increase in the wage share).

The following figures give a rough idea of the possibilities of achieving further changes in the vertical income distribution by means of tax policy. Among incomes of 20,000 kronor a year and more, the groups earning more than

Table 3-3.   GNP per Head and Wage Share of Value Added, 1953-69

	GNP per Head (US $)	Wage share of value added[a]				Rank order of		
		Percentage			Percentage change	GNP per head		Wage share
	1969	1953	1960	1969	1953-69	1953	1969	1969
Canada[b]	3,260	56.7	59.0	62.3	9.9	2	3	4
Japan	1,630	45.6	45.4	46.6	2.2	16	13	16
USA	4,660	62.4	63.3	65.4	4.8	1	1	3
Austria[b]	1,690	52.8	52.8	59.8	13.3	12	12	7
Belgium[b]	2,360	48.7	50.9	56.3	15.6	5	8	10
Denmark[b]	2,860	51.2	52.9	60.8	18.8	7	4	5
Finland	1,940	54.4	50.2	56.1	3.1	9	11	11
France	2,770	50.7	51.3	54.8	8.1	4	5	13
West Germany	2,520	52.4	54.6	57.2	9.2	10	7	9
Ireland[b]	1,160	49.8	51.4	56.0	12.4	13	15	12
Italy	1,520	43.3	46.9	51.4	18.7	14	14	15
Netherlands	2,190	47.9	50.9	60.1	25.5	11	9	6
Norway	2,530	51.8	55.3	58.8	13.5	8	6	8
Sweden[c]	3,490	60.9	62.8	72.1	18.4	3	2	1
Spain	870	46.5	49.0	52.9	13.8	15	16	14
United Kingdom[c]	1,970	64.0	66.4	70.1	9.5	6	10	2

Source: OECD national accounts, 1953-69.
Notes:
   [a]Wage share of value added = compensation of employees ÷ GNP at factor cost.
   [b]Figures for the year 1968 instead of 1969.
   [c]Figures for the year 1954 instead of 1953.

50,000 kronor represent about one-tenth of one percent of the number of income earners and about one-fourth of total income. A 10 percent increase in taxes on the groups above 50,000 kronor would correspond only to 1.5 percent of GNP. In contrast, the relation between the change in general government revenue and the change in GNP in Sweden has by now arrived at values of 0.6-0.7. Thus, it is easy to see that growth in income *automatically* puts into the hands of the government resources of quite another magnitude than could ever be achieved through changes in tax rates under conditions of stagnation.

It is recognized that the features described above vary considerably in importance between countries. But, on the other hand, the mechanisms described and their implications for growth and distribution are, of course, valid also for the relations between rich and poor countries. Even in a small, rich, and industrialized country there remain many needs to be met. But at the international level the needs and problems become tremendous. The importance of continued strong growth becomes evident. It is impossible to think in terms of reducing economic growth to a considerable extent, although this does not make a discussion about the forms, content and direction of growth superfluous.

In fact, such a discussion becomes increasingly important if growth is to be seen more in a distributional context.

CONCLUDING REMARKS

When asked about an apparent reversal in economic policy, a prominent Swedish politician once answered—partly in jest—that economic policy mainly consisted of "successive corrections of earlier mistakes." While certainly not fully satisfactory, this definition illustrates one side of the political conditions which are the starting point of planning and which to a large extent determine the interplay between different planning horizons and political goals.

Political goals are mostly given merely as a direction in which to go during an undetermined future. Definite specification of the time when the goals should be attained is rare, and so also are detailed descriptions of the actual implications of the goals. They are rather presented in general terms. such as less inequality in the distribution of income, better environmental protection, greater social security, improved health care and so forth. Ways and means to reach those goals are studied in a long-term perspective without, however, a fixed time-schedule. Through such studies, annual budgetary appropriations are decided on.

If the specific items of the annual budgets are seen as parts of a long-term strategy, these items, as well as budget policy and the economic policy as a whole, will be continuously adapted and corrected in response to changes in the external conditions. In this process of adaption and correction the five-year plans have a special and very significant function. With respect to the various aspects of uncertainty, planning with a medium-term perspective seems to have particular advantages because the combined effects of uncertainty in the short run and in the long run are minimized in that perspective. For those reasons, examination of the development being achieved in the five-year plans provides a useful basis for an evaluation and testing of the various components of economic policy. A precondition for such a scrutiny is, of course, that the five-year plans include the effects of the prevailing policy, at least in the first stage. If the testing of the policy results in certain problems of adaptation or conflicts being defined, an analysis of alternative policies can then be made.

At the beginning of this chapter the importance of long-term planning and its close connection with sectoral planning were pointed out. The five-year plan can be used partly as an instrument for checking and reevaluation of long-term political goals and ambitions. But there is also quite another side to the interplay between medium-term and long-term planning. A five-year study, whether it is done by econometric methods or not, presupposes the values of a number of variables as exogenously given and many institutional conditions as unchanged. Here it is long-term planning that takes the role of complement and instrument of checking the realism of such assumptions by revealing their long-term consequences. The possibility to draw up a medium-term plan of the type common in Western Europe depends partly on the validity of the assumption of a certain inertia in the institutional framework, in the preferences of the individual, in the stock of real capital, and so forth. The important test of checking the consequences of these assumptions rests with long-term planning. Given the differences in scope and tasks, it is thus natural that methods and approaches used in planning in the longer term cannot be the same as those used in the five-year studies.

NOTES

1. See "Problems of Co-ordination of Long Range Sectoral Planning" (by I. Ståhl and B.C. Ysander) in United Nations, Economic Commission for Europe, *Long-term Planning* (Papers presented to the Seventh Meeting of Senior Economic Advisers to ECE Governments) (New York, 1971), p. 162.
2. E. Lundberg, "Störningar i tillväxtprocessen" [Disturbances in the Growth Process], in *Svensk ekonomisk tillväxt* [Growth in the Swedish Economy] (Lund: Kungl. Finansdepartementet, 1966), pp. 133–68.
3. The Swedish contribution to the Tenth Session of Senior Economic Advisors to ECE Governments in March 1973 on "Economic Growth and Distribution," to be published by the United Nations Economic Commission for Europe.

Comments on
Erik Höök's
Chapter

Per Sevaldson

Mr. Höök's interesting and readable paper is full of common sense, and of statements which are evidently based on considerable experience in work with the problems of planning over varying horizons. It is consequently not easy to find points on which to disagree and to start an argument. This problem for the discussant is accentuated by the rather broad generality of most of the formulations—a generality which sometimes borders on vagueness and which I consider the main weakness of the paper. Instead of trying to argue against the author, I will take up the general issues in his paper for scrutiny from a slightly different point of view.

I will start with something as fundamental as the very concept of planning: When we use the word "planning" with reference to a person or to a business firm, there seems to be little danger of being misunderstood. But when the same word is used with reference to the economic activities of the government of a country, there is a large variety of interpretations. There is a rational or simplistic interpretation, which uses the word in analogy with its use in other fields of human activity. The reasoning goes approximately like this: In most of the countries of our present world, the governments dispose of a considerable proportion of the national income through incomes and expenditures of public budgets and through regulation of the spheres of activity of independent decisionmakers like private consumers and business firms. As a consequence, government decisions are of great importance for the entire economic situation of a country at all times, and government economic policy cannot be evaluated without an analysis of its effects on all aspects of the national economy. In order to be able to carry out a rational policy, the authorities must agree on aims for the entire economy and make plans designed to achieve these aims to the extent possible. Government economic planning will consequently be the working out of an action program for the government aiming at specific, politically chosen goals for the economy, and taking into account the effects of such a program on all aspects of economic structure and development.

On the other hand, there is an ideological interpretation of the word "planning," associated with the controversy between adherents of a "free enterprise economy" and a "socialist economy." According to the former, government interference can only disturb the working of the free market, whereas the latter view presupposes active government steering of the entire economy. As a consequence, "planning" has come to be associated with strong government interference in the economy, and, at the extreme, with organizations like the "centrally planned economies" of Eastern Europe. But with this politically and emotionally charged use of the word—which exists partly in confusion with, partly to the exclusion of, the more rational interpretation—it has become difficult to talk about planning in the rational sense of the word, as is required in economies of the West European type. Among the offsprings of this neurotic situation are the diffuse concept of "indicative planning" and the idea that in a market economy "planning should be concerned only with the public sector."

Höök's paper is not entirely clear at all points regarding which concept of planning he is discussing. However, even with a rational interpretation there are several purposes that planning may serve in a market economy, and the importance and role of the time perspective must depend on the weights given to the various purposes:

1. If the role or main purpose is to work out an action program for the government, then the period for which actions should be determined by the plan ought to be relatively short, since new and better programs can and should be worked out when new information becomes available. Beyond the action period, the plan should be concerned only with conditions which are important for determining the best choice of program for the action period. This would lead to an effort to draw up a relatively detailed and comprehensive picture of expected economic developments in the period immediately after the action period, but a picture with less and less details for periods farther and farther away in the future. And the ideal would be a process of rolling plans revised for each new action period (e.g., the budget year or even shorter terms).

2. If the main purpose of the plan is to serve as a political declaration of what purposes the authorities will aim at achieving over a given period, the role of the time perspective will, of course, be rather different. The "planning period" may be politically determined, e.g., the period between two elections, and the specification of intended concrete actions may be quite vague.

3. As a third alternative, we may think of a plan intended to provide information and guidelines for independent decisionmakers, most likely the

managers of independent enterprises. These decisiónmakers will be interested in two aspects of the plan: as a forecast of general economic conditions, and as a declaration of the policy the government is going to carry out. The policy declarations may be either (a) in terms of the goals which the government intends to achieve, or (b) in terms of the actions it is going to carry out. In the former case, developments beyond the control of the authorities may make it impossible to achieve the aims, or make it preferable to change the goals. In the latter case, uncontrollable events may make it necessary to change the action program. In either case, the probability that a change will be needed will increase with the length of the planning period. But if it is important to maintain the credibility of the plan, the policy changes in relation to the plan should not be too extensive or frequent.

We thus see that each purpose leads to a separate set of considerations concerning the time-horizon problem. The horizon problem should accordingly be discussed in relation to the various purposes of planning, and to the relative importance of each.

In his paper Höök discusses the purposes of planning in Western-type economies in a section on target-setting and the need for flexibility. But from the outset he adopts a very restrictive framework. He excludes the possibility of "setting up specific and rigid targets for the larger part of production and utilization of resources" except in areas "where government has direct entrepreneurial responsibility." The general aim is "to create favorable conditions for overall economic development." In addition he mentions other general purposes, such as "full employment, balance in external payments, a proper income distribution, 'fair' regional development, and reasonable price stability." One gets the feeling that planning is thought of as the process of drawing up relatively generally formulated aims for such broad categories, but not the working out of specific policy programs designed to achieve the targets. On the contrary, he suggests that the nature of economic uncertainty is such that a specific policy program would in any case have to be adjusted to actual developments, and thus be more of a hindrance than a means towards a successful policy.

Such a description may represent the current view in Sweden and many other West European countries (though certainly not Norway among them). But in my opinion it deprives planning of a major part of its potentialities as an instrument for steering economic development, even in this type of economy, and it also detracts from the fruitfulness of a discussion of the length of the planning horizon. The more the plan degenerates towards a listing of targets in terms of broad macroeconomic characteristics which we think can be achieved and which we will aim for, but without telling how, and without spelling out the consequences for today's government policy, the less interesting, in my view, is the question whether the perspective is one, five or fifteen years.

Within the framework of this concept of planning, I think I am willing to accept the author's apparent preference for the five-year perspective as something of an ideal. I find relevant his arguments about the influence of business cycles and the gestation period for new productive capital. However, when a more "operative" concept of planning is adopted, such as that of working out an action program for economic policy, one is led to ask whether, and if so why, a distinction between planning over a number of discrete time perspectives should be made at all. And, as already mentioned, different purposes may call for different considerations in regard to the horizon problem.

In addition, the cost of working out plans may be important for the choice of horizon. By dividing the process of plan preparation into the preparation of a number of plans over varying horizons, it may be possible to reduce the amount of work required for plan preparation, since the plans over the longer horizons may be less susceptible to the need for revision in the light of current developments. A five-year plan may perhaps need only minor adjustments in the first two or three years, and a fifteen-year plan may stand unchanged for five years. The logic must be to assemble in the short-term plan those variables which must be revised at short intervals. in the medium-term plan those which need only be the subject of (major) revisions over the medium term, and in the long-term plan those variables which are expected not to need revision even in the medium term. But what is a proper definition of short, medium, and long term from this point of view?

Chapter Four

Economic Planning Under Uncertainty: Recent Theoretical Developments

Roy Radner

INTRODUCTION

This is a survey of recent developments in mathematical theories of economic planning under uncertainty, and related research in mathematical economics. The presentation is essentially non-mathematical, but I cannot pretend that it will not be technical or abstract. I knew before I started preparing this chapter that the theory of national economic planning under uncertainty is in its infancy, and that it is still far from true applicability at the national level. This impression was confirmed as I reviewed the relevant literature. Nevertheless, I believe that the infant theory has some insights to offer the student of planning who is willing to make some investment in mathematical technique, and I hope this chapter will give some hints regarding what the literature has to offer.

The sources of uncertainty in planning include all of the uncertainties faced by the economy, as well as any uncertainties there may be about the role of the planners in the economy. It is customary to divide the uncertainties faced by the economy into two groups: (1) uncertainty about variables that are exogenous, i.e., not affected substantially by the actions of the economic agents within the country, such as weather, some conditions of world trade and politics, etc., and (2) uncertainty about the behavior of the economic agents themselves, including the behavior of some economic agents outside the country, such as important trading partners. The distinction is that variables in the second group may be significantly affected by the plan, whereas variables in the first group are not.

The original plan for this chapter was to concentrate on uncertainties of the first type, and in fact the title in the preliminary program for the conference was listed as "Planning under Conditions of Uncertainty about Economic Variables External to the Plan." As I shall argue below, it is doubtful whether one can in

This chapter is based on research supported by the National Science Foundation.

reality decouple the two types of uncertainty, even though the distinction may be valid from a conceptual point of view.

By far the bulk of the theoretical literature on economic planning under uncertainty deals with various problems of optimal allocation of resources, and this is reflected in the relative length of the section, "Characterization of Optimal Paths of Economic Growth Under Uncertainty," which is devoted to this class of problems. Upon reflection, I am not convinced that this emphasis (by present-day theorists) is merited, and I believe that the problems described in the other sections, although less finished and more speculative, will eventually attract as much, if not more, attention from mathematical economists. However, progress usually involves building on what has come before, and I hope I can give you a feeling for the progress that remains to be accomplished, without in any way minimizing the importance of what has been already achieved.

INTERACTION BETWEEN PLANNING AND IMPLEMENTATION

Mathematical theories of resource allocation planning at the national level have rarely considered explicitly the relations between planning and implementation. Mathematical planning theories have been primarily concerned with *optimal decisions*. First, we have theories that attempt to characterize optimal allocations of resources, e.g., in terms of shadow prices, present value, corresponding "profit" maximization, etc., or in terms of state valuation functions, as in dynamic programming, or even in terms of explicit formulas for optimal allocations in simple cases. Second, we have theories about the properties of alternative procedures (algorithms) for the *calculation* of optimal allocations (mathematical programming, linear and nonlinear decomposition, dynamic programming algorithms, etc.). These procedures could be interpreted as methods of preparing a plan.[1] Most of the literature on this topic does not consider uncertainty. The focus of attention is on properties of convergence, and sometimes on the interpretation of steps of the algorithm as activities of the various agents involved in the process of preparing the plan. A third group of theories deals with uncertainty explicitly, and focuses on the characterization or calculation of optimal *decision rules* for allocation. Such decision rules (as in the theory of optimal inventory control) typically require the decisionmaker to periodically take account of new information as it is observed, and could be interpreted as models of operating systems, that is to say, models of "implementation" of policy.

In practice, the activities of planning and implementation are typically carried on by different administrative units, especially in the case of planning at the national level. Plans are in the form of forecasts of what would be desirable and feasible trajectories of economic magnitudes (inputs, outputs, consumption, prices), but they rarely take explicit account of uncertainty, and more rarely provide explictly and formally for the revision of planned decisions during the period covered by the plan.

The gap between theory and practice has created tensions at both ends. Planners and decisionmakers are aware of the desirability, in principle, of more formal and explicit links between planning and implementation, and of increased interdependence and feedback between plans and decisions (e.g., "rolling plans"). But they are also aware of the overwhelming requirements for exchange and processing of information that are implied by serious, continuing feedbacks between planners and decisionmakers. Further, they are aware of the conflicts of interest and power that so often create obstacles in the way of effective exchange of information and the corresponding revision of plans and decision rules.

Theorists, too, are aware of these organizational problems. Indeed, the theories of games, teams, and statistical decision would appear to provide the tools for a more sophisticated approach, but thus far only the simplest examples have yielded to theoretical analysis.

These remarks are not intended to minimize the importance of the insights that planning theory has provided, nor the increased power provided by advances in methods of mathematical programming, computation, and information processing. Subsequent sections of this chapter will be devoted to describing some of these theoretical insights, and the models from which they arise. Nevertheless, it is my view that the theory of planning under uncertainty cannot make much further progress without an explicit attack on problems of *organization*. The incorporation of uncertainty into theoretical models of planning almost forces one, sooner or later, to face up to questions regarding the organization of the diverse activities of observation, communication, information processing, forecasting, and actual decisionmaking.

It may be that a continued exclusive reliance on a framework of optimal decision will not be fruitful for planning theory. On the one hand, a concern for economic planning seems to imply, almost by definition, a concern for a *rational* approach to the organization of economic activity. On the other hand, the *optimal* solution of economic decision problems on a national scale, taking account of uncertainty, seems totally beyond our capacities, now and in the indefinite future. A promising approach to the resolution of this dilemma is suggested by Simon's concept of "bounded rationality." As he defines it, ". . . Theories that incorporate constraints on the information-processing capacities of the actor may be called *theories of bounded rationality*."[2] These constraints refer not only to what is often described as the cost of information, but also to the limited capacities of humans (and machines) for imagination, computation, and other aspects of internal information-processing. Thus far, this concept has not significantly penetrated the theoretical literature on national economic planning.[3]

CHARACTERIZATIONS OF OPTIMAL PATHS OF ECONOMIC GROWTH UNDER UNCERTAINTY

A Model of Economic Growth Under Uncertainty

Before describing various characterizations of optimal economic growth under uncertainty, it will be useful to give a sketch of a theoretical framework within which one can discuss these results.

Consider an economy at successive dates (years, quarters, or months, etc.), starting from date zero. At each date there is a fixed list of conceivable commodities (goods and servies), which we may, for convenience, take to be the same at all dates. The production possibilities at each date will be represented by an activity analysis model. At each date, each activity will be "operated" at some "level." The level of an activity at a given date determines the quantities of all the inputs at that date, and also determines the outputs, which are available for consumption or input into production *at the next date*. In other words, in this "period analysis," the production that results from the level of an activity at one date is assumed to take place during the period between that date and the next. If the period is short relative to the "period of production," then the list of commodities must include all unfinished goods, or goods-in-process, at different stages of production.

At each date, some quantities of *resources* are supplied exogenously to the economy. Negative resources would represent commitments undertaken before date zero to supply commodities to the outside world. *Consumption* at each date is what is left over from this date's resources, plus output from the previous period, after substracting the inputs for current production. Consumption may be constrained in some fashion, e.g., to represent a minimum standard of living, or a required rate of growth, etc. A consumption program satisfying such constraints will be called *acceptable*.

Uncertainty about production is introduced by assuming that the inputs and outputs at each date depend not only on the levels of the corresponding activities, but also on certain random variables. Uncertainty about resources is similarly introduced by assuming that the resources at each date are random variables. The complete specification of all of the random variables that influence production and resources at any date will be called the *state of the environment at that date*. A *partial history of the environment through date t* specifies the states of the environment up through date *t*. A *complete history of the environment* specifies the states of the environment at all dates.

The last date envisaged will be called the *horizon*. For "practical" purposes, one might suppose that the horizon could always be taken as finite. However, in many situations the horizon might be very distant, or difficult to specify, and in both these situations it might be mathematically convenient, and a good approximation, to take the horizon as infinite.

Thus uncertainty of resources and production is represented in terms of a (finite or infinite) sequence of random variables, the history of the environment. These random variables need not, of course, be mutually independent, in a statistical sense, nor need corresponding random variables at different dates have the same probability distribution. All that we assume is that (1) the joint probability distribution of the random variables can (in principle) be specified, and (2) the evolution of the history of the environment is not affected by any economic decisions (activity levels). Assumption (2) is really in the nature of a convention. All "variables" in the world are divided into three groups: (1) decisions (activity levels), (2) environment, and (3) all others, which are assumed to depend on decisions and the environment.[4]

At each date, the activity levels are to be determined on the basis of information about the partial history of the environment up through that date. The rule according to which an activity level is determined is called a *decision function* at that date. A *policy* (or *strategy*) is a sequence of decision functions, one for each date and activity level at that date.

The more information the decisionmaker will have at any date about the partial history of the environment up through that date, the richer is the set of decision functions that he can use. A *completely centralized* economy is defined as one in which, at every date, every activity level may be determined on the basis of full knowledge of the partial history of the environment up through that date. An economy will be called *decentralized* to the extent that different activity levels are determined on the basis of different information about the environment. I should emphasize that I am speaking at this point of *informational* centralization and decentralization. The decentralization of authority will be discussed in the last section of this chapter.

For the remainder of this section, I shall confine my attention to the case of completely centralized economies, as just defined. In my view, a realistic approach to planning under uncertainty must inevitably deal with informational decentralization. However, theoretical research on this topic is relatively recent, and not at all as well-developed as is research on the model of informational centralization (see the section "Decentralization of Information"). [5]

It follows from the definition of complete centralization that, at each date, the decisionmakers know the *resources* at that date, and know the *inputs* required by each activity at any level. However, the decisionmakers may still be uncertain about the *outputs* from activities at the time those activity levels are determined. This is expressed by assuming that the outputs from activities at one date may depend on the partial history of the environment up through the *next* date.

Once a particular policy is chosen, *all* of the variables in the economy are determined by the evolution of the environment, either directly, as in the case of the resources, or indirectly, as in the case of inputs, outputs, and consumption. Thus, for a given policy, all of the variables in the system are random variables, with a joint probability that is determined by (1) the initial stocks of the economy, (2) the initial state of the environment, (3) the joint probability distribution of the successive states of the environment, and (4) the policy.

Thus far, nothing has been said about a criterion for choosing among alternative policies. Of course, the first requirement for a policy is that it lead to consumption sequences that are acceptable, whatever the state of the environment. Beyond that, theories of *optimal* decision assume that the centralized decisionmaker (planner) has preferences among alternative probability distributions of consumption sequences, or of final stocks of capital, or both. Such preferences imply preferences among alternative policies. For example, a popular assumption is that (1) there is a "utility function" ("social welfare function") that determines a "utility of consumption" at each date, (2) the utility of a consumption sequence is the sum of the (possibly discounted) utilities at the different dates, and (3) one policy is preferred to another if it leads to a larger expected total utility of consumption.

In this context, the *grand decision problem* of the planner is to choose a preferred policy among all those that lead to acceptable consumption sequences. Such a policy will be called *optimal*. The next three subsections deal with four topics in the characterization of optimal policies: (1) dynamic programming and the state valuation function, (2) certainty equivalence, (3) shadow prices, and (4) explicit solutions.

Note. The criterion of expected total (discounted) utility of consumption is so commonly used in theoretical work that some brief interpretive comments are in order concerning this criterion. First, the assumption that preferences can be represented in the form of *expected utility* implies assumptions of independence of tastes and beliefs (as well as certain technical assumptions of continuity, etc.)[6] Second, the assumption that preferences among sure consumption sequences can be represented in the form of a sum of (discounted or undiscounted) one-period utilities implies an assumption of independence of preferences as among consumptions at different dates. In particular, the discounting of future utilities implies a preference for present over future consumption, and thus (possibly) a "discrimination" against future generations.[7] In some problems it may make a difference whether at each date the utility of consumption is computed as (1) a utility of total consumption, (2) a utility of per capita consumption, or (3) a utility of per capita consumption multiplied by the number of consumers. Finally, the introduction of an infinite horizon may introduce special problems of convergence, continuity, etc., and the possibility of incompatibility among various properties that preferences among finite sequences of consumption naturally have. The limitation of space does not permit a more extended discussion of these questions here, but a full understanding of the difficulties inherent in a theory of planning under uncertainty requires some sophistication in these matters.[8]

Dynamic Programming and the State Valuation Function

Dynamic programming is a useful tool for both theoretical analysis and computation in many dynamic decision problems. For the purposes of this chapter, my interest in dynamic programming concerns the associated idea of the state valuation function, which provides insight into the theoretical structure of planning under uncertainty, and also may suggest useful *heuristics* for the solution of planning problems. As defined below, the state valuation function is a theoretical construct that imputes to each current state of the economy a "value," which is the maximum expected total discounted utility that can be achieved starting from that state. The importance of the state valuation function is that it enables the decision-maker to transform a many-period decision problem into a sequence of two-period problems.[9]

It is not my intention to review the theory of dynamic programming, but a few basic concepts are needed for an understanding of the significance of the state valuation function.[10] Suppose that the sequence of successive states of the environment forms a Markov chain,[11] with an infinite horizon. Suppose also that preference among policies is represented by the expected total discounted one-period utilities of consumption (see the above section on a model of economic growth under uncertainty). Assume that the transition probability law is the same at each date, and that the one-period utility function is the same for all dates, with a constant discount factor. In this situation, with sufficient regularity conditions, one can show that there is an optimal policy that is *stationary*, in the sense that, at each date, the optimal activity levels are a function of the current state of the environment and the current stocks of commodities, and this function is the same for each date.[12] The *state of the economy* at each date can therefore be adequately represented by the pair consisting of the state of the environment and the vector of stock levels. Denote this state, at date t, by e_t. For any policy π, let $V\pi(e_t)$ denote the expected total discounted utility of consumption *from date* t *on* that is implied by using the policy π, if the state of the economy at date t is e_t. The function V_π is called the *state valuation function associated with the policy* π. The function V_π satisfies an interesting and important recursive equation. Starting from the state e_t at date t, and using the policy π, let c_t denote the resulting consumption at date t, and let e_{t+1} denote the next state of the economy. At date t, the consumption c_t is known with certainty, but the planner is uncertain about the next state of the economy. The expected total discounted utility from date $(t+1)$ on is $EV_\pi(e_{t+1})$, where the symbol E denotes mathematical expectation with respect to the (uncertain) next state e_{t+1}, *and the discounting starts only at date $(t+1)$*. Let $u(c_t)$ denote the one period utility of the consumption c_t at date t, and let δ denote the planner's discount factor. Then the expected total discounted utility starting from date t is a sum of two terms: the utility $u(c_t)$ in the current period, and the discounted expected future utility, $EV_\pi(e_{t+1})$. Hence we have the recursive equation,

$$V_\pi(e_t) = u(c_t) + \delta EV_\pi(e_{t+1}) .\tag{4-1}$$

The state valuation function corresponding to an *optimal* policy plays a special role in the theory of dynamic programming, and is simply called *the* state valuation function. I shall denote it here by V^*. Corresponding to (4-1), there is the so-called *functional equation* of dynamic programming, which characterizes V^*. This functional equation can be motivated as follows. At date t, the current consumption is determined by the current state of the economy, and the current vector of activity levels, say ℓ_t. The choice of a vector of current activity levels will also lead to a vector of (uncertain) outputs at the next date, and thus to a new (uncertain) state of the economy at the next date. If the planner follows an optimal policy from date $(t+1)$ on, the expected utility, discounted from $(t+1)$ on, will be $EV^*(e_{t+1})$. Hence the optimal choice of activity levels at date t must maximize the sum of the utility of current consumption and the discounted expected optimum future utility, i.e.,

$$V^*(e_t) = \max_{\ell_t} [u(c_t) + \delta EV^*(e_{t+1})] ,\tag{4-2}$$

which is the functional equation of dynamic programming. Under appropriate conditions, V^* is the unique solution of the functional equation (4-2).[13]

Furthermore, knowledge of V^* is equivalent to knowledge of an optimal policy, in the sense that if one knows V^*, then one can determine the best activity levels for any state of the economy by choosing the activity levels that maximize the expression in square brackets on the right-hand side of (4-2). Thus, knowledge of the state valuation function would enable the planner to reduce the problem of finding an optimal *policy* to a sequence of two-period problems, in each of which it is required only to find an optimal vector of activity levels.

In a practical planning problem of any size, the apparent simplification of computation provided by the state valuation function may be illusory, since it may be just as much work to calculate the state valuation function as it is to calculate the entire optimal policy. Nevertheless, the functional equation yields an important insight into the structure of the problem. *Implicit in any optimal policy is a valuation of states of the economy that reflects completely the repercussions of current action on future utilities,* and this valuation completely characterizes an optimal policy. Indeed, implicit in any policy, optimal or not, is a corresponding valuation, and higher valuations correspond to better policies.

The functional equation corresponds intuitively to many heuristic attempts to solve dynamic optimization problems. For example, suppose that one makes a guess as to the correct valuation of states, and this guess is represented by a function, say U^0. One can then calculate what would be the optimal current actions if the *next* state were valued according to U^0; this would imply a valuation of *current* states according to some new function, say U^1. Now replace the function U^0 by the function U^1, and repeat the above procedure, obtaining a third function, U^2. Indeed, one can show that, under suitable conditions, the sequence of functions obtained in this way converges to the (true) state valuation function, V^*. If the first guess, U^0, is not too bad, a good approximation to V^* may be obtained after only a small number of iterations.

Following up this idea, the activity levels planned for the *beginning* of a long-term plan may be quite good, even if the planners have not correctly evaluated the final stocks at the *end* of the planning period. Of course, the planned actions will typically become worse and worse as one proceeds into the planning period, unless one constantly revises the plan, with a new planning horizon at each revision ("rolling plans" again!).

The state valuation function is also intimately connected with shadow prices, as will be indicated in the next subsection.

Shadow Prices

The concept of shadow price is familiar from mathematical programming (Lagrange-Kuhn-Tucker multipliers), theories of optimal allocation of resources, and, in particular, theories of optimal growth.[14] The extension of the theory of shadow prices to optimization under uncertainty is, in some sense, straightforward, although a general treatment can give rise to considerable mathematical difficulties.[15] In this subsection I shall briefly review what is known about the theory of shadow prices for our particular problem of optimal growth under uncertainty, and interpret the implications of this theory for planning.

A *price system* for our model of economic growth under uncertainty associates to each commodity, at each date, for each partial history of the environment at that date, a number, or price. Thus a price system determines a *stochastic process* of prices, i.e., a sequence of random prices, whose joint probability distribution is determined by the joint probability distribution of the states of the environment. These prices are to be interpreted as *discounted* prices, with the discounting taking place from date zero. Given a price system, one can calculate the *expected (discounted) profit* for an activity at that date, conditional on the partial history of the environment up through that date, as follows. The *cost* of the activity is the cost of the current inputs, calculated according to the vector of prices associated with the current date and partial history of the environment. The *expected revenue* of the activity is the *expected value* of the outputs of the activity at the next date, calculated according to the *conditional* probability distribution of prices at the next date, given the partial history of the environment at the current date. The expected discounted profit is the difference between expected revenue and cost.

A price system will be said to *sustain* an optimal policy if, for each partial history up through that date, and each activity, the optimal activity level maximizes expected discounted profit. In this case, I shall also say that the price system is a system of *shadow prices* associated with the given optimal policy.

Notice that, in the calculation of expected profit for an activity at a given date, *all* inputs and outputs must be priced. In particular, one must calculate the costs and revenues corresponding to used capital goods and goods-in-process. However, an alternative calculation is possible, extending over the entire period of the plan (or any shorter period), if the goods-in-process and used capital at a given date are actually used by the activity, and not disposed of elsewhere. In this calculuation, the expected discounted profit of an activity over the period of the plan is equal to the sum of the expected values of the *net* outputs at each date. The net output of each commodity at each date is, of course, the difference between the output of that commodity (from the previous period) and the current input. Note that, in the case of goods-in-process and used capital goods that are actually used, the net output is zero, and hence shadow prices for these commodities are not needed in order to calculate the expected discounted profit for the entire planning period.

One can show that, under the usual assumptions of convexity, etc., to every optimal policy there corresponds a system of shadow prices, provided that (1) the planning horizon is finite, and (2) there are only finitely many states of the environment at each date.[16] In principle, these last two assumptions are not restrictive, since an infinitie horizon and an infinite set of states are, in some sense, only mathematical idealizations of a very large finite horizon, and a very large set of states, respectively.

As a technical digression, it might be noted that infinite horizons are often analytically convenient in the theoretical treatment of growth, especially for examining the "long-run" properties of growth paths. Also, infinite sets of states are common in even elementary probability models (e.g., the Gaussian and Poisson distributions). On the other hand, the introduction of such infinities into the theory of optimal growth leads to special mathematical difficulties, as already noted, and the theory of shadow prices in such models is still incomplete.

I turn now to some implications of the theory of shadow prices for planning under uncertainty.

Expected profit maximization.   It should be emphasized that the appropriate criterion for each activity is expected profit. In other words, with the correct probability distribution of shadow prices, *no adjustment for risk aversion is needed.*

The rate of interest is stochastic.   As already noted, the shadow prices are to be interpreted as *discounted* prices. In other words, the system of shadow prices reflects, not only relative prices at each date, but rates of interest between different dates. In general, since the shadow prices at difference dates will not be proportional (except by accident), there is no unique natural definition of interest rates. Corresponding to each choice of numeraire, or each choice of price index, there will be a different system of (shadow) interest rates.[a] To be more precise on this point, we need a little notation. Let p_{ht} denote the discounted price of commodity h at date t; the prices p_{ht} are, of course, random variables. The *own-interest rate for commodity* h *at date* t is defined as

$$r_{ht} = \left[\frac{p_{ht}}{p_{h,t+1}} \right] - 1 .$$

(4-3)

Analogously, for any price index with strictly positive weights v_h, there is a corresponding *average rate of interest at* t, defined by

$$r_t = \left[\frac{\sum_t v_h p_{ht}}{\sum_t v_h p_{h,t+1}} \right] - 1.$$

(4-4)

Thus, the sequence of interest rates, however defined, forms a stochastic process.

Current relative prices are stochastic. Using again the weights v_h, define the *current* shadow price of commodity h at date t by

$$p_{ht} = \frac{p_{ht}}{\sum_k v_k p_{kt}} .$$

(4-5)

The current price of commodity h at date t reflects only the price of that commodity *relative to* the prices of other commodities at the same date, in the sense that the weighted sum of the current prices is always unity. The sequence of current shadow prices also forms a stochastic process.[17]

Price flexibility and probabilistic forecasts. The preceding remarks show how the sequence of stochastic discounted shadow prices determines corresponding sequences of interest rates and current prices, given a set of weights. Indeed, it is easy to see that, for a fixed set of weights, the interest rates and current prices completely characterize the discounted shadow prices, i.e., one can calculate the sequence of shadow prices from the sequences of interest rates and current prices. It follows from the preceding remarks that, if the planners or

[a]See, however, note 17 with regard to stationary stochastic programs.

decisionmakers are to use shadow prices as guides to planning and allocation, *then they must be prepared to (1) change current prices and interest rates from one date to the next, according to observations of the state of the environment, and (2) make probabilistic forecasts of future current prices and interest rates,* i.e., forecasts of these variables must be in terms of probability distributions, or at least characteristics of such distributions, such as means, variances, correlations, etc.[18] As far as I am aware of actual practice, price "flexibility" and forecasting of this type would be unusual in planning, and would even be regarded with some skepticism by planners. Some pros and cons of such use of shadow prices will be discussed below, especially in the section "Decentralization of Information." In any case, one may question the practicality of calculating shadow prices, a point to which I shall now turn.

Calculation of shadow prices. The shadow prices associated with an optimal policy give information about that policy, and are closely connected with the state valuation function discussed in the previous subsection. Indeed, whereas the state valuation function characterizes the optimal policy *globally,* the shadow prices characterize it *locally.* To that extent, the remarks in the previous subsection concerning the calculation of the state valuation function are applicable as well to the shadow prices. Since the shadow prices contain less information than does the state valuation function, they may in some cases be easier to calculate or estimate. These problems are not different, in principle, from the corresponding problems in the case of certainty, although the sheer size of the calculation problem may be orders of magnitude greater! Problems and pitfalls in the estimation of shadow prices are, of course, familiar from studies of cost-benefit analysis.[19]

Certainty-Equivalents

Because of the difficulty of calculating optimal policies (or the associated state valuation functions, or the shadow prices) in dynamic planning models of any complexity, there is a great incentive for discovering classes of problems that permit simplified calculations, or at least simplified approximations. One intuitively attractive method consists in the replacement of the various random variables in the decision problem by corresponding *nonrandom* variables, thus converting a problem of decisionmaking under uncertainty into one under certainty. (For example, each random value might be replaced by its expected value.) In such a procedure, the nonrandom variables are called the *certainty-equivalents* of the corresponding random variables; I shall call the corresponding decision problem (under certainty), the *certainty-equivalent problem.*

The solution of a certainty-equivalent problem will yield specific *decisions* for both the present and future dates, rather than decision rules or policies. The decisions for date zero will be implemented; the calculated decisions for future dates may be called the *planned decisions.* All of these calculated decisions will reflect the information available to the decisionmaker at date zero. When one arrives at date one (the second date), new information will typically become available. The decisionmaker is not constrained to implement, at date one, the planned decisions for date one that were calculated at date zero. A natural extension of the certainty-equivalent procedure at date one would be to reformulate a new certainty-equivalent problem, based upon the new information. (For example, one might replace the random variables at future dates by their conditional expected values, given the partial history of the environment through date one.) The solution to this certainty-equivalent problem at date one could be interpreted as a *revision of the plan* that was adopted at date zero. Proceeding in this manner from one date to the next, the decisionmaker formulates a sequence of certainty-equivalent problems, the solutions of which represent successive revisions of the original plan in the light of newly available information at each date. Thus the successive decisions do indeed reflect new information; in other words, *the sequence of certainty-equivalent problems defines a policy*, which I shall call the *certainty-equivalent policy*. Notice, however, that each successive certainty-equivalent problem is solved under the implicit assumption that no new information will become available in the future!

The certainty-equivalent approach has obvious computational attractions, which I shall now illustrate. For example, suppose that at each date t the decisionmaker observes the state of the environment at that date, and also remembers the partial history of the environment up to that date, and suppose further that at each date there are K possible states of the environment. There are therefore K^t partial histories of the environment up through date t, assuming that the state of the environment at date zero is fixed. A policy must determine what decision to take at date t for each of the K^t alternative partial histories up through date t. In other words, for each date t, there are K^t "unknowns" to determine, in order to specify a policy. If the horizon is T, then in total a policy must specify

$$\sum_{t=0}^{T} K^t = \frac{K^{t+1} - 1}{K - 1} \tag{4-6}$$

unknowns. Notice that this number grows geometrically with the horizon, T.

In the certainty-equivalent approach, however, the first certainty-equivalent problem has $(T+1)K$ unknowns, the second has TK unknowns (K for each remaining date), the third has $(T-1)K$ unknowns, etc. The total number of unknowns is therefore

$$\sum_{t=0}^{T} (T + 1 - t)K = \frac{(T + 1)(T + 2)}{2} K \tag{4-7}$$

which increases only like T^2.

Under what conditions is the certainty-equivalent policy optimal? Under what conditions is it approximately optimal? More generally, what are the directions of the errors made when one uses a certainty-equivalent policy rather than an optimal policy?

An answer to the first question is provided by the Simon-Theil theorem.[20] If (1) the criterion function whose expected value is to be maximized is a quadratic function of the decision variables, for every history of the environment, (2) the coefficients of the second degree terms do not depend on the environment, (3) the usual second-order conditions are satisfied, and (4) the certainty-equivalents at each date are taken to be *the conditional expected values of the coefficients of the zero and first degree terms* of the criterion function, given the partial history of the environment up through that date, *then the certainty-equivalent policy is optimal.* Furthermore, the planned decisions at each date (i.e., the calculated values of future decisions in the certainty-equivalent problem) are equal to the conditional expected values of the corresponding decisions as determined by the optimal policy, given the partial history of the environment up through that date. In other words, at each date, the "revised plan" gives the expected decisions, in the precise sense of mathematical expectation.

The quadratic case covered by the Simon-Theil theorem is, of course, quite special, but the same method could yield good approximations in more general cases. Indeed, if the criterion function were twice-differentiable in the decision variables, then it would be approximated by a quadratic function in the "neighborhood" of any sequence of decisions, and if the uncertainty about the coefficients were sufficiently small, then one would expect this approximation to be adequate. This idea can be made precise, as was shown by Theil in the static case and by Malinvaud in the dynamic case. [21]

Unfortunately, it is difficult to obtain information about the directions of the errors caused by using the Simon-Theil certainty-equivalent policy instead of the optimal policy. This question is equivalent to the question: how are the optimal decisions affected if uncertainty about the coefficients in the criterion function increases in a way that leaves the expected values of these coefficients unchanged? The answers to these questions appear to depend on the third and higher derivatives of the criterion function with respect to the decision variables, and these are parameters of a planning problem that are rarely known with precision. Malinvaud gives some interesting examples of this in the paper just cited.

Explicit Solutions

I am not aware of explicit (closed form) solutions of classes of problems of economic planning under certainty in any generality. Three special classes of problems might be mentioned here, however. First, some examples of optimal savings and portfolio choice might be interpreted as one-sector, i.e., macroeconomic planning models. These examples generally involve utility functions that exhibit constant risk aversion.[22]

Explicit solutions for a multi-sector dynamic linear-logarithmic model with uncertainty can easily be adapted from the solutions in the certainty case, provided that the uncertainty in production is confined to multiplicative coefficients of the production functions in each sector. (These solutions have not, however, been published.)[23]

Third, the vast literature on optimal inventory policies may be interpreted as a special subfield of economic planning under uncertainty. Nevertheless, the examples for which closed form explicit solutions are available are still much simpler than what would be needed to plan large-scale inventory systems, with many economic agents.

DECENTRALIZATION OF INFORMATION

Plans as Information Signals

I have defined an economy to be *informationally decentralized* to the extent that different activity levels are determined on the basis of different information about the environment. According to this broad definition, every economy is informationally decentralized to some extent. From this viewpoint, a national plan provides a set of information signals to economic agents, but these signals complement other information that is available only at the levels of the ministry, enterprise, plant, shop, etc. No national plan can hope to be based on complete information about the environment, even at the time it is drawn up, nor can one hope to develop procedures that will keep plans perfectly up-to-date. Therefore, when we think seriously about planning under uncertainty, we are forced to consider the nature of the information transmitted in the plan to the economic decisionmakers, the delays in this information, and the feedbacks (if any) from decisionmakers to planners at the national level. Unfortunately, theoretical research along these lines is recent and fragmentary, and does not typically make much of a distinction between planning and implementation.

The few studies on which I shall report below may be interpreted in terms of a simplified "model" of planning and information flows. The planners sit in an office and receive information about the environment, production, demand, etc. They make periodic computations, and periodically send out to various economic decisionmakers (or other planners at intermediate levels) information signals in the form of production targets, shadow prices, forecasts of demand, etc. They also periodically receive signals from the decisionmakers concerning estimates of current or past values of these and other variables (or perhaps also forecasts of them). The lags involved in these signals may be anything from weeks to years. The resulting economic decisions (e.g., activity levels) form a stochastic process. Two different planning procedures are to be compared in terms of the character of the two stochastic processes of decisions that they generate, and in terms of the corresponding costs of observation, computation, and communication.

Price Signals

Much of the literature on "market socialism," decentralized planning procedures, and decomposition methods for mathematical programming has emphasized the possibility of using prices as information signals from planners to decisionmakers (in a context of certainty). [24] In the typical procedure of this type, at each date the planners send price signals to the production managers (and possibly to the consumers), and receive in turn information about supplies and demands. If such procedures were to be used in real time, under conditions of uncertainty, the environment would change stochastically during the period of time required for each iteration. In other words, the environment would not stand still while the procedure converged to an "optimal" solution. Hence we are led to study the performance of such a system under conditions in which decisions about allocation and production are taken before the shadow prices have reached their "optimal" or "equilibrium" values. Since the performance of the system is stochastic, we may ask whether the resulting process is stochastically stable, and if so, calculate such measures of performance as (steady state) average output, variance of output, etc.

Once the problem is formulated in this way, it is natural to study the *optimal* decision rules, given the system that generates the information. If the price signals are not equilibrium prices, i.e., if supply does not equal demand at those prices, then decisions must be taken regarding how the existing supply is to be allocated, if it is less than demand, or what to do with excess supply, if supply exceeds demand. Furthermore, enterprise managers may have to make various local decisions before they know what their supplies will be for the current period.

The performance of such price signalling procedures, and the characterization of the corresponding optimal decision-rules, have been studied by Groves and Radner, under quite restrictive assumptions, using the methods of the theory of teams. The pattern of information exchange is one in which a central "resource manager" sends out price signals at each date to the "enterprise managers," who respond with "demands" that would maximize a suitably defined "shadow profit" criterion. At this stage, the enterprise managers must also make decisions concerning some "local" variables, before knowing the quantities of all the resources that will be allocated to them by the central manager. On the basis of the information he has received up to that point, the central manager determines the allocations of the resources to the enterprise managers. New observations of their respective parts of the environment are then made by all the agents, and the cycle is repeated. The aspects of the environment that vary from date to date are the quantities of centrally allocated resources, and the technical conditions of production in the enterprises. The criterion is long-run average output.

Groves and Radner actually studied a "static" version of this model, in which the agents have no "memory," and start afresh each date, but with a different environment, of course.[25] This is equivalent to studying the average or expected performance of an adjustment process (algorithm) in which only a single iteration is allowed before decisions must be made, and these decisions are chosen optimally, given the limited information provided by that single iteration. Under an assumption that the production functions of the enterprises are quadratic,[b] it is shown that *optimal decisions based on the price and demand signals yield as large an expected output as could be achieved by a complete exchange of information between the enterprises and the center.*

Groves studies a dynamic version of this model,[26] as described in the next to last paragraph, and showed that when the decisionmakers have memories, and prices are partially adjusted from date to date according to the perceived differences between supply and demand, then the simple result of the Groves-Radner "static" case no longer holds. However, for his model, he was able to show that if the enterprises send to the center forecasts of future demand, as well as estimates of current demand, then the resulting system is again as good as complete exchange of information between the enterprises and the center. A further result was that, *as the number of enterprises grows large, the percentage loss as compared with complete information (complete informational centralization) approaches zero.* (This result also was valid in the Groves-Radner model.)

The results just described have been derived for a highly simplified model, and appear to depend heavily on the quadratic assumption for their exact validity. However, Groves[27] has proved for the Groves-Radner model a result analogous to the approximate-certainty-equivalence theorems derived by Theil and Malinvaud in the case of a single decisionmaker. To the extent that these approximation results are robust, they suggest that *price and demand signals are strikingly efficient in conveying the information needed for good allocation decisions, even out of equilibrium.*

Production Targets and Decomposition Algorithms

If production functions are close to linear, then small changes in prices may generate large changes in demand. Under these conditions, in the case of certainty, adjustment processes that rely exclusively on price signals to the enterprises may oscillate excessively during convergence to the optimal solution. This unpleasant property has the consequence (among other disadvantages) that at some iterations the enterprises will be proposing plans that are far from their current experience, and also far from the final inputs and outputs to which the process eventually converges. This difficulty has led, in the mathematical programming literature, to the study of algorithms that involve computation at the center of production targets for the enterprises, possibly in addition to price signals.[28]

[b]The precise assumptions are similar to those that permit the use of certainty equivalents; see the section "Characterization of Optimal Paths of Economic Growth Under Uncertainty."

The appropriate mathematical model for the study of such problems would seem to be the linear programming (linear activity analysis) model. In this model, the inputs and outputs are linear functions of the activity levels. In addition, there are constraints corresponding to factors or inputs whose supplies are fixed. Unfortunately, the solutions of linear programming problems can rarely be expressed in closed form as functions of the parameters. This makes difficult the analytical study of problems of uncertainty in which the parameters are themselves random variables. For such problems, methods of simulation and numerical analysis seem indispensable, at least given the theoretical techniques that are currently available.

Hogan [29] studied the performance of several decomposition algorithms in the same spirit as in the Groves-Radner investigation, but using numerical methods. Between iterations of the algorithm, the environment changes according to some probabilistic law (possibly incorporating serial correlation). As in our previous discussion, each iteration of the algorithm in question is interpreted as an exchange of information between planners and enterprises, as well as the results of decentralized computation within the planning unit and the enterprises. Performance of the procedures was tested using ranges of parameters suggested by input-output tables for five different countries.

The results of Hogan's study are too complicated to summarize fully here. He was able to confirm the stochastic stability of the algorithms, and to demonstrate that such numerical simulation is feasible and sufficiently accurate with moderately long histories of simulated iterations. The most surprising results were that

> *as the variance of both the technology and the resource supplies increases, and as the accuracy of the starting information (at each iteration) becomes poorer, the performance of (the) procedures becomes better.* This result is due to the fact that the decomposition procedure tends to converge to the optimal plan quicker when the starting vectors are farther from their optimal configuration. This results (in turn) from the fact that the prospective indices shift more under these conditions, so that the range of vectors contained in the memory of the central board is greater and the known portion of the production sets is also greater. This allows quick convergence in the early iterations. [30]

UNCERTAINTY AND
DECENTRALIZATION OF AUTHORITY

The theories of planning under uncertainty that have been considered thus far in this chapter have explicitly or implicity assumed the existence of a single overall objective or criterion to be maximized, even though there may be a number of different decisionmakers with different information. In this respect, these theories fall within the framework of the theory of *teams* rather than the theory of *games*, the latter of which deals explicitly with conflicts of interest among the decisionmakers. The theorist may invent decision rules that are optimal, given the limitations on the information available to the different agents in the economic system, but one must still face the problem of providing the incentives for the agents to follow these decision rules and provide the required information. Indeed, the postulated information system may itself fall victim to, or be manipulated by, the power struggles of the members of the organization.[31]

Students of bureaucracy—and bureaucrats—are well aware of the power that may go with limited information.[32] Under conditions of uncertainty and limited information, it will typically be difficult for a supervisor (or organizer) to determine whether a particular decisionmaker is providing correct information or is following the prescribed decision-rules, since to achieve this would require the supervisor to have all the information that is available to the subordinate decisionmaker. In other words, *informational decentralization leads to de facto decentralization of authority.*

If the behavior of decisionmakers in situations of conflict of interest were perfectly predictable, this would not introduce any additional uncertainty into the organization. In fact, there is considerable uncertainty about the behavior of individual decisionmakers in conflict situations. Furthermore, the theory of games has not even been able to produce an agreed-upon definition of "rational" behavior in conflict situations. These considerations lead me to conclude that, in an organization, uncertainty about the environment brings with it uncertainty about the behavior (decision-rules) of the members of the organization. These two classes of uncertainty may be distinguished conceptually, but not separated in practice.

If informational decentralization generates decentralization of authority, and if modern economies are too complex to be operated with information centralization, then it follows that no modern economic system can be operated with complete, or even nearly complete centralization of authority.[c] (On the one hand, this is a platitude, but on the other hand, it contradicts the official position of many large economic organizations, although by this date the myth of the "command economy" has perhaps at last been laid to rest.)

This proposition poses a dilemma that is particularly acute for a socialist economy. An effective system of incentives must allow decisionmakers to share the benefits that derive from the improvement of information, decisions, and decision-rules. But the accumulation of these benefits leads to inequalities in income, power, etc. Such inequalities are typically self-perpetuating, and are contrary to the spirit of socialism. An analogous phenomenon is familiar in capitalist economies. To provide the incentives for firms to make improvements, one must be willing to let them reap some monopoly profits from such

[c]This does not deny that there may be significant differences in centralization of authority among different economic systems.

improvements, if only in the short run. Thus, under conditions of uncertainty, the effective operation of a capitalist economy is inconsistent with "perfect competition."

The proposition may also be paraphrased as follows. Under conditions of uncertainty, information is a valuable input into production, i.e., it is one of the "means of production." Since the decentralization of information is unavoidable, there will inevitably be decisionmakers who "own" information that is not owned by others. In this sense, *under conditions of uncertainty, pure public ownership of the means of production is impossible*, at least with the currently available technology of observation, communication, and computation.

CONCLUDING REFLECTIONS

We have seen in this brief survey that most of the theoretical literature on economic planning under uncertainty deals with various problems of optimal allocation of resources and optimal growth (investment policy). This literature can be viewed in perspective as an extension of "mathematical programming" models to the case of uncertainty. As some of the other chapters in this volume show, the use of mathematical programming models is not unknown in applied work on economic planning, and one can anticipate that such applications will gradually be extended to cover cases of uncertainty. This development will be facilitated by the dramatic rate of increase in computational power that continues to characterize the development of the computing industry, in terms of both hardware and software.

Although I have questioned here the relevance, in some deep sense, of optimization models to planning, two observations in defense of optimization models should be emphaiszed. These observations are based upon the relatively long history of the use of such models in operations research, and the shorter history in national economic planning. First, the application of mathematical programming models stimulates more intense empirical research on the *quantitative* relations in the economic system. In these applications, econometric, mathematical, and computational progress must go hand-in-hand. Second, in responsible applications of optimization models, the optimization is done "parametrically": a family of solutions is calculated corresponding to a range of parameter values in the objective function (the optimization criterion). In this way, policymakers can see how the optimal policy depends on the crucial parameters of the objective function, and are provided with a family of alternative policies whose consequences can be studied quantitatively and qualitatively in terms of various criteria that are not explicitly incorporated into the objective function.

The theory of optimal planning also has *qualitative* implications for the structure of the planning process, especially in the formulation described in the section "Characterizations of Optimal Paths of Economic Growth Under Uncertainty" as "dynamic programming." Optimal planning under uncertainty calls for "rolling plans," i.e., sequential planning strategies that involve the updating of planned actions as new information about the environment and the economic system becomes available. The frequency and comprehensiveness of this updating should, of course, depend upon the associated informational and computational costs.

A particular form of sequential updating was described in the section "Characterizations of Optimal Paths of Economic Growth Under Uncertainty" as the "certainty-equivalent" approach. This approach will usually be less demanding in terms of information and computation than a fully optimal sequential strategy, and under certain conditions will provide a good approximation to an optimal strategy. It is my impression that the certainty-equivalent approach corresponds in some sense to the informal practice of many planners, but I am not prepared to document that impression in this chapter.

In spite of the rapid progress of information processing technology (in the broadest sense of the term), a large gap remains between the information processing requirements of fully optimal planning strategies and the capabilities of real man-machine planning systems, now and in the foreseeable future. Indeed, I support the view that, from a deeper methodological point of view, the concept of "fully optimal planning" is meaningless. In any case, I speculate that the most significant next advances in the *theory* of economic planning will focus on the organizational and behavioral aspects of information processing and decentralization.

Some recent research on the mathematical theory of informational decentralization was described in the section "Decentralization of Information." To date, behavioral approaches to the theory of planning and resource allocation have primarily used the tools of computer simulation,[33] and computer programs will probably continue to constitute an important form for the expression of behavioral theories of decisionmaking. In addition, reports of recent research (largely unpublished) suggest that theories of bounded rationality are also amenable to more traditional forms of mathematical analysis.[34] If so, then we are on the brink of a new stage of rapprochement between theory and practice in the field of economic planning under uncertainty.

NOTES

1. See, e.g., E. Malinvaud, "Decentralized Procedures for Planning," Ch. 7 in *Activity Analysis in the Theory of Growth and Planning,* ed. M.O.L. Bacharach and E. Malinvaud (London: Macmillan; New York: St. Martin's Press, 1967), pp. 170–210; J. Kornai and T. Liptak, "Two-Level Planning," *Econometrica* 33, 1 (January 1963):141–69.

2. H.A. Simon, "Theories of Bounded Rationality," Ch. 8 in *Decision and Organization,* ed. C.B. McGuire and R. Radner (Amsterdam: North-Holland Publishing Co., 1972), pp. 161–76.

3. See, however, J. Kornai, *Anti-Equilibrium* (Amsterdam: North-Holland

Publishing Co., 1971); his criticisms of general equilibrium theory are at some points in the spirit of bounded rationality.

4. This is the now familiar model of statistical decision theory; see, e.g., L.J. Savage, *The Foundations of Statistics* (New York: John Wiley and Sons, Inc., 1954).

5. For discussions of concepts of informational centralization and decentralization, see J. Marschak and R. Radner, *Economic Theory of Teams* (New Haven: Yale University Press, 1972), Chs. 4, 6, 8, and 9; also R. Radner, "Normative Theories of Organization: An Introduction," T.A. Marschak, "Computation in Organizations: The Comparison of Price Mechanisms and Other Adjustment Processes," and L. Hurwicz, "On Informationally Decentralized Systems," Chs. 9, 12, and 14 in *Decision and Organization,* ed. McGuire and Radner; see, also, references cited in Hurwicz, "On Informationally Decentralized Systems," pp. 334–36.

6. See, for example, Savage, *Foundations of Statistics;* Marschak and Radner, *Theory of Teams,* Ch. 1; and K.J. Arrow, "Exposition of the Theory of Choice Under Uncertainty," Ch. 2 in *Decision and Organization,* ed. McGuire and Radner.

7. T.C. Koopmans, "Representation of Preference Orderings with Independent Components of Consumption" and "Representation of Preference Orderings Over Time," Chs. 3 and 4 in *Decision and Organization,* ed. McGuire and Radner.

8. On the last two points, see T.C. Koopmans, "On the Concept of Optimal Economic Growth," and E. Malinvaud, "Croissances optimales dans un modèle macroéconomique" [Optimal Growth in a Macroeconomic Model], both in *The Econometric Approach to Development Planning,* Pontificiae Academiae Scientarium Scripta Varia, October 7–13, 1965 (Amsterdam: North-Holland Publishing Co., 1965), pp. 225–88 and 301–78.

9. The term "state valuation function" is to be distinguished from the term "state preference function" that one finds in some literature on the economic theory of socialism; see, e.g., J. Drewnowski, "The Economic Theory of Socialism," *Journal of Political Economy* 69, 4 (August 1961):547–58. In the latter term, the reference is to the (political) state, whereas in the former it is to the state of the economy at a particular date. The "state preference function" corresponds to what has been described above as the preferences of the planner (social welfare function).

10. For an introduction to the theory of dynamic programming, see, e.g., S.M. Ross, *Applied Probability Models with Optimization Applications* (San Francisco: Holden-Day, 1970).

11. In a Markov chain, at any date, the conditional distribution of the future, given the partial history of the environment up through the present date, depends on the partial history only through the present state of the environment. See, e.g., W. Feller, *An Introduction to Probability Theory and Its Applications, Vol I,* third edition (New York: John Wiley and Sons, Inc. 1968), or any other introduction to stochastic processes.

12. For this and other facts about optimal policies for the present case, see P. Jeanjean, "Optimal Growth with Stochastic Technology in a Multisector

Economy," Technical Report No. 16, Center for Research in Management Science, University of California, Berkeley, August 1972.

13. Again, see Jeanjean, "Optimal Growth," for sufficient conditions for the functional equation to characterize optimal policies.

14. For an introduction to mathematical programming methods and their relationship to economic theory, see M.D. Intriligator, *Mathematical Optimization and Economic Theory* (Englewood Cliffs, New Jersey; Prentice-Hall, 1971). An advanced treatment is found in K.J. Arrow, L. Hurwicz, and H. Uzawa, *Studies in Linear and Non-Linear Programming* (Stanford: Stanford University Press, 1958). T.C. Koopmans, *Three Essays on the State of Economic Science* (New York: McGraw-Hill, 1957), Ch. 1, provides a good introduction to the relationship between prices and resource allocation. A basic reference for shadow prices and optimal growth is still E. Malinvaud, "Capital Accumulation and Efficient Allocation of Resources," *Econometrica* 21, 2 (April 1953):233–68; see, also, E. Malinvaud, "Efficient Capital Accumulation: A Corrigendum," *Econometrica*, 30, 3 (July 1962):570–73. An important duality theorem not mentioned in these references is in D. Gale, "A Geometric Duality Theorem with Applications," *Review of Economic Studies* 34, 1 (January 1967):19–24.

15. For a treatment of uncertainty with finitely many states of the environment, see G. Debreu, *Theory of Value* (New York: John Wiley and Sons, Inc., 1959), Ch. 7. More advanced treatments are surveyed in M.K. Majumdar and R. Radner, "Shadow Prices for Infinite Growth Programs: The Functional Analysis Approach," in *Techniques of Optimization,* ed. V.L. Balakrishnan (New York: Academic Press, 1972), pp. 371–90.

16. A result of this type follows immediately from Chs. 5 and 7 of Debreu, *Theory of Value.*

17. Such price processes can be quite general, even in simple cases. Even if the states of the environment are independent and identically distributed, the sequence of shadow prices will typically not have this property (see J. Schechtman, "Some Applications of Competitive Prices to Dynamic Programming Problems Under Uncertainty," Operations Research Report No. 73–5 and Ph.D. dissertation, University of California, Berkeley, March 1973). If the states of the environment are Markovian, then the sequence of pairs (state, price vector) will in general also be Markovian, *but the price process by itself will not.* If the environment is stationary, then under certain conditions it is known that the price process will be stationary, or asymptotically stationary (see R. Radner, "Optimal Stationary Consumption with Stochastic Production and Resources," *Journal of Economic Theory* 6, 1 [February 1973], pp. 68–90; and R.A. Dana, "Evaluation of Development Programs in a Stationary Stochastic Economy with Bounded Primary Resources," Technical Report No. 19, Center for Research in Management Science, University of California, Berkeley, February 1973; to appear in *Proceedings of a Symposium on Mathematical Methods in Economics,* ed. J. Los [Amsterdam: North-Holland Publishing Co., 1974]). In this case, the time-average of the rate of interest is zero, for all price indices.

18. In the pure form of "indicative planning," the planners attempt to make forecasts of prices and quantities such that, if the various economic decision-

makers believe these forecasts, then they will behave in such a way as to confirm the forecasts for the history of the environment that is actually realized. The theoretical possibility of making such "self-fulfilling" price forecasts (which must, of course, be probabilistic) has been demonstrated by Radner, "Existence of Equilibrium of Plans, Prices, and Price Expectations in a Sequence of Markets," *Econometrica* 40, 2 (March 1972):289–304, for an economy with *incomplete* markets for future and contingent delivery.

19. A good illustration of these issues in the context of project analysis, primarily for the case of certainty, can be found in I.M.D. Little and J.A. Mirrlees, *Manual of Industrial Project Analysis in Developing Countries, Vol. II: Social Cost-Benefit Analysis* (Paris: Development Center of the Organization for Economic Cooperation and Development, 1968).

20. For the original contributions, see H.A. Simon, "Dynamic Programming Under Uncertainty with a Quadratic Criterion Function," *Econometrica* 24, 1 (January 1956):74–81; and H. Theil, "A Note on Certainty Equivalence in Dynamic Planning," *Econometrica* 25, 2 (April 1957):346–49. A general account is given in Marschak and Radner, *Theory of Teams,* Ch. 7, Sec. 2.

21. H. Theil, *Optimal Decision Rules for Government and Industry* (Amsterdam: North-Holland Publishing Co., 1964); E. Malinvaud, "First-Order Certainty Equivalence," *Econometrica* 37, 4 (October 1969):706–18. A precise statement of their results would require more space and technical apparatus than are feasible for this chapter. I should also point out that neither the exact nor the approximate certainty-equivalent results require that the criterion function be separable in time, as was assumed in the model we have been considering in this chapter.

22. For examples of savings and portfolio problems, see D. Levhari and T.N. Srinivasan, "Optimal Savings Under Uncertainty," *Review of Economic Studies* 36, 2 (April 1969):153–64; H.H. Hakansson, "Optimal Investment and Consumption Strategies Under Risk for a Class of Utility Functions," *Econometrica* 38, 5 (September 1970):587-607. Further references can be found in D. Levhari, "Optimal Savings and Portfolio Choice Under Uncertainty," in *Mathematical Methods in Investment and Finance,* ed. G. Szegö and K. Shell (Amsterdam: North-Holland Publishing Co., 1972), pp. 34–48.

23. The multi-sector linear-logarithmic model under certainty is treated in R. Radner, "Optimal Growth in a Linear-Logarithmic Economy," *International Economic Review* 7, 1 (January 1966):1–33.

24. B. Ward, *The Socialist Economy* (New York: Random House, 1967); T.A. Marschak, "Centralization and Decentralization in Economic Organization," *Econometrica* 27, 3 (July 1959):399–430; and Malinvaud, "Decentralized Procedures."

25. T.F. Groves and R. Radner, "Allocation of Resources in a Team," *Journal of Economic Theory* 4, 3 (June 1972):415–41.

26. T.F. Groves, "Market Information and the Allocation of Resources in a Dynamic Team Model," 1972, to appear in *Review of Economic Studies.*

27. T.F. Groves, "The Allocation of Resources Under Uncertainty: The Informational and Incentive Roles of Prices and Demands in a Team," Technical Report No. 1, Center for Research in Management Science, University of California, Berkeley, August 1969.

28. For a discussion of some of these problems in the case of certainty, see, e.g., Malinvaud, "Decentralized Procedures"; and M. Weitzman, "Iterative Multilevel Planning with Production Targets," *Econometrica* 38, 1 (January 1970):50–65.

29. T.M. Hogan, "A Comparison of Information Structures and Convergence Properties of Several Multisector Economic Planning Procedures," Technical Report No. 10, Center for Research in Management Science, University of California, Berkeley, May 1971.

30. Ibid., p. 8; the emphasis is mine. The papers by Groves ("Incentives in Teams") and Hogan ("Comparison") are the only ones with which I am familiar that deal with the dynamic "real-time" properties of models of iterative procedures for economic planning under conditions of uncertainty. However, at a recent seminar at the University of California, Berkeley, Professor Kornai announced that research on this subject was currently being done in Hungary. Related models of the dynamics of decisionmaking in teams were analyzed in Ch. 7 of Marschak and Radner, *Theory of Teams,* where one can also find references to other (moderately) relevant literature.

31. For a comparison of the theory of teams and the theory of games, and for an introduction to the concepts of normative theories of organization, see R. Radner, "Teams," Ch. 10 in *Decision and Organization,* ed. McGuire and Radner, pp. 189–215; or for a fuller treatment, Marschak and Radner, *Theory of Teams.* See, also, T.F. Groves, "Incentives in Teams," *Econometrica* 41, 4 (July 1973):617–32, for a provocative study of incentives in teams.

32. See, for example, the insightful study by M. Crozier, *Le phénomène bureaucratique* [The Bureaucratic Phenomenon] (Paris: Editions du Seuil, 1963).

33. Simon, "Bounded Rationality," p. 174; R.M. Cyert and J.G. March, *A Behavioral Theory of the Firm* (Englewood Cliffs, N.J.: Prentice-Hall, 1963).

34. R. Radner, "Aspiration, Bounded Rationality, and Control," Presidential Address, Oslo Meeting of the Econometric Society, August 1973, to appear in *Econometrica;* R. Radner, "Satisficing," paper presented to the IFIP Technical Conference on Optimization Techniques, Novosibirsk, July 1974; and R. Radner and M. Rothschild, "Notes on the Allocation of Effort," Technical Report No. OW-1, Center for Research in Management Science, University of California, Berkeley, May 1974. See, also, the references cited in the first two of these papers.

Comments on Roy Radner's Chapter

Richard Portes

Professor Radner has given us a lucid and honest survey of his subject, as we should expect. It conveys the essential theoretical points without oversimplification which would make them meaningless or trivial. Yet its technical level should be accessible to nonspecialists. This also reflects his honesty: He does not conceal behind technique the severe limitations of existing theory in prescribing methods for solving planning problems in an uncertain world, or even in describing realistically the context in which such planning is actually carried out.

Radner first sets out the standard conceptual framework for dealing with dynamic systems under uncertainty. Although this seems familiar now, the contemporary theorist could legitimately remind impatient critics that it all dates only from the first postwar decade, the remarkable construction of von Neumann, Savage, Koopmans, Marschak, and others. This framework helps to clarify the *sources* of uncertainty in the environment (resource supplies and technology) and in human behavior. This is a first step in dealing with uncertainty. Typically, we think of the former as exogenous random variables to be predicted (in the sense of specifying their probability distribution), and the latter as a "structure" which we can specify so as to estimate its parameters. The division is to some extent conventional, however. Indeed, planners can consciously attempt to reduce uncertainty by bringing some of the "exogenous" variables at least partly under their control. The converse is less common, but perhaps equally important—efforts to *predict* structural change, which may require broadening our specification of economic relationships to include more variables representing "noneconomic" behavior.

To give a taxonomy to the work he surveys, Radner distinguishes between the *characterization* of optimal paths, optimal *decision rules,* and procedures for *calculating* optimal allocations. He stresses that an optimal policy is a strategy, a sequence of vectors of decision functions—not a set of decisions made at $t = 0$ to cover the entire period up to the planning horizon. With all its implications, this notion of planned but flexible adaptation to the consequences of past decisions and to new information as it becomes available is much more subtle than it appears. It underlies all that the theory of planning under uncertainty has to offer practitioners. Rigid plans and planners have too often chosen decisions rather than policies and adhered to them, at great cost, long after a sensible strategy would have dictated tactical adjustments.

Radner goes on to outline the main theoretical results of dynamic programming, efficiency pricing under uncertainty, and the Simon-Theil first-period certainty equivalence theorem—all in the context of complete informational centralization. Dynamic programming tells us that if the vectors of random variables describing successive states of the environment form a Markov chain with constant transition probabilities, then the policy maximizing the discounted sum of expected utilities is *stationary:* the vector of decision functions is constant over time, and at each date its arguments are only variables characterizing the state of the economy at that date. The optimal policy is defined by a (conceptually) simple first-order recursive functional equation whose solution, the state valuation function, embodies all the effects of current actions on future utilities. This simplicity is deceptive, however, and the practical applicability of the technique is limited by the difficulty of actually calculating the state valuation function in all but relatively straightforward cases, which are unlikely to appear in national economic planning. Nor are many of the variables which a planner must treat as exogenous likely to obey the very restrictive probabilistic hypothesis, if only because they may themselves be economic variables with complicated autoregressive behavior. Nevertheless, as Radner points out, the approach gives some intuitive insight into the structure of the planning problem and suggests one line of argument for "rolling plans."

The theory of shadow pricing under uncertainty has even less operational content than dynamic programming. Considering the immense and controversial literature on appropriate principles for shadow pricing in a deterministic setting, the propensity of programming models to yield implausible and unstable shadow prices, and the reluctance of practical planners to take seriously shadow prices for just two or three basic resources—one must be rather skeptical of theory here. As always, the efficient price system is dual to the optimal policy and characterizes it locally, but its intertemporal behavior will be complex and seems to admit no useful generalizations. While I can at least imagine planners thinking in terms of optimal policies defined over quantity variables, I cannot see them using an appropriate shadow price system in the way that Radner indicates; to be fair, neither can he.

The certainty-equivalent policy looks more useful, as Theil has often argued. It amounts to making decisions each period on the basis of the expected values of the relevant random variables, and to that extent ignoring their stochastic character. This too is a version of planning with continual revision. But, the conditions under which this policy is optimal are again rather strong, in particular the requirement of fixed (nonrandom) coefficients of the quadratic terms in the objective functions. I believe that this would typically be violated in multi-period programming models with capital accumulation. Moreover, as Radner emphasizes, it is difficult to evaluate the loss from using the certainty-equivalent policy or to estimate the sensitivity of this loss to increased variance of the random coefficients in the objective function.

After citing some examples of explicit solutions to planning problems under uncertainty, Radner turns to the situation in which information is decentralized, so that there is no single decisionmaker who can determine all activity levels in full knowledge of the partial history of the environment through the period in question. Most of the literature on decentralized planning procedures deals with *tâtonnements* taking place in computational time and eventually converging to optimal plans, which are then implemented. In real time, however, the environment would change stochastically during iterations, and Radner discusses two interesting studies of how iterative procedures perform in these circumstances. His own results in a team model are quite encouraging in that they suggest that price and demand signals transmit information effectively even in a disequilibrium context. Hogan simulated the behavior of various decomposition procedures in a probabilistically varying environment and found not only that their stability properties were robust, but that convergence actually became quicker when the variance of the technology and resource supplies increased. I find Hogan's explanation puzzling, unless he was working only with non-monotonic procedures, but the results are good all the same. In order not to seem too optimistic, however, I should mention that practical experience in applying iterative multilevel procedures to national planning in Hungary encountered great difficulties. I have discussed in detail elsewhere why these procedures are still far from being useful for current allocation in centrally planned economies, even ignoring uncertainty.[1]

I shall return below to some of Radner's perceptive more general introductory and concluding remarks. We must surely agree with his overall assessment that the theory of national planning under uncertainty is still in its infancy and can at most give insights into general features of planning problems. Specific models and solution procedures require highly restrictive assumptions, a multitude of sophisticated data, and very complex calculations. The literature itself is impenetrable to all but mathematical economists, although they may be able to convey some of its flavor to their more practical colleagues (if they are as good at it as Radner). All this could be contrasted with the growing use, in both underdeveloped and centrally planned economies, of multi-sectoral deterministic planning models. Even here, there are problems in getting policymakers to assimilate and use the output of these models (as Augustinovics' chapter explains), but uncertainty clearly presents theoretical and practical difficulties of a much higher order of magnitude.

Yet, the world, at least as it appears to us, is undeniably stochastic—and some philosophers (as well as modern physics) would drop the qualification and hold that it is ineradicably so. Planners must and in many ways do take account of uncertainty.

Mathematical planners calculate multiple plan variants on varying assumptions about the state of the environment, as expressed in the constraint system. They engage in parametric programming and sensitivity analysis to discover where the loss from taking suboptimal decisions under uncertainty is likely to be greatest. They use interval rather than point forecasts and make explicitly probabilistic statements about future events. Undoubtedly these relatively primitive approaches cannot give even a first-order approximation to a truly optimal policy, but they do represent progress over only a few years ago.

"Traditional" planners and policymakers (following East European terminology) occasionally *have* ignored uncertainty—confidently, obstinately, and unsuccessfully. But the excessive optimism about "scientific" planning (cf. Lindblom's chapter) was in part politically inspired, and experience has, in fact, moderated it to the point where it is now mainly rhetorical. In centrally planned economies, the plans are now more cautious. They allow for uncertainty by providing "reserves"—a margin of excess capacity in the form of stocks of commodities and foreign exchange—so that random shocks do not create bottlenecks whose effects, spreading through the economy, far exceed the size of the initial disturbance. Indicative planning, of course, finds its raison d'etre in uncertainty. The object of the exercise is precisely to reduce uncertainty in a decentralized system, at both micro and macro levels, by dissemination of information and coordination of decisions.

Both Eastern and Western planners seem increasingly attracted by the idea of "rolling plans." Radner has indicated some theoretical justification for this from dynamic programming and the certainty equivalence theorem. Another argument (somewhat similar to certainty equivalence) comes from the theory of deterministic multi-period planning.[2] Suppose we have a set of planning problems with different planning horizons, i.e., covering t periods, where $t = 1$, ..., T, ... All have the same quadratic criterion function and linear constraint system. Let the optimal first-period solution be x_1^T for any given T and x_1^∞ for the infinite horizon case. Then by choosing T large enough, x_1^T can be made as close as we like to x_1^∞. Thus, the conceptually more satisfactory but mathematically complicated infinite horizon problems can be replaced with a finite horizon problem (for sufficiently large T), without introducing arbitrary influences through the choice of terminal condition—*provided* we continually revise the plan each period, so we use only first-period solutions. In practice, T may not have to be too large in order to get a good approximation to x_1^∞, in which case this procedure also limits the uncertainty introduced by very long (or infinite) horizons.

Planning with continual revision does mean a lot of work for the planners—in the Hungarian view (according to Morva) so much that the procedure is feasible only for the long-term (fifteen–twenty year) plans, but not for the five-year plans. Moreover, neither rolling plans nor calculating ex ante many plan variants can tell the planners what to do *during* the (minimum) plan period when significant random disturbances appear. The discrete time model hides this problem. For a given current period, the plan is a set of decisions, not a policy—yet the planners may be forced to readjust during the period. This will obviously occur often in the context of a five-year plan—there are two extreme examples for Czechoslovakia during the 1960s alone. On the other hand, frequent intervention during the plan period may be just as destructive to the plan as exogenous shocks. It is easy to construct models in which "fine tuning" is destabilizing, and it may *create* uncertainty for decentralized decision makers (cf. the Hungarian desire to maintain stability of the "economic regulators" during the five-year plan, in order to provide a firm basis for enterprise decisions).

Planners may also respond to uncertainty by adapting the structure of the planning and plan-implementation mechanism. Information and control systems may be superimposed upon each other—e.g., we may find planners transmitting not just price or quantity signals, but both, perhaps together with value targets as well; information may flow not just "horizontally" or "vertically," but between units in all directions; "success indicators" may proliferate, each additional one being designed to control some aspect of behavior which the planners find unpredictable. This type of response can be useful, if it creates new sources of data or cross-checks on existing ones. It may also be dysfunctional, however, as information becomes not more complete and comprehensive, but rather contradictory and garbled. A series of ad hoc reactions to unexpected or "uncontrolled" phenomena can eventually generate systems of baroque complexity, as East European planning has occasionally demonstrated (the history of the Polish success indicator system provides some particularly egregious examples).

The mechanism may also adapt through decentralization, by choice or necessity. The planners may recognize their inability to predict some types of data or behavior, or to react quickly to uncertain events as they occur. They may then turn to Lindblom's "strategic" planning, allowing decentralized units to take decisions as new information appears to them, under constraints and following rules prescribed by the center. The planners themselves may move away from making comprehensive decisions well in advance of events, towards sequential planning with feedback. But this is just what the theory of planning under uncertainty suggests: attempts to formulate optimal *policies* and sets of decision rules.

Here we return to Radner's view of the present state of the art. Since it will in the foreseeable future be impossible to design truly optimal policies for national economic planning, he suggests that we shall have to be content with some degree of "bounded rationality" (in Simon's phrase)—so he and Lindblom converge from quite different standpoints. Moreover, uncertainty implies that even the limited information available about past and future states of the world cannot be fully known to a single central decisionmaker, so informational decentralization is unavoidable. We therefore need a theory of the organization of information-processing and decision-taking in planning. Since the objectives of participants may differ, the model of a team is only a first step, and the theory must go on to incorporate conflict and incentive problems in a game-theoretic way. He argues that uncertainty precludes full knowledge by a supervisor of whether his subordinate is providing correct information and following the prescribed rules, so that authority is inevitably decentralized. Our inability to predict decisionmakers' behavior in conflict situations therefore makes the syllogism run directly from uncertainty about the environment to uncertainty about the behavior of participants in the planning and plan-implementation process. Finally, he draws conclusions which will be unpalatable at least to socialist planners: uncertainty, he maintains, implies that decentralized decisionmakers will "own" information essential to proper functioning of the economy, and in this sense *full* public ownership is impossible. Accordingly, to elicit new or better information from decentralized units requires allowing them to share as "owners" the economic rents which this information will create.

Reluctantly, I find this argument compelling, and it is supported in practice by the poor performance of socialist-planned economies in innovation. Despite the supposed advantages of central planning in organizing research and development, directing it toward economic priorities, and propagating innovation without the encumbrances of patents and private property, the record, in fact, suggests that here lies the major weakness of centrally planned economies. I myself should hope, however, that reforms which improve the incentives to innovate in these economies will be accompanied by measures to mitigate their inegalitarian effects.

I would suggest, however, that in his conclusion Radner may have overemphasized the importance of uncertainty about the environment. Although his conclusion implies some decentralization of information and decisionmaking authority, another equally sufficient condition for such decentralization is the imperfect and limited capacity of the "center," which is after all a human being or group of them. Even if each decentralized unit had perfect past knowledge and foresight about the time paths of a subset of environmental variables, the union of which would form a complete history of the environment relevant to economic planning, no central decisionmaking body could ever assimilate and process all this information and make decisions based on it. So, the inherent limitations of human central planners are an independent source of their uncertainty about the environment and the behavior of other units in the system, to whom some decisionmaking authority must therefore be delegated.

NOTES

1. R.D. Portes, "Decentralized Planning Procedures and Centrally Planned Economies," *American Economic Review* 61, 3 (May 1971):422–29.

2. This point is discussed at length in L. Nyberg and S. Viotti, "Quasi-Dynamic and Dynamic Methods in an Economic Planning Problem" (Seminar Paper No. 29) (Stockholm: University of Stockholm Institute for International Economic Studies, May 1973).

Chapter Five

Integration of Mathematical and Traditional Methods of Planning

Mária Augustinovics

INTRODUCTION

In this chapter the word "planning" will be used for what it literally means: the process or procedure of preparing a plan. Within this, the subject of the chapter is confined to *central economic planning*, that is to the process of shaping a consistent and comprehensive image of the future economy in order to prepare social (legislative, government) action aimed at directing the economy's future.

Whether the economy is a "planned economy" or not, depends on social, economic, and political conditions for plan implementation. Given these conditions, means and methods applied in implementing the plan depend on the actual management system of the economy. Methods of planning, in turn, will reflect all these components of the general setup; moreover, they should be purposefully designed and developed in accordance with them.

Methods of planning, however, do have a certain *autonomy,* simply because the interdependencies of the economy are given and planning—if it is to draw up the comprehensive image of the future economy—must reflect these interdependencies. (Nobody would imagine a planning process in any country, at any time, that does not deal with the level of GDP or national income, or neglects the relation between investment and production.) Clearly, the autonomous contents of the methodology relate it to the economy and to economics rather than to the actual institutional and political framework, the latter being more specific for individual countries and periods. Methods of planning will be discussed in this chapter mainly from the former, more general aspect, with due respect to the principally social—and by no means technical—character of the planning procedure as a whole.

I shall try to concentrate on what I believe to be rather general. I should stress, however, that the analysis of planning practice given in this chapter is based on a knowledge of planning in a few countries and on personal experience in only one.

THE METHODOLOGICAL PROBLEM

The basic methodological problem that central economic planning has to face is the relation between the economy *as a whole* (as an entirety) and its *parts* (units, individuals, fields).

The "parts" have never been acting blindly: they have always been "planning" their future. Even a modestly good housewife—the "individual consumer"—would know what the next day's dinner will be and what the family's savings will be spent on. Agricultural production even at the most primitive level always required at least one year's foresight or "planning" in the temperate zone. Modern technology requires much more: nowadays large corporations in many countries are well ahead of their governments in planning their long-term future. The difficulty is that these "plans" have always affected each other and many of them have affected the interests of the society. Marx's wording "anarchy on the market" might sound exaggerated under modern circumstances, but it still came much nearer to reality than the paradise of perfect information on the perfect market. Therefore, the *historically new element* in the task of central economic planning is to plan the *total process*[a] in its complexity, so that its parts could develop consistently, and subordinated to the interests of the society.

How can the total process be grasped? The economy is an infinitely complex and sophisticated system. For reasons of size and complexity, this system in its totality is beyond every individual human mind and is as yet very poorly comprehended by the "collective human mind," by science. The forms, intensity, and sometimes even the nature of many interdependencies are unknown. The system cannot be dealt with in the proper way that a huge system should be dealt with according to modern ideas of systems analysis and control theory.

Economics (and statistics) has since long worked out two compromise approaches. One of them is—let us call it the *aggregate totals approach*—to represent the total process by its most aggregate indicators, which are supposed to correspond to the ultimate performance of the system, e.g., the growth rate of GDP, the global capital-output ratio, total consumption or consumption per head, etc. This approach is really comprehensive and dynamic, helps to capture a few decisive tendencies, and lends itself conveniently to formalization, even to using refined, nonlinear mathematical forms. However, all this is achieved at the price of losing sight of even the most important structural parts of the system. Therefore, it is descriptive rather than explanatory, more useful ex post than ex ante.

[a]Throughout this chapter, I shall use the term "total process" in the belief that it is the best English equivalent for the German *Gesamtprozess*.

The other one is—let us call it the *additive consistency approach*—to look at the totals as sums of the respective parts. Total production is indeed the sum of the activities of individual units. Aggregation can be arranged according to any convenient hierarchy (branches, sectors, regions, etc.). If the same total is shown in two different breakdowns, that is if its structure is shown in two aspects (e.g., the GDP as the sum of various final uses), then we have a balance sheet. To compile the planned balance sheets of various products and aggregates is called the *balance method*, so much praised and also looked down upon as the "major" method of traditional planning and so generally accepted, for example, in the system of national accounts.

In this additive world we at least gain some insight into the structural pattern of the total system. However, it is a static world. It describes a certain state of the system but does not provide any clue to its transition from one state to another, because it has nothing to say on how and why the parts—to be summed up—are such as they are and how they depend on each other. Applied ex ante as a consistency-check of the provisional plans of individual units, it can tell us that these provisional plans should be altered because they are inconsistent, but it does not help either in first drawing up those provisional plans or in altering them in the right direction.

It should be noted that even at present, economic theory and mathematical model-building have produced only very few, and rather weak, links between the elegant, dynamic world of logarithmically related or exponentially growing total aggregates and the tiresome static world of additive consistency. This is probably so because the links are hidden among those nonadditive interdependencies between the elementary parts that neither of these approaches is able to grasp.

Both compromise approaches have always been active components of "traditional" planning. It was in the earliest "tradition" to consider them seriously, as is shown by the pioneering works of Feldman and Popov.[1] They continue to serve and help planning up to the present: the aggregate approach at the starting and final phases in each stage of the planning process, the additive consistency approach in between. The latter—as the "balance method"—has also been said to be the principal method of traditional planning, but this is, in my view, an overestimation of the impact of this method on the results and an undue underestimation of the entire performance of planning.

However, these compromises are not sufficient for practical planning. Though planning has to grasp the total process, the purpose of this exercise is to come to correct conclusions about the *parts,* because parts are the targets of action.[b]

[b]If the economy is guided by directive plan targets for individual enterprises, in this case the "parts" are mainly the productive units. But also if the economy is to be guided or oriented by indirect methods, these methods should hit certain strategic points that are expected to bring about the desired results. In this case, the "parts" would be a few—hopefully well known—interdependencies rather than productive units; nevertheless, action would be directed at "parts," simply because no government can directly work on "growth," "prosperity," "welfare," and so forth.

Therefore, planning has to grasp *the total system as an entirety consisting of mutually interrelated parts.*

THE TRADITIONAL METHOD

The "traditional" solution of the almost unsolvable task is to plan in great detail for the parts, to coordinate the major direct relations among these plans, and finally to submit them to an overall coordination by the techniques called the "balance method." On the one hand, this is a combination of what the individual units could and would do for themselves anyway in the first place, plus what the "additive consistency approach" can accomplish in grasping the total system. On the other hand, it is much more, because it also implies the tracing of the significant direct interdependencies between connected parts.

All this is carried out by what may be called a "man-man" system. In this system human beings think and act on behalf of smaller or larger groups of economic units, and certain types of interdependencies. In fact, they include representatives of the units themselves, experts at various levels of the management hierarchy, and finally people within the central planning agency. The division of labor and of influence among them depends on the organizational pattern of the particular planning exercise, which in turn reflects the management system. Within the central planning agency, those representing production units belong to the "sectoral" or "branch" departments; those thinking in terms of specific cross-sectoral interdependencies work in the so-called "functional" departments (e.g., investment, finance, foreign trade, etc.); and the few who are supposed to be in charge of the total process form one or two "coordinating" or "synthetic" departments.

As rather detailed information and knowledge are expected at each point, the central planning agency is usually large (the number of personnel varying from a few hundred to a few thousand) and has like every other organization—a tendency to grow that must be either continuously checked or cut back from time to time.

The Planning Process

The procedure of traditional planning is an *iterative procedure by its nature.* There are many aspects implied in the procedure: the iteration between past and future, between what is given and what is still open for decisions, between "physical" and "synthetic" consistency, between changing volumes and changing values, etc. The following description will concentrate on one aspect of this iterative character: the iteration between provisional plans for parts of the economy (detailed planning), and the economy as a whole (coordination).

The controversy on the starting point of the planning procedure is as old as planning itself. Should it begin "from above" or "from below"? That is, should it start by collecting plan proposals from the individual units through the two- or three-level hierarchy of the management system, or by working out centrally the "control-figures" to be disaggregated through the same hierarchy? Arguments are given pro and contra, and both variants, each of them in many subvariants, have been experimented with.

However, this is a question of the control and management system rather than that of planning itself, because whatever the institutional procedure might be, the procedure of planning must start "from below"—logically if not always also formally. Thus, even if the central planning agency initiates the planning process, it must begin by thinking in terms of individual producing units rather than macroeconomic aggregates. This very initial phase, that of *detailed planning* for the parts, is the hardest to describe and the least impossible to simulate in model-building. It is based on information on past and present; on statistics, reports, periodicals and books; on formal and informal personal contacts in the respective fields; and in many cases on life-long experience. Literally millions and millions of bits of information flow through a number of minds, dozens of alternative possibilities and maybe hundreds of constraints are considered by each, until figures, describing tentatively the future state and activity of that particular "part" of the economy, get first shaped.

Every participant has to have a private model of his own in his mind for this process, though very probably he would not be aware of it. But obviously there are certain (far from linear) relations to be reckoned with, there are constants, and there are "variables." Each participant will rely upon certain fixed points and build the rest of it around them.

What the "fixed" points should be would be partly specific to the given field (e.g., geological capacity in mining, the total population in labor resource planning, etc.), but partly depending on the general situation, on habits, and on orientation received beforehand. For a long period, in planning for productive units, for example, the usual approach was to set future production at the highest technologically possible level and request supply of materials, manpower, and investment accordingly. However, this can be changed very flexibly. It may be assumed that investment funds will be limited or even fixed, that the highest possible exports are desirable, that labor force will be scarce, that the most up-to-date technology has to be achieved, and so on.

What "the rest of it" to be built around the "fixed point" should be depends largely on methodological instructions, issued by the coordinating department beforehand. Outputs for various purposes, primary and secondary inputs, various technological and efficiency indicators, etc., would be listed. This is done, on the one hand, to characterize the desired future performance of the given unit or field, and, on the other hand, to relate it to the total system.

Naturally, it is not only in the minds of those planning for production and productive units that this busy thinking on details is going on. Service sectors, household and public consumption, money flows, manpower resources, foreign trade relations—all significant "parts" of the total process will be dealt with similarly.

A great amount of *partial coordination* between neighboring parts is going on already at this initial stage of the planning process. Direct interdependencies are supposed to be checked with the respective partners. All balances that do not require economy-wide aggregation, most physical balances in fact, are supposed to have been calculated by the departments in charge of planning the production of the product in question. In other words, certain aspects of the "total process," at least the most obvious ones, do have a feedback on the individual tentative plans already when the first steps are made.

The next phase, that of *synthetic coordination*, is easier to describe. This is the stage of checking additive consistency and analyzing the results. Estimations or proposals of individual "parts" are hierarchically aggregated and forwarded to the various "functional" departments and to the coordinating department. They would sum up whatever can be summed up of the primary information and prepare the first variants of the synthetic balances (e.g., the GDP balance, the international payments' balance, etc.).[2] Equilibrium would be analyzed and also the provisional "performance" in terms of growth rates and the main proportions of the total aggregates. It is only natural that balances will not be completely balanced and total aggregates and proportions will not seem satisfactory at this stage. This is only the first step in a long iterative procedure.

At this point, *decisions* have to be made, and they will be political decisions by nature, regardless of the decisionmaking body. (The latter might be within the planning agency at the earlier stages; but later it will be some consulting body of the Council of Ministers or the Council of Ministers itself.) Provisional plans for the various parts of the economy should obviously be altered if they are inconsistent, but the direction in which they should be changed is not determined by the fact of inconsistency itself. Therefore, this is the checkpoint —and such points occur many times during the whole iterative process—where economic policy influences plan-coordination, where the whole tiresome procedure of visualizing the future of the economy is confronted with its social aims.

As to the follow-up, there are two possible cases from the methodological point of view. (1) The representatives of the "parts" might be given some qualitative instructions on the major lines and told to start again. (2) A few quantities might be fixed, on the basis of the previous balances. For example, if there had been a shortage of resources in the GDP balance and the decision was to solve it by reducing investment, then investment quotas might be fixed for every branch for the next phase of the planning process. But, the "parts" have to start again in the latter case too; only their "fixed points" have been changed and exogenously given. They must do the same thinking on constraints, interdependencies, and alternatives, in the same way as earlier. Obviously there is nothing to guarantee that the new results would meet the consistency-check in the next stage. Therefore, the whole procedure will be repeated at least a few times, until consistency and an acceptable—with respect to general conditions— performance will have been approximated.

In each distinct stage of this iterative process, the much-discussed balance method provides the accounting framework for synthesis and consistency-check, but it is far from being anything like "principal" or "major." It somehow keeps the thing stretched out, like a skeleton. But living flesh and blood are put on it by what happens before and after balances, by detailed planning of the parts, by partial coordination and by political decisions.

It should be noted that during the multi-phase iteration between "parts" and "total," the mainstream of quantitative information flows always upwards "from below," while the information flowing downwards "from above" is mainly qualitative. For example, the overall consistency check might suggest that import quotas have to be reduced or that a faster increase in productivity would be desirable. Such instructions can be given "from above." But, the overall consistency check does not tell us "where," "when," and "how much" would be feasible. To determine these, detailed thinking on the parts has to start again. There is a very simple algorithm to produce total aggregates of detailed plan information: it is addition. There is no algorithm in the traditional system of planning to go the other way round. Quantitative conclusions regarding the parts, derived from the aggregated future image of the economy, can be reached only by setting the whole "man-man system" in motion repeatedly.

The Model

Planners often claim that they deal with "reality" as opposed to the unrealistic abstractions of mathematical models. Though the practice of traditional planning is indeed capable of dealing with a large number of specific details, its image of the total economic system is still, quite naturally, a very simplified image itself, containing rough abstractions—a model of the economy, and not the economy itself. It is a model of enormous size and complexity, too big and too sophisticated for complete formalization and for any existing computer. However, it is a model.

The extent of disaggregation in this model varies from country to country and from time to time, but internally it changes less than is usually assumed. The number of physical balances to be worked out, or the number of branches to be dealt with, may be increased or reduced drastically according to changes in the system of managing the economy, but there are limits to aggregation in planning for forecasting technological change, in calculating income distribution or territorial labor migration.

The system of economic interdependencies reflected by this model depends partly on the degree of complexity the economy itself has reached and partly on the time horizon of the plan to be prepared. There is no need for lengthy arguments on how planners in a country with a $100 per capita GDP and a few railroads have to consider other problems than their colleagues in a country with $1,000 per capita GDP and a puzzlingly sophisticated financial super-structure. It is also obvious that what is exogenous in the short run might be endogenous in the long run.

The model of traditional planning is very flexible with respect to the focus and degree of abstraction. Aspects or phenomena or processes that were non-decisive and therefore passed over yesterday, may come into the spotlight and get the proper detailed treatment today, if necessary. It is also flexible with respect to distinguishing between constants and variables. To remove an oppressive constraint might become a temporary objective, to fulfill a social aim might become a constraint. Since in the future everything is subject to change, the selection of what should be treated as a constant is arbitrary and might be adapted to the actual situation. This extreme flexibility, as compared to formalized models, is the major advantage of this "model"—the main reason why it is able to come near to reality.

However, flexibility is accompanied by disorder. Lists of sectors, products, and indicators are usually not synchronized for the different parts and have never been properly classified or at least documented. Exactly which inter-dependencies are considered and which are neglected, which hypotheses and assumptions are considered—all this has never been systematically revealed. Partisans of the new ideas of systems analysis have already launched many unsuccessful attacks to "map" the field, by distributing questionnaires of the "please kindly specify . . ." type, inquiring about input-information, output-indicators, etc. The replies, if any, did not fit into a proper block diagram to be programmed for a computer. In the last decade a considerable progress could have been observed—to a large extent under the influence of incoming mathematical model-building—in slowly but methodically improving the situation at least with respect to the central "skeleton," that is, the synthetic balances and their direct inputs. However, the model as a whole is still far from being well-defined and so far resists everything except being solved in the humanly ingenious and untidy manner of the "man-man" system.

"Solution" in a case like this means "approximation." Even if the model were properly defined, nobody could solve a system of ten-thousands of nonlinear equations. Approximative iteration is capable of making a few converging steps but not of reaching the point of convergence. Major chains of interrelations can be traced, but never the total system of indirect interdependencies. This is why the method fails to supply decisive "downward" flowing quantitative infor-mation. Because of the lack of a unique solution, the values of most variables remain arbitrary and can be determined only by repeated detailed planning, as has been shown in the previous section.

Selecting Alternatives

It may sound surprising, but decisionmaking, as an integral component of the traditional planning process, is decentralized. It is selective and hierarchic. This is true from the institutional aspect if we look at the planning process at its extensive stage when quantitative information (forecasts, proposals, projects) flows "upwards" from a wide circle of enterprises, ministries, etc. But from the logical aspect it is true even if everything happens within the central planning agency itself, if every tiny bit of decision were made by "central planners" themselves—which has never been the situation. The point is that, in the "man-man system" of traditional planning, "information" already implies "decision" at least in the sense of "selection." Each individual mind refuses a number of possible alternatives when selecting the one it is going to work out, and so do the other minds. They have to do so at the very beginning, and once they have done so, there is no chance for anybody to study another set of alternatives.

In the course of hierarchic aggregation and partial coordination more and more such decisions have to be made; because there is a chance again when combining smaller parts in various ways, but only one of these ways will be selected for further aggregation and for deals with further partners. By the time the whole picture fits together, comparatively little remains open for those decisions that can be derived as conclusions from the whole picture. Naturally, since the process is iterative, decisions are not final and can be revised during the next phase, if the selected set of alternatives were proved to be inconsistent or insufficient. But there is little chance for the decisionmaking bodies to point to other alternatives, particularly in quantitative terms, since most of the parimary alternatives have not been worked out and checked for consistency and performance.[c] In other words, the traditional method cannot supply alternative, consistent plan-variants for the total process, although obviously the future of the economy is not *so* determined that only one course of events and actions would be possible.

What might be even more important, there is no mechanism to assure that decisions have been subordinated to social interests or overall policy aims. Even if everybody had selected the alternative that seemed the best to his knowledge, the combined set of the neglected second or third bests might turn out to be much superior from the overall viewpoint. So we have the following contradiction: while the purpose of planning the total process is to come to correct conclusions regarding the parts, the impact of the total system of interdependencies on partial decisions is weaker than it should be. This impact is stronger and enforced better (though not fully) where consistency is concerned. The impact is less well enforced with respect to overall efficiency or optimality (whatever it might be), and with respect to the ultimate purpose of the planning exercise: to subordinate parts to the whole.

Conclusions

The man-man system of traditional planning is much superior to every existing formalized model in grasping the utmost complexity of the economy,

[c]This might be one of the reasons for the very questionable practice of deciding on important partial issues (big investment projects, for example) outside the regular planning procedure—which again limits the chances for planning to deal with alternatives: a vicious circle.

because in place of transistors it applies the most perfect learning automatons, human minds. Despite all methodological shortcomings, this system has been able to do the job: to highlight those varying strategic chains of interdependencies that are vital in the actual situation and crucial for economic policy. However, from the methodological aspect, such planning methods seem to be better in grasping details than in conceiving the total process and deriving conclusions from it. The historically new element of the task is not fully accomplished as yet.

Why are these methods better in grasping details? There are several reasons. Planning for an individual unit of the total system has tradition, there is experience, it has always been practiced. To do it in a centralized system does not differ so much from doing it within and by the same unit as it is generally supposed. (Able and competent experts in a field are not necessarily inferior to their colleagues simply because they sit in the building of a central agency instead of being permanently on the spot; what they lose in internal information, they may gain by knowing external relations. And they are backed by a large number of institutions, agencies, ministries, and the enterprises themselves.) What appears to be "central" in this respect is mainly collected and aggregated from "decentralized" sources. Also, the institutional element seems to work in favor of detailed planning, to stress its priority, to be more demanding in this respect. There is no minister, bank director, enterprise manager, or TV commentator to speak up for indirect interdependencies, but a proposal on a certain investment project, particularly a negative one, may provoke widespread excitement.

On the other hand, planning the total process is, historically speaking, still a new task, and there is very little background for it, not only from the intellectual but also from the institutional aspect. The small team doing the synthetic part of the job is, even in terms of bare numbers, outmanned by the large network of detail specialists. But what is more important, the methods themselves are the weakest where they should be the strongest: in synthesis. Additive consistency, even if more or less fairly approximated by iteration, is a poor weapon against the complexity of the total economic process. This complexity calls for more sophisticated methods, and this is the point where planning urgently needs major methodological improvement.

Many planners believe that introducing mathematical models and methods into planning is a temporary fashion. Partly this is a comforting belief for people who have the vested interest of life-long experience with the "traditional" methods. Partly this belief seems to be justified, because there is much pseudo-scientific "showing off" in this field. However, not to make use of techniques that would strengthen the impact of social aims and goals on partial decisions would be a luxury that society cannot afford. Therefore, although the integration of mathematical models and methods into planning may seem fashionable, in fact it is inevitable.

MATHEMATICAL MODELS AND METHODS

It is not the purpose of this chapter to give a full description of models and methods that are helpful and should be applied to planning. That would be hopeless, anyway, because every model might be helpful if it reveals a significant relation, even if only qualitatively, and makes the planner understand the economy more deeply. This brief discussion will be limited to the mainstream of models and methods that seem ready to be *integrated into plan-coordination.* "Integration" means that the model or method is no longer just an additional burden and decoration, i.e., not merely something very nice but dispensable. Integrated use is a stage at which a certain part of the planning process is accomplished by a model, regularly and exclusively. Excluding now a number of significant groups of models and methods from this discussion—e.g., aggregated nonlinear growth models, stochastic models, the entire field of econometric models, and many others—does not imply any view about their future in relation to planning practice, since it is too early to predict the future in this field. The present state of affairs is, however, characterized by the advance of input-output and mathematical (mainly linear) programming into the everyday life of central planning. Perhaps the reason is that these two are ready to absorb and process planned information.

Input-Output: A Model

Input-output was accused of smuggling the evil of Communist planning into the free democratic economy and the evil of bourgeois ideology into the socialist economy. It was said to be unsuited for planning, both for being too rigid and deterministic as well as for assuming too much freedom. It was looked down upon for being simple-minded—only linear—and yet the interpretation of the inverse matrix has been too sophisticated for many an economist.

The facts are that collecting input-output information is now a regular practice of official statistics in many countries, and where the authorities fail to do so, private business comes to the rescue with data banks. International organizations (EEC, OECD, CMEA, ECE) have their standardized systems of input-output tables. Partisans of decision-models as well as econometricians are busy building input-output relations into their models, and practical planners are busy calculating their planned input-output tables. Input-output has been interpreted according to Walras, according to Marx, and according to the balance-method of planning. It has been extended to prices, to income and money flows, to demographic processes, to education and pollution. Its triumph over doctrine and snobbery is a fact which should be explained.[3]

Quite obviously, it is the basic framework—rather than the additional, surrounding mathematical forms and economic abstractions—that really counts. Open static, closed static, open dynamic, and closed dynamic models have all been presented, and systems of differential or difference equations have been formulated within the same basic framework. Optimal control techniques seem to find their way into input-output model-building and, at the same time, a simple input-output table without any mathematics at all can also be considered a useful tool for many purposes.

The term "input-output model" does not refer to any particular form of it, not even any longer to Leontief's original version. It refers to the basic framework, to the very simple idea of looking at outputs as inputs for other outputs, and at inputs as outputs produced by other inputs: in other words, the idea of arranging *mutual* economic interdependencies into a square matrix, whereby the also very simple technique of inverting a matrix will do the trick of revealing the propagating indirect interdependencies and following them infinitely up to the point where they converge.

By its origin, this basic framework belongs to what I took the liberty to call the "additive consistency approach" in this chapter. An input-output table itself is just a set of systematically arranged balances. However, this is the first opportunity for this approach not just to sum up individual parts of the total system, but to gain insight into the direct and indirect relations between the parts, to look at the set of parts as *a system*. Therefore, it is something qualititatively new. Venturing more innovations in terminology, I could say that the input-output model represents the *interrelated consistency approach* to the total economic system.[d] Obviously, it is much superior to bare additivity while implying the latter. This is, in my view, the major contribution of the input-output model to economic theory as well as to empirical analysis and planning. It is not by pure chance, nor a temporary fashion, that practical planning—and statistics, for that matter—is absorbing this model in a more or less natural manner. Planning was prepared for it and was in urgent need of it, no matter how difficult it is to accomplish in practice what seems to be quite obvious in theory.

Linear Programming: A Method
Linear programming tells us that from the feasible solutions of a system of linear inequalities (under certain mathematical conditions) a single one can be selected that makes the value of a linear function of the variables maximal or minimal. This is helpful enough if a linear system is to be dealt with and this is always the case when—at the factory, farm, enterprise, branch or economy-wide level—the economist is willing to assume linearity in order to get a chance to deal with a complex system. Originally the method was applied for the optimal production-programming of a Leningrad factory.[4]

Over-interpretation with respect to economics did more harm than good. That the objective function reflects overall social preference, the primal solution

[d]With due respect to assumptions on homogeneity, linearity, etc., of course. But who has ever produced anything approximately comprehensive for nonlinear systems consisting of nonhomogeneous parts?

is the optimal plan to be implemented, and the dual solution the optimal price-system to be introduced—all these provoked endless protests and arguments rather than energetic action in making full use of an extremely useful method.[5]

A more realistic and more modest approach takes us further. What the objective function, the constraints and variables, the primal and dual solutions really do express depends on what has been built into the model: the economic content should be properly interpreted in each case, and this is not determined by the programming technique. If a model for economic planning is to be built, it should grasp what planning is up to, not only in general, but also in the particular period characterized by particular problems. Building linear programming models for planning requires the careful analysis of the planning process itself, and a respectful limitation of the area where the model may be expected to compete.[6]

There is, however, indeed one underlying general assumption in applying this technique to any system of economic interdependencies: namely that the system is not fully determined but open—under given constraints—for purposeful intervention. The technique is supposed to reveal the course of intervention leading to the best possible result, to specify how the individual parts should behave in order to maintain consistency and make the total system optimal. And so the technique does, subject to the condition that chances for correctly weighing the constraints and the purposes have not been overestimated. In other words, as it is in principle impossible to build a "perfect" model of the economy as a whole, every model will always have its "deficiencies." Therefore, it is not advisable to attach unjustified economic significance to just one, single, optimal solution of one particular model. The heart of the matter is that with linear programming techniques, alternative solutions—with alternative objective functions, under alternative constraints—can be computed and analyzed so as to learn about the *sensitivity of the system to various conditions and to various preferences.* This is, I believe, the major contribution of linear programming to economic analysis and planning.

Much has been said against linearity. Little can be said for it, except that no economics, no mathematics and no computer techniques exist for handling large-scale nonlinear systems. The case of indivisibility is fortunately now an exception. For it, mixed programming methods (handling continuous and integer variables at the same time) are now accessible on available computers, and model-building seems to be rather quick to make use of this technique. In this sense, with respect to the near future, the epithet "linear" could even be omitted when discussing practical planning models.

The Place of Mathematical Models and Methods in Planning

A typical planning model for coordination would imply an input-output system extended to as many types of economic interdependencies as can be treated as endogenous (time-horizon, information, etc., permitting). More often than not, there would be alternatives (more variables) for the same activity, distinguished mainly by input structure. The alternatives could be mixed under some constraints (if represented by continuous variables) or be selected in a yes-no manner (if represented by integer variables). This system would then be surrounded by constraints that are considered exogenous. (Experience shows that a "properly behaving," "realistic" model usually contains more constraints than variables.) Then, there would be alternative objective functions, many of them related to a few variables only, reflecting the fact that most sectors of the economy affect the final outcome—living standards or the balance of payments, for example—only through the entire system and not directly.

The word "typical" in the above roughly simplified description is meant to say both that it is quite logical to build up a planning model in this manner and that actually most models presented and computed in recent years for practical planning purposes have been of this type. The word "planning" emphasizes that the information digested by the model refers to the future and not to the past. This is obvious as far as lower-upper bounds on the right-hand side are concerned. But coefficients should also refer to the future relation between variables—future technology or consumption pattern, for example.

A model like this would be able to trace the entirety of indirect interdependencies; to solve the problem simultaneously, so that decisions (selection) need not be made separately, hierarchically; to supply thereby the missing link of "downward" flowing, unambiguous quantitative information; to produce many consistent variants for the system as a whole, in a short time. In other words, this model would supply a "skeleton" much superior to the simple balance-method and would eliminate the tiresome procedure of iterative, approximative plan-coordination.

However, and this is the vital point, it will not put "living flesh and blood" on the bones. No planning model will ever prepare its own parameters, coefficients, and upper-lower bounds, because the parameters themselves already reflect an anticipated future process or situation that had to be previously visualized, forecast, estimated, calculated, and checked several times by a human mind.

The range of the orderly arranged and simultaneously solved interdependencies can, of course, be extended. It is not advisable to increase the size of a central model beyond reasonable limits, not so much because of computational difficulties but primarily because a model also requires human minds of limited capacities to deal with it. But it is possible and desirable that a central planning model be supported by satellite models, deriving most of its parameters from the latter, and feeding back its results to them.[e] In fact, much of recent research and experiment has proceeded along these lines.

[e]This seems to be a more generalized approach than multilevel programming by decomposition methods. First, because there are vital fields (consumption, demography, etc.) that are not represented by any "level" in the hierarchy of the management system but should be modeled. Second, because the term "decomposition" refers to disintegrating one huge problem rather than to dealing with many interrelated problems.

The formalized system cannot, however, be extended so far that it should not have boundaries. Even if the links between the central model and the satellites and the latter's satellites and so on were fully formalized and computerized, somewhere outside there must be people feeding this monster with primary information. And the more complex the system grows, the more vulnerable it is, the more sensitive to the quality of the primary information.

To sum up briefly, models will improve planning techniques, but will never do the whole job. Where models are superior, they must be integrated into the planning process, where the total system's interdependencies have to be handled. Where detailed expert knowledge on particular parts, experience, and intuition are required, and also where the results obtained by models have to be reasonably interpreted, there the human element will prevail. Planning should be converted into a "man-machine" system, combining the two.

THE PROCESS OF INTEGRATION

Planning institutions, as all existing institutions, are rather resistant to anything new coming from outside. The integration of mathematical methods into the everyday practice of central economic planning is a slow and gradual process, as yet not fully accomplished anywhere. Thus far, three stages of this process may be distinguished, namely the experimental, the parallel, and the integrated use of models.

The Experimental Stage

Integration begins by convincing planners to experiment. The initiative usually comes from research institutes, and is supported by a few planners who are aware of the deficiencies of the existing practice. A wider circle of planners, leading officials primarily, have to be convinced that it is worthwhile to take the trouble and cost of experimenting with new methods. Articles, books, conference papers, internal documents, proposals, and motions point out the advantages of mathematical planning models. The ease of producing consistent variants, speed, and relief from manual computations are mainly emphasized. This is the stage of raising illusions beyond realistic expectation, causing disappointment later on.

However, the dialog between planners and model-builders begins. The *input side* is on the agenda: what should the model be like and how can it be fed with information from the planning process. The structure of the particular model has to be formulated, the variables and the interdependencies (constraints) have to be specified. In due course the model will take shape as an inevitable compromise between what would be desirable and what is possible.

The next step is to collect, or rather prepare, input data. No matter how carefully the model-building considered the needs and means of the existing practice and how far it went in compromising, it will inevitably turn out that the necessary information does not exist. It can be prepared because there is plenty of similar information, but never in the particular breakdown, classification, and form required for the model.

At this point a very important and lasting controversy begins: any formalized model is *rigid* as compared to the utmost flexibility (and disorder) of the non-formalized model. Obviously, if it is to weigh various parts and various alternatives, it needs the *same* information about all of them, though what is especially significant for one part may be secondary for the other part and therefore never previously considered and calculated for the latter. Every formalized model, even the most flexible one, has a tendency to *uniformity*, inherent in any approach that wants to grasp the total system. On the one hand, this is a major advantage. On the other hand, each individual planner, responsible for planning one particular part or field, will always claim that the model requires unnecessary information while it neglects the real issues, and he will be right from his viewpoint.

In any case, quantitative information must be prepared for the model. Very often a wide circle of experts from various institutes, government agencies, and enterprises will be invited to do the job, possibly with planners from the central planning agency participating. For the latter group, this will be an additional burden, whether willingly accepted or not, and the work for the model will always be postponed—quite naturally—since the on-going practical planning process comes first. It seems to take ages to get together the input-data for the model, which causes the first disappointment concerning speed—often for the small team of determined model-builders themselves.

By that time the ship has usually departed. The particular planning task for the particular time period has been completed with traditional methods, the plan has been discussed and accepted. Feeding the information into the computer, solving the model, and analyzing the results would follow the usual working methods of research rather than those of practical planning. Results would be compared to the final plan that had been accepted and they would turn out to be somewhat better on the whole but unacceptable at a number of points. Since the plan is already approved and on its way to be implemented, this does not provoke much excitement anyway. Conclusions bear more on the model than on the plan.

It is indeed the major result that the properties and behavior of particular models are investigated—not only discussed ex ante in journals, but actually experimented with on existing computers, with existing data. Careful analysis of various solutions reveals deficiencies in the structure of the models and indicates directions of improvement. Particular conclusions are, of course, specific to the models, time-periods, and the whole set of actual circumstances. But there are a few general conclusions to be drawn and applied for the next stage.

One of the general conclusions might be, for example, that it is possible in model-building to repeat the failures of the practical process, whereas its purpose is to eliminate them. Namely, even models or systems of models can be better in the parts than on the whole. Since branch models preceded economy-wide models in time and experience, it is an obvious idea to build a large network of them, and once they have covered the field completely, to link them in an overall system of models. But if the links are weak then the result might be poor exactly with respect to what needs major improvement, namely synthesis. Furthermore, delay in any individual sector might prevent the whole effort from being rewarded by overall, synthetic results, and confidence, patience, and persistence might be exhausted too soon or submitted to a dangerous test.

Therefore, the next stage would quite often begin with aims less ambitious in size and extent, but more ambitious in practical usefulness—with a strategy of starting from the heart of the matter and extending the range gradually.

Parallel Use

At this stage, the use of mathematical models becomes an officially declared part and tool of the planning process, in an additional and auxiliary capacity. Models are expected to supply additional results in analyzing past and future, but at the same time plan-coordination goes on in the usual, traditional way.

As providing information for the models becomes a regular part of the work, the standardizing effect of model-building begins to be reflected in classification —in a more uniform breakdown, in a certain stability regarding types and forms of indicators, etc. A typical example is the use of the planned input-output table, based on bilateral information on both inputs and outputs, as a regular consistency-check.

The major issue at this stage is, however, the race for time. Input-data for the model are still delayed, because the non-formalized (untidy but relevant) information for the traditional process comes first, and indeed it must exist before it can be arranged for the model. Nevertheless, output-results should be ready by the time that plan-coordination comes to the checkpoint of decisions, if they are to affect the conclusions and decisions. The time left in between is impossibly short for collecting, checking, correcting, punching, checking, and correcting again on punched-cards and magnetic tapes a terrible mass of data; for testing and running the model with them; for checking the results and finding the errors; for arranging and analyzing final results in a way comprehensible enough to affect practice.

The second disappointment concerning speed is caused by the fact the computerized data processing is slow, particularly as compared to no data processing at all. At this point another important and lasting controversy begins. The use of models requires, within the planning agency, the *centralized handling of detailed information* that had never left the individual desks before. In the traditional process, it is only the partial result and the conclusion that are forwarded, while initial data (assumed coefficients, capacity-limits, etc.) remain decentralized; they can be checked, corrected, altered during coordination, partly as a consequence of coordination. Centralized processing of detailed information corresponds inherently to the purpose of simultaneous decisions, that is, to the major advantage of using models. On the other hand, it requires such care in preparing the data as was never necessary before, because it deprives the individual planner of the chance for subsequent, continuous revision without losing face.

The first disappointment concerning the belief that models and computers are designed to save work is that the use of models requires an extra amount of tiresome manual work, both in preparing and in processing data, which was unknown in the traditional process.

Anyway, the chances that the model will be used parallel with traditional practice are small. The best possible outcome is that a number of solutions can be turned out, insufficiently digested and analyzed, but still in time to reach a few minds before final decisions. The rest of the output will be produced after the plan will have been accepted. More solutions will be computed in a systematic way, the series of solutions will be analyzed, documented. Methods, results, failures, conclusions will be summed up and published in the regular, scholarly manner.

However, those first results received in time were interesting and promising. They gave something to think about. If there was also a chance for a brief dialog, if a few synthesizing minds could have asked questions of the "and what, if . . ." type and received sensible answers, then the battle was won, at least until the next stage.

Preconditions for Integrated Use

During years of experimental and parallel model-building and use, sufficient experience has been accumulated to sum up the preconditions on the "input-side" for integrated use. They are briefly the following:

1. Since there is little hope for inventing the absolutely perfect planning model in the near future, *model-building itself must become flexible.* Various models have to be applied to various purposes, even to investigate various aspects of the same problem. Some of them may have satellites; others may not. Links between various models can vary; formalized decomposition, feeding each other with information *via* the human mind, and bare comparability of final results are all acceptable. It should be easy to modify any of them if new information or new problems occur. Without this high degree of flexibility, models might be superior to the traditional coordination in dealing with indirect interdependencies, but they will certainly remain inferior to it in the dialog with those who are in charge of formulating the final, synthetic results of the whole planning procedure.

In this happy family of flexible models, however, one member should be designed primarily for coordination, since it is hardly possible to come to unambiguous, straightforward quantitative results with a series of loosely connected exploratory computations. This particular model should imply as few assumptions as possible beyond the familiar assumptions applied in planning for the parts, and its results should be converted as directly as possible into quantitative conclusions on the parts. In other words, this model should replace and surpass traditional coordination in its capacity of leading the dialog with planners of the individual parts.

2. Flexible building and use of models is required, but the supply of input information can not be equally flexible. Therefore, it is not the parameters of one particular model—still less of every model to be applied—that should be prepared and collected, but instead a certain carefully designed and well-defined *set of basic information,* which will provide the possibility of quantifying models for a wide range of problems.

Meanwhile, preparing initial, detailed planned information separately for "planning" and for "the model" must be stopped, because this leads to the feeling that models are something distinct and different from planning, and because it makes the interchange of problems and results intolerably slow and difficult. There must be a *unified* set of primary information, used both by model-building and by what remains outside of it. In designing and implementing a unified framework of basic information, disorder and individual convenience must yield to order and discipline, on the one hand. On the other, the desire for uniformity must not be pushed beyond reasonable limits, and requirements should be confined to information that is available and comprehensible to the individual planner.

3. Information about the *past* in the same framework is equally necessary, partly because it is the starting point of thinking about the future, and partly because final results about the future will have to be compared with past performance. In other words, planning for consistency has to be backed by consistent statistics.

4. From this common pool of basic information there is a long way to go before the proper computer input of any formalized model is ready. The pool must be properly arranged in a data bank and the road from it to model-inputs (also the road in the opposite direction) must be paved by flexible, ready-made *computer programs* that almost everybody can easily handle on his own. Manual data processing is out of the question if results are to be available in time, but there is also little hope for every model-builder to have three computer-programmers behind him, busily programming his last-minute brain waves.

Initial Experience with Integrated Use of Models

To my best knowledge, long-term planning for the period 1971–85 in Hungary has thus far been the only experiment with integrated use of models. In this particular planning process, quantitative coordination with traditional methods has been replaced by a family of models, with one of the family designed particularly for coordinative purposes. One single example would not justify general conclusions; in addition, this exercise should be considered as rather special for several reasons.[f] Nevertheless, a few elements of the experience gained may be worth mentioning, those which seem to be on the general rather than the specific side.

First steps in integrated use seem to shift trouble from the "input-side" of the models to their "output-side"—a considerable progress. Information supplied by models used to be interesting but dispensable and unexciting at earlier stages. Now it becomes vital because of its monopoly of quantitative synthesis, and crucial because of its potential bearing on the plan, on decisions that shape economic policy.

Information supplied by the models must be fed back into the planning process as fast as possible or even faster. But this is information of a never-experienced quantity and needs careful interpretation as opposed to the simple, familiar sort of narrow information supplied by a balance that is not balanced. The technical difficulties connected with the usual quantity and form of the information can be solved sooner or later; this part of the procedure can be speeded up as the input-side had been speeded up previously. But the third and incurable disappointment concerns speed. The human mind that has to do the thinking and puzzling over the results is slow, and there is no computer program to cure this. People are accustomed to straightforward figures, and unprepared for dealing with several variants. To digest them, to draw the correct and relevant conclusions from them, is quite a different sort of work, but it is hard work; hence the second disappointment in "labor-saving" computers and models.

First tentative conclusion: recommendations on the use of mathematical models in planning will probably have to be revisited. Central economic planning is not like bookkeeping, where time- and labor-saving computers can keep the same records faster and more cheaply. The use of mathematical methods in planning is time-consuming and labor-intensive. Emphasis should be placed where it belongs: that the new technique helps accomplish something that has never been accomplished before—to trace the indirect interdependencies of the total economic system and to investigate the system's sensitivity to preferences and external conditions.

Nevertheless, the results are there and should be accepted in place of the usual results of coordination. As long as they correspond to expectations based on experience and common sense, there is no problem. (But why do we need all those sophisticated models for such trivial results?) However, the results might

---

[f]The fifteen-year time-horizon is a novelty itself in planning. In fact there is no "traditional" procedure, no established practice for dealing with the quite specific problems of such a period. Even the need for a long-term plan to be consistent—that is, the need for coordination—was said to be questionable by several economists. Those who said that consistency was necessary have also agreed that it should not be interpreted in the same way as for shorter time-horizons. Finally, the planning process has not been concluded yet, as the time-horizon has been extended to 1990 and the planning process for this new horizon is regarded as a direct follow-up of the work accomplished so far.

deviate from widespread beliefs and make well-established priorities question-able. They might suggest decisions that threaten various partial interests.

At this point, the most important controversy is highlighted. Models may be said to relieve planners from the burden of the tiresome procedure of coordination. However, it turns out that planners do not feel relieved; on the contrary, they feel deprived of having their word in, and exerting their influence on, coordination. It turns out that plan-coordination is much more than the technical procedure of iteratively approximating consistency: it is the ground where views and values, interests and priorities are confronted and gradually synchronized. The result of traditional coordination is more than a technically feasible variant: it also implies a more or less general agreement on what should be done, that makes the particular variant feasible in the social and political sense.

This social and political—also personal—element is missing from the "alienated," "computerized" coordination carried out by models. The ground of confrontation and agreement is shifted to the discussion of several variants, equally feasible from the technical aspect, but each of them depending on various alternative assumptions in a sophisticated way, each of them offering a particular path to the society and the economy, at a particular price. The contents and the nature of the decisions to be taken will have to be modified. This, after all, has been the purpose of the exercise. However, to build vital decisions on model-supplied results requires confidence in the model. This, in turn, will require widely extended participation in model-building and ex ante confrontation and agreement on input-data.

Second tentative conclusion: although the use of the new technique is concentrated on plan-coordination, it still affects each individual phase of the planning process, from the very initial detailed thinking on individual parts up to the final political decisions. The impact is inevitable and desirable. Nevertheless, it will take time for planning to adapt itself to the new requirements and new opportunities.

NOTES

1. G.A. Feldman, "K teorii tempov narodnogo dokhoda" [On the Theory of Growth Rates of National Income], *Planovoe khoziaistvo*, No. 11 (1928):146–70, and 12 (1928):151–78. *Balans narodnogo khoziaistvo SSSR, 1923/24 gg.* [Balance of the Economy of the USSR 1923/24], ed. P.I. Popov (Moscow: TsSU SSSR, 1926).

2. Due criticism of methodological shortcomings of this procedure might have confused a few readers. An example of undue interpretation: ". . . the secret of how the 'planned' socialist countries solved their 'synthetic balance' has been resolved by the revelation that they didn't know how." Abba P. Lerner, "Some Thoughts on Landauer's Theory of National Economic Planning," in *Essays in Socialism and Planning in Honor of Carl Landauer*, ed. Gregory

Grossman (Englewood Cliffs, New Jersey: Prentice-Hall, Inc. 1970), p. 40. To know that something is difficult and hence not perfectly accomplished does not mean not to know how to do it.

3. Some of the latest results in this field are summed up in *Input-Output Techniques,* ed. A. Bródy and A.P. Carter (Amsterdam: North-Holland Publishing Co., 1972).

4. L.V. Kantorovich, *Matematicheskie metody organizatsii i planirovaniia proizvodstva* [Mathematical Methods of Organizing and Planning Production] (Leningrad: LGU, 1939).

5. In regard to discussions in the Soviet Union, see, e.g., "Matematicheskie metody v ekonomike: Nauchnoe soveshchanie po primeneniu matematicheskikh metodov v ekonomicheskikh issledovaniakh i planirovanii" [Mathematical Methods in Economics: Scientific Conference on the Application of Mathematical Methods in Economic Research and Planning], *Voprosy ekonomiki,* No. 8 (1960):100–28.

6. A few examples: Krzysztof Porwit, *Zagadnienia rachunku ekonomicznego w planie centralnym* [Economic Optimal Calculations in Central Planning] (Warsaw: Panstwowe Wydawnictwo Ekonomicne, 1964). The English version is *Central Planning: Evaluation of Variants,* trans. Józef Stadler (Oxford, New York: Pergamon Press, 1966).

András Bródy, *Az ágazati kapcsolatok modellje* [The Model of Interindustry Relations] (Budapest: Akadémiai Kiadó, 1964), and *Érték és ujratermelés* [Value and Reproduction] (Budapest: Közgazdasági és Jogi Könyvkiadó, 1969). The English version of the latter is *Proportions, Prices and Planning: A Mathematical Restatement of the Labor Theory of Value* (Amsterdam and London: North-Holland Publishing Co., 1970).

János Kornai: *A gazdasági szerkezet matematikai tervezése* [Mathematical Planning of the Structure of the Economy] (Budapest: Közgazdasági és Jogi könyvkiadó, 1965). The English version is *Mathematical Planning of Structural Decisions* (Amsterdam: North-Holland Publishing Co., 1967).

"Union of Soviet Socialist Republics: The Use of Macro-economic Models for Production and Investment Planning," in United Nations, Economic Commission for Europe, *Macro-economic Models for Planning and Policy-making* (Geneva, 1967), pp. 91–95.

Comments on
Mária Augustinovics'
Chapter

Michael Manove

Dr. Augustinovics' chapter describes traditional planning, mathematical planning, and the problems of integrating the two from the practical point of view of an experienced mathematical planner. The chapter is good medicine to cure those of us who believe deep down inside that any good computer with a few smart people to run it ought to be able to plan better and faster than an army of clerks and bureaucrats. Augustinovics convincingly explains why this notion is false. At the same time she presents a strong argument for the necessity of integrating mathematical models and computerized data-processing into the planning process. Since there is little in her chapter I would dispute, I will take this opportunity to present some of my own ideas on the topics she discussed. As I am not a planner, the reader is advised to regard my ideas as armchair speculation.

1. One of Augustinovics' more important observations is that traditional planning methods tend to be extremely flexible and applicable to a wide range of situations, while mathematical models are quite rigid by comparison. Although this is not surprising on an intuitive level, the reasons why it is true are far from clear.

One factor which tends to increase the flexibility of the traditional planning process is that traditional planners need not specify a planning model (or, more precisely, a planning strategy) in advance. The traditional planner can gradually shape his model to suit his data and his intermediate results. The planner using a computerized mathematical model cannot take such liberties. To a much larger extent, he must *plan* the planning process in advance. There are two factors which taken together make such advance planning necessary: the man can build or modify mathematical models but slowly, and the computer is as yet too stupid to build or modify them at all. Thus, mathematical models must be built before the data are received and processed; therefore, the models may turn out to be inappropriate to the economic circumstances the data describe. The way to remedy this problem is to increase the capacity of the planner to modify his model *ex post*. Until computers become smart enough to make such modifications themselves, the planner must be able to work more closely with computers (a point expressed by Augustinovics). Computer programs and programming languages designed for interactive use (i.e., use from a terminal) would, I expect, be of considerable help to the planner, provided he knows how to use them.

Another reason for the apparent rigidity of mathematical models is the constraints imposed by the requirement of mathematical tractability. One might wonder why a planner with a sound knowledge of mathematical technique and a computer should be more constrained in his model-building, by the requirement of tractability, than would be a traditional planner with neither mathematical skills nor a computer. The answer, I think, is that the mathematical planner demands exact or almost exact solutions of his model, whereas, as Augustinovics points out, the traditional planner is often satisfied with only a crude and incomplete approximation to a solution of his model. In other words, the traditional planner can create a very complex model because he does not intend to analyze it thoroughly. Perhaps mathematical planners could improve the quality of their results by imitating their traditional counterparts and accepting less exact solutions to more complex models.

A third reason why mathematical planning is less flexible than traditional planning is that the data used in mathematical planning are less flexible than those used in traditional planning. To a traditional planner, relatively few parameters seem completely fixed. When circumstances require it, he shifts the parameters a little this way or that. This does not mean that the traditional planner is being dishonest for the purpose of obtaining desired results (although that is a possibility). Rather, the traditional planner is in a position to see that many parameters which would be treated as exogenous in the "alienated" mathematical model are, in fact, slightly endogenous and can be influenced. It is difficult to imagine how a mathematical model could capture this type of flexibility.

2. Augustinovics observes that traditional planning is not merely a technical procedure. "Views, values, interests and priorities are confronted and gradually synchronized." In "alienated" mathematical models, she goes on, the alternative values and interests should be embodied in the "variants" offered to the political authorities. Note, however, that the decisionmakers in the two cases will be different. In the *traditional* process, decisions are made throughout a large bureaucracy, and in many cases the decisionmakers are close to those most affected by the decisions and they accordingly reflect the interests of the latter. On the other hand, the political authorities who choose between the variants of *mathematical* plans may have values and interests which are quite different. If the mathematical models are good, decisions based on those models will be made on the basis of more complete information than decisions reached in the

traditional way. But we cannot say that those decisions will be better, or more just, as a consequence.

3. Augustinovics deliberately restricts her discussion of mathematical models to input-output programming models. What role, if any, is there in a planned economy for econometric forecasting models of the type being applied to advanced market economies? There are two aspects to this question. First, can this sort of model successfully simulate the institutional framework of a planned economy? And, if so, could such models be put to worthwhile use in such a framework? Assuming that the answer to the first question is yes, I would like to suggest that the answer to the second question is also affirmative.

The planning models discussed in the chapter are intended to be used for decisionmaking, whereas forecasting models are intended for use in predicting future economic trends, with important decisions by governmental authorities usually treated as exogenous data. Picture the following scenario: On the basis of results produced by mathematical planning models, the political authorities make economic policy decisions and adopt an economic plan. Then, the economic forecasters go to work. They plug the most recent decisions into their forecasting model and predict future values of important economic indicators. Of course, the values predicted by the forecasters differ from the values for the same indicators embodied in the official plan (which was shown to be consistent and feasible by the planning models). Is this a tragedy? Only if the planners and the forecasters are armed, and honest citizens are caught in the crossfire. In fact, such disagreeable forecasts ought to be extremely useful to the planners as an independent check on their models and data. Without an independent forecast, planners must wait until the real-world results of the plan are known before they can correct their mistakes. By then, it is often too late.

Chapter Six

Planning in France

Claude Seibel
(Translated from the French by Elizabeth Henderson)

A system of public planning was inaugurated in France after the Second World War. A decree dated January 3, 1946 provided for the establishment, within six months, of "a first overall economic modernization and investment plan for metropolitan France and the overseas territories." At the same time, planning machinery was set up in the form of a Conseil du Plan and a Commissariat Général, the latter headed by Jean Monnet as Commissaire Général du Plan. It certainly was Jean Monnet's influence which led the French government to plan at that time not only in terms of making good war damage, but of modernizing production methods. The major innovation was a break with traditional bureaucratic methods by the creation of Modernization Commissions, in which experts chosen by the Commissariat du Plan from among employers' and trade union groups joined government officials on a footing of equality. But this decree must be seen in the much broader context of a whole set of measures which profoundly altered and strengthened the role of the state in the control and direction of economic development (e.g., the nationalization of key sectors of the economy). More than twenty-five years have gone by since then, and the initial approach has gradually changed in the light of experience. Forecasting methods have improved, the scope of planning has widened, and planning machinery has become more prominent in government departments—but the plan itself has become less and less imperative, and also more difficult to formulate. With France open toward Europe and markets more and more international, uncertainties increased, while the debate was shifting from "means" to "choices" within society. All this challenged the very nature and the philosophy of planning.

What started out as the "Nation's Plan" became a "medium-term government program," but in fact it appears that the plan is a very weak reference point for

The author was Chef du Service des Programmes at the Institut National de la Statistique et des Etudes Economiques (INSEE) when he wrote this chapter.

short-term economic policy, even if it tries to describe theoretically a set of alternative strategies. The major themes outlined in the First Plan are still there, themes such as modernization, productivity, productive and social investment, regionalization; but the approach has become more qualitative. Concern has shifted to the aims of growth and to its social consequences, and gradually a balance is being struck between economic development and social planning.

As a means of state intervention in the mechanism of a market economy, French planning appears to outside observers to be at the same time innovatory and ambiguous in its relevance to the realities of development. Strictly speaking, it should be discussed in the wider context of the relations between state and society. French planning is one form of these relations, a form peculiar to our country.

It is from this point of view that French planning will here be discussed. The observer of this planning system is struck by the highly pragmatic processes by which it is established and adjusted. It is perhaps its flexible adjustment to the political and social debate which lends public planning in France its essential strength. As will be shown in the first section, pragmatic adaptation has for twenty-five years governed planning methods and targets as much as prior discussion of the plan and its implementation. In the second section, the example of the preparation of the Sixth Plan will show, over a shorter period, how the diagnosis and the picture of the future drawn from economic models are gradually reinterpreted in discussions which lead, in addition, to the adoption of a set of "social norms" as a basis for the plan eventually promulgated by the government. The third section, finally, will examine the approach now taking shape with respect to the Seventh Plan and show how French planning strives to take into account and to solve the new problems of economic and social development in France. But this latest approach, which implies a shift toward diversification and intensification of public action, comes up against two contradictions; sectoral policies in particular fields have to be combined with overall targets in government action, and public action has to be reconciled with market forces at a time when economic growth no longer seems to be regarded as the essential aim of development.

CHANGES IN THE AIMS AND METHODS
OF FRENCH PLANNING

The aims and methods of French planning have changed profoundly since the Second World War, but no body of theories can be identified by which to explain these gradual changes. As time went on, planning covered wider fields; new and more efficient planning methods made it possible to tackle new problems; a change took place in the significance and purposes of prior consultation, or, as it is called in France, *concertation;* and in spite of the government's stated intention to turn the Plan into a medium-term program of action, official action in fact makes only partial use of planning studies.

All these changes gradually came about in the course of twenty-five years of planning and five successive Plans; no revision of them is called for by the current implementation of the Sixth Plan.[1]

The Main Themes of Successive Plans

The First Plan: "Modernization or decline."[2]   By the end of the Second World War, the French economy was shaken to its roots. Fifteen years of stagnation, with the Great Depression of the thirties and then the destruction wrought by the war, had left their mark. But the French people emerged from the sufferings of the war and the struggles of the Resistance movement with a passion for renewal, manifest in the wave of enthusiasm which followed the liberation. The idea of planning, which had taken shape in the National Resistance Committee, linked up with certain prewar concepts, such as those developed by the group X-Crise,[a] or by the *planistes,* and did not conflict with the setting up of the Resistance's "organization committees" during the war. It was no doubt Jean Monnet's personal influence which persuaded General de Gaulle to introduce a system of planning. This first Plan was supported by all social groups, including especially the trade unions. Given the presence of Communist ministers in the government, the nationalization of key sectors of the economy (electricity, transport, etc.), the wider coverage of the social security system and the establishment of joint management committees with worker participation, the Plan indeed appeared to some as the harbinger of a socialist economy.

With *dirigisme* in full swing, Jean Monnet set up the so-called Modernization Commissions as a forum of discussions between government, employers, and the trade unions, and launched the idea of a "concerted economy."

The central theme of the First Plan (1947–1950, later extended to 1953) was reconstruction. The planners' choices were highly selective, since the main emphasis was on raising production in major basic sectors, whose growth conditions expansion in all other economic activities. The chosen sectors were coal, electricity, steel, cement, farm machinery, and transport. While protectionism ruled supreme, the Plan spoke of the need to move towards an opening up of frontiers.

The Second and Third Plans: "From growth to international competition." The Second Plan (1954–1957) [3] and later the Third Plan (1958–1961) [4] were of less consequence than the First and commanded less support; but they

[a]A group organized at the time of the 1929–30 crisis by former students of the Ecole Polytechnique, including Alfred Sauvy, Jean Ullmo, Pierre Massé, and Louis Wallon. The group advocated active state intervention and planning.

served to put across the idea that economic growth can and must be pursued after the completion of postwar reconstruction. The result was a fundamental change in the attitude of the French people, and more especially of its ruling classes.

Modernization of the economy and expansion remained the major aims. Both Plans tried to promote certain structural reforms, called "basic actions" in the Second Plan, and "imperative tasks" in the Third. There were no decisions, strictly speaking, but rather general guidelines and recommendations regarding such things as vocational training, research, the organization of agricultural markets, investment, and the sources of investment finance, etc.

One of the dominant ideas was the reintroduction of competition, followed by the opening up of the economy to the outside world in connection with the beginnings of the new Europe. As the Third Plan proclaims (para. 20): "Our country cannot choose a policy of protectionism and reliance on its own resources without at the same time incurring the danger of finding itself in a few years' time impoverished, isolated and, as it were, left behind by history."[5] The preparation of the Plans thus helped to replace the image of a stagnating or crisis-prone economy by one of a growing economy.

The Fourth Plan: "A less incomplete concept of man." [6] The recovery of the French economy after the 1957–58 recession, the entry of France into the European Economic Community (EEC), the rejuvenation of the labor force predictable from the postwar baby boom, the political stability of the early years of the Fifth Republic and General de Gaulle's predilection for the idea of economic planning all combined to create a favorable climate for the Fourth Plan. It became an act of political faith sanctioned by a vote of Parliament and described by General de Gaulle as a "passionate commitment." Consultation between government, employers and trade unions in the Modernization Commissions gained new vigor.

The Fourth Plan (1962–1965) stressed the social aspects of planning. The "modernization and investment Plan" turned into an "economic and social development Plan." Beyond expansion, modernization, and priority for investment, two new themes appear for the first time: concern with the distribution of the fruits of expansion, and regional development. Alongside a high overall rate of growth (5.5 percent annually), we find a target rate of 10 percent annually for social investment (housing, education, health)—a target which, incidentally, was met by and large.

But the implementation of the Fourth Plan got into serious trouble as early as 1963, when prices soared and the balance of payments got into deficit. A policy of stabilization by demand containment became necessary, and preparations for the Fifth Plan began in the inauspicious atmosphere of the stabilization program introduced by the Finance Minister, Valéry Giscard d'Estaing. Both partners in industry—labor and management—disliked the idea of an incomes policy and were in no mood to discuss, let alone "concert," anything with the planners.

The Fifth Plan: "This competitive world . . ." At the Incomes Conference late in 1963 the Planning Commissioner, then Pierre Massé, tried to reconcile expansion and price stability by an incomes policy. But nobody seemed ready to take this road—not the trade unions, nor the employers, nor even the government.

By that time, the French economy began to open its borders, and the maintenance of its competitiveness by strict control of domestic price rises was given top priority, the more so since France's membership in the EEC greatly restricted the use of other, traditional means of reducing the external deficit, such as import quotas, custom duties and, as a last resort, devaluation. If domestic prices are to be prevented from rising too fast, the growth of money wages has to slow down, and this might have been achieved by an active policy of structural reform (through employment policy or the reorganization of firms). But knowing that this would take a long time to put into effect, and doubtful about the scale of the results, the authors of the Fifth Plan proposed another way, namely, "a certain amount of slack on the labor market." It was hoped that this, without involving too much unemployment, would keep down wage increases sufficiently to slow down the price rise.

This was the reasoning behind the Fifth Plan. In practice, it led to the choice of an annual growth rate of 5 percent[b] between 1965 and 1970, "slightly below the physical limit of our capacity" (Report on the Fifth Plan, p. 6).[7]

In the absence of agreement on an incomes policy, the Fifth Plan set out "indicative norms" regarding the desired pace of income growth, together with a consistent set of targets for the real distribution of the fruits of expansion among consumption, productive and social investment, and the external balance on goods and services account.

Anxious to submit the Plan to a more democratic discussion, the government arranged, a year ahead of its adoption, for a Parliamentary debate on its options, that is to say on the major policy lines underlying the preparation of any plan as such.

The implementation of the Fifth Plan was proceeding more or less on course, when the social upheavals of May and June 1968 disrupted every economic balance as well as the implementation of the Plan. The overall results of the Fifth Plan are briefly summarized in table 6–1. It is true that expansion of gross domestic product slightly exceeded the target, and productive investment got even more priority over consumption than had been planned; but social investment fell badly behind, as the chief victim of the budget cuts of November

[b]The growth rate of 5 percent calculated by the 1959 system of national accounts corresponds to 5.7 percent annually if recalculated by the new 1962 system.

Table 6-1. France: Indicators of the Implementation of the Fifth Plan, 1966-70[a] (annual growth rate, percentage)

	Plan	Results						
	Fifth Plan	*Annual national accounts*					*Average for the period*
	1966-70	*1966*	*1967*	*1968*	*1969*	*1970*	*1966-70*

(a) Expansion and its uses: main items (in volume terms at 1965 prices)

Gross domestic product	5.7	5.9	5.0	4.6	7.6	6.0	5.8
Consumption by households	5.3	4.8	5.2	3.9	6.3	4.8	5.0
Productive investment	6.0	10.3	6.3	6.7	12.9	6.6	8.6
Investment by government	10.4	8.2	13.0	3.7	6.1	4.7	7.1
Housing investment	3.8	6.5	5.4	8.6	3.4	3.9	5.6
Exports	7.5	5.6	6.0	12.4	17.2	18.1	11.9
Imports	8.4	12.4	5.7	13.8	24.7	7.3	12.8

(b) Prices and incomes

General price level	1.5[b]	2.8	2.7	4.1	6.6	5.2	4.3
Hourly wage rates[c,d]	3.3[b]	3.1	3.0	6.8	4.4	4.8	4.4
Average net wage (excluding employees' social security contributions)[c]	3.8	3.3	3.0	6.1	4.0	4.8	4.2
Gross income per non-agricultural entrepreneur (excluding production expenses)[c]	3.8	6.4	6.4	3.7	4.1	5.1	5.1
Gross returns per farmer (including productions expenses)[c]	4.8	4.9	7.1	1.0	3.8	4.6	4.3
Social benefits (pensions, sick pay, etc.)[c]	7.3	7.3	6.9	6.4	7.9	6.6	7.0

Notes:

[a]These indicators are calculated for the French Commissiat du Plan in order to evaluate the implementation of Plans.
[b]Political norm.
[c]Corrected for the rise in the general price level.
[d]Income flow as evaluated in the national accounts.

1968 and the 1969 devaluation. Price and income movements diverged widely from the indicative norms. The guidelines for prices, somewhat unrealistic to begin with, were completely disregarded, and so were those concerning wage restraint and the upgrading of farm incomes; only social benefits followed the course laid out by the Plan.

But it was not merely the consequences of May 1968 that called the Fifth Plan in question. It would be more correct to say that the origins of the social crisis called in question the logic of the Fifth Plan. In a society undergoing such profound changes as the French, mainly under the impact of international competition, strains like unemployment and restrictions on purchasing power gains enabled an explosive situation to develop.

The Sixth Plan: "The industrial imperative."[8]   In spite of the shock generated by the social crisis, a start was made in October 1969 with the preparation of the Sixth Plan. At once the employers made it clear that they wanted strong expansion and priority for industrial development. "The industrial imperative" for the progressive group of employers, "the imperative of the industrialists" for the trade unions—these were the slogans to which the contents of the Sixth Plan had to be fitted. Balanced growth was no longer expected from containment of domestic demand, as in the Fifth Plan, but rather from an "active policy of stimulating supply." Social policy remained timid, placing the stress mainly on help to the most underprivileged groups (increase in the lowest wages and in old-age pensions, care for the handicapped).

Prospects for the Seventh Plan: "Growth—to what end?"   At a time when international monetary difficulties and inflationary pressure throughout the Western world are surrounding the outcome of the Sixth Plan with mounting uncertainties, society is beginning to ask itself what is the point of all this economic growth so dear to the planners (the British economist Andrew Shonfield speaks of French planners as an "expansion lobby"). And so French planners, as they get ready to prepare the Seventh Plan, are faced with a challenge. They must allow not only for the necessary economic consistency, but for new social and ecological aims dictated by the present stage of development.

Changing Methods for a Wider Range
of Problems
The preparation of French Plans has always been accompanied by a host of planning studies and economic projections. As the range of issues treated by the planners widened and became more diversified, better tools of analysis and forecasting became available to them thanks to improvements in economic information (statistics and national accounts). Actually, progress in information and in planning systems is closely connected for, to a large extent, it was the

questions the planners asked which called forth—not always very quickly—more detailed information.

Input-output tables have been used since the Second Plan, and even more so the Third, as the primary means of presenting a synthetic picture of the quantitative aspects of the economy. The First Plan made do with such fragmentary data as were needed for forecasting output in the priority sectors, but subsequently the planners wanted full coverage and were thus led to work out detailed projections of the volume of output and its uses. The required input-output table was drawn from the national accounts. This technique had its heyday at the time of the Fourth Plan, when it was used as a basis for a "general market study." This, in the view of Pierre Massé,[9] then Planning Commissioner, was to provide economic agents with all the information, in global and in detailed terms, they might need on the growth prospects of private and public demand and of production.

The problems of income distribution and price formation in time focused attention on the need to work out an overall economic table (*tableau économique d'ensemble*—TEE). This had to do with the transition from a protected to an open economy. Once France's membership in the Common Market began to show its effects, it intensified the pressure of international competition on the French economy. It was no longer enough to produce in order to sell; one must produce at competitive prices.

State intervention, too, gradually underwent a change in the direction of *indirect* influences on the market mechanism (e.g., by fiscal and budget policy). The detailed effects of such state intervention do not show up at the stage of equilibrium in volume terms (output and its uses), but at that of the formation of incomes, expenditure and prices on different markets.

Beginning with the Third Plan, but mainly on the occasion of the Fourth, the construction of an overall economic table made it possible to study the saving-investment equilibrium as well as problems of income distribution.

The study of financial consistency requires projections in a table of financial operations (*Tableau d'opérations financières*—TOF). Taking overall real and financial equilibrium for granted, a consistency test account is constructed to check whether planned investment can be financed within the framework of existing (or proposed) financial institutions, due allowance being made for the rigidity and separation of financial circuits, which are rather pronounced in France. Such a table was prepared experimentally for the Fourth Plan and came into effective use in the Fifth, when the government was proposing to channel its intervention in the financing of productive investment through the private banking sector. There was much talk at the time about the "disengagement of the Treasury," and it became clear that this meant that the private banks would have to "transform" a major part of the short-term funds accruing to them into medium- and long-term loans to enterprises for the purpose of financing productive investment.[10]

Alongside these studies designed to test the consistency of the norms set by the government for its own action, experimental work was started on the financial analysis of enterprises by sectors,[11] with a view to improving sectoral price projections. Each sector was examined to see if the price forecasting was consistent with the financial assets and the possibilities for self-financed investments required by growth. This work brought to light inconsistencies in the financial flows of certain sectors which might have compromised these sectors' investments.

Formal model-building: The physical-financial model FIFI.[12] Without a formal exposition of the behavior of economic agents, the macroeconomic projections were unable to play their part of verifying the consistency between the government's chosen norms and the behavior of agents. In any case, it was a slow and clumsy business to calculate all these projections by hand, and it was impossible to show more than a very few volume-value interdependences. Taking advantage of the new, more sophisticated econometric models and of computer calculation, French planners, when preparing the Sixth Plan, worked out a semi-global (seven enterprise sectors) medium-term simulation model for the whole of the French economy. The model is built so as to show the impact of international competition on the French economy. Assuming that in industry, the sector fully exposed to such competition, there is a constraint on domestic price formation, the model shares out the market for industrial products between financially possible domestic production and substitutable imports. That is, the model determines domestic production and demand, and imports are obtained as the difference. This is in effect a transposition of the neoclassical theory of the firm to the scale of an entire sector, because the sector faces given prices and its production is determined by its financial possibilities. In the other sectors price is a variable which can be influenced at will either by government (administered prices) or by firms (sectors sheltered from international competition). For the latter case it is assumed that cost and profit changes are passed on to the medium-term supply price of firms according to a Keynesian-type mechanism of inflationary gap. By stressing the medium-term importance of the French economy's price competitiveness, the FIFI model suggested that priority should be given to policies susceptible of increasing price competitiveness, that is, of stimulating the supply of marketable output, especially in industry.

Toward a system of medium-term models. The synthetic macroeconomic model was not the only one prepared for the Sixth Plan. Around the central model are grouped a number of peripheral ones, which can provide detailed information in response to questions asked by certain working parties and commissions. There exists, for example, a set of models for the national and local governments and the social security system;[13] these are compatible with the central model but much more detailed. They are used to study fiscal and financial policies, for example, how to obtain equilibrium in the social security system. Similarly, the output projections of the FIFI model's seven enterprise sectors did not tell the production commissions all they needed to know, and so detailed projections were worked out for twenty-nine branches, subject, of course, to consistency with the semi-global equilibrium of the overall model. It may well be that in the future we shall build more such articulated systems of models, which together will furnish detailed medium-term projections whose consistency will be safeguarded by their being fitted into one global model.

Present trends in macroeconomic model-building. Three further developments are afoot in France at present. (1) Simultaneous description of economic equilibrium and financial circuits in the model FIFI-TOF.[14] This is the central tool in the preparation of the Seventh Plan, and it is hoped to subsequently integrate in its structure the effects of the money-creating mechanisms and the financial repercussions on the physical and economic elements of equilibrium (productive investment, housing investment, price formation, etc.). (2) Combination of regional and spatial development aspects in the model REGINA (REGIonal-NAtional)[15] should make it possible to test the effects of regional development policy on national equilibria, by distinguishing five major regions of France and three urbanization zones in each of them. (3) Clarification of the relations between medium-term projections and short-term forecasts in a short-term/medium-term model called STAR,[16] on which research is now in hand in the Forecasting Division of the Ministry of Finance; the idea is to lengthen the forecasting horizon of the "economic budgets" (forecasts of economic accounts for the next one or two years) and, in the course of Plan implementation, to analyze the reasons of any divergences from medium-term projections.

Microeconomic tools occupy a less important place in French planning. However, the sort of economic calculation which public enterprises have long used in investment choices is increasingly finding its way into government departments under the influence of what the Americans call Planning, Programming, Budgeting System (PPBS) and the French call *Rationalisation des choix budgétaires* (RCB). These techniques are used in an attempt to introduce economic calculation into more detailed official programming. Decentralized short- and medium-term "program budgets" should add realism to the national plan, but would certainly involve problems of synthesis when it comes to choices among different fields of public activity.

From Dirigiste to Indicative Planning

French planning very quickly broke away from the postwar *dirigisme* of economic policy. The latter was still much in evidence in the methods by which the First Plan was implemented, e.g., the use of Marshall Aid counterpart funds for investment, import licenses, etc., but this was no longer true of the Second

Plan, when the Commissariat Général du Plan was able to exert only an indirect influence on the chief instruments of *dirigiste* policy applied by other divisions of the Ministry of Finance (to which the Planning Commission belonged until 1962, when it became attached directly to the Prime Minister's office). Short-term difficulties in plan implementation as well as political vicissitudes explain why, as the years went on, planning became more and more "indicative" with respect to short-term policy, for which the Ministry of Finance retained responsibility. During the period of the Third Plan, the advent of the Fifth Republic and France's entry into the Common Market made it necessary to resort to an interim plan for the years 1960 and 1961. No sooner had the Fourth Plan (1962–1965) got under way, than it was seriously upset by the introduction of a stabilization program. And as regards the Fifth Plan (1965–1970), finally, the upheavals of May and June 1968 produced a shock so strong that the initial design had in effect to be abandoned.

From warning signals to review procedures. Faced with these repeated vagaries of economic reality, the planners tried to do two things. They chose a few of the more important plan targets and then tried to obtain firmer commitments from the government with respect to this hard core of targets. These preoccupations are the origin of the system of warning signals, which give notice of any significant departure from the planned targets in matters of expansion and equilibrium. In the intention of its authors, this system was to be an element of economic strategy in plan implementation; any significant overshooting of the point where the warning signal flashed would *automatically* lead to a decision either to abandon the target or else to apply corrective policy. As is shown in table 6–2, the warning signals of the Fifth Plan were indeed able to indicate divergences in plan implementation, but official reactions were apparent only in ministerial communiqués. The bodies responsible for short-term

Table 6–2. France: Time Table of Monthly Warning Signals during the Implementation of the Fifth Plan, 1966-70

Subject	Danger point for activation of signal	Date of warning
General price level	Retail price increase 1 percent in excess of that of major trading partners (for three consecutive months).	January 1968 to February 1970
Foreign trade balance	Less than 90 percent of total imports covered by exports for three consecutive months.	April 1969 to April 1970
Growth of industrial production	Twelve-month growth of less than 1 percent (for three consecutive months).	July to November 1967
Employment situation	Unemployment exceeding 2.5 percent of the working population (for three consecutive months).	August and September 1968

economic policy—the Ministry of Finance and its main Services—refused to take the Plan as a point of reference for their actions, and the original Plan figures were neither defended nor revised. In addition, the practice of monthly checks was clumsy and eventually became almost meaningless because it was done too frequently.

It spite of difficulties in Plan implementation, the monthly warning signals flashed rarely, and the annual ones (gross domestic product and productive investment) never, though admittedly the danger point at which the latter were to be activated was set very low (GDP, 2 percent; investment, 2.5 percent).

The relative price increase in France compared with prices abroad exceeded the 1 percent limit for three consecutive months in January 1968, as a result of the extension of the value-added tax to retail trade. It did not drop back below this limit until February 1970, but this may be explained by the high rate of world inflation (6 percent annually).

The other signals were less restrictive and flashed after a time lag of six to twelve months.

In view of these difficulties, the system of warning signals was replaced by a mid-course "Plan Review," to which the government committed itself in advance and which was to be the subject of a Parliamentary debate. In addition, a new set of quarterly indicators is published and widely distributed by the National Institute of Statistics and Economic Studies (Institut National de la Statistique et des Etudes Economiques—INSEE)[17] and the Commissariat Général du Plan. This system is explained in the next section.

Hard-core targets in plan implementation.   In their formulation, French Plans have been, and are tending to become, more and more *comprehensive* as regards both the range of problems and the detail in which they are treated. But at the same time the Planning Commission has, among other things, been anxious to place stress on *selectivity* with respect to measures to be introduced or applied in the course of plan implementation. Accordingly, a distinction is made, in the figures of macroeconomic projections, between mere forecasts and targets to which the government commits itself. The clearest example is the introduction to the report on the Sixth Plan,[18] which summarizes only those of the planned targets to which the government has committed itself (cf. the next section). Similarly, an attempt was made in the Sixth Plan to concentrate intervention in the field of public finance, while encouraging regional and local decentralization in Plan implementation.

The most sensitive area is that of public investment, which can fall victim to short-term policy more easily than current operating expenses, such as wages and salaries and other current expenditure. The device adopted for the Sixth Plan in this respect was to set an overall figure for public investment as a Plan target without specifying completely the share for each function (health, education, transport, etc.). Part of the investments for each function, ranging from 15 to 40 percent, is considered variable, and the list of projects included is subject to a "priority declaration." On the other hand, a number of programs (with all their expenditure on investment, staff, and operation) were completely planned because of their strategic character; examples are the activities of the National Employment Agency, of the road safety squad, etc. Decentralization in Plan implementation was to be encouraged by recent "Plan contracts" signed by the government and a small number of local authorities grouped in urban communities. The national government grants subsidies to these communities to carry out a public investment program over a three or five year period.

Planning and decisionmaking. In spite of all precautions, it seems certain that the implementation of an indicative Plan in a market economy will always involve the planners in some tricky problems. The Plan is part of the varied means of government intervention in development. Yet it has no direct control over any of the other means employed. Nor is planning a continuous process, and hence it is a decisionmaking one only to a very limited extent. Planning can probably more aptly be described as the opening move in a process of discussion and consultation among government departments and between them and spokesmen of social groups. This process serves to test the approximate consistency of the policies of various government departments, and at the same time to lay down an overall set of general guidelines binding upon government and strengthening its ability to resist the demands of interest groups during a certain period, at most throughout Plan implementation. A case in point may be recalled in connection with the preparation of the Sixth Plan. At that time, the idea gradually gained ground that "tax pressure"—that is, the incidence of taxes, social insurance contributions, and the like—on production, should not increase during the period of the Plan. This rule was put into practice, step-by-step, through a series of tax decisions and has become a benchmark of the implementation of the current Plan.

The Shift from the "Concerted Economy" to a Government Program
Participation of spokesmen of social groups in Plan preparation was an ingredient of the philosophy of French planning from the outset. On the occasion of the First Plan this was spelled out quite clearly:

> Since the implementation of the Plan will require the collaboration of all, it is indispensable that all the nation's vital elements take part in its formulation. This is why a working method is proposed which, for each sector, involves joint discussions by officials of the government department concerned, prominent experts and representatives of professional groups (workers, managerial staff, employers) . . . . [19]

This is what was meant by a "concerted economy" in contrast to a *dirigiste* one run on bureaucratic or corporative lines. To give effect to this conception, the

Commissariat Général du Plan set up and kept at work a large number of commissions and working parties, some of them within the Civil Service.

Planning machinery. As the range of issues brought within the purview of planning in successive French Plans increased, so did the number of Commissions and Working Parties involved.

Eventually, by the time of the Sixth Plan, the system was reformed in an attempt to enhance the unity and efficiency of the whole body of Commissions. These are now of three kinds (see table 6–3): the "horizontal" Commissions, which are responsible for problems common to all activities (e.g., employment, research, etc.), and among which the Commission for the General Economy and Financing takes care of synthesis on the basis of the relevant overall planning studies; the "vertical" Production Commissions, much reduced in number but now including a new single Industry Commission concerned with synthesis and with industrial policy; and the Budgetary Commissions, also called "Commissions of Collective Functions," which deal with major fields of public services (e.g., education, health, etc.). Within separate Commissions, the study of specific problems or those concerned with sectoral activities is delegated to specialized Committees (e.g., a Foreign Trade Committee, twenty-two sectoral Production Committees under the umbrella of the Industry Commission) or to Joint Working Parties in the case of problems common to two or more Commissions (e.g., the Joint Working Party on Vocational Training of the Employment and the Education Commissions). Finally, some of the major Commissions have arranged for technical and production studies to be discussed by Technical Working Parties made up of experts from government departments, employers' associations, and trade unions.

Two new features in the preparation of the Sixth Plan were the development of *long-term study groups*, whose discussions generally preceded those of the Plan Commissions, and the establishment of *administrative groups*, which met

Table 6–3. France: Commissions for the Sixth Plan, 1971–75

Seven "horizontal" Commissions: general economy and financing, employment, social benefits, research, economic information, National Commission for Regional Development *(Commission Nationale d'Aménagement du Territoire*–CNAT), overseas territories.

Eight "Production" Commissions: agriculture, agricultural and food industries, industry, transport, communications, trade, professions and crafts, tourism.

Nine "Budgetary" Commissions (or "Commissions of Collective Functions"): rural areas, towns, social action, sports and activities of social education, cultural affairs, water, education, housing, health.

Attached to these Commissions are a number of Committees (Committees on competition, foreign trade, and financing; technical group of the Commission for the General Economy and Financing; twenty-two sectoral Committees of the Industry Commission, etc.) as well as Joint Working Parties (vocational training, industrial financing, etc.). The Commissions themselves set up many Working Parties of their own.

---

before the Commissions, prepared the latter's work and coordinated the position of government departments. The most important among these administrative groups are the Finance-Plan Groups, which have done much to give more prominence to the medium-term view in the work of the Ministry of Finance, to increase the exchange of information between its divisions and the Commissariat Général du Plan, and to define its position in relation to the Sixth Plan.

The extent of participation in Plan preparation. The social groups which were to take part in the preparation of Plans actually do so in varying degree, according to the view they take of the functions of planning and to the position they occupy in French society. Most participants agree that planning is useful as a means of economic and social information,[c] but opinions differ as to what commitments are to result from the planning process. *Farmers* regard planning as an important stage in their traditional discussions with government. Farmers' associations, for example, warmly supported an incomes policy during the Sixth Plan, even though the Fifth Plan had failed in this respect. The attitude of *employers* changed in the course of time. At first they were rather hostile because of the seemingly *dirigiste* complexion of the whole venture of planning, but later their associations took an active part in the preparation of the Third and Fourth Plans, when the "general market study" was a valuable source of information for them. However, the Conseil National du Patronat Français (CNPF), which in principle represents all private enterprises but in actual fact only the biggest ones, did not abandon its reserved attitude until the Sixth Plan. At that time it publicly took a strong stand in favor of vigorous growth based on industry, because it was anxious to have the Sixth Plan give priority to industrialization; yet its position remained ambiguous owing to an internal conflict of interests between a forward-looking group of large industrialists and the bulk of the owners of small- and medium-sized firms who looked with misgivings at the far-reaching structural changes in French industry.

Trade unions likewise changed their attitude, but in the opposite direction from employers. At first, they liked the apparently socialist implications of planning, but later they increasingly contested the use made of it by government, so much so that sometimes they withheld all participation. The Confédération Générale du Travail (CGT)—which, despite its importance among the unions, was excluded by the government from the planning process until the Third Plan—and its breakaway group Force Ouvrière (FO) adopted the same attitude towards planning, in spite of their divergent ideologies (Communist in the first case and reformist-socialist in the second). Both take part actively in meetings, and both withhold collaboration—the one by refusing to agree to

---

[c]The whole set of Commission, Committee, and Working Party reports published by the Commissariat Général du Plan in 1971 constitutes a valuable source of recent studies and information on most aspects of the French economy.

anything in the first place and opposing final decisions, the other by paying lip service to agreement but refusing to be committed by it. The Confédération Française Démocratique du Travail (CFDT, the socialist-inspired successor of the Confédération Française des Travailleurs Chrétiens, CFTC) changed course more radically. While it played an active part in economic management in 1962 and raised a claim for "democratic planning," it held aloof from the Sixth Plan when its socialist orientation became stronger. It was so critical of the whole approach of the Sixth Plan that in September 1970 it refused to take any part in the second stage of its preparation.

As regards the *government* and the *planners* themselves, the discussions of the Plans fulfill a certain number of functions, though these, too, have gradually changed in time. The collection of information has lost much of its importance as a result of the general improvement of the whole system of economic and statistical information. The Planning Commission relies more and more heavily on the macroeconomic studies of the National Institute of Statistics and Economic Studies and of the Forecasting Division of the Ministry of Finance. And most government departments have developed their own information programs in connection with PPBS, research and programming units, etc.

Conciliation in the interests of compliance. The efforts to conciliate the differing points of view of social groups at the stage of Plan preparation aim at increasing compliance with the Plan. For a long time the planners tried to achieve a *social consensus* regarding the general lines of the Plan, witness Pierre Massé's ambition of a "Nation's Plan." But now it has become clear that the rules of the game of our society are contested at the root by some of the social groups which are part of the planning machinery. Inevitably, this altered the significance of the Plan itself, for its choices and targets increasingly became those of government. The Plan now is to all intents and purposes a medium-term action program for government. Plan discussions still have their function, but it is a function of *social simulation* by which the government's choices are confronted with the preferences (or objections) of social groups in order to test the impact of reform projects and to amend them prior to final decision. This is necessarily a partial process, because five-year planning for fixed dates can take account of only a part of government policies, and because many important decisions are taken outside the procedures of Plan preparation and hence are a datum for them rather than a variable to be influenced. But all in all this seems the lesser evil in comparison with a sort of "rolling" planning in which basic choices would be in danger of being watered down in day-to-day action.

These recent changes in French planning are well illustrated by the preparation of the current, Sixth Plan (1971–75). Its main features are discussed below together with its mid-course implementation.

THE SIXTH PLAN, ITS PREPARATION
AND IMPLEMENTATION

French planning received a severe setback by the social crisis of May and June 1968, when the Fifth Plan was abandoned de facto. Nevertheless interest in planning revived in the years 1969 to 1971, when the Sixth Plan was in preparation. On a number of essential points government policy since then has been directly inspired by the targets of this Plan, and the latter, therefore, is progressing well in spite of much stronger inflationary pressures than had been foreseen.

A Revealing Diagnosis of the Problems of French Society

Continuity of structural reform. Work on the preparation of the Sixth Plan was influenced by a number of inter-ministry teams which the Planning Commission sponsored between 1966 and 1968. In three fields joint exploration led to recommendations which were to a large extent followed by the eventual choices of the Sixth Plan. In the field of *employment policy,* an unpublished report by a team led by François-Xavier Ortoli, then Planning Commissioner, advocated the reinforcement of agencies intervening in the labor market through the creation of a National Employment Agency (Agence Nationale pour l'Emploi—ANPE) as well as new vocational training and retraining schemes. The *industrial policy* recommended by the Industrial Development Committee (Comité de Développement Industriel—CDI)[20] took account also of the general obstacles to industrialization in France. And the Committee of Public Enterprises (Comité des Entreprises Publiques)[21] tried to redefine the contractual relations between the state and public firms so as to give their management more autonomy in decisions on price, wages and investment policy.[d] These analytical studies and the ensuing government decisions demonstrate how the Planning Commission can, in between two Plans, exert an influence on structural policy.

Strengths and weaknesses of the French economy. On the eve of the Sixth Plan, a number of studies sponsored by the Planning Commission brought to light certain deficiencies, but also certain assets of the French economy with reference to the level of industrial development. It became clear, for instance,

---

[d]It was not a case of genuine decentralization, except possibly for the big public enterprises, for, in connection with Plan preparation, investment and development programs were drawn up for each of the principal public enterprises and submitted for discussion to the government department concerned (Ministry of Finance, Ministry of Industry, Ministry of Transport, etc.). Local authorities (e.g., for a *département* or municipality) belong to another level of decentralization, which regional planning at the time tried to organize and coordinate, still imperfectly, with the national level.

that the production apparatus had not really recovered from the effects of increased competition. Its competitiveness had weakened since the two devaluations of 1957 and 1958 when the Common Market for industrial products came into force, witness the growing deficit in the trade balance of manufactures and the more rapid pace of price rises in France than elsewhere in the EEC. The 1969 devaluation to some extent ratified this loss of competitiveness.

But this weakness, it seems, was not due to excessively high costs,[22] but to structural imperfections in the production apparatus (like firms of insufficient size, inefficient management) and to an environment unpropitious to its development (social overhead capital, research, impact of public revenue and expenditure). These structural imperfections were highlighted especially by the American economists John H. McArthur and Bruce R. Scott in a study on behalf of the Planning Commission.[23]

But as against these problems, the French economy had certain assets: the demographic structure was such that a rapid increase of the labor force could be expected, the reactions of firms to the booming demand of the years 1968–1969 favored productive investment, and the above-mentioned structural reforms were beginning to take effect.

While the Sixth Plan was in preparation, other factors gradually led to a change in the emphasis placed on the problems of industrial development. It became clear that a structural renewal of the production apparatus, particularly in the industrial sectors, would be associated with a whole series of changes in the nation's social fabric, and came up against latent or sometimes violently expressed opposition (e.g. on the part of farmers, small shopkeepers, and, more recently, skilled and unskilled industrial labor). Concomitant policies had to be devised to deal with these changes and to help the most vulnerable groups.

There was growing public concern, too, at gross inequalities in the distribution of income and at the unsatisfactory living conditions of certain groups (like the elderly, immigrants, large low-income families), for which there was little prospect of spontaneous improvement. The "rejects" of economic growth thus came to the fore among the serious issues to be dealt with by the Sixth Plan.

The Stages of Plan Preparation

The problems requiring solution were thrown into relief by the first macroeconomic projection tests which the Commissariat Général du Plan submitted to the Commissions for discussion in the autumn of 1969. This so-called initial account presented trend projections for 1975 worked out with the help of the FIFI model, and combined an extrapolation of the behavior trends of economic agents with unchanged policies of public revenue and expenditure. The prospect it outlined for the end of the planning period was that of a mediocre and unbalanced situation (weak growth, very high prices and incomes, external trade deficit, budget deficit). A number of variants, similarly worked out with the help of the model, showed the effects of possible corrective policies, and, as was to be expected from the model's economic logic as described earlier in the first section, the policies which appeared favorable were those designed to stimulate the supply of marketable output especially in industry.

Discussion in the Commissions, between October 1969 and March 1970, proceeded partly on a branch-by-branch basis. In each individual field an attempt was made to define the targets specific to it and to find an approach likely to help eliminate the imbalances which the projections had revealed for the economy as a whole. For instance, in the field of energy, Commission debates soon suggested that investment would rise less than the past trend-line would indicate for coal-mining and hydroelectric power; this made room for a corresponding reduction of subsidies and hence of the budget deficit. Even though it later became necessary to take a less sanguine view of the expected potency and effects of these corrective policies (like reducing investment), it is clear that sectoral policies in each individual field were meant to be geared to the removal of macroeconomic imbalances.

In general discussions the employers' representatives made themselves the champions of vigorous growth, then termed "Japanese-style growth." As regards the government, the Ministry of Finance advocated a strictly balanced budget, a reduction in total public expenditure such as to leave the rate of tax pressure unchanged, and a vigorous export drive to sustain overall economic growth.

At that stage, in February-March 1970, the physical-financial model was used to work out for the Commission for the General Economy three synthetic variants corresponding to three alternative growth models.

1. The so-called *accelerated structural change model* was based on the assumption of a very active policy to stimulate industrial growth. An annual growth rate of 6.5 percent was to be associated with vigorous employment and vocational training policies. But this model entailed sizable risks both of an economic kind (soaring prices and wages, labor shortage) and of a social and political one (faster social change possibly leading to heavy political strain).

2. The so-called *prudent model* kept close to the growth strategy of the Fifth Plan. Its annual growth rate of 5.5 percent was well below physical growth capacity (and also involved high unemployment), but it kept the public finances in strict equilibrium at unchanged tax pressure and also showed balance-of-payments equilibrium in spite of the assumption of a no more than moderate growth rate abroad.

3. An *intermediate model* foreshadowed the recommendations which the Planning Commission was in fact preparing for submission to the government. This combined the essential choices of the two other variants namely, (a) to stimulate an expansion of competitive supply, and (b) to maintain budget equilibrium with a view to controlling demand. At the same time, however, the

model assumed less spectacular results from policies under (a), and also a slightly higher rate of tax pressure than in the past for the benefit of concomitant policies by which it was hoped to offset the damaging consequences of social changes associated with economic growth.

The choices and targets of the Sixth Plan thus gradually took shape in Commission discussions both in overall terms and with reference to individual fields. Once the government had made its policy decisions, these were submitted to Parliament and debated by it in accordance with the precedent established when the Fifth Plan was being prepared. In May–June 1970, Parliament debated and approved by vote the major policy lines of the Sixth Plan; a year later, after another debate, it enacted the Plan itself. The hard core of the Plan's targets, which is described in the Introduction thereto,[24] reflects the themes mentioned earlier: stimulation of competitive supply in an open economy, control of demand, public finance equilibrium at constant tax pressure and gradual shifts in the structure of expenditure, corrective measures to offset the harmful effects of change, aid to the elderly and handicapped, and slight adjustments in the division of time between work and leisure.

Quantification of Plan targets went hand-in-hand with their definition for the government. Both the report on policy lines and the report on the Sixth Plan as such were accompanied by macroeconomic projections for its terminal year 1975. In June 1971, the *Plan Account* put together the "projections associated with the Sixth Plan" [25] and provided quantitative estimates consistent with the targets defined in the report approved by Parliamentary vote. Most of the figures in these projections are in the nature of technical forecasts. Thus the increasing distinction between targets and forecasts found expression in the planners' own conjoint work on two separate documents, the *Rapport du Plan* and the *Projections associées au Plan.* The chief quantified targets of the Sixth Plan are recapitulated in table 6–4; but they are not, in themselves, enough to define the Plan, for an essential element of it resides in the economic policies by which these targets were to be achieved in practice.

Medium-term economic policy associated with the Sixth Plan was in fact closely geared to its main targets, to wit expansion of competitive supply, control of demand, and a better deal for the underprivileged.

The government pursued two lines in its effort to speed up the growth of profitable output. (a) It took steps to influence the environment of industrial enterprise by such means as an active employment and labor training policy, the reorientation of research toward competitive industrial products, a special investment effort in the field of social overhead capital (roads, telecommunications, ports, etc.), encouragement for saving and for industrial investment finance from banks, and further industrial mergers together with the promotion of dynamic medium-sized firms. (b) It marked out priority sectors chosen either because of their strategic role or because of their special difficulties; in industry, these were mechanical engineering, chemicals, electronics, and the agricultural

Table 6-4. France: Targets of the Sixth Plan, 1971-75

Subject	Target	Observations
Growth	Average annual rate of growth: gross domestic product (GDP), 5.8–6.0 percent; industrial production, 7.5 percent. Creation of 250,000 new jobs in industry.	
Employment	Full employment resulting from growth (no quantitative target).	
Vocational training	Doubling of after-work training facilities.	
Working hours	Reduction of work week by 1½ hours over the Plan period (from 44½ to 43 hours).	
Productive investment	7 percent annual growth rate for the economy as a whole. Rate of industrial investment to rise from 14.7 percent (1965) to 16.7 percent (1975).	The rate of investment is the ratio of gross fixed capital formation to the corresponding value added.
Domestic saving	Rate in excess of 30 percent of GDP.	
Prices	Political norm: 3.2 percent annually.[a]	Rate of increase equal in the medium term to that of France's main trading partners.
Foreign trade and external payments	Trade surplus of 1,000 million francs. 1 percent of GNP to be allocated to aid to developing countries.	Balance-of-payments equilibrium.
Public finances	Government borrowing requirement: nil. Maintenance of existing tax pressure (about 40 percent of GDP).	
Total consumption	Growth rate of 5.5 percent annually.	
Housing	Completion of 510,000 new dwellings. Modernization of 250,000 existing dwellings.	

Note:

[a]This figure was chosen as a political norm and became an exogenous variable.

and foods industries, and elsewhere, nuclear energy, tourism and shipping (to help the balance of payments).

Control of demand was no longer, as under the Fifth Plan, expected from an incomes policy, since this had been rejected by all social groups except possibly the farmers. Instead, the government went for active support of competition especially in such fields as services and building, which are protected from international competition. The main ingredient, however, was budget policy.

Strict balance of revenue and expenditure involved a limitation of public expenditure on social schemes, which in practice meant no increase in the rate of obligatory social charges on production. The structure of public expenditure was altered with particular reference to the requirements of development: current subsidies were curtailed and an effort was made to improve the efficiency of the public administration.

As regards a better deal for the underprivileged, the priority aims were faster than average rise of the lowest wages, and a rearrangement of social transfers so that more of the steadily increasing total should go to the old, the handicapped and, to a lesser extent, family assistance. This involved curtailment of other social expenditure, in particular for sickness insurance and rent allowances.

The authors of the Sixth Plan were much concerned with the need to be able to cope with unforeseen events, and to this end proposed a strategy of Plan implementation. Implementation was to be improved, in particular, by a mid-Plan review and, if necessary, revision, in the middle of 1973.

The Mid-Plan Review

Halfway through the Sixth Plan, the chief problems encountered in its implementation were brought to the attention of the government by the Planning Commission on the basis of a set of studies carried out early in 1973 and using the technique of short-term economic budgets. As will be seen from table 6–5, which is an extract from the control panel of Plan implementation, the macroeconomic figures hold out the prospect that the chief targets of the Sixth Plan can be achieved at least in volume terms, though not in terms of value—for the initial projections assumed an annual price rise of 3.2 percent for GDP, whereas the actual rise since 1970 has been 5.5 percent annually. This price divergence is explained not merely by the political nature of the price guideline adopted by the government for the Sixth Plan, but also by the fact that the French economy actually developed along lines very different from the "competitive" model on which the Sixth Plan was based. As things turned out, at least the early years of Plan implementation were free from international constraints in the form of price competition. The two reasons for this were the devaluation of the franc in August 1969 and strong inflation elsewhere in Western economies. Prices on international markets did nothing to force down French prices, and the latter rose at much the same rate as those of France's trading partners (5 to 6 percent annually on the average).

But the fight against inflation was, and is, not the main element of short-term economic policy. Admittedly, at the beginning of 1973 the government agreed to a sharp cut in indirect taxes, especially on food products, but this measure, costly as it was for the public finances, achieved no more than a temporary halt in the general inflation. But this type of measure makes it more difficult to implement the budgetary aspects of the Plan. The shortfall of revenue resulting from anti-inflationary tax cuts has made it impossible for the government to allocate enough funds for financing the public investment

Table 6–5. France: Indicators of the Implementation of the Sixth Plan, 1971–75 (annual growth rate, percentage)

	Plan	Results			
	Sixth Plan	*Annual national accounts*			*Average for the period*
	1971–75	*1971*	*1972*	*1973 (estimated)*	*1971–73 (estimated)*
(a) *Expansion and its uses: main items* (in volume terms at 1970 prices)					
Gross domestic product	5.9	5.6	5.6	6.2	5.8
Consumption by households	5.4	6.1	5.6	5.8	5.8
Productive investment	6.8	7.1	7.2	7.2	7.2
Investment by government	7.6	2.8	6.1	9.1	6.0
Housing investment	4.6	4.9	6.3	5.5	5.6
Exports	10.0	10.9	11.6	12.9	11.8
Imports	9.3	7.3	12.8	13.6	11.2
(b) *Prices and incomes*					
General price level	3.2	5.3	5.6	5.5	5.5
Hourly wage rates[a,b]	3.9	5.2	6.1	6.8	6.0
Average net wage (excluding employees' social security contributions)[a]	4.5	4.3	4.4	6.2	5.0
Gross income per entrepreneur[a]	6.3	5.2	8.5	6.6	6.8
Social benefits (pensions, sick pay, etc.)[a]	7.8	7.1	7.5	9.3	7.9

Notes:

[a]Corrected for the rise in the general price level.

[b]Income flow as evaluated in the national accounts.

program of the Sixth Plan, even though that program represented a government commitment ratified by Parliamentary vote (see table 6–6).

In all, the picture of the implementation of the Sixth Plan at the halfway point in mid-1973 is one of overall growth on target, much stronger inflation than expected, and a less than desired rearrangement of public expenditure to the benefit of public investment. Although at the time of writing, in early summer 1973, the government has not yet taken new decisions, these divergences from planned targets do not seem to entail a revision of the Sixth Plan, more especially since in the course of the preparation of the Seventh Plan (1976–80) the whole machinery of French planning is gradually being polarized.

PROSPECTS FOR THE SEVENTH PLAN (1976–80): "ECONOMIC GROWTH–TO WHAT END?"

As the Sixth Plan got under way, it became progressively clear that new problems, which were still latent at the end of the sixties, required solution. The perennial challenge to French planners is merely updated: will they be able to

Table 6-6. France: Public Expenditure and Taxes and Other Compulsory Levies under the Sixth Plan, 1971–75

	Plan	Results			
	Sixth Plan	Annual budget and national accounts			Average for the period
	1971–75	1971	1972	1973 (estimated)	1971–73 (estimated)
(a) *Public expenditure* (annual growth rate percentage, in real terms)[a]					
Ordinary civil expenditure	6.1	6.4	6.4	7.1	6.6
Investment	7.6	0.6	6.3	8.6	5.2
Social transfer payments (pensions, sick pay, etc.)	7.7	7.1	7.4	8.6	7.7
Economic transfer payments (subsidies, etc.)	4.0	0.9	4.6	5.6	3.7
Other expenditure	3.8	2.5	9.8	2.1	3.4
Total	6.5	5.2	7.2	6.4	6.3
(b) *Taxes and other compulsory levies* (percentage of GDP)					
National government	20.7	19.7	20.2	19.3	
Local authorities	3.8	3.7	3.6	4.3	
Social security system	15.1	15.1	15.2	15.5	
Other agencies	0.1	0.1	0.1	0.1	
Total[b]	39.7	38.6	39.1	39.2	

Notes:
[a]Corrected for the rise in the general price level.
[b]Includes nonconsolidated figures of taxes and social contributions paid by one government department or authority to another.

pinpoint the major issues of the seventies? Will they be alert and imaginative enough to propose solutions? Will they, finally, find enough political support to get reform going in good time?

But the planners are coming up against a contradiction. While subjects such as "control of the social aspects of development" or the "redefinition of the role of the state" can be studied in depth at national level, the growing internationalization of production and finance raises the more and more insistent question whether national planning still makes any sense at all. These three points kept recurring during the early stages of the preparation of the Seventh Plan, and it seems useful therefore to discuss them in more detail.

National Planning and the Internationalization of Production

The new forms of international specialization, especially the rapid spread of multinational firms, present the planners of all nations with considerable problems. National governments are finding it difficult to arrive at a common and consistent view of these developments. There is a time lag between, on the one hand, the forecasting and programming capacity of the managements of companies operating on the continental or even world scale, and on the other, the means of action and reaction at the disposal of government in each individual country. To be sure, some partial forms of political coordination are gradually being devised, one of the most instructive examples being the creation of the European Economic Community, first of six and now of nine members. But experience shows that such groupings, at this stage, have neither common views and interests, nor common means of action by which politicians might deal at a suitable level with the increasing internationalization of production and finance.

The Third Medium-term Economic Policy Program (1971–75) of the European Economic Community might have provided an opportunity for aligning national policies with respect to industrial strategy and relations with multinational firms. Nothing of the kind actually happened. Right from the outset discussion got bogged down in a comparison of macroeconomic variables without any genuine concern for consistent economic policy. For some, the whole thing was an attempt to reconcile four aims: low prices, balanced external payments, strong growth, and absence of unemployment—but this method of the so-called magic square was rather like wanting to square the circle. And yet the long-run future of the countries of the Common Market is conditioned by the agreements which one after the other get concluded and by the policies which become established (or disestablished) in the fields of agriculture, energy, new industries, etc. Similarly, the common monetary policy may, in spite (or perhaps because) of international monetary crises, prove to be a major factor of cohesion in medium-term economic policy.

Thus European economic policies are, for the time being, only very partially subject to overall regulation and alignment, and the methods of their coordination are very far from those used in French planning. Does national planning in France thereby become altogether illusory? This is a question worth considering at a time when preparations for the Seventh Plan are beginning.

European economic integration is bound to accentuate the partial character of French planning. On the assumption that the establishment of a common market proceeds, if not steadily, at least irreversibly, French planning will have to adapt its content and methods to this new situation. There will be more and more community machinery for enforcing regulations common to all the countries concerned, and its impact on French economic policy will have to be analyzed (e.g., the medium-term impact on the French economy of the creation of an economic and monetary European union). But this argument works in both directions. The growing interdependence of European economies will likewise oblige French planners to study the impact of unilateral national decisions on France's partners. For instance, on the occasion of the Washington agreements in the fall of 1971, the French authorities preferred not to devalue the franc in the wake of the dollar, so as not to widen the already appreciable gap between French and German prices. However, even if French planning should manage to take more account of the new economic interdependencies in Europe, there is reason to expect that, under pressure from the big firms and regional policies, a growing proportion of decisions concerning production, finance and monetary matters will in practice be withdrawn from the scope of planning (unless the planners greatly widen the field of their intervention at the level of the European Communities). It cannot, of course, be taken for granted that community policy will be active enough to impose a desired pattern on the internationalization of production and finance at the European level. At the national level, meanwhile, planning must remain an essential means of taking account of changing social demand and defining the role of the state in development.

Social Aspects of Development and Social Planning

The critics of economic growth state their case more or less sharply in different countries. They say it is impossible to pursue growth in the very long period, for reasons discussed below. These debates seem to go beyond a rethinking of the economic mechanisms and to reflect a crisis of society. There are indeed always optimists and pessimists in every society, and it would be interesting to discover why, at different times, the limelight is taken by one or the other of the opposing arguments (Herman Kahn or J.W. Forrester).

Attention is certainly focused nowadays on the place of man in nature (pollution, exhaustion of natural resources, food shortages); but even more prominent in the social debate, it would seem, are the problems of the relation of people to their work and to each other (cultural and social inequalities, developed and developing countries, etc.).

The fragmentation of the work process is a result of the industrial revolution. But there are alternatives to the assembly line and the whole subject of the working methods of industrial production is again open for discussion, with reference to the length of working time, the pace and intensity of work, and the manner of its organization. Similarly, the effect of economic growth on economic and social disparities is seen as ambiguous, if not as "negative." Although there is not nearly enough information on these matters, people are aware of great social inequalities and this reinforces their feeling of social injustice. The general improvement in the standard of living and the increase in the volume of disposable goods and services are not enough to counterbalance these grievances.

The inclusion of social planning in French Plans should seek to meet these concerns. The first discussions at the Planning Commission early in 1973 stressed three points: the evolution of social demand (i.e., consumption and collective services like education and health) and of the contribution of the market and nonmarket sectors; the development of collective functions in response to the needs of individuals and groups (e.g., in the fields of health, education, culture, consumer protection, etc.); and the reduction of inequalities by transfer payments and redistribution policies. The idea was to open the debate by the publication of a Social Report to be requested by the government and to serve as an official statement to be submitted to the Development Commission as the focal point in the preparation of the Seventh Plan.

But even supposing that there is enough political determination in the government to define significant aims in this field as well as means to achieve them, the planners are likely to come up against methodological difficulties. It is not so easy to quantify the social aspects of development, and there are no instruments of measurement. The Planning Commission is playing a leading part in promoting research on social indicators, both global and for separate fields. The Statistical Institute, in its turn, is trying to broaden economic models by the inclusion of social aspects; examples are the measurement of income inequalities (in connection with a medium-term projection), the analysis of the labor market and working conditions, etc. Existing economic models like FIFI will, furthermore, make it possible to test the economic consistency of social policies such as the raising of the lowest wages, alternative immigration policies, etc., but this is bound to remain a minor part of the relevant planning studies.

These methodological difficulties may well serve as a pretext in case social planning fails, but the decision to integrate social with economic planning actually raises much wider problems. French planning has always accorded a privileged position to production, and economic growth has been one of its main themes. Can the planners now reverse their customary order of priorities? And if so, will they be able to make these new aims acceptable to the ruling classes of French society and will it all lead to appropriate political choices? The preparation of the Seventh Plan will provide the first indications of what is likely to happen in these fields. If the aims are clearly defined, their achievement will no doubt entail some changes in the system of public intervention in the market economy of France, such as those discussed below.

Redefining the Role of the State in Development

Plan preparation is a gambit in the social debate. It raises, explicitly or implicitly, the question of the role of the state in the overall guidance of development. The Keynesian prescripts are losing force nowadays when governments are finding it so hard to control growth (which follows a relatively rigid path in each country) and even harder to get the better of inflation (whose pace is quickening everywhere) by means of budgetary and fiscal policy (which is supposed to regulate demand but is not very effective in doing so). Nor has monetary policy fulfilled the hopes of its advocates. There are some who ascribe these failures to the internationalization of production. Is this correct? Is the disruption of the international monetary system a cause or an effect? What, in this situation, are the responsibilities of governments, especially the most influential ones among them?

In the medium-term view, which is the one governing French Plans, the structural impact of public intervention on development is an essential element. But it is difficult to identify, because of the historically close interdependence between development in a market economy and the proliferation of government intervention. The role of the state appears decisive in the process of economic growth, but at the same time it both contradicts and consolidates the development of the market.

The norm (i.e., limit) of tax pressure formulated in the preparation of the Seventh Plan corresponds to current views on the role of public finances in growth. It serves as an overall indicator of the division between private and public activities, and acquired normative force once it had been analyzed by social groups and accepted by the government in terms of taxation and other fiscal levies. But this view of public revenue, which causes all the more resentment the higher it is, completely obscures the counterpart of that revenue, that is, the role and significance of public expenditure in development.

The extension of social planning envisaged under the Seventh Plan will no doubt lead to a change in that norm so as to enable government to meet the new responsibilities it is to take on. It appears quite possible, too, that certain expenditure now financed directly by the state will in future be financed by the private sector (e.g., telecommunications) or even revert to the market (e.g., nonurban motorways). These ideas are the subject of strong political controversy, for there are no real criteria by which to justify such shifts in the division between the public and the private sector. The more profitable activities, according to market criteria, tend to elude the public sector and there is a danger, therefore, of reinforcing inequalities in access to goods and services. Whatever happens to public expenditure and to the sources from which it is financed, the state thus has a function of vital importance in transfer payments and the redistribution of incomes.

Decentralization of decisions is another thorny problem for the planners. The problems of coordinating global and sectoral policies in the preparation of the Sixth Plan were difficult enough and found only an imperfect solution, yet they were a good deal easier than those of ensuring consistency in national and regional policies in case the government opted for genuine decentralization of decisions at regional and local levels. Planning studies on regionalization have so far always been concerned with the regional consequences of national choices in such matters as the location of jobs and the distribution of public investment. Genuine decentralization might well lead to inconsistent choices made, respectively, by local and national authorities. In preparing the Seventh Plan, therefore, new methods will have to be developed so as to allow for the government's regional reforms.

CONCLUSION

French planning is one particular form of the practices of overall economic management current in developed countries. In the case of France, the most striking feature is the public discussion associated with this system of planning, compared with the informal and unpublicized relations maintained in other countries between the managers of large concerns and government departments. Actually, this public discussion which is known as *concertation* in France does not lead to consensus among the social groups. Furthermore, planning remains partial in that a good many decisions are taken outside its purview, which means that the planners must take account of them rather than influence them. It seems difficult to determine the impact of French planning either on government economic policy or on the decisions of firms about output and investment.

Because planning deals with medium-term trends, its influence on economic policy is seldom direct. However, the pursuit of rapid growth and the curtailment of unemployment, stemming from the Plans, has certainly played an important role in French economic policy since World War II. In the same way, the "Industrial Imperative," the main theme of the Sixth Plan, inspired the decisions to restructure industrial branches which the industrialists concerned have gradually been carrying out with the assistance of the Ministry of Finance and the Ministry of Industry. Finally, the public investment programs included in the Plan serve as a point of reference for the ministries concerned during annual budget discussions with the Ministry of Finance.

Firms are less influenced by planning, first because only a small number of French enterprises prepare medium-term plans, and second because it is chiefly the big firms that are acquainted with and use the national plan. A study in 1967 of 2,000 firms showed that about 40 percent of the firms used medium-term forecasts (for four years or more), especially for investment, finance, and production; but the influence of the forecasts in the Plan was perceptible only in the big firms, most of which have planning departments and economic research departments.[26] Indirect influences also operate here because the business press and trade associations in each sector perform an intermediary role in transmitting the forecasts of the Plan. The situation is obviously different when a very oligopolistic sector elaborates a rather precise plan for the development of the market, which often is directly taken into account in the national plan (for example, energy, ferrous metallurgy, automobiles). In the competitive sectors with small firms, the impact of national planning is much weaker because the factors of poor plan implementation discussed above operate fully in these sectors.

In short, the effect of indicative planning on the decisions of economic agents appears particularly weak in the French case, and it is difficult to speak of a "self-validating" forecast.[27] At the most, one can assert that indicative planning is a way of giving directions and guidelines for economic and social development.

The political force of French Plans, therefore, is weak, but they do play an essential part in the formulation of "social norms" which, for a limited period and in any given phase of development, rule the behavior of social groups and establish a frame of reference for government action.

In preparing the Seventh Plan, French planners will have to define more precisely just where national planning finds its place between the international level, where production is in the course of powerful transformation, and the decentralized level to be expected as the result of the proposed regional reforms. The extent of social change and the current doubts about economic growth will perhaps widen the field of planning to take in the social aspects of development. Nevertheless, the difficulties of forecasting and the reserved attitude of both sides of industry work in the direction of reducing the scope of planning, and of formulating the Plan as a set of general guidelines rather than as a detailed program of economic and social policy.

NOTES

1. There are a number of good studies on the earlier experience of French planning, including Claude Gruson, *Origine et espoirs de la planification française* [Origin and Hopes of French Planning], (Paris: Dunod, 1968); Pierre Bauchet, *La planification française: du premier au sixième Plan* [French Planning: From the First to the Sixth Plan] (Paris: Editions du Seuil, 1970); and John and Anne-Marie Hackett, *Economic Planning in France* (London: Allen and Unwin; Cambridge, Mass.: Harvard University Press, 1963). Therefore, this chapter will concentrate on the current Sixth Plan and beyond.

For this first section, I have drawn on the three following recent studies of French planning: (a) Atreize (collective work organized by Paul Dubois), *La planification française en pratique* [French Planning in Practice], (Paris: Collection "Economie et Humanisme," Les éditions ouvières, 1971); (b) Yves Ullmo, "La planification nationale et les institutions politiques en France" [National Planning and Political Institutions in France], to be published in English in *Planning, Politics and Public Policy*, ed. Jack Hayward and Michael Watson (Cambridge: Cambridge University Press, forthcoming); and (c) Gabriel Mignot, *La planification française aujourd'hui* [French Planning Today], internal memorandum (Paris: Commissariat Général du Plan, 1971, duplicated).

2. France, Présidence du gouvernement, *Rapport général sur le premier Plan de modernisation et d'équipement* [General Report on the First Plan of Modernization and Equipment] (Paris: Imprimerie des journaux officiels, 1947).

3. France, Présidence du gouvernement, *Deuxième Plan de modernisation et d'équipement (1954–1957)* [Second Plan of Modernization and Equipment (1954–1957)], Law of March 27, 1956 (Paris: Imprimerie des journaux officiels, 1956).

4. France, Premier ministre, *Troisième Plan de modernisation et d'équipement (1958–1961)* [Third Plan of Modernization and Equipment (1958–1961)], Decree of March 19, 1959 (Paris: Imprimerie des journaux officiels, 1959).

5.*Troisième Plan,* p. 26.

6. France, Premier ministre, *IVème Plan de développement économique et social (1962–1965)* [Fourth Plan of Economic and Social Development (1962–1965)], Law of August 4, 1962 (Paris: Imprimerie des journaux officiels, 1962).

7. France, Premier ministre, *Vème Plan de développement économique et social (1966–1970)* [Fifth Plan of Economic and Social Development (1966–1970)], Law of November 30, 1965, 2 vols. (Paris: Imprimerie des journaux officiels, 1965).

8. France, Commissariat Général du Plan, *Rapport sur le VIème Plan de développement économique et social (1971–1975)* [Report on the Sixth Plan of Economic and Social Development (1971–1975)], Law of July 15, 1971 (Paris: Imprimerie des journaux officiels, 1971).

9. Pierre Masse, *Le Plan ou l'anti-hasard* [The Plan or Anti-risk] (Paris: Collection "Idées," Gallimard, 1965).

10. France, Commissariat Général du Plan, *Rapport du Comité du Financement pour le Vème Plan* [Report of the Committee on Finance for the Fifth Plan] (Paris: La Documentation française, 1967).

11. Raymond Courbis, "Prévisions des prix et étude sectorielle des entreprises pendant la préparation du Vème Plan" [Price Forecasting and Sectoral Study of Enterprises in the Course of the Preparation of the Fifth Plan], *Etudes et Conjoncture* (Paris: INSEE, November 1968).

12. Michel Aglietta, Raymond Courbis, and Claude Seibel, *Le modèle FIFI, Vol. I, Présentation générale et utilisation* [The FIFI model, Vol. I, General Description and Methods of Use] (Collections de l'INSEE, comptes et planification, C. 22) (Paris: INSEE, 1973).

13. Michel Mousel, "Système de modèles à moyen terme–Administrations" [System of Medium-term Models–Administration], *Statistiques et études financières,* série Orange, No. 10, second quarter of 1973 (Ministère de l'Economie et des Finances).

14. Antoine Coutière, Denis Fouquet, Philippe Rossignol, and Patrick Roux-Vaillard, *Le modèle FIFI-TOF (version non intégrée)* [The FIFI-TOF model (Non-integrated Version)] (Paris: INSEE, Direction de la Prevision, 1973, duplicated).

15. Raymond Courbis and Jean Claude Prager, *Analyse régionale et planification nationale: le project de modèle REGINA* [Regional Analysis and National Planning: Draft of the REGINA Model] (Collections de l'INSEE, série No. 12) (Paris: INSEE, 1973).

16. France, INSEE, Groupe de recherche macroéconomique de la Direction de la Prévision, *Présentation de STAR (Schéma théorique d'accumulation et de répartition)* [Presentation of STAR, a Theoretical Model of Accumulation and Distribution] (Paris: Ministère de l'Economie et des Finances, 1972, duplicated).

17. France, INSEE and Commissariat Général du Plan, *Les indicateurs*

associés au VIème Plan, revue trimestrielle [The Indicators Associated with the Sixth Plan, Quarterly Review] (Paris: INSEE).

18. *Rapport du VIème Plan,* pp. 20–39.

19. *Rapport général sur le premier Plan,* pp. 100–101.

20. France, Commissariat Général du Plan, *Le développement industriel* [Industrial Development] (Paris: La Documentation française, 1968).

21. France, Comité interministériel des entreprises publiques, *Rapport sur les entreprises publiques* [Report on Public Enterprises], often known as the NORA Report (Paris: La Documentation française, 1968).

22. Jean Jacques Branchu, "Les charges des entreprises françaises, essai de comparaison internationale" [The Costs of French Firms, Attempt at an International Comparison], *Economie et Statistique,* No. 4 (Paris: INSEE, September 1969).

23. John H. McArthur and Bruce R. Scott, *Industrial Planning in France* (Boston: Division of Research, Graduate School of Business Administration, Harvard University, 1969; Paris: Les Editions d'organisation, 1970).

24. *Rapport sur le VIème Plan,* pp. 11–30.

25. These projections are set out, with comments, in the following two documents: (a) France, Commissariat Général du Plan, *Projections économiques pour 1975 associées au VIème Plan* [Economic Projections for 1975 Associated with the Sixth Plan] (Paris: La Documentation française, 1971); (b) France, Institut National de la Statistique et des Etudes Economiques, *Rapport technique sur les projections associées au VIème Plan* [Technical Report on the Projections Associated with the Sixth Plan] (Collections de l'INSEE, C.24–25) (Paris: INSEE, 1973).

26. Cf. Jean-Jacques Carré, Paul Dubois, and Edmond Malinvaud, *La croissance française* [French Growth] (Paris: Editions de Seuil, 1972), Ch. 14 on the role of economic planning and information, pp. 577–82.

27. Cf. Fernand Martin, "The Information Effect of Economic Planning," *Canadian Journal of Economics and Political Science* 30, 3 (August 1964): 339; and Richard B. Du Boff, "The Decline of Economic Planning in France," *Western Political Quarterly* 21, 1 (March 1968): 99.

Comments on
Claude Seibel's
Chapter

E.S. Kirschen

Seibel's excellent chapter on French planning raises a problem of definition: what is the common denominator, if any, between Western and Eastern planning?

In socialist countries, planning is a central part of economic policy, for both theoretical and practical reasons: the marketplace, while providing most useful information on consumers' preferences and on foreign supply and demand, does not help much in the choices affecting investment and technology.

In the West, with the exception of France and the Netherlands (for something like five years in the late 1940s), planning is that small fraction of economic policy which concerns the objective of growth and the ancillary objective of industrial modernization. It may also include an element of centrally made regional policy and pretend to be busy with the fads of the day, e.g., nuclear power in 1955 (much too early) or aid to agricultural or industrial lame ducks.

In my mind, the term planning does cover very different concepts, and the confusion is mainly due to the French (a rare situation for the heirs of Descartes).

THE FRENCH CIRCUMSTANCES OF 1946

The first postwar French election provided a Parliament consisting roughly of 30 percent Communists, 30 percent Socialists, 30 percent Christian Democrats, and 10 percent various factions of the former Right and Center. The decision to plan the economy—or rather the economic reconstruction of the country—is the child of three fathers, Attlee, Pétain, and Stalin.

The British prime minister in those days enjoyed in French eyes all the prestige owed to the leader of an unconquered and victorious country, and the non-Marxist socialism which nationalized British coal, electricity, gas, and railways appealed to the French government without antagonizing the French industrialists, who did not mind throwing overboard money-losing colleagues.

Hiding behind Pétain's cloak, a number of enterprises (but not entire branches of activity) had thrown their luck in with the Nazi European concept. Thus, the nationalization of the Renault works and of some large banks was not based on overall economic concepts of control by the state, but conceived as punishment for specific "collaborators" and as revenge for their more patriotic employees.

Lastly, Stalin's Soviet Union had borne the full weight of the German military onslaught, and its industry had survived. Soviet central planning, much derided in France when it was started in the early thirties, had proved remarkably resilient. It provided a logical and coherent framework, supplementing British empiricism and French stochastic lack of patriotism.

The head planner chosen was the strong willed industrialist Jean Monnet, of later European fame. With good political backing and an efficient group of civil servants, he produced a central plan emphasizing modernization (the French had entered the war in 1939 with an economy not much changed since 1913) and concentrating on a small number of key sectors, while the rest was supposed to follow. There was hardly any national accounting, no input-output, no econometrics, no academic background.

The French economy did improve, but not faster at first than that of, let us say, neighboring Belgium, for which central planning was then anathema.

PLANNING IN THE FIFTIES AND THE SIXTIES

Political influences in favor of planning faded away very quickly from 1948 onwards in France. The Socialist party became weaker, while the Communists, though remaining numerous, were left in perennial opposition. The Center and later the Right reasserted themselves.

In the government administration, the traditional Ministries—mainly Finance, but also Economic Affairs and Agriculture—regained the powers they had yielded to the upstart Planning Commissariat. Monnet's successor fell afoul of De Gaulle, and gradually the name of the central plan manager became less and less known in France at large.

Meanwhile, the sophistication of the successive plans increased enormously. The university caught up with the times, and provided intellectually stimulating discussions. But planning was reduced to the status of providing a rather useful talking forum between government and some industries. No binding decisions are taken, whether on the government's own investment plans, or on industrial commitments (with the possible exception of steel), or on wages—as the labor unions do not feel part of a system which to them smacks of paternalism.

The all important objective of growth has several times been sacrificed to price stability or balance of payments equilibrium, and anyhow the West German example shows that fast expansion and modernization are possible without planning.

But, like old soldiers, administrative institutions never die.

THE FRENCH SIXTH PLAN

The objectives of that plan are shown in Seibel's table 6–4, about which I shall make a few comments.

1. The plan is medium-term, does not include yearly installments, and has no formal links with the yearly state budgets. In fact, short-term forecasting seems to fall between two stools.

2. Full employment is emphasized as a fundamental objective, but the marginal worker, in France as in the whole of continental Northwest Europe, is now an immigrant from a Mediterranean country.

3. Some of the objectives mentioned are genuine, in the sense that they are closely linked to the choices of the voters, e.g., growth, full employment, the reduction of the workweek, price stability, and investment in housing. Other "objectives" are in fact policy instruments, e.g., public finance (although credit and the exchange rate are not mentioned), while others still are intermediate (irrelevant in Tinbergen's terminology) variables, e.g., savings. Thus, the terminology is somewhat confusing.

4. What about the regional aspects?

THE FRENCH SEVENTH PLAN

1. Here the impression is that planning is running after politically important subjects, but not providing any leadership. Kudos are sought by introducing humanism, and the priority of the growth objective, evident in the First Plan and stressed in the following ones, is now questioned—just as in Britain where intellectuals now pretend, in sour grapes fashion, not to be really interested in the elusive "expansion."

2. French planning seems now to be retreating not only from politics, but also from forecasting in figures. The role of the State in the economy seems to be withering (but without a Marxist revolutionary phase) and France feels itself, according to Seibel, becoming a part of integrated Europe (may he be right!).

3. Social indicators would be a most useful innovation in economic theory as well as in economic policy. Everybody is getting bored with the concept of a Gross National Product which is moving further and further away from National Welfare. The main problem is to arrive at a set of meaningful and consistent indicators—for the East just as much as for the West. The usual mixture of

suicide rates, divorce rates, crime rates, water pollution (what about wine pollution?), and auto ownership rates is very difficult to interpret (an increase in divorces may be a good thing in Italy and a bad thing in Sweden). May the French planners insert their social indicators during the lifetime of their Seventh Plan, and French planning will live forever through its by-products.

Chapter Seven

Planning in Japan

Ryutaro Komiya

When people speak of "economic planning" in Japan they usually have in mind the national economic plan prepared by the Economic Planning Agency once every two or three years. Yet in my view these national plans are not so much a "plan" in the usual sense of the term, and are not as important as they appear at first. Those who are not well informed about economic policymaking in Japan might think that the Japanese government largely follows its medium-term (usually five years) national economic plan when making annual or day-to-day economic policy decisions. In fact, this is not the case. In recent years especially, the national economic plan is becoming less and less relevant to actual economic policy, at least so far as macroeconomic and sectoral quantitative indices are concerned.

This does not mean, however, the Japanese economy is run without much governmental planning. The Japanese government intervenes widely in individual sectors, industries, or regions, and there is much planning on industry as well as regional bases. Many of the plans in individual fields appear to be quite effective in channeling resources into particular industries or regions.

In the following three sections of this chapter, Japan's national economic planning, regional planning, and planning for individual industries will be discussed respectively. In the last section a few concluding remarks will be made.

NATIONAL ECONOMIC PLANS

The Multiplicity of Plans and the Reasons for Underestimation

The multiplicity of Japan's national economic plans is perhaps well known. During the eighteen years from 1955 to 1973, the Japanese government

Financial support for this study from the Research Fund of the Faculty of Economics, the University of Tokyo, is gratefully acknowledged.

announced seven medium- or long-term national economic plans. Table 7–1 gives a brief summary of these plans.[1]

Some of the Japanese words appearing in these plans are rhetoric without much substantive meaning and are difficult to translate into English. Even so, the words in table 7–1 still indicate what Japanese plan-makers considered the most important policy goals at the time of preparing each plan, and reflect the changing atmosphere of economic policymaking in postwar Japan. In the early postwar years, the emphasis was on industrial growth, saving, investment, and export. Later the priority shifted to "balanced growth" (whatever that means), price stability, and international cooperation, and more recently, welfare, quality of life, and environment have been included among most important policy goals.

The natural question will be raised why there are so many national economic plans. An immediate answer is that although each of the plans listed in table 7–1 (except the ten-year National Income Doubling Plan) covered about five years, after its introduction the actual rate of growth surpassed the planned rate substantially, especially in the case of earlier plans, and planning indices became obsolete within a year or two after implementation.[a] Especially in the case of plans II, IV, and V, the actual level of private investment in plant and equipment by far surpassed the planned targets. Later an unexpected rapid increase in exports and huge balance-of-payments surpluses were the main factors which made the plans obsolete very quickly. Also, rapid and unexpected changes in the socioeconomic as well as external conditions made it necessary to change the policy goals declared in the national economic plan.

Why then have Japan's national economic plans persistently underestimated the rate of growth, at least until around 1970? First, in the period immediately after the war, most Japanese were not confident not only of the future of the economy but also of the nation and themselves. The prewar level of per capita real income was regained only around 1955: of the nations which fought World War II, severely defeated Japan took the longest time to recover from war destruction. The target rate of growth of 5 percent given in the Five-Year Plan for Economic Self-Support, the first official economic plan, was severely criticized as too optimistic and as unrealistic by intellectuals, journalists, and leaders of nongovernment parties. Such a criticism was not unrelated to a Marxian view of "monopoly capitalism," according to which the world capitalist system, which entered the period of "a general crisis of capitalism" in 1930, was bound to fall into stagnation and could not continue to grow without undergoing a proletarian revolution or at least a drastic social reform.

Second, having experienced unusually high rates of growth for some time

---

[a]How the plan underestimated the growth rate may be illustrated by the fact that if the "ambitious" (according to the criticisms at the time of its announcement) National Income Doubling Plan had been carried out as planned, the real GNP in 1970, the terminal year of the Plan, would have been only about 70 percent of its actual level.

Table 7-1. Japan: Summary of National Economic Plans

Name of Plan	*Planning period and date of publication*	*Planned and actual real rates of growth (percentage)*	*Objectives of Plan*	*Major policy problems to be solved*
I. Five-Year Plan for Economic Self-Support	1956–60; December 1955	5.0; 9.1	Economic self-support (meaning growth without U.S. aid); full employment.	(a) modernization of productive capacity, (b) development of international trade, (c) increased domestic supply (of raw materials), and (d) economy in consumption (increased saving).
II. New Long-Range Economic Plan	1958–62; December 1957	6.5; 10.1	Maximum growth; improvement of living standard; full employment.	(a) Strengthening of industrial base, (b) expansion of heavy and chemical industries, (c) promotion of export, and (d) increased supply of saving.
III. National Income Doubling Plan	1961–70; December 1960	7.2; 11.0	Same as in Plan II, above.	(a) Investment in social overhead capital, (b) modernization of national industrial structure, (c) international trade and cooperation, (d) betterment of human capabilities and advancement of science and technology, and (e) mitigating the so-called dualistic structure[a] and increasing social stability.

(continued)

Table 7-1 continued

Name of Plan	Planning period and date of publication	Planned and actual real rates of growth (percentage)	Objectives of Plan	Major policy problems to be solved
IV. Medium-Term Economic Plan	1964–68; January 1965	8.1; 11.0	Correction of distortions (arising out of rapid economic growth).	(a) Modernization of low-productivity sectors, (b) efficient use of labor force, and (c) improvement in the quality of life.
V. Economic and Social Development Plan	1967–71; March 1967	8.2; 12.0	Development toward a balanced and enriched economy and society.	(a) Price stability, (b) economic efficiency, and (c) advancement of social development.
VI. New Economic and Social Development Plan	1970–75; May 1970	10.6	Establishing a humane economy and society through balanced economic development.	(a) Improved economic efficiency through international specialization, (b) price stability, (c) promotion of social development, and (d) maintenance of proper rate of growth and cultivation of the basis for further development.
VII. Basic Economic and Social Plan	1973–77; February 1973	9.4	Enhancement of civil welfare; international cooperation.	(a) Creation of a rich environment, (b) ensuring a comfortable and stable civil life, (c) price stability, and (d) international cooperation.

Sources: Japan, Economic Council, *Economic Planning in Japan* (in Japanese) (Tokyo, 1969); and Japan, Economic Planning Agency, *The Basic Economic and Social Plan, 1973–77* (Tokyo, 1973).

Note:

aThe dualistic or dual structure of the Japanese economy refers to the coexistence of modernized big business, on the one hand, and more or less traditional, labor-intensive small business and small-peasant agriculture, on the other. The disparity in wage rates between the big-business and small-business sectors is generally considered a reflection of the dualistic structure of the Japanese economy.

immediately after the war, still an overwhelming majority of knowledgeable Japanese did not believe that such high rates would continue to prevail. Especially those who belonged to the older generations (those who finished university education before the war) continued to criticize the target rates of growth in national economic plans as overly optimistic well into the mid-1960s.[b] It was argued that a high rate of growth was possible in the reconstruction period because capital expenditures to repair war-damaged plant, equipment, and social overhead capital could raise GNP very quickly, whereas after the reconstruction period the increase in GNP could be achieved only by substantial new net investment and/or technological progress.

Another argument was that the Japanese economy was in a catching-up process immediately after the war, making use of a large backlog of new technologies developed in the United States and Europe during the war. Once such a backlog was exhausted, technological progress in Japan would be slowed down.

Pessimists also emphasized the balance-of-payments constraint. They thought that Japan's exports could not continue to grow indefinitely at a much faster rate than the total volume of world trade, and therefore the rate of growth of Japan's raw material and fuel imports, vital for Japan's industrial growth, would be restricted.

Looking back from the hindsight of today, it is obvious that the majority, including the plan-makers, underestimated not only the growth potential of the Japanese economy, but also the adaptability of the economy to changing circumstances and the resultant structural changes. The national economic plans predicted more or less correctly the directions of the changes in the industrial structure, the industrial distribution of the labor force, and the composition of exports, but almost always underestimated the extent of such changes.[c]

Contents of a National Economic Plan

To facilitate the understanding of the nature of national economic planning in Japan, I will briefly describe the contents of the latest *Basic Economic and Social Plan*. The Plan is published as a government document of about 170 pages, and consists primarily of two components. The first two tables of the Plan, reproduced here as tables 7–2 and 7–3, summarize these two components. First, table 7–2 gives the plan targets for various items in each of the four major planning areas. For example, under the heading of "creation of a rich environment" (see the column for "major policy problems to be solved" in table

[b]Osamu Shimomura, Tadao Uchida, Hisao Kanamori, and I were among the minority optimists.

[c]Hence it is a mistake to think that the Japanese government intentionally underestimated the growth rate in order to boast about the overfulfillment afterwards. Not only the government but also the majority of Japanese underestimated the growth and structural changes, and those critical of the government often did so more than the plan-makers.

Table 7-2. Japan: Targets of the Basic Economic and Social Plan, 1973–77

Area	*Item*	*Targets to be reached in 1977*
I. Creation of a Rich Environment		
Preservation of the environment	Air pollution due to sulfur oxides	(a) Environmental Quality Standards more stringent than those presently in force shall be established to avoid adverse effects on human health. (b) In the Big Three Bay Areas[a] the amount of discharge shall be reduced to about half of the 1970 level.
	Water pollution	(a) At least the present water quality standards or the provisional targets shall be met during the period of the plan, with a view to restoration of a situation of no adverse effects on health or living environment by 1985. (b) In the Big Three Urban Areas[b] the BOD[c] discharge load will be reduced to about one-half of the 1970 level.
Living environment facilities	City parks	4.7 sq.m. per capita (estimated figure for 1972, 3 sq.m.; goal for 1985, 9 sq.m.).
	Sewerage systems	Service to 42 percent of the population (estimated figure for 1972, 19 percent).
	Disposal of refuse Human wastes	Within areas covered by plans: 100 percent sanitary disposal in 1975 (estimated figure for 1972, 87 percent).
	Combustible refuse	100 percent disposal in 1980 (estimated figure for 1972, 81 percent).
Nationwide transportation and communications network	Super Express Railways (*Shinkansen*)	Extension to total length of approximately 1,900 km. in operation (construction target by 1985, about 7,000 km.).
	National Expressways	Extension to total length of approximately 3,100 km. in operation (construction target by 1985, about 10,000 km.).
	Telephone subscription	Catching up with backlog demands.
Improvement of agricultural and forest environments	Agricultural land	Doubling of hectarage which supports highly efficient farming (approx. 1.2 million ha. in 1972).
	Reserve forests	Designation of 10 percent more reserve forest area (6.9 million ha. in 1972).
II. Ensuring a Comfortable and Stable Civil Life		
Social security	Ratio of transfer income to national income	8.8 percent (estimated figure for 1972, 6.0 percent).

Table 7-2 continued

Area	Item	Targets to be reached in 1977
	Pensions[d]	
	Employees' Pension Plan	From 1973, a standard monthly pension of ¥50,000, with further improvements thereafter.
	National Pension Plan	A level commensurate with that of the Employee's Pension Plan.
	Non-contributory Old Age Pension	¥5,000 a month in 1973, ¥10,000 a month in 1975, and further improvements thereafter.
	Social Welfare facilities	Expansion of facilities so as to accommodate all of those elderly bedridden people, the seriously mentally or physically handicapped, and others who need care in them.
Housing	Publicly financed housing	Construction of four million new units.
	Housing developments	Early completion of large-scale "New Town" housing developments and other smaller projects already under way in the Tokyo and Osaka metropolitan areas covering approximately 30,000 ha. (to accommodate a total population of about four million), and commencement of other new projects.
Work week and retirement	Five-day work week	Promote general adoption by employers.
	Raising of compulsory retirement age	Promote general adoption of compulsory retirement at age 60 (presently 55).
Education and sports	Educational facilities	Improvement of facilities for kindergarten, primary, and secondary compulsory education, and higher education. To establish at least one medical school (or Faculty of Medicine in a university) in every prefecture.
	Community sports facilities	Provision over a period of about 10 years of readily accessible sports facilities such as athletic grounds, gymnasiums, swimming pools, playgrounds, etc.
III. Price Stability		
	Consumer prices	Average annual rise of not more than 5 percent.
	Wholesale prices	Stability: at most a moderate, unaccelerated rise.
IV. Promotion of International Collaboration		
	Balance of Payments	Equilibrium in the basic balance (balance on basic transactions) within three years.

(continued)

Table 7-2 continued

Area	Item	Targets to be reached in 1977
	Economic aid	Early realization within the period of the plan of a flow corresponding to 1 percent of gross national product (GNP).
	Official development assistance	Raising its ratio to GNP to a level comparable to those of other countries by an early date, attainment of the international goal of 0.7 percent over a longer period, and improvement of the terms and conditions of assistance.

Source: Table 1 of *The Basic Economic and Social Plan 1973-77*, pp. 15-17, with a few changes in wording.

Notes:

[a]The Big Three Bay Areas: areas along Tokyo Bay, Osaka Bay, and the northern part of Ise Bay.

[b]The Big Three Urban Areas: the part of the Kanto Area along the coast, the Tokai coastline, and the Osaka-Kobe area.

[c]BOD: biochemical oxygen demand; an index of water pollution.

[d]The Employees' Pension Plan covers employees in larger establishments, and the National Pension Plan covers those not included in the Employees' Plan: self-employed and their family workers, day laborers and workers in very small establishments. (Footnote supplied by the author.)

7-1), the target levels for improvement in air pollution, water pollution, city parks, etc., are stipulated. Similarly target levels are given for times under the other three broad planning objectives, "ensuring a comfortable and stable civil life," "price stability," and "international cooperation."

Later in the Plan, the policy measures required for achieving each target are explained. But the explanation given in the Plan is largely qualitative rather than quantitative, and sometimes quite vague. Rhetorical and euphemistic words difficult to translate, or almost meaningless words such as "take necessary measures," "promote coordination," "consider improving such and such," appear repeatedly. Moreover, on important policy issues hotly debated currently, the Plan often avoids indicating the future directions of government policy. For example, on the problem of the price of land, which has been rising very rapidly recently and causing social unrest among urban population, the Plan says little beyond what has already been said. On the price policies of public corporations such as national railways and on the problems of cartels and resale price maintenance, all of which are considered by many Japanese as the crucial areas for policies to curb inflation, the Plan spends several paragraphs, but says almost nothing meaningful. Or, while emphasizing very strongly international cooperation and avoidance of protectionism, the Plan says nothing about Japan's own agricultural protection. But, as explained later, the national economic plan under Japan's present institutional setting is bound to be elusive on such specific policy issues.

Second, table 7–3 gives what is called by the Plan a "profile" of the Japanese economy in 1977. Here the figures in 1977 for GNP (in current and constant prices) and its components, the balance of payments, the price deflator for household consumption, the ratio of taxes and other obligations to national income, and several other items are given. These figures are backed up by more detailed figures in later tables and an appendix of the Plan, which are based upon extensive macroeconometric simulation studies. The appendix of the Plan gives detailed national income accounts and an industry breakdown of output and employment in 1977. It is the failure of this part of the earlier national plans to predict the future course of the economy accurately enough that caused the large discrepancies between actual and planned figures within a few years after the introduction of the Plan, and quickly made the Plan obsolete. Earlier plans gave these figures as "planned" or "targets," but in recent plans these figures for the terminal year of the planning period are called "predicted" or "estimates."

Apart from the large discrepancies in the past, some academic economists are critical of the procedure by which the estimates in recent national economic plans were derived. Although the general framework of the macroeconometric model used in the projection was made public, the procedure in deriving the predicted figures for 1977 was not. Only a few of the values for exogenous parameters and policy variables used in the predictions are explicitly given in the Plan (see table 7–3). It is difficult, therefore, for outsiders to evaluate the overall validity of the predictions. The premises under which the predictions are made should be made public, according to the criticism. Especially in the case of the estimates for price deflators, some doubts have been entertained as to compatibility with other estimates: it is generally thought that for an obvious political reason the government chose artificially low figures for the rate of price increase.

Process of Plan-making

To clarify the nature of Japan's national economic plans, it is necessary to describe the process by which the plan is prepared and announced.

The formal process is that first the prime minister requests the Economic Council to prepare a national plan, and then the Council presents its report to the prime minister. In the case of the latest plan, Prime Minister Kakuei Tanaka requested the Council in August 1972 to prepare "a new long-term economic plan which aimed at enhancement of civil welfare and promotion of international cooperation, in view of rapid changes in the domestic and external circumstances."

The Economic Council is an advisory committee reporting to the prime minister, and consisted in 1972 of about thirty members outside of the

Table 7-3. Japan: Profile of the Economy in 1977[a]

	1970 Actual figures	1970 Percentages	1977 Estimates	1977 Percentages	1973-77 Average annual rate of increase (percentage)	1961-70 Average annual rate of increase (percentage)
I. Given Conditions and Policies						
Labor force (persons)	51,700,000		54,100,000		0.8	1.3
Government fixed capital formation (1965 prices)	¥5 trillion		b		15.5	13
Government transfers to households (current prices)	¥3 trillion	(percentage of national income, 5.3)	¥12 trillion	(percentage of national income, 8.8)	22.0	18
Private investment for pollution control (1965 prices)	¥0.2 trillion		¥2 trillion		34.1	
II. Profile of Economy						
Gross national product (1965 prices)	¥58 trillion		¥105 trillion		about 9	11
Gross national product (current prices)[c]	¥73 trillion	100	¥183 trillion	100	14	16
Personal consumption expenditures	¥38 trillion	51	¥95 trillion	52	14	15
Government fixed capital formation	¥6 trillion	9	¥23 trillion	13	18	18
Private plant and equipment investment	¥15 trillion	20	¥28 trillion	15	11	17
Private housing investment	¥5 trillion	7	¥17 trillion	9	20	22
Exports of goods and services and factor income received from abroad	¥9 trillion	12	¥21 trillion	11	14	17

(less) Imports of goods and services and factor income paid abroad	¥8 trillion	11	¥19 trillion	10	17	16
Balance of payments on current account[d]	$2.4 billion		$5.9 billion		not more than 5	5.7
Personal consumption expenditure deflator[e]	132		187			
Deflator for private inventory stocks[e]	109		126		about 2	1.4
Ratio of social insurance premiums to national income (percentage)	4.6		7.3			
Tax and non-tax (social insurance premiums, etc.) obligations (as percentage of national income)	21.7		f			
Balance of government revenue and expenditure (current prices)	0		-¥6 trillion[g]			

Source: Table 2 of *The Basic Economic and Social Plan, 1973–77,* with a few changes in wording.

Notes:

[a] All figures are for the fiscal year, April 1 to March 31.

[b] Cumulative amount of investment between 1973 and 1977: ¥90 trillion (1973 prices), including Okinawa.

[c] Figures in 1977 include Okinawa Prefecture. Elsewhere Okinawa has not been included unless otherwise noted.

[d] Difference between receipts and payments on current account; positive figure indicates a surplus.

[e] Index figures with 1965 = 100.

[f] The Plan envisages a 3 percent increase from 1973 to 1977.

[g] Negative figure indicates a deficit.

government. Its overwhelming majority were presidents and chairmen of big corporations and ex-government officials.[d] Its *Basic Economic and Social Plan* was reported to the prime minister in February 1973, and at the Cabinet meeting a few days later the Plan was formally adopted without any modification "as the guiding principle for managing the national economy during fiscal years 1973 through 1977."

The above might give an impression that the Economic Council or its members are responsible for preparing the plan. In reality, it may be said without much exaggeration that the Council members' involvement in plan-making is minimal. In the first place, the Council has many subcommittees. The total number of members of these subcommittees amounted almost to two hundred in the case of the latest plan. They are again dominated by men from big business and ex-government officials. Preparation and deliberation of the plan were done mainly at meetings of these subcommittees. The Council itself met only a few times: usually it simply approves whatever is prepared by subcommittees or by the secretariat. Membership on the Council is largely honorary. After all, most members are very busy men with their own business or profession and can afford little time to study national economic problems carefully. The last point also applies to the members of the subcommittees.

Hence, second, it is only natural that the secretariat for the Council, the Economic Planning Agency (EPA)—or more precisely its Bureau of Comprehensive Planning—dominates the process of plan-making. In addition to the officials of EPA, officials of various ministries and agencies attend the meetings whenever matters on which they have jurisdiction are discussed. Together with officials of EPA, they act as the secretariat of subcommittees: they collect necessary materials, prepare documents, and draft plans. Indeed, the ministries and agencies have a very strong voice on subjects relevant to them.

It might be asked what happens if the opinions of the members of the Council or its subcommittees are opposed to those of government officials. Such a conflict rarely happens. All members know that the officials of ministries and agencies have virtual vetos, and do not waste time fighting against them. To begin with, EPA selects as members of the Council or its subcommittees only those who will behave well, that is, those who cooperate with government officials. It is easy to recruit cooperative and more or less capable members, since being a member of the Council, one of its subcommittees, or any other governmental committee carries some public (rather than professional) prestige, although pecuniary remuneration is negligible. Also, for those outside of the

[d]Eighteen members were from big business (most of them presidents or chairmen of firms); four, previously high-ranking government officials; five, academics (four of them professors emeriti, that is, retired from universities); and two, labor union representatives. Even this distribution is more diversified than the situation before; at the time of the Medium-Term Economic Plan (1965), of thirty members of the Council all were executives of big business or ex-government officials, except two professors emeriti.

government, the access to information is often an important advantage drawn from being a member of a government committee.

The Nature of the National
Economic Plan

The two components of Japan's national economic plan mentioned above must be distinguished in discussing the nature of the national plan. On the one hand, the national plan is a compilation of current opinions on economic policy issues, and to the extent that the planning targets for specific policy aims (see table 7–2) reflect the conclusions which have been reached by the various councils and ministries having jurisdiction over them (see p. 209), such targets in the plan are more or less thought of as something to be achieved through governmental efforts during the planning period. But since such planning targets are discussed and set by the respective councils and ministries first, and since the national plan is simply a collection of such planning targets in individual fields already at hand, with little attempt at coordination and elimination of inconsistencies among targets, it is misleading to consider the national plan as setting binding policy targets in individual policy areas.

On the other hand, the national economic plan gives "estimates" for macroeconomic variables such as the rate of growth of real GNP, its components, the balance of payments, the price indices, and so on during the planning period. This part of the plan is a prediction or a long-term forecast, as reliable or unreliable as a long-term weather forecast, of the future state of the economy, with some flavor of wishful thinking added.

The national economic plan is not binding: nobody feels much obliged to observe, or be responsible for, the figures given in the plan. This is especially true of estimates for macroeconomic variables (in table 7–3), but is true also of planning targets for specific policy aims (in table 7–2). The Ministry of Finance, the most powerful government ministry in economic policy matters, has not been enthusiastic about rigid economic planning, and for understandable reasons. Other government offices too have considered the national economic plan as primarily a forecast rather than a rigid plan which must be followed faithfully. I will explain the reasons why the national plan has been considered as nonbinding, first in regard to the private sector, and then in regard to the public sector.

Private Sector. Past macroeconometric experience shows that it is difficult to predict variables pertaining primarily to the private sector more or less accurately for planning purposes beyond the time span of six months or at most one year. Two major sources of errors in macroeconometric prediction are (i) changes in the economic structure over time, or the failure of behavioral equations in the macroeconometric model used to give good estimates for the future, even when exogenous variables to be given from outside the model are correctly predicted; and (ii) errors in predicting exogenous variables. My general impression is that for private investment in plant and equipment, certain categories of inventory investment, and price deflators, errors due to (i) are substantial; whereas for exports and the balance of payments, the main source of errors is (ii).

The fact that errors of type (i) have been substantial, indicates that we do not yet know the mechanism of the economy accurately enough for the purpose of planning. Private firms in contemporary Japan are still a fertile source of energy and creative initiatives, and their activities can often be unpredictable.

Suppose, for example, that in one year private investment in plant and equipment in a certain sector rises sharply beyond the "planned" level. Should private investment then be restrained, and if the answer is yes, by what means? At least in Japan, in most cases the government does not know whether it is desirable from a national economic point of view to restrain such an unexpected rise in private investment beyond the "planned" level. The government may tighten the money supply if it expects overall inflationary pressure to develop as a result of a general rise in private investment. Or it may intervene in a particular sector if an obvious excess capacity situation is foreseen as a result of too high a rate of investment there. Generally speaking, however, the "planned" figures in the medium-term national economic plan have never been considered as binding targets according to which the government should regulate the variables pertaining to the private sector.

In addition to unexpected developments from within the Japanese economy, there are errors of type (ii), that is errors in predicting exogenous variables. From a planning point of view, the international economic conditions surrounding Japan several years ahead are especially difficult to predict. Unpredictable changes in world economic conditions can affect substantially the course of an economy, such as the Japanese, heavily dependent on international economic relations.

For these reasons the Japanese government has not paid much attention to the national economic plan when making short-run policy decisions affecting the private sector. Its macroeconomic policies, fiscal and monetary policies in particular, are determined primarily by considering the levels of domestic effective demand and employment, the balance of payments and movements of price indices. When the government steers fiscal and monetary policies watching these macroeconomic indicators, it can naturally end up with overall and sectoral growth rates which are quite different from those given in the medium-term plan, and discrepancies accumulate as time goes by.

It must also be noted that for many variables pertaining to the private sector, the government may not really have at hand policy instruments which can be used to correct effectively the actual course of these variables when they deviate from their "planned" course. Just consider, for example, Japan's huge balance-of-payments surpluses in the last few years, and how difficult and painful it has been to reduce them. Another example is price inflation: not only in Japan but in many countries of the world governments are having great difficulties in restraining the rise in prices.

Public Sector. It might be asked whether the government follows the plan at least as far as variables pertaining to the public sector: what is the use of the plan if the government itself does not feel obliged to observe, for example, the planned level of its own public investment in individual fields?

There are several reasons why even the planned levels of variables pertaining to the public sector are not closely followed by government ministries and agencies, except possibly at the very beginning of the planning period. First, when the actual GNP, the level of private investment, the balance of payments, and so on differ substantially from their predicted levels, it is meaningless or even harmful to stick to the plan only so far as the public sector is concerned. To do so will destroy the balance between the public and private sectors.[e]

Second, the government budget and "investment and financing plan" are voted upon by the National Diet on a rigid annual basis. Only in very special cases does the Diet allow the government to make commitments on capital expenditures beyond the fiscal year. In a democratic society, the Diet and the government budget should respond to the changing needs of its citizens, and the principle of annual deliberation of the government budget has never been challenged. In particular, the parties opposing the government party are against long-run commitments and planning, in the hope that they will win power in the next election and will change economic policies drastically.[2]

Third, the Ministry of Finance, and especially its Bureau of Budget, the most influential government office on the matter of economic policy, has a tradition of economy in, and non-commitment to, public expenditures. Officials of the Bureau of Budget always try to economize and curtail public expenditures in the face of other ministries' and agencies' requests for appropriations. Budget officials think that if the Ministry of Finance once in some way commits itself to a long-term expenditure plan, it would be difficult to cancel or reduce the expenditures for a certain item previously agreed upon in the plan, whereas there will always be requests for new or additional appropriations when circumstances change. Thus according to their view a long-run plan for government expenditure or public investment will give rise to an expansionary bias or a tendency for "increasing fiscal rigidity" which they want to avoid.[f]

[e]This is what actually happened to some degree. As a result of an unexpectedly high rate of growth of the private sector, the public sector in general has been lagging behind, and especially public investment in social overhead capital and public policies against environmental pollution have so far been very inadequate.

[f]This is also the reason why Ministry of Finance officials purposely try to underestimate the rate of economic growth in the government's annual economic outlook, which is the basis for the government budget. If a high rate of growth is expected, tax revenue will also

Also, not only do officials of the Ministry of Finance have an inclination to dislike long-term fiscal planning, but long-run planning is really difficult in regard to certain fiscal expenditures. Certain items in the budget, such as rice-price supports, national medical insurance, price and investment policies of national railways, social security and welfare programs, and national defense plans, have long been difficult political issues, and very hotly debated during the process of budget compilation every year. Anyone who knows the political conflicts on these issues can understand that it is really difficult to make a long-run quantitative plan for these expenditure items.

Forecast Rather than Planning

Thus nobody considers the national economic plan as a rigid, binding plan which must be followed by the government. When the Ministry of Finance makes decisions on the annual budget, the Bank of Japan on money supply, and the Ministry of International Trade and Industry (MITI) on industrial policies, they pay little attention to the national economic plan. There is not much substance in the national plan which can be usefully referred to when government ministries and agencies make important policy decisions in their respective fields. Or putting it differently, it appears that government ministries and agencies other than the Economic Planning Agency tend to try to incorporate in the national economic plan as little as possible of those elements which they consider may bind them rigidly and undesirably in the future.

Therefore, Japan's national economic plan should be interpreted as a long-term forecast, with some flavor of wishful thinking of plan-makers, as far as its quantitative aspects are concerned. Interpreted in this way, it is not surprising that the government publishes a five-year national plan as often as once every two or three years. This is similar to a long-run (one to three months) weather forecast announced once or twice a month.

The Reason for the National Plans
and Their Effects on Growth

If the national economic plans have not been intended to regulate the variables pertaining to either the private or the public sector, one might ask, first, what is the reason for or the use of such plans—what functions are they

---

be expected to increase substantially, the income-elasticity of tax revenues being greater than unity. This will invite bolder requests for appropriations as well as for tax relief. Obviously such purposeful underestimation is not a rational step in planning if a single optimizing body is going to make a plan. But since the budgetary process is essentially a political game, the attempt to underestimate tax revenues may well be rational from the viewpoint of Ministry of Finance officials, who want to leave something in reserve in order to avoid inflationary developments in the face of irresponsible pressure groups demanding big public expenditures and tax relief.

Incidentally, in recent years the government's budget bill has never been modified by the Diet. What is submitted by the cabinet is always passed by the Diet, so that the real budgetary process is in preparing the government's budget bill.

supposed to perform—and second, what is their effect upon Japan's economic growth.[g]

My immediate reaction to the first question is that in a democratic society in which various political forces of different strength are at work, the existing institutions such as economic plans, the tariff system, and price controls—or the government agencies responsible for them—are not always performing useful functions from the viewpoint of the economy or the society as a whole. Quite often they are established, or continue to exist, as a result of politically influential groups acting in their own interests, or simply as a political compromise between powerful pressure groups. This is a great difference from the situation in which a single optimizing entity makes consistent, rational decisions. A democratic society cannot be supposed to behave always consistently and rationally, as an individual or as an enterprise might be.

Moreover, illusions, misunderstandings, and wrong theories, sometimes willfully cultivated and exploited by certain groups to their advantage, often play an important role. Therefore, one must not suppose that there is always a good "reason" for the existing economic plans or that they always perform some useful functions for the society.

In the period immediately after the war, the Japanese majority's confidence in the functioning of price mechanisms was at a low point, and great hopes were entertained for national economic planning. Once the Economic Planning Agency was established, it became very difficult to curtail its personnel or to change its name to "forecasting" or "research," instead of "planning"—not to speak of abolishing it. EPA and plan-making became a convenient platform for information exchanges among government ministries and between the government and the private sector, although national economic plannning has turned out to amount to little more than forecasting.

From the private sector's point of view, there is little reason to object to the present setup. The big businesses obtain information through their representatives participating in the plan-making process. Nongovernment political parties are strongly against the national economic plans published by the Conservative government, because of the growth-oriented, pro-business bias of the plans, but they are not against economic planning as such, for obvious ideological reasons.

Turning now to the second question of the effects of the national plans on economic growth, it seems to me that what is called the "announcement effect" of the national economic plans might have been quite substantial, especially in the case of the "Income Doubling" ten-year plan in 1960. However, the announcement effect would have depended not so much on the contents of the plans as on the government's political will, expressed in the plan, to give a top priority to industrial growth. It is sometimes argued that indicative planning

[g]These questions were put to me at the Bellagio Conference by many of its participants.

would promote growth by reducing uncertainty and business risks through information exchanges. But apparently this has not been the case in Japan, as earlier national economic plans persistently underestimated both the growth rate and structural changes substantially, and therefore one cannot say that uncertainty was reduced much by economic planning.

The Income Doubling Plan was much publicized by the then Prime Minister Ikeda, and probably carried a considerable propaganda effect. It looked more or less plausible and prompted private firms to invest more boldly than before. For some time after its publication, it became fashionable among larger companies to publish their own overall long-term management plan for a five- or ten-year period. When making companies' plans, the national or sectoral rate of growth was taken for granted, so to speak, and each company added a plus factor to the industry average rate of growth, hoping for an increasing market share for itself. But here again in practice few companies paid much attention to their long-term plan in making actual investment decisions, since most such plans turned out to underestimate growth potentials. Shortly afterwards, long-term management planning went out of fashion.

Thus the Income Doubling Plan may be said to have had a considerable impact on Japan's growth in the early 1960s. However, what was important was not so much the contents of the national plans as the political will to promote industrial growth. Even without national plans, if the government would have made clear its willingness to promote growth, and fiscal, monetary, and industrial policy measures for that purpose, almost the same effect would have been obtained. The situation would then have been similar to West Germany in postwar years.

Japan's national economic plan thus amounts to little more than a long-run forecast. Yet this does not mean that the Japanese economy is an over-whelmingly free market economy run without much governmental planning. In fact, the government intervenes extensively in particular industries and markets, but governmental planning or policy is primarily organized on an industry or sectoral basis. Before turning to this question, however, I shall discuss briefly Japanese regional plans, which are similar in important respects to national plans.

REGIONAL PLANS

Regional planning is quite extensive in Japan. Roughly speaking there are at least three different kinds of regional plans. First, there have been long-term nationwide regional plans concerned with regional distribution of population, industries, and national income. The National Comprehensive Development Plan published in 1962 and the New National Comprehensive Development Plan published in 1969, both prepared by the Bureau of Comprehensive Development of the Economic Planning Agency, are two overall regional plans hitherto adopted by the government. The 1969 Plan, for example, gives projections of income and population of seven major regions of Japan in 1985, on the one hand, and describes those policies affecting regional distribution of population and industry which are deemed desirable by plan-makers, on the other. Plans of this type are similar to national economic plans in character: that is, a combination of forecasts, wishful thinking and prevailing opinions. For each region the 1969 Plan lists almost indiscriminately all kinds of measures which are supposed to be desirable from a regional development point of view: such as public investment in roads, railroads and port facilities; modernization of agriculture; development of dairy farming, fishery, forestry, manufacturing, and tourist industries; and prevention of pollution, investment in housing, and so on. But the Plan gives almost no figures at all, except a very rough regional breakdown of national income and population, nor does it commit the government in any way.[3]

Second, in certain types of the central government's regional programs, (i) certain areas are designated as covered under the program, and (ii) special incentives, such as tax relief and low-interest loans from government financial institutions, are given to private firms in the areas, or to firms which will build new plants in the areas. Also, (iii) special grants or funds from the central government are allocated to local governments within the areas, and (iv) priority is given to the areas covered by the program in central government investment in roads, port facilities, railways, industrial water supply, and other social overhead capital.

For example, under "New Industrial Cities Program" introduced in 1962, fifteen areas out of more than forty applications from all over Japan were designated as "new industrial city" areas, and measures (ii) through (iv) which were supposed to promote industrialization were adopted. One "new industrial city" area usually comprised several cities and towns, and fifteen such areas were selected as new areas for immediate industrial development. For this type of plan the Economic Planning Agency has the final responsibility, but the Ministry of Finance, Ministry of Local Governments, MITI, and local governments concerned participate in the planning process.

This type of plan includes fiscal measures (ii), (iii), and (iv), and whether they are successful or not in promoting regional development as planned,[h] the government is committed to implement the plans at least to some extent, and it appears that some plans are often effective in channeling resources to particular regions. Private enterprises and population are often attracted by incentive measures and public investment in infrastructure, but usually it is not easy to separate their effects from other factors in regional development.

Third, there are programs involving only the central government's assistance to the local governments. For example, under a program begun in 1970 to assist

[h]For example, a few of the "new industrial cities" have not been successful in developing as industrial centers.

communities suffering from a rapid decline in population, any town or village losing more than 10 percent of its population in a five-year period is eligible for special grants-in-aid or low-interest funds from the central government.

The above are examples of nationwide regional programs. There are also regional plans for particular areas in which the central government participates. Proliferation of regional planning has reached such a stage of overlap that the overall total area covered under various regional plans authorized by the central government is said to be several times the total area of Japan.

It may be mentioned in this connection that in Japan public finance of local governments (prefectures, cities, towns, and villages) is highly integrated with that of the central government. Its Ministry of Finance and Ministry of Local Governments are in a very powerful position to influence local governments' finance, and the degree of fiscal autonomy of local government is very limited.

INDUSTRIAL POLICIES[4]

It is perhaps well known that the Japanese government has developed an elaborate system of industrial policies to promote industrial development, intervenes in industries and markets extensively, and cooperates closely with private firms. But how decisionmaking on industrial policies is organized, what kinds of policy measures are used, and what the real contents of industrial policies are, seem to be little known outside of Japan. Even in Japan the overall system of industrial policies has rarely been explicitly explained, and matters which are common sense for insiders are often little known to the general public (including academics), although fragmentary information is abundantly reported in newspapers from time to time. It is therefore quite difficult to describe the system. This section attempts to give a general idea of the system of industrial policies in postwar Japan.

The term "industrial policy" as used here refers to government policy undertaken to change the allocation of resources among industries, or the levels of certain productive activities of private enterprises in individual industries, from what they would be in the absence of such a policy. An industrial policy is concerned with encouraging production, investment, research and development, modernization and reorganization in certain industries, and discouraging such activities in others. Protective tariffs and excise taxes on luxuries are "classic" examples of the measures of industrial policies so defined.

The system of industrial policies has been steadily changing in postwar Japan. Especially in the last few years it has been undergoing a rapid change. The following describes the state of affairs predominant in 1960s.

The Process of Policymaking

Generally speaking the National Diet does not fulfull its formal function in formulating industrial policies. The parties in opposition to the government are not much interested in industrial policies, apart from their overall accusation about the government's "preoccupation with production to the neglect of civil welfare," or the government's collaboration with "monopoly capitalists." Almost any bill prepared and presented by the government (administration) is approved by the Diet, so that the real policy decision is made within the government, or jointly by the government and the industry.

The principal entities which exert important influence in the process of industrial policymaking are: (i) the government's *genkyoku* offices and (ii) its coordinating offices and, on the side of the private sector, (iii) industry associations and (iv) councils. Also, (v) the *Zaikai* (the central businessmen's circle)[i] and (vi) banks supplying funds to the industry may have some influence on industrial policies. Usually no one entity has an overwhelming influence, and the game of industrial policymaking is played primarily through mutual persuasion, coordination, and sometimes threats. If one group can persuade others concerned that a certain policy is desirable for the national economy or for the industry—very often these two are intentionally mixed—it will succeed in putting the policy into effect.

The Genkyoku and Coordinating Offices. One of the notable characteristics of industrial policymaking in Japan is an important role played by the government offices generally called *genkyoku*. The word *genkyoku* may be literally translated as an "original bureau" or an "original government office," meaning the government office having the primary responsibility for the industry in question.

To each industry there corresponds a *genkyoku*, which supervises the industry, and is responsible for policies toward the industry. Quite a few capable and dedicated government officials in the *genkyoku* work on the policy problems of that particular industry.

MITI is the largest *genkyoku* ministry and is subdivided into smaller *genkyoku* offices. As of 1970, five of MITI's nine "bureaus" were *genkyoku* bureaus: namely, the Bureau of Heavy Industries, Bureau of Chemical Industries, Bureau of Textiles and Sundries,[j] Bureau of Coal and Other Mining, and Bureau of Public Utilities. These bureaus are further divided into divisions, most of which are *genkyoku* divisions in charge of particular subdivisions of industries. For example, the Bureau of Heavy Industries has divisions of iron and steel, industrial machinery, electronics, automobiles, aircraft, rolling stock, and several others.

[i]An informal, not too well-defined group of top-ranking, well-informed businessmen, who meet and consult with each other quite often and act as the spokesmen of the big business community. Most of them occupy prominent positions in formal business organizations.

[j]"Sundries" refers to household goods produced by more or less labor-intensive, small-business light manufacturing industries, such as footwear, leather goods, stationery, and most items sold in variety stores.

Not all bureaus of MITI are *genkyoku* bureaus, which are sometimes called "vertical divisions." Again as of 1970, MITI's "horizontal division" bureaus were: the Bureau of International Trade, Bureau of Trade Development, Bureau of Enterprises, and Bureau of Pollution and Safety. These "horizontal division" bureaus and the Minister's Secretariat *(Kambō)* often have their own policy ideas and take leadership. They also act as coordinators and mediators within MITI.[k]

MITI is not the only *genkyoku* ministry supervising manufacturing industries. Besides agriculture, the Ministry of Agriculture supervises the forestry, fishing, food processing, and nonalchoholic beverage industries. The pharmaceutical industry is under the Ministry of Welfare, and shipbuilding (not only shipping) is under the Ministry of Transportation. The Ministry of Finance is naturally the *genkyoku* for banking, security dealers, and insurance, but it also supervises the alchoholic beverage industry.

A *genkyoku* office is responsible for policy planning related to the industries which it supervises. First, special laws concerning particular industries—such as the "Petroleum Industry Act" (1962), the "Law on Temporary Measures for Promoting Machinery Industries" (1956), a similar law for electronics industries (1957), and another for textile industries (1967)—are prepared and administered primarily by the *genkyoku* offices. Second, the plans for (1) special tax incentives given to particular industries, (2) changes in tariff rates, (3) policy on import liberalization, and (4) policy on liberalization of foreign (inward) direct investment are first prepared by the *genkyoku* offices. Third, authorization of (5) individual patent and know-how contracts, (6) joint ventures between foreign and Japanese companies—most of which have been subject to screening and authorization case by case until recently—and (7) new productive facilities—where such authorization is mandatory as in petroleum refining, shipbuilding or electric power supply—rests primarily with the *genkyoku* office. Fourth, on the allocation of low-interest funds from government financial institutions, especially the Japan Development Bank, the *genkyoku* office and the Ministry concerned have an almost decisive voice.

The policy on (1) through (6) above prepared by the specific *genkyoku* office is discussed and coordinated first at the ministry level, and then goes to Ministry of Finance. On (1), the Bureau of Tax; on (2) and (3) the Bureau of Tariffs; and on (4), (5) and (6) the Bureau of International Finance—all of the Ministry of Finance—have final responsibility within the government, and exercise some coordinating function. But it is often difficult for Ministry of Finance officials to change what has been decided and requested by the respective ministries.

The Fair Trade Commission is in charge of antitrust policy, and is another important government agency in the process of industrial policy making. In the 1950s it was largely neglected, but during the 1960s its relative strength within the government rose substantially.

[k]MITI underwent an extensive reorganization in 1973. See pp. 225-26.

Industry Associations. The industry associations such as the Japan Iron and Steel Federation, Japan Automobile Industry Association, Japan Shipbuilding Industry Association, and hundreds of similar and often subdivided associations are counterparts of the respective *genkyoku* offices. Usually the industry association collaborates closely with the *genkyoku* in charge of the industry, but the relation between them varies from one industry to another. From the industry's point of view, or from the point of view of its leading firms, whose presidents or chairmen alternate as the president of the association, the chief function of the industry association is to persuade the *genkyoku* to take measures favorable to the industry. From the *genkyoku's* point of view, the industry association and its members should cooperate with the *genkyoku* in the latter's execution of industrial policies, and persuade disobedient or dissident members. Sometimes, however, an industry association has diversified opinions, or the *genkyoku* office and the industry may be opposed to each other. In industries dominated by small business, firms in the industry may not be able to organize an association by themselves and may ask the help of the *genkyoku* office to organize one. Typically the industry association and the *genkyoku* spend much time negotiating with, and trying to persuade, each other to reach a satisfactory solution to the industry's problem.

Councils. Just as the Economic Council reports to the prime minister on national economic planning, there are many councils which report to each minister on specific problems. In the case of MITI, as of 1970 there were twenty-seven councils and investigation committees composed of members from outside the government which advised the minister on specific issues. Fifteen of them were to report on problems of industrial policies: Council on Industrial Structure, on industrial policies in general; and Councils on Machinery Industries, Petroleum, Mining, Coal Mining, Promotion of Electronic Data Processing, Technologies in Light Industries, Industrial Location and Water Supply, and various others, on policies in their respective fields.

The nature and role of these councils, the composition of their membership, their deliberation procedures, and the role of the secretariat are more or less similar to those of the Economic Council, and therefore need not be discussed here.

Industrial Policies and the National Economic Plan

Not only on industrial policies but also on other important policy issues there are councils reporting to the minister in charge, and the national economic plan reflects the opinions of these councils to the extent that they have already reached conclusions acceptable to government officials. The national economic plan is, for one thing, a compilation of such opinions, as noted in the first section above. But it often happens that councils reporting to various ministers are still discussing their assigned problems when the national economic plan is drafted. Then the statement in the national plan on such problems can hardly be anything but obscure and elusive.

Thus to some extent the national economic plan reflects industrial policies in individual fields. On the other hand, when making decisions on industrial policies, ministries and councils take into account the growth rate and other macroeconomic and sectoral planning indices, as well as the order of policy priority expressed in the plan. ·Especially in the year in which a new national economic plan is published, the national plan is referred to when *genkyoku* ministries negotiate with the Ministry of Finance on budgetary appropriations. However, the national plan is in no way binding on the government, as explained in the first section, and is referred to primarily as a sort of official forecast. Since the plan has tended to underestimate the growth rate as well as structural changes, if ministries stuck too much to macroeconomic and sectoral indices in the national plans, they would have ended up with insufficient appropriations. The national economic plan has been considered, therefore, as no more than a long- or medium-term forecast when ministries make annual decisions on and execute industrial policies.

Types of Industrial Policies

Industrial policies in postwar Japan are quite extensive and are concerned with different needs (or what government officials and industry representatives consider as such) in a wide variety of situations. It is not easy then to classify them into a few principal categories of policies, but I will list some of the more frequent types of industrial policies.

Development of a New Industry. To develop new industries in Japan—such as iron and steel, shipbuilding, petroleum refining, synthetic fibers, automobiles, petrochemicals, certain types of machines, electronics, computers, and so on—at one time or another the government gave them special tax incentives (accelerated depreciation privileges, special low tax rates on profits, exemption from tariffs on imported machines used in such industries),[5] and supplied low-interest funds through the Japan Development Bank, Japan Export-Import Bank, and other government financial institutions. At the same time, imports competing with the products of these industries were restricted by import quotas and tariffs, and the entry of foreign firms into Japan was severely limited by restrictive policies on foreign (inward) direct investment,[6] to protect indigenous "infant" firms. Also, the firms in new industries to be encouraged were given preferential treatment in the allocation of import quotas and authorization of patent and know-how contracts.

Direct subsidies given to new industries have been relatively rare. Only research and development activities in a few areas and certain "large-scale" (research) projects have been subsidized by the government in recent years.

In developing a new industry, the government may make a plan over a period of one to several years giving the levels of the industry's output, productive capacity, and investment, but such a plan is more often a loose blueprint than a rigid plan to be faithfully followed. If the industry expands faster than the givernment considers it desirable—such a case is relatively rare—the government can limit its expansion by restrictive measures.[1] But there is no effective means, besides the incentives measures listed above, to push the industry into faster growth.

Industry Modernization Program. Sometimes called an "industrial reorganization" or "structural improvement" program, this type of policy is concerned with industries characterized by a relatively large number of firms operating at a smaller-than-optimum scale and/or producing too wide a variety of products in small quantities. A modernization or reorganization program consists of encouraging modernization investment to introduce new technologies, on the one hand, and promoting mergers and cooperation among firms and specialization by individual firms in fewer products so as to attain economies of scale, on the other. A cartel, called a "rationalization cartel," which is exempted from antitrust prosecution under certain conditions, is often organized to achieve cooperation and specialization among firms.

When this type of policy is undertaken for a particular industry, a "basic plan" covering several years and an annual working plan may be prepared after consultation with related councils, and those firms cooperating with the plan may be granted special tax privileges or low-interest funds.

This type of policy has been extensively applied to some machinery, textile, and chemical industries.

Control of Excessive Investment. During the 1960s one of the major concerns of MITI was to avoid what was called "excessive competition in investment" in certain industries. "Excessive competition in investment" tends to develop in industries characterized by heavy overhead capital, homogeneous products, and oligopoly. Examples are iron and steel, petroleum refining, petrochemicals, certain other chemicals, cement, paper and pulp, and sugar refining. The reasons why such a tendency toward excessive investment developed in these industries are quite complicated and cannot easily be explained in a brief discussion.

However, it may be pointed out, first, that from the late 1950s to the late 1960s, large Japanese companies were generally very optimistic about the growth of demand. On the whole, they made better judgments than journalists, economists, and government officials who tended to underestimate growth

[1] Examples of restrictive measures for this purpose are compulsory cartelization, quotas on raw material imports, restrictions on exports (when exports increase too fast and cause "market disruption" in an overseas market), and so-called "administrative guidance" on investment.

potentials. Moreover, the fact that optimistic and aggressive companies were more successful than others in earlier years induced most companies to invest more boldly in later years.

Second, the separation of ownership and management in large corporations is more pronounced in postwar Japan than in most other countries including the United States, and Japanese executives are more growth-oriented and less-profit-conscious than their colleagues in other countries. It is remarkable that during the 1960s the profit rate was very low in many fast-growing industries, for example, iron and steel, shipbuilding, and petrochemicals. Japanese executives have been more concerned with growth and market shares than with short-run profits. They depended heavily on borrowed funds, and the fact that banks and other financial institutions, most of which were also run by management separated from ownership and were likewise growth- and market-share-oriented, willingly supplied funds for aggressive expansion is another important factor.

But these factors are more or less common to most industries and do not explain why "excessive competition in investment" has been observed primarily in industries such as those listed, producing homogeneous, non-differentiated products using heavy fixed capital, and has rarely been a problem in some other fast-growing oligopolistic industries such as automobiles, household electrical appliances, heavy electrical machinery, pharmaceuticals, shipbuilding and beer-brewing.

The "excessive competition in investment" in an industry appears to me to depend on the following three factors: (i) the products of the industry are homogeneous, not differentiated; (ii) the size of productive capacity can be expressed readily by a single index such as monthly output in standard tons, daily refining capacity in barrels, number of spindles, etc.; and (iii) such an index of productive capacity is used by the supervising *genkyoku* or by the industry association for administrative or allocative purposes. If, for example, import quotas for crude oil are allocated on the basis of refining capacity at a certain time, this encourages oil companies to expand their refining capacity beyond the limit justified by market conditions, in the hope of gaining both market shares and profits. That productive capacity has actually been used or referred to for administrative or allocative purposes in direct controls, administrative guidance, or cartelization, and that companies rightly or wrongly expect this to be repeated in the future, seem to be the real cause of the "excessive competition in investment." In industries where products are differentiated or made to order, so that marketing efforts are the determining factor in gaining market-shares, or where it is difficult to express the size of productive capacity because of a wide variety of products (e.g., pharmaceuticals, machine tools), excessive investment has rarely been observed.

The principal means by which the government tries to control excessive investment is simply to persuade firms concerned. Persuasion was more or less effective in the 1960s since the government maintained direct controls on imports of raw materials and on patent and know-how contracts between Japanese and foreign firms. In some industries, such as petrochemicals, it was impossible to build new plants or to expand productive facilities without foreign patents and know-how, and the government control over patent and know-how contracts was the last resort when persuasion failed to restrain excessive investment.

Assistance to Declining Industries. Apart from agriculture, declining industries which need public assistance have been relatively few in contemporary Japan. Coal mining is an example. In the period immediately after the war, coal mining supplied a major share of energy, and was one of the four industries given the highest priority in the reconstruction program. As petroleum imports rose sharply beginning in the late 1950s, coal could not compete with petroleum as a source of energy, as was the case in many other countries.[m]

The Japanese government policy toward coal mining in recent years has been to maintain annual coal output, so as to avoid a sharp increase in unemployment of coal miners, who are said to be less mobile than other workers, and to enable an orderly withdrawal of labor from coal mining. For this purpose the government granted and is still granting extensive subsidies and low-interest loans to coal mines. Also, the government requests electric power companies and some other consumers of coal to burn more coal than cost considerations justify. Power companies cooperate with the government, because they are given preferential treatment in regard to taxes and allocation of funds. The Bureau of Coal (later Bureau of Coal and Other Mining) of MITI prepares and administers a detailed annual coal mining plan, giving the levels of coal production, investment, consumption, inventories, and employment in each district. Since the plan is backed up by subsidies and low-interest funds, it is very closely observed by coal mining companies.

The government also gives aid to workers moving to other industries, subsidizes their retraining, and promotes industrial development of coal mining areas. The funds necessary for these policies towards coal mining are raised by a tariff (10 percent) on petroleum imports.

Another example of the government's assistance to a "declining" industry is provided by certain textile industries which suffered a loss of exports as a result of the conclusion of the Japanese-American Textile Agreement in 1971. The government decided to make low-interest loans (for modernization investment) and to purchase (for scrap) surplus textile machines over a three-year period, as compensation for the industry's loss of exports.

[m]Domestic coal accounted for about 48 percent of Japan's total energy supplies in 1953, but declined to 6 percent by 1970.

Planned Shipbuilding. The policy of "Planned Shipbuilding" undertaken by the Ministry of Transportation is rather unique among the Japanese government's industrial policies in the scale of government funds involved and its continuation over a long period. Planned Shipbuilding was started in 1947 when Japan was under the Allied Occupation, and is still being carried out in basically the same way, although minor changes in the details have been frequent.

Under Planned Shipbuilding, the government announces every year the total tonnage of each of the major types of ships (liners, tramps, tankers, ore bulk-carriers, and LPG-carriers) to be built under the plan, and selects qualified shipowners and shipbuilders from among applicants. A certain percentage— recently 50–80 percent, depending on the fiscal year and the type of ships—of the total funds necessary for new ships is supplied by the Japan Development Bank under terms substantially more favorable than ordinary financing. The ships are then built in Japanese shipyards.

Japanese shipowners have also built ships outside of Planned Shipbuilding, especially in years of prosperity in shipping, but more than two-thirds (in tonnage) of ocean-going ships now carrying the Japanese flag were built under Planned Shipbuilding. Ships for export are outside of Planned Shipbuilding, but the Japanese Export-Import Bank supplies low-interest loans to shipbuilding companies, to finance their deferred payment credits extended to foreign shipowners.

Besides supplying low-interest loans under Planned Shipbuilding, since 1953 the government has been granting extensive "interest subsidies" on loans from the Japan Development Bank and commercial banks for ocean-going ships, in order to lighten "interest burdens" of shipowners who have generally been in financial difficulties.

In 1963 and 1964, under new legislation enacted in 1962, the government carried out what was called the "Plan for Reconstruction and Consolidation of Marine Transportation." The plan consisted of encouraging mergers, coalition, and cooperation among shipping companies, in order to reduce "excessive competition" in marine transportation and to "strengthen the financial basis" of shipping companies, Firms which cooperated with the Plan were given deferred payment privileges for interest on loans from the Japan Development Bank, and were treated favorably under Planned Shipbuilding.

What is the purpose of these extensive policies to assist shipping and shipbuilding? In the early postwar period, the officially announced aim was "reconstruction of Japanese marine transportation" or "to secure Japanese tonnage." Development of the Japanese shipbuilding industry may have been another purpose. In the 1950s and the first half of the 1960s, when Japan's balance of payments often showed deficits, the objective was said to be to reduce the balance-of-payments deficit on invisible trade. In recent years, when Japan's overall balance-of-payments surpluses (instead of deficits) became a serious problem, and the Japanese shipbuilding industry has fully grown up to build about half the total newly launched tonnage of world, the purpose has become obscure. Some people argue that it is necessary or desirable to raise the share of cargo carried by Japanese ships in Japan's exports and imports,[n] but why it is so has never been made clear.

CONCLUDING REMARKS

Japan's medium- or long-term national economic plans prepared and published by the Economic Planning Agency should be viewed primarily as a sort of official forecast, accompanied by a collection of current opinions on certain policy issues. They have not been intended as a plan ot be followed more or less faithfully by the government in making annual or day-to-day decisions on matters of fiscal, monetary, industrial, or other economic policies.

The nationwide "Comprehensive" regional plans of 1962 and 1969 are also more a forecast than a plan in the usual sense of the term. The 1969 Comprehensive Development Plan gives estimates for regional distribution of population and income in 1985, and lists all kinds of measures considered desirable from the viewpoint of each region's development, but it includes little if any attempt at implementation, and the quantitative estimates and policy measures in the Plan remain unrelated to each other. Also, the contents and planning process of the "Comprehensive" regional plans are largely unrelated to those of the national economic plans, although they are published by the same government agency—the Economic Planning Agency (but by different bureaus in it).

Both national economic plans and the "Comprehensive" regional plans are referred to and taken into consideration by government ministries, agencies, and local governments, as well as by private firms and industry associations, when they make their own plans and decisions. But nobody feels obligated to observe these plans. They consider these plans primarily forecasts as reliable or unreliable as a long-term weather forecast. The fact that national plans underestimated substantially both growth rates and structural changes in the past and had to be replaced within two or three years after their announcement, in spite of their official coverage of five to ten years, limited the usefulness and the prestige of these plans as long-term forecasts. But, in an economy like postwar Japan's, which has been undergoing rapid growth and structural change, on the one hand, and is heavily dependent upon international economic relations and therefore subject to external disturbances, on the other, the task of economic forecasting is admittedly a very difficult one.

Since Japan's national economic plan is primarily a forecast, asking about its effects upon economic growth is like asking about the effects of weather

[n]Thirty-nine percent for exports and 45 percent for imports in 1970; if chartered foreign ships operated by Japanese shipping companies are included, 55 percent and 63 percent respectively.

forecasting upon agricultural production. A forecast, whether economic or meteorological, must be useful to the extent that it predicts the future accurately. In the case of Japan, however, the additional advantage of having a central economic plan—beyond what is done by research organizations, individual government ministries, and private firms—seems to have been relatively small, since the forecasts given in national economic plans cannot be said to have been much superior to those by others, especially in earlier years.

It must not be thought from the above, however, that the postwar Japanese economy is predominantly a free enterprise, market economy run without much governmental planning or intervention. Much planning and intervention are conducted at sectoral levels. The Ministry of International Trade and Industry, other ministries, and their subdivisions, acting as *genkyoku* offices having supervisory and planning responsibilities over individual industries, intervene extensively in their respective areas of administrative jurisdiction. Industrial policies planned and administered by them appear to have been quite effective in channeling resources into particular industries or sectors. Also, some of the central government's regional programs— which give grants-in-aid, low-interest loans, tax-incentives, and priority for social overhead investment to local governments and certain private firms in particular regions—must have been effective at least to some extent in reallocating population and industries among regions.

Evaluating the Effects of Industrial Policies

What then are the effects of the Japanese government's industrial policies and regional planning upon growth? It is very difficult to answer this question, because it is generally very difficult to infer what would have been the situation if certain policies were not undertaken or if some other policies different from those actually adopted were undertaken, and to prove or disprove the beneficial effects of certain policies. The mere fact that the Japanese economy has grown rapidly does not constitute a proof that Japan's industrial and regional policies contributed to growth: the Japanese economy might have grown in the absence of extensive intervention, or in spite of some negative effects of wrong policies.

In order to evaluate the effects of industrial and regional policies on growth, the analysis should perhaps proceed in three steps. First, it is necessary to estimate the amounts of subsidies, grants-in-aid, tax relief, low-interest loans, and other assistance given to each industry and region. It is also necessary, in the case of regional analysis, to estimate other interregional flows of resources directly controlled by the central government, such as public investment in transportation facilities.

Second, for each industry or region the effects of such government assistance upon industrial and regional development must be evaluated. Some industries might badly have needed government assistance at a critical point in their development, and might have been quite responsive to incentives given by the government. On the other hand, certain government assistance might have had little effect on the industrial or regional development process. Some industries might have developed more or less the same way in the absence of such assistance,[o] or government policies might have failed to develop a new industry or a backward region, in spite of a considerable amount of public funds devoted to it.

Third, the fact that the government's industrial policy toward a certain industry was successful in developing it or accelerating its growth does not necessarily mean that such a policy is contributing to economic growth and beneficial to the economy as a whole. Most industries or regions will be able to develop, or their growth will be accelerated, if massive assistance is given and heavily protective measures are taken for them. Since the costs of such assistance and protective measures are to be borne by others within the national economy, there must be a specific reason or reasons to help or protect a particular industry or region at a sacrifice to others. It must be asked, therefore, first, whether the industries which have received government assistance in various forms merit preferential treatment at the cost to others, and second, whether such assistance to a particular industry was given in the most appropriate forms and in the right amount.

There are few studies addressed to these questions, which are most important in evaluating industrial or regional policies, and little is known to make a judgment about their positive or negative effects on growth. This is true not only of Japan but of other countries too.

In the absence of careful studies with the three steps described above, I can only offer a few remarks on industrial policies from my general impressions.[p]

Protection of Infants or Adults?   In the early stage of development of new industries, the government's protective policies for industrial development described in the third section above have often been effective and probably beneficial to the national economy in many cases. In the absence of protective measures, some of the new industries would have encountered much greater difficulties in establishing themselves in Japan.

Having thus acknowledged the importance of the policy of infant protection, one may, however, point out first that some of the rapidly expanding "new" industries, the products of which have been increasingly exported all over the

[o]An example may be huge tax-exempt profits which accrued to a synthetic fiber company making nylon in the 1950s under the special tax provision of "exemption of income from the sales of important new products." The company was enjoying a monopoly position, and it appears that nylon would have been introduced into Japan more or less the same way in the absence of that particular tax incentive.

[p]I know much less about Japan's regional development policies than about industrial policies, and no attempt will be made to evaluate the effect of regional planning. It may be noted that the main objective of regional development policies in the 1960s was not to accelerate Japan's overall growth, but to alleviate the increasing disparity in the per capita income level between the prosperous central regions and the stagnant periphery.

world recently—such as motorcycles, bearings (especially miniature bearings), transistor radios, TV sets, tape recorders, pianos, and zippers—received relatively little government assistance even in their infancy periods. By and large these industries were able to stand up by themselves, with little government protection or planning.

Second, the protective policies which were probably necessary and desirable in the very early years have tended to be continued for too long. Since the process of policymaking on protection in regard to a particular industry is dominated by the *genkyoku* office in charge of the industry and the representatives of the industry in question, the motives to check unwarranted continuation of protectionism are always weak. Thus, for example, the steel industry was given preferential treatment well into the mid-1960s, when MITI had to try hard to persuade steel companies to slow down their rate of investment. Also, the policy of low-interest financing of exports of ships and heavy plant and equipment, which was initially pursued for a balance-of-payments reason and was helpful to the development of the shipbuilding and industrial machinery industries, was continued in the days of huge balance-of-payments surpluses.

Lack of Consistency. Planning and decisionmaking on industrial policies take place industry by industry, without a clear statement of the basic principles of industrial policies. By the latter I mean the principles in regard to what types of industries or economic activities should be encouraged and what types discouraged, what measures should be used in what situation, and to what extent and how the government should intervene to "reorganize" industries and market mechanisms.

For individual industries and *genkyoku* offices what is important is that they receive favorable treatment, and any ad hoc reasons or pretexts are used so long as they are helpful in persuading others concerned. As reasons for protection or government assistance, often such very general slogans as to increase the international competitive power of Japanese industries, to promote exports, to improve the balance of payments, or to advance or modernize Japan's industrial structure have been used indiscriminately to protect a wide variety of industries.

Since the Japanese economy in the postwar years has been in a state of nearly full employment, protecting an industry implies discouraging other industries. If the government takes measures to protect most industries, such measures will largely cancel each other out. That might be not too far from what actually happened. Few government officials in charge of industrial policies have understood a simple economic truth that protecting all industries equally is protecting none of them.[q]

[q]It was suggested at the Bellagio Conference that for a closed economy a policy of protecting all industries equally may be protecting none of them, but for an open economy like Japan's such a policy may result in protecting and giving advantages to many of them in

However, the degree of protection has been unequal among industries. Politically influential industries and especially industries cooperating closely with the government since the prewar years, such as iron and steel, shipbuilding, and shipping, have apparently been more heavily protected. Also, the *genkyoku* offices within ministries other than MITI tend to be more insular and protective towards their industries, whereas MITI supervises many industries and tends to have a wider and longer perspective.

Another example of a lack of consistency may be provided by the following. During the 1950s and early 1960s when Japan's balance of payments often showed deficits, the government gave special tax privileges to incomes earned from exports. These special tax privileges were introduced in order to encourage exports, and were substantial until 1963. It is inconsistent, however, to give such tax relief when the exports in question are under voluntary or compulsory export restriction. It is a matter of simple economics that implicit subsidies due to such tax privileges will shift the export supply curve upwards, and that when there is a quantitative restriction on exports, the upward shift of the supply curve will simply increase the special premium accruing to those receiving export quotas, without accomplishing any useful function. Such an inconsistency could arise because the export restrictions and the tax measures were administered by different government offices.

The System of Information Exchange. Whatever the demerits of the system of industrial policies in postwar Japan, it has been a very effective means of collecting, exchanging, and propagating industrial information. Government officials, industry people, and men from governmental and private banks gather together and spend much time discussing problems of industries and exchanging information on new technologies and domestic and overseas market conditions. People at the top levels of the government, industries, and banking circles meet at councils, and junior men meet at their subcommittees or less formal meetings. Probably information related to the various industries is more abundant and easily obtainable in Japan than in most other countries. Viewed as a system of information collection and dissemination, Japan's system of industrial policies may have been among the most important factors in Japan's high rate of industrial growth, apart from the direct or indirect economic effects of individual policy measures.

---

their competition with foreign industries. In the short run it may appear that the above is true: a country's exports can be increased and imports suppressed by protective measures and government assistance to industries, giving an impression that such a policy is helping the economy to grow faster than otherwise. However, in the long run, exports and imports, the major components of the balance of payments, must largely be balanced in some way, and a country's exports cannot be increased beyond imports indefinitely. Moreover, to the extent that a country's balance of payments continues to show surpluses, the country is making low-interest loans to the rest of the world. Clearly, such a policy is not promoting the economic growth of the country in question.

The Problem of Equity

As explained in the first section, the process of decisionmaking about industrial policies in postwar Japan is, first, organized predominantly on an industry-by-industry basis, and, second, dominated by the officials in the *genkyoku* offices and representatives of the industries in question. This means that individual industries' interests or producers' interests tend to be promoted more or less in disregard of the interests of other groups affected by such policies and industrial development.

Particularly serious has been the disregard of harmful effects of environmental pollution. In spite of warnings by quite a few people, the government officials in charge of industrial policies persistently belittled the harmful effects of pollution until around 1970, when environmental pollution caused by industries reached a very serious and almost unmanageable dimension.

Consumers' interests have also been largely ignored. A famous representative of the steel industry once said that steel was the nation, meaning that anything good for the steel industry was good for the nation. Although they have never said so blatantly, the *genkyoku* officials have often behaved as if they consider that anything good for the industry which they supervise is good for the country. Not only the interests of consumers in the sense of households, but also the interests of users of the products of the industry in question, have received little attention. For example, users of electronic computers were asked simply to cooperate with the government's protective policy to develop Japan's own computer industry. Various councils on industrial policies have always been dominated by producers' interests. The *genkyoku* offices, which are formally supposed to supervise their respective industries, often act as an advisor, a protector, or a deputy for them.[1]

Another dimension of the problem of equity is that Japan's industrial policies tend to favor leading firms in the industries concerned. When the government makes plans or rations quotas, the usual criterion as to each firm's share is the past record. Thus industrial policies or planning tend to freeze the status quo in regard to the relative shares of individual firms. Industry associations and councils which play important roles in the process of industrial policy making are dominated by presidents and chairmen of the leading firms having largest shares in the respective industries. Industry associations, councils, and the *genkyoku* offices spend much time trying to ·persuade all the firms in the respective industries, in order to be fair and impartial and to avoid criticisms that policies or planning are unfair or partial, but usually the individual firms' shares change little. This means that industrial policies of the postwar Japanese type tend to suppress new entrants and aggressive expansion of smaller but more

[1]In the early 1960s a young official in one of the *genkyoku* divisions of MITI told me that he sometimes felt as if he were a financial manager for companies which were under the supervision of his division, since much of his time was spent in negotiating on loans for the companies with other MITI offices and the Japan Development Bank.

vigorous firms. At least, the changes in the relative shares of firms are moderated by government intervention.

Also, for the same reason, the system of industrial policies is often incompatible, at least in principle, with antitrust policy. The former emphasizes mutual persuasion, collaboration, and mergers among firms, whereas collusion and mergers in restraint of competition must be prosecuted under the latter. In fact, MITI was often in conflict with the Fair Trade Commission in the 1950s and early 1960s, when the system of industrial policies was in its heyday.

It must not be thought, however, that the system of industrial policies is, as claimed by some Marxists, a scheme whereby the government and capitalists collaborate to exploit workers and the public at large. Although the Marxian argument of "state monopoly capitalism" cannot be dealt with easily, a few relevant points may be noted.

First, the ownership and management of firms are probably more thoroughly separated in postwar Japan than in most other countries, including the United States. Only very few of the large companies are run by owner-managers. Generally, salaried executives rather than capitalists dominate the management of big business. They pay less attention to profits and lay more emphasis on growth of the firm than managers in other countries, so long as the profit rate is higher than a certain minimum considered as acceptable to the industry. This is one of the reasons why Japanese firms compete to invest very heavily, even with borrowed funds. Both the government offices in charge of industrial policies and the management of firms are manned overwhelmingly by middle-class intellecturals who are graduates of a few leading unversities. They are managers, administrators, and technocrats, and do not think that they themselves are "capitalists," or capitalists' agents, nor that they are serving the interests of wealthy capitalists.

Second, most industries where the government has intervened extensively, such as iron and steel, shipbuilding, shipping, petroleum refining, chemicals, petrochemicals, and electric power, have been characterized by a low rate of profit throughout the 1960s. Their profit rates have been substantially lower than the average for manufacturing industry. Because of lively competition, government assistance in various forms to these industries has largely been passed on to the purchasers—some of them foreigners—of their products or services. As a result of industrial policies favoring them, these industries and firms have grown and their wage rates have risen rapidly, but their profit rates have remained relatively low.

Third, Japan's ruling Conservative government has been closely associated with the interests of big business and the relatively rich, and has done many things which are considered to be favorable to them and little if anything which was opposed by them. However, the functioning of the highly competitive market mechanism of the postwar Japanese economy is such that big businesses cannot retain for themselves all or most of the benefits of industrial policies which are supposed to be favorable to them. Smaller firms have grown about as rapidly as big ones, and the degree of industrial concentration remains largely unchanged. It appears that in the process of rapid economic growth two counteracting forces are at work, one increasing the advantages of large-scale production and marketing, the other creating new openings and opportunities within the economy for new and smaller firms to develop and prosper. Apparently these two forces have been more or less balanced so far.

Another point which may be mentioned here is that income distribution in postwar Japan is a relatively equal one among industrialized countries. Although the reliable statistical data on income distribution are scarce, and international comparison of income distribution is extremely difficult both in practice and conceptually, it appears that income is more nearly equally distributed in Japan than, say, West Germany or France. There is no doubt that Japan's income distribution is now much more nearly equal than in prewar years. This is due to the land reform, Zaibatsu dissolution, and the once-for-all capital levy enforced immediately after the war, on the one hand, and high progressive income as well as inheritance taxation in postwar years, on the other.

Historical Background and Applicability in Other Countries

The system of industrial policies in postwar Japan is closely related to the tradition of "strong government," or the dominant and pervasive role played by the government in Japan. As is well known, since the Meiji Restoration in 1868 the Japanese government has been the main driving force in Japan's industrialization and modernization. The Meiji government was organized by samurais of lower strata of a few leading anti-Tokugawa feudal clans which overthrew the Tokugawa Shogunate and won the civil war. Between 1868 and 1890 the Meiji government organized the national army and navy based upon a national conscription system, established the Bank of Japan and a commercial banking system, introduced a compulsory education system, a national postal system, a system of local governments, and so on. Thus the Meiji government took all kinds of measures to change a feudal country divided into nearly three hundred clans into a modern nation-state. Yet during this period there was no popularly elected national Diet or Congress.

The first national Diet was elected in 1890, but in this election only about one percent of the population was given the right to vote. Throughout the prewar years suffrage was expanded only gradually, and the power of the Diet to check the government (administration) remained very weak, constitutionally as well as in practice, until World War II. In prewar years, therefore, the Japanese government was more or less an absolutist government, nearly omnipotent in pursuing whatever policies it chose. The traditions of free enterprise and economic liberalism were almost nonexistent in prewar Japan. Businessmen were generally viewed as a social group whose status was lower than that of government officials or the military.

During World War II and the period immediately after the war, extensive direct controls were a necessity, as in many other countries. This led to further extension of government intervention in industries and markets. The decontrol process after the war was much slower in Japan than in other countries. The Allied Occupation enforced a series of democratization measures, a drastic and successful land reform, less thoroughgoing but still quite effective dissolution of the Zaibatsu, and the introduction of an antitrust law. Also, the constitutional status of the Diet in regard to the government budget and economic policies was substantially strengthened. Yet, the extensive involvement of the government in economic affairs, its powerful position vis-à-vis the private sector, its close relationship with business, and the public attitude toward the government-business relationship were not affected much by the democratization measures.

The elaborate system of industrial policies in postwar Japan must be understood in the light of this historical background. It would be difficult, if not impossible, to introduce Japanese-type industrial policies and planning in countries with much different cultural and political traditions.[5]

Recent Trends and Prospects

Although the interest of the general public in the Japanese government's national economic plan has been declining gradually, the government is likely to continue to prepare and publish a medium-term national economic plan once every two or three years. In fact, it was reported in the press that in view of the impact of the recent oil crisis on the Japanese economy the Economic Planning Agency is now contemplating the revision of the Basic Economic and Social Plan, and has made a "trial" calculation of the likely effects of the oil crisis on Japan's rate of economic growth and other macroeconomic indices.[7] Since the national economic plan appears to many people to be helpful as a sort of official forecast, and since the plan-making process is a useful ground for information exchange and communication, there is no prospect of a substantial change in the present institutional set-up of plan-making in the near future.

The medium-term national economic plan will be viewed more and more as a forecast rather than a plan in the usual sense of the term. But any attempt to change the name from the "national economic plan" to, say, the "national

[5]A necessary condition for Japanese-type industrial policies to succeed is the existence of a bureaucracy capable of planning, implementing, and administering complicated policy systems. There must be an abundant supply of honest, intelligent, and dedicated bureaucrats. It may be noted that there have been very few cases in which high officials in charge of industrial policies were involved in bribery. For government officials it does not pay to receive bribes. For one thing, acceptance of bribes is severely punished, and also although their salaries are surprisingly low, government officials are under the lifetime employment scheme, and high officials can take prestigious and well-paid jobs after retirement from the civil service.

economic projection" or "forecast" will be strongly resisted by "plan"-makers in EPA. Such a change would be considered by the "plan"-making officials as degrading the importance of their work.

The public interest in regional planning is increasing in Japan. This is because of excessive congestion and pollution problems in heavily industrialized and overpopulated areas, the increasing disparity in income levels between the industrialized center and the predominantly agricultural periphery, and the resulting large outflow of population from peripheral regions. Whether or not Prime Minister Tanaka's ambitious "Remodeling the Japanese Islands" program is successfully enacted into new legislation, the government's already extensive intervention and planning in the process of regional allocation of industries and population will be intensified in the future.

On the other hand, in the last few years the Japanese government has been dismantling and reorganizing its elaborate system of industrial policies. It has been in the process of disengagement from excessively protective and overly paternalistic policies. At the request of foreign governments, especially the United States, to liberalize tight controls in various spheres of the economy, since around 1969 the Japanese government has moved to abolish or reduce considerably quantitative import restrictions and direct controls on patent and know-how contracts and foreign direct investment in Japan. Toward the end of the 1960s Japan's trade balance showed large surpluses. Many Japanese industries, well protected and given various forms of assistance under the elaborate system of industrial policies, have already become full-fledged export industries acquiring increasingly larger shares in the markets of industrialized countries. Environmental pollution and disruption caused by industry became very serious in many regions of Japan. All this led to a sudden but belated change in the order of priority among policy objectives. Industrial development can no longer be the primary objective of industrial policies. Prevention of pollution and disruption of human life, consumers' interests, harmonious international economic relations, and price stability are now considered as important policy objectives in preference to industrial development and technological progress.[t]

NOTES

1. There were national plans drafted before 1955, but they were not officially adopted. For a brief history of Japanese national economic planning in English, see Tsunehiko Watanabe, "National Planning and Economic Develop-

[t]An extensive reorganization of MITI in April 1973 symbolizes the changing objectives of industrial policies. The number and the relative importance of verticial *genkyoku* bureaus and divisions were substantially diminished and those of horizontal ones were increased. Now only three out of the eight bureaus of MITI are vertical *genkyoku* bureaus, as compared with six out of ten in 1965.

ment: A Critical Review of the Japanese Experience," *Economics of Planning* 10, 1–2(1970): 23–30.

2. J.E. Meade asks but does not answer the following question. "Moreover, what is the legitimate use which, in a democratic society, one government may make of its own social welfare function? Should it rigidly commit resources to uses which will satisfy its own ideas about future social welfare without leaving any flexibility for them to be turned to the satisfaction of alternative objectives favored by the opposition party which may well in turn become the government—presumably because of some change of social values among the electorate itself?" Meade, *The Theory of Indicative Planning* (Manchester, Eng.: Manchester University Press, 1970), p. 72.

3. I was asked about the relationship between the "National Comprehensive Development Plans" (CDP) and the national economic plans (NEP). It seems to me that national regional planning and national economic planning are two separate and almost unrelated ventures. The former (CDP) assumes that Japan's real GNP will quadruple or quintuple over the twenty-year period from 1965 to 1985, and considers the pattern of regional development under that assumption. The latter (NEP) is concerned with a much shorter period of five years, and pays little attention to regional aspects of the Japanese economy.

A large volume (more than 700 pages) entitled *Shiryo: Shin-Zenkoku Sogō Kaihatsu Keikaku* [Documents Related to the New National Comprehensive Development Plan], edited by A. Shimokobe, the chief plan-maker of the 1969 plan, includes only a few vague words discussing the relation between CDP and NEP (pp. 373–78). It appears to say that CDP was formulated almost without reference to medium-term (five-year) national economic plans, and to try to justify that.

If either CDP or NEP is a plan with substantive content to be followed more or less faithfully by the government, the plan-makers belonging to the same EPA could not have ignored one of them in formulating the other.

4. This section is an elaboration of a section in the author's earlier study, "Japan and the World Economy," to be published as Ch. 12 in *Toward a New World Trade Policy: The Maidenhead Papers*, ed. C. Fred Bergsten (Lexington, Mass.: D.C. Heath and Co., 1975).

5. For detail, see Ryutaro Komiya, "Japan," in *Foreign Tax Policies and Economic Growth*, Conference Report of the National Bureau of Economic Research and the Brookings Institution (New York: National Bureau of Economic Research, 1966), pp. 39–90.

6. For detail, see Ryutaro Komiya, "Direct Foreign Investment in Postwar Japan," in *Direct Foreign Investment in Asia and the Pacific*, ed. Peter Drysdale (Canberra: Australian National University Press, 1972), pp.137–72.

7. *Nihon Keizai Shimbun*, December 11, 1973.

Comments on
Ryutaro Komiya's
Chapter

Robert F. Dernberger

At the very outset of his discussion of economic planning in Japan, Professor Komiya downgrades the "national economic plan" on the ground that, although an official government document which specifies targets or estimates for major types of economic activity, it has become less and less relevant to economic policymaking. Not only is the national economic plan not binding on those who do make economic policy, but the plan targets represent little more than wishful thinking within the context of current public opinion. Because the targets in the plan are too aggregate to be operational and they have a record of becoming out-of-line with reality very quickly, economic policymakers do not pay much attention to the plan. I find this argument convincing and in accord with my knowledge of Japanese planning.

However, Komiya goes on in the bulk of the chapter to present evidence supporting his contention that a considerable amount of what he calls planning takes place within various agencies of the government, despite the ineffectiveness of "national" economic planning. Komiya's examples of this effective planning include the adoption of specific tax exemptions, subsidies, tariffs, and low-interest loans to stimulate desired and discourage undesired behavior in the private sector. Another type of planning, which he calls regional planning, includes those policy decisions which affect the flow of financial transfers between the central and local units of government in Japan. This regional planning is said to be the natural result of the very crucial role of the central government in financing the economic projects of the local governments, due to the lack of local fiscal autonomy. Again, Komiya presents specific examples of the various governmental agencies involved and the process by which economic policies are formulated.

In his evaluation of this effective planning, Komiya argues that the resulting industrial policies have worked to protect and assist the established industries, rather than help infant industries; have failed to pursue a common objective or balance demands and supplies, but have led to an excess demand for labor in an economy already at full employment; have transferred income to preferred producers whose ability to increase output was limited by some exogenous constraint; and have served to promote the interests of big business against other interests in society. This is a substantial indictment of planning in Japan. About the only significant contribution made by planning to Japan's remarkable record of economic growth is found in the collection, exchange, and propagation of information.

Although I do not have the necessary expertise to challenge Komiya's factual presentation of planning—i.e., policymaking—in Japan, I believe it is possible to accept his account and still to question some of the more important implications of his analysis for a general evaluation of planning in the world today. First of all, should we include Japan's experience in such a general evaluation of planning—i.e., is it really meaningful to use the word "planning" to identify the various economic-policymaking activities described in Komiya's chapter? The national economic plan in Japan always has been an exercise in forecasting, not planning, and Japan's experience merely serves to point out the many problems forecasters face when making forecasts for an economy undergoing tremendous dynamic changes: forecasts become out-of-date shortly after they are made. On the other hand, even if the forecasts had been more accurate, we have no evidence that those who were engaged in actual policymaking had any intention of using the forecasts.

The regional planning discussed in Komiya's chapter involves rather crude regional estimates of the distribution of population, income, and employment, for the purpose of identifying certain areas as deserving preferential treatment when the central government works out its fiscal program and financial allocations for local units. Presumably, the purpose of this regional planning is to achieve a more equitable or desirable regional distribution of population, employment, and income. However, the chapter does not indicate whether or not these results have been achieved.

In describing the various industrial policies, Komiya provides several arguments to support his contention that interactions and negotiations between representatives of the government and business interests indeed are an important means by which economic policy is formulated in Japan. On the other hand, he notes the partial or particular concern of these interactions and negotiations, the absence of an attempt to coordinate the resulting policies in regard to the achievement of well-defined social and economic objectives, and the frequent counterproductive or contradictory effects of these policies. However, for these shortcomings one should not hold responsible those who advocate planning as a meaningful and useful tool in mobilizing and allocating resources.

This same argument applies to an analysis of the national economic plan in Japan. We should recognize as such those exercises in planning which are for purely political purposes, and should not label exercises in political decisionmaking as "planning" merely because they result in a policy decision. And we should not judge planning to have failed when the planners and the plan are given no role in the determination of economic policies. My own reading of the Japanese national economic plan is that it is a political platform of the prime minister and his party, demanded by the electorate as the government's promise of things to come. It is allowed to be biased in the downward direction, so that what actually happens makes the government's record look even more remarkable. In addition, the plan can even be specified by the prime minister, with the planners assigned only the task of working out the details. Thus, the "doubling-national-income in ten years" plan was initiated by the prime minister, who asked for a plan with exactly those results even though it called for a rate of growth below that being realized in Japan's economy at the time!

I do not mean, however, that exercises in planning cannot have an important impact on the economy when the plan and the planners are not an integral part of the decisionmaking process. French planning presents a good example where this is the case. Another example is the very first Japanese economic plan, which is not included in Komiya's chapter. This plan was drawn up in the early 1950s and was little more than a simple estimate of Japan's needs and capabilities, i.e., an exercise in arithmetic, not planning. Never intended to be operational or to determine economic policy, this plan nonetheless had a very significant impact on later developments in the Japanese economy. Emerging from the Second World War a defeated nation, with the economy "over-destroyed" by American bombs, the Japanese population was demoralized and was dependent on foreign supplies for its very livelihood. The future seemed to offer little hope, except the unhappy choice between generous foreign aid or starvation. By merely specifying a few simple yet not unreasonable assumptions, and by making a few crude estimates about future trends in productivity, investment, and supplies from abroad, this first plan showed the Japanese that they could hope to return to the standard of living they had enjoyed in the 1930s. The plan thereby contributed in no small way to a significant change in Japanese attitudes which made possible the sustained and successful efforts to rehabilitate and industrialize the Japanese economy.

These remarks about the arguments presented in Komiya's chapter, as well as in other chapters in this volume, lead me to propose a possible distinction between three types of planning which may help to clarify or even eliminate the many semantic debates in discussions about planning. When talking about planning as we observe it in the world today, we should carefully specify whether we mean (a) an economic activity intended actually to alter the allocation of resources in a coordinated manner to achieve some well-defined objective (*allocation planning*); (b) a political activity intended to give the impression the government is making rational policy decisions and to gain support for its economic policies and leadership (*propaganda*); or (c) an educational activity intended to provide decisionmakers in the public and private sectors greater information about possible developments in the future (*forecasting*).

Finally, Komiya concludes with the observation that the Japanese planning process would be most difficult to introduce in other countries because of their very different cultural and political traditions, especially due to the atypical power position of the central government in Japan's economy. After reading Komiya's study of planning in Japan, I find it somewhat difficult to see why another country would want to follow Japan's lead. Rather, Japan's experience, as depicted by Komiya, presents very good arguments both for those who oppose planning and for those who favor it.

If, on the one hand, the maximum rate of growth is the single goal of a society, the Japanese were very wise to ignore the possible contribution of the planners and to give free rein to the conservative Ministry of Finance and Ministry of International Trade and Industry, which pursued a policy of easy access to bank advances for the accumulation of fixed assets by big business, with only the level of foreign exchange reserves as a serious constraint. With the exception of a few periods of tight money, the profits of oligopolistic industries and large advances supplied by the banking system provided the Japanese with a remarkable rate of capital accumulation and growth—a rate of growth any planner would be proud to achieve. Furthermore, Japan was able to have its cake and eat it too, becoming the third largest economy in the world, embarrassed by an ever-growing accumulation of foreign exchange.

If, on the other hand, a society's objectives include not only growth but also the provision of social overhead capital, social welfare, equitable income distribution, and the reduction of pollution, the Japanese experience in the absence of coordinated comprehensive planning, would indicate its desirability.

Comments on
Claude Seibel's and
Ryutaro Komiya's
Chapters

Witold Trzeciakowski

It is interesting to compare the sequence of development strategies in France and Japan. The starting point of the economies in terms of national income per capita was different, but both countries needed reconstruction and in both the governments accepted full responsibility for the promotion of development and full employment. France accepted a strategy of high, but at the same time balanced, growth, while the Japanese economy reached unprecedented growth rates of 9–12 percent per year. Any outsider who would like to discover the theoretical explanation of this striking phenomenon is left with the impression that the Japanese historical experience is not applicable to other countries. The samurai tradition transplanted to the management of large corporations; the exceptional discipline of Japanese society; the high level and widespread character of higher technical education; the containment of consumption and, consequently, the enormous internal savings, devoted totally to development with no armaments expenditures; finally the long historical tradition of a very strong central government—all these factors together can give, at least partially, an explanation of the Japanese "miracle." However, what is interesting is that, in spite of the differing paths of development, both economies are now reaching the stage when the same basic question is posed: growth—to what ends?

How to eliminate existing economic and social disequilibrium, especially in the domain of the environment; how to improve the quality of life; how to abolish the drastic discrepancies between the rich and the poor—these are the fundamental problems that are becoming the growing concern of planners in both economies. There is a common consensus that there exists no economic mechanism which could solve these growing social and environmental problems automatically. Hence, it becomes necessary to enlarge the sphere of central planning; to put greater stress on *social ends* than—as hitherto—on *economic means*; and to strengthen governmental intervention in regard to social problems. Predictions only "as reliable as a long-term weather forecast with some flavor of wishful thinking added" will probably not suffice. Whether these changes are compatible with the contemporary corporation-dominated market remains to be seen.

Let us consider the different possible relationships between planning and decisionmaking. In centrally planned economies, planning is basically not separated from decisionmaking. On the other hand, both the French and the Japanese systems show a strict demarcation line between planning and government intervention or government industrial policymaking. Seibel looks at planning as part of the varied means of government intervention in development, with no direct control over any of the other means employed. Nor is planning considered as a continuous process. Rather, it is viewed as an opening move in a process of consultations among government departments and between them and spokesmen of social groups. Similarly in Japan, the plan is treated as a forecast and is not at all binding. Hence, consistency between long- and short-term planning and decisionmaking, as well as between the overall and the branch or sectoral levels, is sought differently in centrally planned economies and in developed market economies. These divergences may be further deepened if Seibel is right, i.e., if the actual planning evolves from imperative towards less *dirigiste*, more indicative planning.

Both authors stress the increasing role of the "technostructure" (using Galbraith's terminology). It would be interesting to know more precisely whether this tendency is a characteristic feature of an advanced stage of development in any economy, or specifically only of economies with market relationships. Similarly, there is the intricate question whether inflationary processes are a characteristic feature of contemporary market economies with Keynesian concepts of government spending. What are the general conclusions from the evident failure to stop inflation and to introduce a workable incomes policy? Does the "active policy of stimulating supply" without the containment of domestic demand—and the lack of harmonization of national policies at an international level—lead inevitably to monetary disequilibria? Is this, in the authors' view, a structural or only a transitional weakness of the contemporary economic system? What is the potential contribution of the planning system of developed market economies in solving these fundamental problems?

The analysis of development strategies of both economies throws light also on the intricate choice between a protectionist policy and a policy of an internationally open market. Both countries started with a strong protectionist policy and both tried to switch to a policy of international specialization and of opening their domestic industries to external competition. In both cases, the governments were (and still are) facing great difficulties, in the opposition of strong vested interests to the removal of protectionist barriers. In essence both economies have reached the very advanced stage of industrialization when foreign trade liberalization serves best the overall interest of their economies. However, society as a whole, which benefits from trade liberalization, is politically weaker than the economically smaller, but politically stronger, vested interests of specific groups, backed by powerful lobbies. Hence, the constant danger of jeopardizing any healthy attempts to implement a rigorous and effective policy of an open, competitive economy. These internal difficulties are characteristic for developed and developing economies all over the world. Thus, the practical experience of France and Japan in trying to overcome these problems is of great interest and deserves a more detailed description.

The next problem of vital importance concerns the role of the state in economic development. As already mentioned, planning in both countries is a particular form of the comprehensive process of government intervention. The striking feature of French planning is the strong element of public discussion— "concertation"—and, as an ultimate goal—"participation." In Japan, the relationship between the government and the managers of large corporations seems to have a more informal and less public character. In both cases governmental interventionism is relatively much stronger than in other developed market economies, although the government's role in economic decisionmaking is greater in Japan than in France. However, the prospects for the future are not identical. The French planning system faces the fundamental difficulty of how to solve the contradiction between the political sovereignty of the state and the limits on its economic decisionmaking power resulting from the progress of economic integration and the ever growing role of multinational corporations. It remains to be seen how this basic dilemma will be solved in the coming years.

Actually, the crux of all planning systems, including the French and the Japanese, is the thorny problem of decentralization of decisions: the coordination of global and sectoral policies, national and regional policies. No known planning system—whether in the East or in the West—can claim that it has found a fully satisfactory solution to this problem. The French FIFI model can be looked upon as an important step forward in macroeconomic modeling. However, its role is limited to analyzing basic variants of the overall plan and helping to formulate a set of general guidelines rather than a detailed program of economic and social policy. A similar lack of internal consistency between overall macro-planning and sectoral *genkyoku* policymaking in Japan is likewise stressed by Professor Komiya. Paradoxically, one would be inclined to conclude that in these conditions the weakness of the planning system cannot hinder the dynamic development of the economy. Still, the fundamental question persists: growth—to what ends and in whose interests?

Chapter Eight

Planning in Poland

Krzysztof Porwit

PLANNING IN THE SYSTEM OF FUNCTIONING
OF THE ECONOMY

We are concerned here with socioeconomic planning understood as one of the basic functions of guidance over the activities of the whole national economy. It comprises processes of decisionmaking and is closely interlinked with the other two functions of control, i.e., organizing (preparing the system for its activities) and supervising implementation (including adaptive measures).[a]

In the conditions of our socialist sociopolitical system there is a close relationship between the manner of functioning of the economy, on the one hand, and the setup of planning, on the other. When considering the tasks of planning, as well as its methods and procedures, we cannot limit our interest to the questions of general policy at the governmental level. The crucial issue is to implement such policies by shaping the activities of particular segments (subsystems) of the economy in accordance with the lines set in the national, economy-wide plan.

It is necessary to consider such an issue, as there is an obvious inter-dependence between the feasible level of overall, societal goals and the level of efficiency attained by the particular economic organizations. In fact, their contribution to the task of maximizing socioeconomic goals is considered as the basic criterion of efficiency. Simultaneously, there are possibilities to consider this issue in an explicit way because of the predominance of social ownership of the means of production.[1]

The manner in which this issue has to be tackled and solved is subject to different views and opinions. According to my view, one cannot look for

---

[a]I shall use the word "control" in the technical engineering sense, to refer to all kinds of influence exerted by a higher hierarchical level, rather than to imply only direct administrative influence.

positive solutions by making a sharp distinction between either (a) a "pure" command system, with a detailed network of administrative orders and limits set by the central level and determining all the actions for every enterprise, or (b) a "pure" system of parametric regulation, in which the central level would try only to induce the enterprises to behave according to a desired pattern by means of regulating general rules of behavior and influencing the parameters used for micro decisionmaking. There are no "pure" systems but only a predominance of one way of influence and also a possible danger of neglecting the other one. Our experiences allow one to draw the conclusion that a one-sided emphasis on the tools of a command approach leaves in fact a part of socioeconomic processes outside the scope of effective central influence. This exerts a negative effect from the viewpoint of the regulatory mechanism and motive forces for efficiency and socioeconomic development.[2]

In order to be more explicit let us consider the following points.

1. Practical possibilities of central control over activities of particular organizations are limited. Within a comprehensive, economy-wide plan it is possible to master only aggregate indicators of partial activities plus some chosen indicators of more detailed processes. So there remains a wide range of choices which are not decided upon at the center. If the economy-wide criteria of social rationality cannot be directly applied, there remains an open question: who makes the decisions elsewhere, and how?

2. A network of interconnected plan indicators, integrated with the central plan, has to be worked out well in advance of the period covered by the plan. It is hardly possible to keep such a network fixed. A tendency to do so will prevent necessary adaptive measures. Endeavors to introduce such measures create a quite cumbersome formal procedure and make the whole idea of fixed targets and limits questionable.

3. Economic organizations tend to strive for their own criteria of choice and preferences, which may not coincide with those of the central, economy-wide point of view. Having in mind their own preferences, the organizations tend to bargain to get relatively easier tasks and more ample resource allocations.

As the result of the above features, one may make a distinction between two spheres: (a) where the direct forms of central control are really workable and lead to definite effects; and (b) where the assumed instruments of control become illusory, and no other effective instruments and motive forces are in practice available.

It is not easy to draw a distinct border line between such spheres. The first one includes: (a) enforcement of far-reaching structural changes, considered necessary from the viewpoint of long-term development; (b) mobilizing adequate internal resources for this purpose; (c) keeping a policy of social equity in terms of income distribution and availability of social services; (d) implementation of a large number of big investment projects, as well as R&D activities, which are considered as priorities from the viewpoint of increasing national economic potential.

On the other hand, let us label the second sphere with the somewhat vague name of "microstructure," i.e., a great variety of small-scale activities, which primarily concern: (a) current decisions on output and input-mix in conformity with a detailed structure of demand and a prevailing supply of production factors; (b) introduction of technological innovations (in terms of new or improved products, changed technologies, etc.); (c) embarking upon still other activities aimed at maximization of efficiency of every "microunit" (a plant, workshop, work-team, community).

A relative weakness in this sphere not only becomes a problem of an economic and technical nature but also has its sociopolitical implications. The people directly engaged in productive activities do not find enough possibilities to show and implement their own initiative to solve many problems within their own capacities, without having to wait for an order or permission to do so.

The approaches started in Poland in 1971 and now in the stage of development and implementation tend to keep and strengthen the positive forces of central guidance and at the same time to introduce radical changes in the "microstructure" in order to bring more power into the second motive force of development, the one coming "from below."[3]

This line, to be described more fully in the next section, is very closely linked to the change in priorities in general, socioeconomic policy goals, which since 1971 has put a basic emphasis on the satisfaction of human needs (in the sense of ensuring their quickest possible growth without endangering a necessary further development of economic potential). On the one hand, this order of priorities favors changes in the system of planning and management, by bridging a gap between overall and partial goals. Simultaneously, however, the implementation of this policy depends heavily on the success of such changes in planning and management—for example, in increasing the attainable level of efficiency in every economic unit.

Finally, it would be wrong to assume that solutions have been sought in the sphere of market forces as an alternative to central planning and control. We are striving for a number of self-regulating devices to operate within limited scope and subject to central guidance. In this sense there are notions and instruments which are similar to those known in the market economies, but the basic structure is different. Simultaneously, there is an important stream of effort aimed at changes in infrastructural conditions for the economic mechanism, such as restructuring the administrative apparatus, organizational changes, modernizing the technology of management functions, improving the quality of labor and of human relations, etc. In this sense, the tasks of central control and planning are not limited to economic activities within a given (existing) set of infrastructural conditions, but they comprise also the area of reshaping these conditions.[4]

With this perspective, we shall consider in the following sections such main features of the planning system as (a) the respective roles of the center and the enterprises (economic organizations), as well as the ties between them; (b) the functions performed by long-, medium- and short-term plans respectively; and (c) the technology of planning, i.e., its methods and techniques. We shall concentrate on the issues encountered during the last few years and presenting challenges in the years to come.

A MULTILEVEL SYSTEM OF
PLANNING (INTERLEVEL TIES)

Within the socialized sector of Polish economy there exists a hierarchic structure of authority. This sector covers an overwhelming majority of all economic activities—in 1972, 98.3 percent of industrial output,[5] 88.1 percent of contruction,[6] etc.—with the exception of agriculture, where a major part of arable land (81 percent[7]) and of marketable output (82 percent[8]) remains in private ownership. Existence of a hierarchic structure of authority means that the higher levels (up to the central government level) have the right to determine certain activities to be performed within particular socialized enterprises, as well as to limit the inflow of production factors.

Activities and definite actions take place not only within this hierarchic structure but also between its members, on the one hand, and households, private farms, and workshops, as well as external markets (foreign firms), on the other.

In this context, a multilevel system of planning and management and the nature of interlevel ties involve the question of delegation of authority, within the hierarchic structure, to make decisions. The solutions depend on: (a) the scope and nature of information necessary to appraise the problems involved, (b) the nature of criteria of choice used in decisionmaking, and (c) the scope of direct and indirect consequences which a decision may involve in terms of interbranch and intertemporal dependencies. As a rule, the central level has to concentrate on those problems which link the main sectors—socialized, household, private (mainly agricultural)—and their connections with the rest of the world, which have far-reaching interbranch and intertemporal consequences. Next we explain how specific processes subject to planning and their indicators are related to the nature of control instruments applied in the respective fields.

Central Planning of Relations Between Households
and the Socialized Sector

In relation to *households* there are mainly two kinds of control instruments: (a) those related to money incomes and to retail prices of goods and services, and (b) institutional rights of access to free social services and other benefits. The demand for goods and services is influenced by planning and implementing these instruments. At the same time, there arises a crucial problem for the socialized sector of the economy to plan and deliver corresponding supplies.

Thus, the main tasks of central planning in this field comprise: (a) setting the desired growth rate for real wages and consumption (e.g., there was an 18 percent target for the growth of real wages in 1971–75, in comparison with 10 percent achieved in 1966–70[9]), as well as for particular branches of social services; (b) making sure that corresponding supplies will be available from domestic outputs and imports. For this purpose, there was a shift of emphasis towards the output of consumer goods in the plan for 1971–75 (see below, p. 252).

The approaches applied in the central plan in this field are concerned with general and structural equilibrium between the demand and supply on the consumer market. The question of general equilibrium is tackled by a consistency-checking technique known as "balancing of money income and expenditures of the population" for the economy as a whole and its main regions. For the purpose of structural equilibrium planning, analyses and forecasts are made concerning expected demand for main groups of consumer goods and services, which are linked with corresponding policies for income distribution and retail prices. These policies are heavily influenced by socio-political criteria of appraisal and choice. The aim is to ensure a relatively high level of basic items of consumption, especially food, communal, and cultural services. For nutrition, this can be exemplified by the average content of 3400 calories, 91 grams of proteins, and 108 grams of fats in the daily diet for 1970,[10] i.e., a level much nearer to that of highly developed economies than the relative income per capita would suggest (compare fn. 29). All this serves as the basis for targets concerning the development of supplies, from both internal sources and imports. There are, of course, feedbacks, since an assessment of supply feasibility exerts an influence on policies concerning incomes and prices.

This procedure leads to directives informing the respective economic organizations about aggregate indicators of market supplies expected from them. Also, however, the organizations themselves must determine a more detailed specification of their outputs, using their own market research as well as that of specialized trade organizations. Final arrangements are made on the basis of trade contracts between the producers and the trade network.

The way in which an ultimate structure of transactions is formed depends on the nature of the goods and services in question. This in turn is connected with the manner of price formation and control. For a list of goods and services considered as high-order necessities for the consumers, there is control of prices, which are kept stable, often at a subsidized level (as in the case of meat, milk, butter, cheese, and flour).[11] In many instances deliveries of such necessities enter into the specification of targets set for the respective organizations. Outside this range, prices are formed by a producer's cost-plus-profit calculation, compared with an estimate of a demand-price level. Producers tend then to increase and to restructure their sales, according to the specification of demand. Whether and how far they are forced to do this and induced to increase their efficiency, including innovations in product characteristics and technologies, depends, of course, on the conditions of the respective segments of the market—i.e., prevalence of a buyers' or sellers' market. Gradual shifts toward a buyers' market contribute to relative strengthening of efficiency-promoting forces. But in certain segments of the market there is still the necessity to reinforce the buyers' interests by means of stricter price controls and plan targets (e.g., in basic food products, communal services, housing, and standard quality apparel).

Central Planning in the Field of Agriculture

In relation to farmers, the central plan exerts its influence primarily through the policy of purchase prices linked with contracts for deliveries of agricultural products; the policy of selling prices of producers' goods used for farm output and investment, linked with credits; taxation policy; an extension of agro-technical service facilities as well as promotion of cooperative forms of mechanization and trade services. At the same time, there is a more direct influence—mainly through investment policy—on the expansion of capacity in state-owned farms, especially in large-scale livestock breeding and in connection with industrial processing of agricultural products.

Since 1971, a number of important policy measures have been introduced to raise agricultural output.[12] They include abolition of compulsory deliveries of some basic products at low prices and considerable increases in normal contract-purchase prices. Also, supplies of fodder, fertilizers, construction materials, agricultural machines, and equipment increased markedly. Free health services have been extended to cover individual farmers and their families. Territorial administration at the lowest level of rural communities has been reorganized in order to strengthen it and to allow most local problems to be solved there without involving higher administrative levels. As a result of the changes introduced in December 1972, the lowest administrative units (4,368 village and settlement communities) were transformed into 2,365 communities—relatively larger entities the authorities of which took over responsibility for a number of matters belonging formerly to the competence of district authorities. (A district is a middle-level territorial unit; there are 390 districts for the entire area of Poland equal to 312.7 thousand square kilometers and a population of 33.2 million inhabitants at the end of 1972.) These matters, about one hundred in number, involve most questions concerning the contacts of the people with the territorial administration (related to land use, property rights, water use, roads, construction activities, etc.), as well as questions concerned with socioeconomic activities within the community. The latter are subject to coordination according to community development plans, mainly from the viewpoint of linking local services and infrastructural facilities with the activities of organizational units outside the direct control of local authorities.

Considering expected effects of such measures, the plan for 1971–75 included the target of doubling the annual growth rate for agricultural output, from 1.8 percent in 1966–70 to 3.6–3.9 percent in 1971–75.[13] The results, partly due to favorable climatic conditions, have proved to be much higher, as the annual increase in total output for 1971–73 amounts to about 6 percent, with still higher indicators for the purchases of such basic products as livestock (more than 10 percent annually) and milk (more than 11 percent).[14]

The tasks of central planning in this field involve a number of analyses, forecasts, and balancing accounts to set policy and to devise implementation instruments which would induce farmers to act accordingly. They involve also programming methods and techniques related to ensuring supplies and services for agricultural production, as well as to the links between agriculture and industrial processing of its products.

Central Planning in the Field of Economic
Relations with Other Countries

In relation to foreign trade and other forms of international economic cooperation, there is a large set of problems which are considered and decided upon at the central level.

First, there is a group of issues related to basic raw materials, fuel and energy sources, construction materials, basic food supplies, etc. These are the strategic materials of fundamental importance for the present and future functioning of the entire socioeconomic system. No one but the central level can have the responsiblity in this field. The issues are much too complex to be appraised according to profitability criteria of any industrial organization. There are two reasons: (a) There are possible conflicts between short- and long-term considerations, and a predominance of relatively short-term preferences from the viewpoint of partial, sectoral criteria of choice. In sectoral calculations, present or independently forecast prices can be used, whereas a comprehensive central analysis can include induced interbranch implications expected for the future. (b) The managers of particular sectoral organizations do not represent only their own interests. If the decisions involve risks of far-reaching, interbranch and intertemporal consequences, they must be "reinsured" by the government, representing the overall interests of the society.

Second, there is a more general problem of policy choices affecting the best way of utilizing potential benefits of an international division of labor. This involves international agreements. multilateral and bilateral, which set a framework for various aspects of cooperation: trade, industrial, technical, scientific, financial, etc. Also included are a number of major ventures and projects undertaken with foreign partners (e.g., a cellulose plant in the U.S.S.R.; a combed yarn mill in Poland built with the cooperation of the German Democratic Republic; contracts with the U.S.S.R. for gear-boxes for construction and road-building equipment, with the International Harvester Company, Fiat, the Japanese roller-bearing industry, Swedish Machine Tool Co., etc.). [15]

Finally, there is the issue of control over current transactions, where diverse instruments, financial and administrative, are used.

Among the most important problems concentrating attention of central planning are those linked with the implementation of the Comprehensive Program for Socialist Economic Integration adopted in 1971 by the XXVth Session of the Council for Mutual Economic Assistance (CMEA). The measures involved here [16] are related to diverse forms of coordination for plans and policies, as well as joint projects decided upon at the respective central government levels. They are aimed also at facilitating and improving institutional and financial conditions for direct cooperation among enterprises of different countries, as well as for development of multinational enterprises and other economic organizations. The effects up till now, and the efforts for the future, are concentrated in three main areas: (a) solving jointly the problems of energy sources and raw materials, (b) extending and deepening industrial specialization and cooperation, and (c) extending scientific and technical cooperation.

Being primarily concerned with a number of basic policy problems and strategic issues, the central plan does not attempt to solve the question of a full specification of exports and imports for particular organizations (enterprises). It is the job of the latter to find the best ways to respond to external demand, to attain desired quality standards, and to be competitive in terms of costs and prices.

Since 1971 a number of measures have been taken in order to accelerate our foreign trade and develop other forms of international cooperation. Although trade in earlier decades was increasing considerably, the share of Poland in world trade remained at the prewar level of 1.1 percent.[17] At the same time, the economic potential of Poland was developing at a much higher rate, causing a considerable increase (a doubling) of our share in the respective world figures in terms of output. Although our exports were becoming much more diversified, with a growing share for industrial manufactures, nevertheless this trend was not sufficient to give the current earning capacity needed for a more radical restructuring and modernization of our technologies, product specifications, etc. The latter, in turn, was an essential precondition to attain a higher level of foreign exchange earning capacity. Mainly in this context, a policy was adopted to use foreign credit facilities more widely (i.e., to concentrate attention on licenses, cooperation contracts, and other purchases leading to mastering of new or improved technologies, higher quality standards, and so forth).

This approach has been connected with various steps aiming at a closer and more direct impact of foreign trade and cooperation on the efficiency of economic organizations. On the one hand, industrial firms, as well as internal trade organizations, are now more directly interested in the financial profitability of their exports and imports, because they sell and buy at "transaction" prices, i.e., current foreign exchange prices converted into domestic currency at a uniform exchange rate. Formerly, internal (fixed) prices were used, and the positive and negative differences in comparison with values at transaction prices, were handled through a centralized budgetary account. For the time being, this new solution is more generally applied in exports. On the import side there are exceptions, in the sense that the internal purchase prices of imported basic commodities (such as cotton, wool, mineral raw materials, etc.) are fixed for a given period of time (pending a revision), in order to protect individual users from short-term price variations or differentials in particular transactions.

Some organizational measures have been taken also in the direction of linking a number of specialized foreign trade firms with the respective industrial organizations or licensing the latter to engage directly in external transactions (especially in industries dealing with investment goods and equipment). This allows the industry to get a better knowledge and understanding of foreign markets and to ensure more direct links for technical know-how, extending field services for foreign customers, entering into direct industrial cooperation with foreign firms, etc. Similarly, there are now wider possibilities for the domestic trade firms to use exports and imports as more flexible tools to enrich and diversify the supplies in the consumer market (e.g., apparel, cosmetics, confectionery, and canned fish products).

In 1971–73, there has been an acceleration of exports, which were growing at an average annual rate of about 14 percent, in comparison with 9.8 percent in the preceding five years, and a still stronger one for imports, where the earlier annual rate of 9.1 percent has been more than doubled (see below p.256). The policy guidelines for 1974–75 emphasize targets to raise the volume of exports by at least 34 percent, and the volume of imports by the still considerable though smaller amount of at least 24 percent, over the two years.[18]

Central Planning and Control over Transactions among Socialized Enterprises

These transactions represent the major part of intermediate demand and of the investment component of final demand. In this sense they are of a secondary, induced nature in relation to the fields of action discussed above. Consequently they are under the influence of planning and control instruments related to those fields. Through such links, value categories and economic efficiency calculations can and do exert important influence on decisions made within socialized enterprises.

A number of steps have been taken since 1971 in order to strengthen the role of economic efficiency calculations at the enterprise level to guide managerial decisions, especially for short-term problems but also for such future-oriented activities as replacement and modernization of equipment, and development and introduction of new products and technologies—i.e., investment with relatively short gestation periods and relatively less mutual dependence on projects to be implemented elsewhere in the economy. At the same time, the central plan has strengthened its direct links over basic development projects characterized by multiple interbranch relationships.

There are two parallel streams of actions aiming to reshape and improve planning and management. First, a number of big industrial and trading organizations, called "pilot organizations," have already adopted a new, comprehensive system of operating rules.[19] They accounted in 1973 for about 20 percent of total industrial output. In the selection of the enterprises for the new management approach, a policy has been adopted of concentrating on those organizations where there were a full understanding and initiative for these changes. In many cases it was necessary to start with some preparatory measures, e.g., to change organizational structures or some price relationships. It is expected that in 1974 more than 40 percent of industrial output will be produced in enterprises working according to the new rules and that the whole operation of switching to these rules will be completed in 1975.

The second stream of actions comprises a schedule for implementation of general measures—pertaining to the whole economy, not only to selected enterprises—in such fields as organization of investment processes, price control, planning and management of foreign trade, implementation of wage policies, restructuring of territorial and central administration, strengthening of the educational system, reshaping the organizational and financial framework for research and development activities, etc. These measures are considered indispensable to create the proper environment for the successful operation of efficiency targets in enterprises.

One may conclude then that we have adopted in Poland a comprehensive program of measures,[20] which should converge towards a predetermined pattern. This is not conceived in a sense of an historic "optimal model," but rather as a set of historically conditioned and changeable guidelines. The main point is to set in motion self-learning processes leading to gradual adaptation of management methods to the challenges of the future.

Functioning Rules in the Pilot Organizations.[21] The main feature lies in the change of incentives—raising wages and bonuses—from a dependence on the percentage of plan fulfillment to a link with the improvement in performance in comparison with a preceding "base" period. Performance is measured by the indicators of value added and profit. The increase in value added serves as a basis for wage increases, and the increase in profit, for bonuses to managerial personnel.

The organization as a whole is obliged to keep wages in a period t within a limit W_t determined as follows:

$$W_t = \overline{W}_{t-1} \, (1 + r_w)$$

where $\overline{W}_{t-1}$ = wages paid in the base period, and r_w = permitted rate of growth. This rate is determined as

$$r_w = R r_v$$

where r_v = the rate of growth of value added, and R = a centrally set parameter of elasticity of wages in relation to value added. Parameter R is set separately for each organization for a period of three years, usually at the level of 0.6–0.7. If the organization consists of many enterprises, the level of R can be differentiated for particular enterprises. This is decided internally by the management of the higher organization.

With a sufficiently high growth of value added, there will be a surplus of the available wage fund, W_t, over the amount due according to the existing wage rates, $\overline{W}_t$. A part of such a surplus goes to form a reserve fund (to be used in case of a slowdown in growth of output), and another part can be used for extra remuneration related to implementation of targets set internally within the organization. The management is free to shift employment among particular workshops and services, as the distribution of the available wage fund by shops is not specified by higher authorities.

There is a similar mechanism regulating the growth of managerial bonuses, with an additional feature of progressive taxation on them. The fund for bonuses is formed as a predetermined percentage of net profits. A part of this fund (at least 10 percent of the increment over the level of the previous period) goes to form a reserve. The rest is subject to tax at a rate ranging from 10 to 80 percent of the increment. The tax rate rises depending on the ratio of this increment to the base level of bonuses paid previously. The funds forming a reserve are not taxed, and they can be used to neutralize the impact of a decrease in net profits.

Value added is calculated as the value of sales *minus* the cost of materials and services, *minus* the repayment of investment credits. The value of sales is measured as revenue in effective prices (internal prices or transaction prices in the case of exports), *plus* subsidies (if applicable).

The enterprises are expected to be able to sell their products at prices which will give a gross profit allowing them to cover taxes related partly to the value of wages and partly to the value of capital. The net profit after taxes will be used to repay investment credits (if depreciation allowances do not suffice), and to pay managerial bonuses, to form reserve funds, and to create an internal fund for "ex ante" self-financing of investment. The latter part is progressively taxed if it surpasses a certain percentage of the capital stock. The financial position of an enterprise depends then on the prices it gets for its products at home and abroad. This position can be improved if costs are decreased, the output mix is better matched to the structure of demand, and/or new profitable products are introduced.

In other words, there is wide scope for efficiency-promoting initiative on the part of enterprises. However, this may not be true if the producers are in a position to enforce their supply prices on the buyers. Such cases may occur in the conditions of a sellers' market, especially in transactions between productive enterprises (e.g., in many kinds of construction materials and investment goods characterized by a strong and rising demand) and also in some segments of the consumer market (such as meat products and furniture), and price controls serve to counteract them. At the same time, there are instances where the structure of final prices seeks to promote consumption of certain products (especially basic items of household expenditure—both goods and services), and to constrain demand for others (not only for socially less desirable items, such as alcoholic beverages and tobacco, but also some relatively more luxurious goods, such as fashionable clothes, private cars, etc.). In order not to mislead the producers, it is essential then to apply financial and fiscal instruments (subsidies and taxes), as well as explicit plan directives, to guide production. Finally, there is the field of major development choices, where the mechanism based on financial criteria does not suffice and centrally devised and coordinated programs do play a leading part.

LONG-, MEDIUM-, AND SHORT-TERM PLANS

Since 1971 one can see a growing emphasis on the role of long- and medium-term plans—on an increase of their quality and effective impact on socioeconomic development. This does not mean, of course, that the issues of a more distant future are considered as more important than those of today and the immediate future. On the contrary, the main justification comes from a growing understanding that the possibilities to execute control over current processes become heavily limited if there is no sufficiently clear and well-rounded development program for the periods to follow. The question of linking and reconciling short-term (static) and longer-term (dynamic) criteria of efficiency has no easy and straightforward solution. Neither can it be based on the assumption that a series of short-term optimizations will lead to a desired path of development, nor is it possible to determine detailed time schedules extending far into the future and to subordinate short-term actions to them. The plans covering relatively longer time horizons do not correspond just to a series of interlinked plans for shorter periods. They differ in their tasks and nature. Consequently, they also need different methodological approaches.

Long-Term Plans

The main task of a long-term plan for fifteen-twenty years is to identify and to start problem-solving actions which need a long time for their completion and the attainment of their effects. The point is to devise such actions in order to shape the future according to the challenges of the future and not merely on the basis of the past and present. According to our experience, the following features of long-term planning deserve special emphasis:

1. There is a particular need for a whole set of interlinked forecasting studies. We have in mind here exploratory forecasts which outline the probable development of population, of the main fields of science and technology, of

world trade and other external conditions for economic cooperation, etc. Of great importance also are problem-oriented, normative forecasts which outline factors influencing patterns of future social goals and features of the future sociocultural pattern of life in a socialist society.

2. These forecasting studies have to be linked in a comprehensive manner. On the one hand, one must get a systematic picture of qualitative interdependencies—"cause-effect" relations—through appropriate techniques, such as "relevance tree" networks. On the other hand, it is necessary to obtain an approximate picture of demand-supply balance for basic production factors, energy sources, etc. Comprehensiveness does not mean that one tries to cover all future activities. Rather, it refers to endeavors to cover all problems of a *strategic* importance for socioeconomic development. In planning for the period 1971-90, we have concentrated our attention on the following sets of problems: [22]

a. *The human factors of development* are linked with material consumption and social welfare goals. According to actual forecasts there will be a radical change in labor supply conditions. In comparison with a net increase of three million people entering employment in the ten years 1971–80, it is expected that there will be only 600 thousand in 1981–85 and still less, i.e., 300 thousand, in 1986–90. In other words, the net inflow at the end of the eighties will be one-fifth as great as at present. Considering in addition the consequences of a program to diminish the length of the work week as well as of an expected acceleration of the demand for labor-intensive services, planning must give particular weight to measures to increase the rate of growth of labor productivity.

This forms a background for policy choices related to the development of capacities, their structural changes, directions for technological change, etc. However, there is also an emphasis on qualitative changes in the labor force considered from the economic and sociocultural viewpoints. Related programs concerning material consumption, education, health, recreational facilities, and the social and cultural framework for human relations are considered then in the context of a feedback between the social goals ("for the people") and the basic factor of their implementation ("through the people").

b. *Natural and material resources* constitute the next major field, where development programs are considered mainly from the following angles: (i) extending our own material base (especially coal mining) as well as international cooperation links; (ii) wider utilization of substitution (especially synthetic new materials from the chemical industry) and technological innovations to economize scarce basic resources; and (iii) devoting ever more attention to preservation of the natural environment (it is estimated that at least 1.5 percent of national income will be devoted to that purpose in the late eighties).

c. *International cooperation and trade problems* are treated not so much in a context of estimating a desired pattern and volume of trade, but mainly by preparing and setting in motion policies necessary for the attainment of such a pattern. This involves, first of all, various measures to tighten economic integration with the other members of the CMEA—i.e., a coordination of the basic strategies and policies of the respective national perspective plans, as well as a more detailed elaboration of jointly undertaken programs related to raw materials, industrial specialization and cooperation, joint investment ventures, etc. As examples of such measures, one can mention cooperation with Czechoslovakia in the copper industry, projects for joint CMEA investments in the USSR (iron, cellulose, asbestos, nickel), and many cases of cooperation in the machine tool industry.[23] Long-term planning also forms the premises for programs and bilateral agreements for economic cooperation with other countries, both developed and developing.

d. *Investment processes* are considered a kind of lens to focus attention on the factors indispensable for the strategies just discussed. Since capital formation in the period in question will be much greater than the total present capital stock, there are numerous questions about how to utilize this potential freedom of choice in regard to structural changes from the interbranch and interregional viewpoints, technical modernization, etc. Naturally enough one meets a tendency to estimate future investment demand at a level surpassing supply capacities in terms of the growth of GNP and its distribution. In view of uncertainties related to future capital-output ratios, it is hardly possible to assume a strict balancing approach here. Nevertheless, such an approach is useful to check sectoral capital formation programs and also to appraise how far qualitative changes improving capital-output and other input-output ratios are essential to implement desired goals with constrained resources.

e. Among *qualitative factors* promoting development, attention is concentrated especially on scientific research, including channeling the main areas and directions of research, extending the material base for these activities, and strengthening the transmission mechanism between science and economic activities. It is estimated that the number of scientific workers employed in research institutes and universities will amount to 5 percent of total employment in 1990, in comparison with 2 percent in 1970. There will be a strong increase in the general level of skills and professional qualifications of the labor force. An educational program will ensure that, among the age groups over twenty years, people with an education above the basic level will constitute about 66 percent in 1990, compared with 34 percent in 1970. According to the principles adopted in 1973 on the basis of a report prepared by a special Committee of Experts, a general reform of the educational system will be implemented, introducing free middle-level education (of ten years) for all children, as well as a comprehensive set of educational and training activities aiming at continuous up-dating of qualifications.

Many of the problems discussed above are considered also within another framework, that of a *perspective spatial (interregional)* plan. We have adopted a concept of regulated, polycentric concentration of economic activites, primarily in twenty–twenty-five big urban agglomerations (ten already existing, seven in formation, and the remaining to be initiated), which will serve as the main centers for economic, scientific, and cultural development. More detailed urban plans for these agglomerations have been prepared. Also, a greater number of locations for industry in the so-called "centers for accelerated growth" have been chosen. The spatial plan determines guidelines for the specialization of particular regions and for the land use pattern (including 10–15 percent of the total area earmarked for development of tourist and recreational facilities).

From a formal point of view, the perspective plan consists of:

i. Cross-sectional studies and strategy outlines which specify development policies for key issues in the main fields listed above. They are interlinked by means of a set of macroeconomic indicators and accounts. The core of this part consists of GNP projections (from the viewpoints of its creation and distribution) linked with topical studies related to labor, capital, material resources, and external relations. This serves also as a consistency checking analysis for the sectoral development programs (see below).

ii. A number of partial programs, viz.: thirty-two problem-oriented inter-branch programs, such as those related to nutrition, housing, education, raw materials, and energy resources; fourteen branch programs, concerning especially the chemical and engineering industries; and seventeen regional development programs for the respective administrative districts (voivodships) and for three macro-regions, comprising groups of neighboring districts with specific common development problems.

The approach explained above corresponds to actual practice applied in planning for the period up to 1990 and differs from earlier approaches,[24] which were concentrated primarily on economic indicators of macro-proportions of development linked with those of particular branches and regions. The difference consists primarily in greater emphasis recently on the elaboration of the sociocultural pattern of the future society, on problem-oriented interbranch programs, and on regional and interregional programs concerned especially with infrastructural problems. Correspondingly, major changes have been introduced into the procedure and methods of planning. This is reflected, inter alia, in a number of forecasting and futurist studies made by the "Committee Poland 2000" of the Polish Academy of Sciences, as well as in the formation of special commissions and working groups charged with the tasks of preparing well-founded reports on the particular problem-oriented programs. Some of these reports, especially those with wider social implications–e.g., the restructuring of the educational system, housing, the problems of youth, etc.–have been submitted to public discussion and were later appraised by the Central Committee of the Polish United Workers Party (PUWP) and by the Parliament.[25] In this way the foundations, scientific and social alike, for long-term planning have been strengthened.

Medium-Term, Five-Year Plans

These plans shift the accent from outlining problem-solving projects to the tasks of programming and setting in motion a more comprehensive set of development processes covering all the sectors and branches of the economy. The approach to medium-term planning is based simultaneously on two premises: (a) an assessment of the initial position, at the threshold of the five-year period in question, and including expected consequences of action started earlier, and (b) the postulates coming out of the perspective plan and determined by the needs of a more distant future. As a result, there emerge the schedules of actions to be taken during the following years. The point is to set plan guidelines clear enough to organize such actions in a comprehensive manner, but at the same time to leave enough room for flexible adaptations. In comparison with the perspective plan, there is a more explicit and obligatory statement of social targets to be implemented, as well as a wider specification of implementation projects and policies, including tasks and targets addressed to particular sectors and economic organizations.

The Polish plan for 1971–75 adopted the following basic goals, which also defined the main policy principles: [26]

First, to increase substantially the material standard of living of the population, especially to increase real wages by 18 percent. This target was already surpassed during the first three years, and the result is expected to reach above 30 percent in five years.

Second, to treat social aspects of development as equally important and closely integrated with economic and technical aspects, which were given priority in the past. A number of measures were planned and implemented along this line,[27] including: increase of the minimum wage level, extension of free health service to the rural population, gradual equalization of sick-pay rights for all blue- and white-collar workers, extending the length of paid maternity leaves from twelve to sixteen weeks after a first child and to eighteen weeks for additional children, and giving full social security pay for up to sixty days a years for working mothers in case of illness of their children. In the field of housing, the target for 1971–75 was to get an annual average of 6.5 new apartments per 1,000 people (in comparison with 5.8 attained in 1966–70) and to increase construction capacities considerably in order to attain about nine new apartments per 1,000 persons annually in 1976–80 and above eleven in the eighties.[28] The targets for 1971–73 are being exceeded by about 5 percent.

In order to attain such final consumption targets, the plan for 1971–75 specified that the national income should grow at an annual rate of 7 percent, in comparison with 6 percent in 1966–70; the actual rate achieved for the first three years is above 9 percent per annum.[29] In accordance with a change of priorities in final goals, there was a planned shift in favor of consumer goods output—an increase from a rate of 6.6 percent in 1966–70 to 8.3 percent for 1971–75, with a parallel slowing down of the rate for producer goods from 9.3

to 8.6 percent. The rate achieved in the first three years for consumer goods is still higher (10.7 percent), whereas that for producer goods is also slightly higher than in previous period (10.4 percent).[30]

One may note that the crucial task for the period 1971–75 was to achieve an acceleration of economic processes in all their aspects, i.e., consumption, output, foreign trade, and investments. This was necessary both from an economic viewpoint, as the condition to reach higher social goals, and from the sociopolitical angle, as a way to strengthen and sustain a favorable atmosphere for initiative and creative attitudes of the people. Consequently, the policies applied in the consecutive *annual* plan periods during 1971–73 have led to a considerably quicker rate of growth in foreign trade (nearly doubled in comparison with that during 1966–70 and the same increase planned for 1971–75), as well as in investments, which for 1971–75 will be nearly 80 percent higher than in the previous five years.[31]

It has been recognized, however, that such accelerating policies cannot be fully effective unless they are combined with other factors of a more self-sustaining nature.[32] Among such factors, particular emphasis is given to a closer integration of science with the tasks of socioeconomic development, a rationalization of the planning and management system, an improvement in a whole set of institutional and motivational factors strengthening the attitudes of "innovational dynamism."[33] This term has been introduced by Józef Pajestka to depict a whole set of motivational, organizational, cultural, science-induced and material factors, which promote progress through social, technological and economic change. This concept is emphasized as characteristic of a higher stage of socioeconomic development in relation to a former one, when innovations were being "forced" mainly through centrally decided changes in structural and technological features of the economy.

From the technical viewpoint of planning procedures the following issues reflect the reasoning outlined above: (a) the attainable rate of growth in satisfying social goals depends on the growth of capacity and economic potential; (b) the latter can be increased by means of (i) additional inputs, (ii) structural changes, and (iii) improving micro-efficiency in input-output relations. The factors listed under (ii) and (iii) reflect an increase in productivity per unit of input. They are called sometimes "intensive factors of growth" in contradistinction to "extensive factors," i.e., relatively larger inputs reproducing proportionally larger outputs. An increase in productivity may be caused at the macro-level by shifts in output structure (in favor of products with relatively higher and/or faster-rising factor productivities) and also at a micro-level by means of technological and managerial progress leading to increased productivity. In planning and management we have mastered much better the instruments dealing with (i) and (ii), whereas the possibilities to increase the last factor (iii) are not fully explored. In planning procedures, they can be only approximately estimated.

This feature, together with probable impacts of random events, leads to a concept of an "open plan," i.e., a structure open to flexible adaptations. The concept of an "open plan" means that the plan provides a clear picture of ultimate goals (including statements about their preference ordering), together with a program for their implementation. However, the latter is conditional in the sense that it can and should be revised if there arises any new possibility to attain the goals earlier or more efficiently, or to reach higher level of goals within the same time horizon. "Openness" has a meaning similar to "flexibility": an approach within which it is more important to conform with the directions for actions set in the plan, than with every particular indicator prescribing details of such actions and reflecting information available at the time when the plan was made.

This also justifies an emphasis on all the measures aiming at efficiency targets at a micro-level. An emphasis on *measures* means that, together with progressive input-output relations included in the plan (reflecting various aspects of outlays in respect to outcomes), one strives to specify actions leading toward desired changes in these relations. The actions reflect not only the impact of technological innovations, but also more general measures in the fields of management, incentives, training, etc. Exerting an influence on the causes is considered then as equally or more important in comparison with statements expressing the will to have a given change in input-output relations. Finally, it is understood that the implementation of such a concept must involve adequate information channels and data processing procedures for the central management level.

Short-Term Plans

The nature of annual plans with initial policy outlines for the next year, as well as current measures undertaken during their implementation, has been changing as a consequence of the approaches outlined above. The accent has been shifting from concentrating efforts to set forth a detailed network of plan directives and limits toward a deeper reappraisal of basic proportions in relation to the consumer market, foreign trade, and current implementation of development projects. This allows formulating basic policy lines in terms of income, price, foreign exchange and financial policies and setting more specific tasks for particular branches and their economic organizations. The essence of the shifts in approach involves two reasons.

The first reason results from a tendency to ease rigidity imposed by numerous, detailed targets and constraints on the conditions of current management at the enterprise level, i.e., to allow more flexible adaptations in input- and output-mix. Because the process is in transition and the solutions applied in respect to various branches are heterogeneous, it is difficult to express an exact measure of the extent of this shift. Generally speaking, output and/or sales targets are less numerous and are expressed in larger aggregates, whereas the choice of input-mix is less restricted by allocations of specific resources.

There is also a second reason: to get a closer link between the performance of individual organizations and the implementation of basic socioeconomic policies. In this sense, for example, the firms concerned are being made aware of how far an additional increase in their deliveries for the consumer market creates conditions allowing changes in wage-rates and salaries for particular trades, changes in pensions, etc. Thus, there are also twofold motivational links: (a) between higher wages and bonuses in a given enterprise and its economic performance, and (b) between its deliveries (for consumption, for exports, for major development projects) and the feeling of a contribution to the implementation of overall socioeconomic policies.

For example, in planning for 1974 there were the following major issues: (a) whether to continue a policy of acceleration, i.e., of a growth quicker than specified in the five-year plan for 1971–75; (b) how to ensure a continuation of the policy giving priority to consumption goals and also to secure adequate growth for investments and foreign trade. In the field of consumption there was a specific important problem: whether to continue the policy of stable ("frozen") retail prices. From a social point of view, the answer might have been obvious. There was, however, the crucial question of the extent to which intensive factors of growth may gain a leading part in securing higher results, in comparison with the extensive factors (which dominated in the past, and have still kept an important role in the years 1971–73).

An analysis of this question led to the conclusion that the results of investment activities in 1971–73 allow a considerable increase (by 31 percent in 1974 in comparison with 1973) in the value of new capacities and that it is possible to set for 1974 higher targets for the growth rate of labor productivity, i.e., 8.2 percent in industry (in comparison with an annual average of 6.7 percent in 1971–73) and 10.0 percent in construction (in comparison with 8.9 percent).[34] Finally, the proportions set in the plan for 1974 (summarized in table 8–1) express a policy of further acceleration not only in relation to the five-year plan, but also to the growth rates achieved in the first three years. They express also a directive to scale down the growth of investments in comparison with the exceptionally high rate of 1971–73 and to achieve a stronger acceleration of exports in comparison with that of imports. The plan keeps a priority for social welfare targets and continues the policy of stable ("frozen") prices for basic food products on the consumer market.

The practice of planning during the years 1971–73 has gained important new features by supplementing its technical aspects with those of a social process. Measures have been taken towards ensuring better co-participation of the enterprises and their staffs in appraising and solving questions linked with the major issues of the national socioeconomic plan. This is reflected not only in the

Table 8-1. Poland: Growth Rates Planned for 1974 in Comparison with Average Annual Growth Rates Planned for 1971-75 and Those Achieved in 1971-73 (percentage)

Item	Five-Year Plan 1971-75: Average annual growth rate	Average annual growth rate achieved in 1971-73	Growth rate planned for 1974
1. National income	6.8	9.1	9.5
2. Industrial output (sales)	8.4	10.5	11.1
3. Agricultural output (gross)	3.5-3.9	5.8	4.3
4. Exports	9.2	14.5	19.4
5. Imports	9.8	20.0	22.1
6. Gross investment	7.9	17.5	12.4
7. Money income of the population	7.8	12.9	8.8
8. Real wages (average)	3.4	7.6	5.0
9. Supplies for the retail market	7.4	11.1	9.7

Source: "Rok 1974 w liczbach" [The Year 1974 in Figures], *Życie gospodarcze*, No. 49 (1973):6.

new operating principles (see the second section above), but also in a new practice of submitting such questions to public discussion, especially in larger industrial plants. This approach creates closer understanding of interdependencies between the choices made in the national plan and the performance of particular organizations. It has helped to secure in 1972 and 1973 the acceleration of supplies, especially of consumer goods and exports, over levels initially foreseen in the respective annual plans. Similarly, policy issues for the years 1974-75 were subject to consultation with workers' collectives before their final appraisal by the National Conference of the PUWP in October 1973 and the submission of the plan to the Parliament.

THE TECHNOLOGY OF PLANNING

It is obvious that central planning and management functions require a great mass of information, for appraising development policy variants and related decisions, as well as for current control over socioeconomic processes. In order to utilize this information, it is necessary to apply diverse analytical and computational methods, the nature of which depends on the problems subject to analysis. It follows from the nature of central planning tasks that such problems pertain respectively to (a) comprehensive economy-wide proportions of development as well as equilibrium conditions in consecutive shorter periods; (b) activities of particular sectors of the economy (branches, groups of enterprises); (c) interrelations between the respective sectors and economy-wide proportions, including also interregional aspects; and (d) the ways to ensure influence on sectors, by means of various instruments, in order to shape their activities in accordance with a pattern set by the central plan.

Corresponding to these types of problems there are specific kinds of planning tasks, which are performed by separate, specialized organizational units and teams in the planning apparatus. Such tasks may be considered as subsystems in a comprehensive system of the central plan, as shown in figure 8–1. Subsystems (1) and (2) correspond to the first type of planning problems listed above, that of comprehensive, economy-wide accounts. Having such a wide scope, they use aggregated data concerning effects and outlays related to large sectors and branches (usually twenty–thirty in number). On the other hand, relatively more detailed calculations are made in respect to particular branches (groups of economic organizations). These calculations form subsystem (5) of branch planning. In aggregate terms of outputs and inputs, there are direct links among subsystems (1), (2), and (5). However, other linking devices are used, viz. those of problem-oriented and regional programming, as in subsystems (3) and (4). This approach introduces more specific interdependencies reflecting important structural and technological changes and showing interrelations among related development projects. Finally, there is a kind of planning work, reflected in subsystem (6), which concentrates on the links between the desiderata expressed in all the former types of accounts and the implementation instruments, both financial and administrative.

Practical solutions related to data collection and processing and computational methods and procedures have been developed in the light of not only technical and organizational factors (such as availability of data processing and computational facilities), but also the priorities adopted in defining the functions and tasks of the central level in relation to other management levels. There is a feedback loop in this field, because a weakness of computational facilities in the past contributed to a predominance of approaches to planning which relied on partitioned vertical directives and limits—which in turn created obstacles to efforts to modernize computational procedures. Since 1971 there has been a positive interdependence between measures aiming at restructuring the approach to central planning functions and at strengthening the computational apparatus applied in performing these functions.

The main feature relevant in this respect is a shift in emphasis from short-term targets and limits addressed to separate economic organizations towards a more comprehensive treatment of larger sets of development processes aiming (a) to concentrate attention on strategic issues; (b) to influence the causes expected to bring desired outcomes, instead of relying mainly on setting directives for such outcomes; and (c) to master the skills necessary for a current reappraisal of developments and for simulating their most probable path in the future. All this depends obviously on the ability to utilize a great amount of

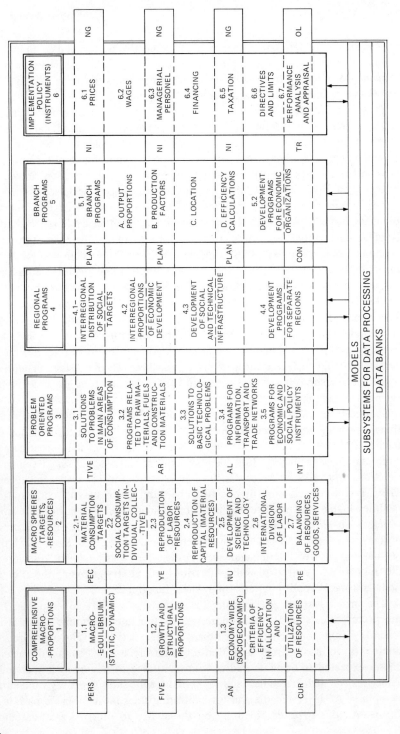

Figure 8–1 Central Plan Structure (Main Subsystems and Problems)

information, which in turn is possible only with the help of powerful computational facilities.

For many years in the past, the central level has had in practice very restricted access to information. This was caused by technical, not institutional, reasons; i.e., potentially available information could not have been properly utilized. Given existing computational capacities, it was possible to collect a great amount of separate detailed information. This was sufficient for a "vertical" analysis of indicators related to particular sectoral activities, as a basis for administrative directives and limits, but it did not permit a comprehensive "horizontal" approach covering interdependencies among various activities. Of course, there existed aggregated data concerning relatively large sectors of the economy, permitting analysis and scheduling of basic macro-proportions, but it was difficult to link them with the processes introducing changes in such proportions. There were, in a way, two parallel sets of analyses and accounts, concerned, respectively, with a list of basic detailed processes (investment and R&D projects, capacity expansions and technical changes for basic products, and so forth) and with aggregated sectoral output, employment, and capital indicators. Mutual links between these sets could not have been expressed in an explicit manner.

These informational and computational conditions made the central level dependent on planning information obtained from below in the form of sectoral draft plans, because the central level was not able to apply the techniques of comprehensive forecasting, simulation or programming covering various inter-related sectors, branches, regions, and enterprises. Partitioning of informational channels and procedures also produced an unfavorable side effect, as there was a tendency to apply different definitions and classifications for identical processes looked upon from various viewpoints. Balancing (consistency-checking) tech-niques have been widely used for separate elements of partial draft plans such as main groups of raw materials and final products, labor, capital, and foreign exchange resources. These techniques have certainly proved very useful, but some difficulties have persisted because of an insufficiently large and uniform data base and also of simplifications imposed by weaknesses in data-processing technology. Because of the large number of separate balances (several hundred), they could not have been made in the form of a set of simultaneous explicitly interrelated equations. The interdependencies were secured only for smaller sets of balances dealing with more important (but not all) links.

Because of all these factors, there was not much demand for computerized data processing on the part of organizational units at the central level dealing with separate, partitioned fields of interest. At the same time, a growing demand for data processing was expressed by other units interested in a more comprehensive approach, e.g., using aggregated national accounts, input-output interbranch analysis, etc. However, these latter units encountered difficulties resulting from a lack of necessary consistency in basic data sets, which had to be reconciled with the approaches adopted by specialized sectoral units interested more in specific, detailed, and diverse intrabranch elements than in a set of unified, aggregated indicators.

Over a number of years numerous steps were taken to overcome these difficulties and to shape the planning technology to correspond better to the principles of a comprehensive and system-oriented approach to economy-wide planning. In some fields progress has been already made, but such fields must be integrated into a more comprehensive whole.

One of these fields concerns macroeconomic *interbranch structural analysis* and has been based on input-output statistics compiled in more detail at longer intervals and in a more truncated form annually. It includes also information on the branch distribution of labor, capital, and foreign exchange inputs. Retrospective and perspective analyses have been made by research units attached, respectively, to the Central Statistical Office and the Planning Commission of the Council of Ministers.[35] The latter have been based on "classic" input-output models (with changes related to the treatment of imports and to the emphasis on supply-demand versus price-generating relations) and also on linear programming models in their single-period and multi-period comparative static and dynamic forms.

A common feature of all these studies was the assumption of "one technology for each sector," so that the analysis was restricted to implications of structural changes and did not involve a choice of input-mix within individual branches. On the other hand, we have used in these calculations estimated future input-output coefficients, especially for labor and capital inputs but also for a number of more important material inputs. These structural studies were made for a time horizon which, with few exceptions, was not longer than five years and for a rather small set of not more than thirty-odd sectors. In their classic input-output form, they have served as a tool to answer such questions as the scope and directions of changes in output, in inputs of production factors, and in primary income distribution—all in relation to given variants of a final demand level and its structure.

This approach has been extended also to include computations of full (direct and indirect) input coefficients for a more detailed specification of final products, which has been found useful in efficiency considerations related to possible structural changes in consumption and in exports. This approach has been applied to a quite wide range of products, the idea being that it allows estimation of "accounting prices" reflecting a uniform distribution of profits (e.g., in given proportions to wages and capital stock). In this way one checks and revises relative efficiency considerations based on existing prices. (The difference may occur, for example, when final product A shows a higher profitability than product B, but the costs of the latter include materials priced with relatively higher rates of profit than the former.)

The studies based on linear programming models have served a similar purpose, the difference consisting in a more systematic and comprehensive treatment of numerous constraining conditions related to labor and capital supply (with intertemporal relations in a dynamic approach), to the supply and demand for foreign exchange, to a permissible range of structural changes in final demand, etc. Given the objective function maximizing the total value of consumption (in constant prices), one could get solutions showing macrostructural proportions considered as optimal in a relative sense, i.e., depending on the assumed technologies (matrices of input-output coefficients) and also on the shape of constraining conditions built into the model. This has proved useful as a tool to get an approximate "feel" of options available in structuring the macro-proportions.

Similar linear programming studies have been made for some sectors of the economy, (e.g., in chemicals, construction materials, food processing, and housing construction). They have served the purpose of determining a relatively optimal pattern of intrabranch output and specification of exports and imports, given a predetermined vector of final demand and demand from other branches as well as some other constraints, e.g., concerning inputs of some production factors. Some of these studies have included the problems of choice among technological variants and also among various possible locations of new capacities. A wider range of models has been used in branch programming—not only a basic linear programming type, but also such forms as integer, parametric, and with a nonlinear ("fixed charge") objective function.

We have also conducted a number of *econometric, analytical, and forecasting studies* related to particular fields, such as consumer demand, foreign trade, and production function analysis. Moreover, several attempts were made to construct and use more comprehensive, multi-equational, economy-wide econometric models. They were developed initially in academic econometric centers in Katowice and Lódź and more recently also in the research units of the central planning commission.[36] The former studies have been quite useful in estimating partial relationships included in the calculations of macro-proportions (described above) as well as in planning procedures performed in more "traditional" ways. The model developed in the Planning Commission (KP-1) is a linear econometric model which consists of forty-one interrelated equations with forty-one endogenous and twenty exogenous variables. The parameters were estimated with the help of OLS and 2-OLS methods on the basis of time-series for 1955–70. The econometric models have helped to make exploratory, conditional forecasts which give an approximate view of possible future development if the relationships of the past continue also in the future. There is already a long tradition of more developed and advanced studies and forecasts in the specific field of *demography*, which is obviously of great importance for the tasks of socioeconomic planning. Continuously revised demographic forecasts for twenty-five–thirty years ahead are published each year by the Central Statistical Office in annual Demographic Yearbooks.[37]

Some of the plan information flows reflecting proposals of respective sectoral units have been covered by *computerized data processing procedures.* [38] At the central, macro-level the scope of such procedures has been very limited up to now, concentrating on output, labor, and capital indicators, as well as relationships among them. Supplementing them with other macro-indicators, related to the main elements in the creation and distribution of GNP, we have attempted to develop a computerized procedure simulating consistency-checking of general proportions and leading to an acceptable solution within certain predetermined tolerance brackets. This procedure simulates growth relationships among output, labor and capital inputs, net exports, consumption, and investment. It consists of ninety steps, within which there are specific points where supply and demand (generated by earlier steps) are confronted. Calculation may proceed further if these two components do not differ by more than a predetermined tolerance range. Otherwise, it must be started again with changes introduced into earlier assumptions. These computerized-processing procedures have been applied more widely to some sectoral problems such as income and expenditure of the population, transport, investment and construction activities, etc.

Besides the work outlined above, pertaining directly to central planning, computerized procedures have been developed extensively in such closely related fields as statistics, technical design, and even operational management functions in larger enterprises. Positive results in the last of these fields have been reached mainly in two directions: (a) planning and control of production processes, (b) record keeping and accounting. On the other hand, it has proved to be much more difficult to develop and introduce integrated management information systems (IMIS) for planning and control of an organization as a whole. The reasons include not only the intrinsic difficulty and complexity of the task, but also another factor. When enterprises were evaluated according to plan fulfillment and consequently were motivated to bargain about the magnitude of the assigned tasks and limits, they were not eager to develop techniques to indicate their maximum productive potential. Recently there has been a much stronger demand for computerized management information systems on the part of economic organizations themselves, because such systems are considered tools to improve economic and financial performance and thus also to increase the earnings of employees and the managerial staff.

Hence there are reasons to conclude that access to computerized data processing and planning calculations has already led to positive results in different fields at various management levels. However, this is only an initial stage on the way towards a more systematic integration of such procedures into the practice of planning and management. At the central level intensive work is under way [39] to set in motion by 1975 three comparatively wide subsystems of computerized procedures, for (a) medium- and short-term planning of macroeconomic proportions, (b) current appraisal of basic economic processes, together with short-term forecasts, and (c) surveys of planning and implementation of investment activities. Similar projects are being carried out for other planning centers such as ministries and large economic organizations, as well as for specialized economy-wide information systems for statistical services, for financial, budgetary and credit institutions, and for population files.

The central planning level has a program to construct gradually an integrated central management information system (ICMIS), but this will certainly need quite a long time to be elaborated in detail and subsequently implemented. Consequently, it would be premature to discuss hypotheses related to the future shape of such a system. However, the experience gained so far indicates that the following features are essential for designing and implementing subsequent subsystems: (a) they must meet the basic requirements of central planning: comprehensiveness, problem solving and integrating social and economic premises; (b) the procedures related to such approaches must be represented by adequate mathematical models, which are indispensable for systemization of information and as a basis for computational algorithms; (c) access to information must be secured along with the possibility to process it flexibly according to the structures of particular models; (d) the nature of models used and of data processing requirements must be coordinated with computational capacities; (e) correct utilization of computerized procedures depends on their integration with organizational structures and modes of communication, both "man-man" and "man-machine." Experience shows that neglecting any of these prerequisites will always considerably decrease the effectiveness of efforts.

Here lies also the clue for an answer to the question of the role of mathematical models in planning. Their indispensability is too obvious to be subject to discussion, but it is not enough to agree on this point, without treating the issue of mathematical tools in a close relationship to the remaining prerequisites listed above. A mathematical model will hardly prove useful, even with numerical computations made and solutions obtained, if such solutions do not answer the questions considered essential by the respective staff units and decisionmakers. Either a model must be revised or the potential users convinced that they should become interested in different questions. The difficulties will still be there, even with a reconciliation of users' questions and the answers procured by a model, if there are informational or computational obstacles to a prompt use of the model whenever such a need arises in practice.

There are obvious reasons justifying the existence of a genuine demand for various mathematical tools in central planning. This follows not only from the great complexity of the problems subject to decisionmaking, but also from a need to follow the development of the economic situation, to assess expected consequences of earlier decisions and presently emerging phenomena. There is also a new field to be explored: how to simulate probable consequences of using appropriate sets of parametric instruments of control and selected instruments of an administrative nature, taking account both of the assumed general economic proportions and of the sensitivity of subjects to the influence of such instruments. The methods and techniques for these purposes must use mathematical tools more advanced than the earlier ones (often called "traditional"), because they must comprise many-sided and multidirectional interdependencies among many elements constituting the socioeconomic system. Without such tools it is possible only to consider separate relationships for particular links of the network formed by interdependent elements, or to forego a more detailed understanding and limit an analysis to very aggregative indicators of socioeconomic processes.

But in order to match this demand with an adequate supply, it is not enough to reach into the vast arsenal of analytical, forecasting, and programming methods provided by mathematics and econometrics. It is essential to base their application on a deep understanding of socioeconomic processes subject to planning and to have adequate information available. Although it is a very hard task, we are striving for solutions which will be more coherent from all these points of view.

CONCLUSIONS

I have tried to indicate that an essential qualifying feature of planning consists of its conformity with the nature of the socioeconomic processes it helps to shape and control. It is well known that such processes represent a very complex system, the elements of which are developing and changing, not only according to already explored technical and economic laws and foreseeable patterns, but also under the influence of new phenomena reflecting diverse social, political, scientific and technical factors. These phenomena reflect also various motivational factors, which shape the attitudes of people deciding about particular actions and performing them. Very often they are under the impact of exogenous developments or random events.

Consequently, one can hardly assume that the whole structure of planning methods, techniques, and institutional conditions, may be set, once forever, according to an ideal, theoretically devised pattern. The changeable nature of planning approaches cannot be considered as a deplorable sign of weakness in the theory of planning, which presumably has not been strong enough to prepare ready-made recipes. Probably it is just the reverse, i.e., there were too many attempts to concentrate research and discussion on pure and abstract models, according to which the socioeconomic system *should* behave. On the other hand, until lately, there was not enough effort to reach a deeper understanding of the *real* behavior of the system, with due consideration of various quantitative and qualitative forces exerting an influence. A will to build planning structures within the framework of such an understanding is, as I see it, one of the principal features of the changes being introduced in Poland since 1971.

This is certainly not a simple and easy matter, especially because it does not mean that a planning system has to be passively adapted to some exogenous and autonomous mechanism which introduces changes into socioeconomic conditions. On the contrary, the planning system constitutes one of the important forces which determine the pattern of socioeconomic processes, usually with time-lags. Consequently, it would be *wrong* to pose the problem in the following way: planning previously used to perform twofold functions, those of a motive force and of control, whereas it should now be concentrated on the tasks of controlling a self-regulating mechanism serving as a motive force. It is rather that there have existed, and will always prevail, other important motive forces of a social, political, and psychological nature, and the main point is to make them converge with a will to implement given objectives. According to my view, there is no contradiction between (a) the postulate to increase initiative and economic independence of enterprises and (b) the targets directly linked with economy-wide goals and a comprehensive program aimed at their efficient implementation. On the contrary, there are reasons justifying the necessity to have such targets, with the following conditions:

1. They should not be applied mechanically, leading to redundancy of information, but must appear only when the sender really knows what he wants to gain.
2. It is important to ensure an understanding by the recipient of why and how the implementation of such targets is essential for the society and consequently also for the people employed in a given enterprise.
3. Economic and financial rules and incentives should be set in a way which neutralizes possible conflicts between the will to improve economic performance indicators and the will to implement the targets.

In order to integrate planning with other motive forces, it has been necessary to set in motion, in limited spheres of activities, self-regulating mechanisms which link economic and financial criteria with material, social, and political motivations.

It is true that the tasks involved are very hard. The steps adopted since 1971 in order to implement them have met with a positive response from the society, not only as a result of shifts in priorities toward consumption goals, but also because they favor creative and active attitudes leading toward the attainment of such goals. They have certainly contributed, in addition to economic policy choices, to the positive results attained in implementing socioeconomic goals in the years 1971–73.

At the same time, it is understood that these steps pose much more difficult challenges to all management centers, including the central one. It might have been easier to set a number of plan figures expressing a desired pattern for a more or less distant future, than to make a comprehensive analysis of diverse factors and motive forces which contribute to such a pattern and to apply diverse implementing instruments correspondingly. However, the latter is precisely the way to make central planning and control more effective in the real conditions of a complex socioeconomic system.

The growing complexity of planning tasks justifies an emphasis on the development of mathematical tools and computerized procedures. Thus, there is hardly a question of choice between the development of such tools and procedures, on the one hand, and the process of restructuring planning and management approaches, on the other. They constitute complementary lines of action, not two comparable alternatives. The planning and management approaches have their foundations in manyfold aspects of the whole socioeconomic system, whereas mathematical methods and computers can plan only a derivative, instrumental role. There is, of course, an open question whether and how far diverse aspects of a future "computerized society" will pose new challenges and necessitate corresponding reappraisals of planning and management structures. This, however, remains to be seen and there is no doubt that the people engaged in research on planning will have a lot of work in the future.

NOTES

1. At present (according to the statistics for 1972) 80.6 percent of the national income comes from the socialized enterprises. Poland, Główny Urząd Statystyczny [Central Statistical Office], *Rocznik Statystyczny 1973* [Statistical Yearbook 1973] (Warsaw, 1973), p. 122.

2. See Jan Szydlak, "Lepsze funkcjonowanie gospodarki—Lepsze warunki życia społeczeństwa" [Better Functioning of the Economy—Better Living Conditions of the Society], in *Doskonalenie procesu planowania i kierowania gospodarką narodową; Materiały z plenarnego posiedzenia Komisji Partyjno-Rządowej dla unowocześnienia systemu funkcjonowania gospodarki i państwa* [Improvement of Planning and Management Processes in the National Economy; Materials for the Plenary Session of the Party-Government Commission on Modernizing the System of Functioning of the Economy and the State] (Warsaw: Książka i Wiedza, 1972), pp. 17–49.

3. These guidelines, as well as other basic directives for development strategy and policy, were set by the Resolution of the VIth Congress of the Polish United Workers Party, published in *Nowe Drogi,* no. 1/272 (1972), 138–85.

4. For a more detailed analysis of qualitative factors of socioeconomic development, see Józef Pajestka, "Ogólne współzależności rozwojowe i społeczne czynniki postępu" [General Development Interrelations and the Social Factors of Progress], *Ekonomista,* No. 1 (1973): 9–38.

5. *Rocznik Statystyczny 1973* [Statistical Yearbook 1973], p. 164.

6. *Rocznik Statystyczny 1973,* p. 227.

7. *Rocznik Statystyczny 1973,* p. 258.

8. *Rocznik Statystyczny 1973,* p. 250.

9. See "W połowie planu pięcioletniego" [In the Middle of the Five-Year Plan], Editorial, *Gospodarka Planowa*, No. 7 (1973): 433–40.

10. Zygmunt Żekoński, "Wyżywienie jako element modelu konsumpcyji" [Nutrition in a Consumption Model], in *Problemy długofalowej polityki wyżywienia w gospodarce planowej* [Problems of Long-Term Nutrition Policy in a Planned Economy] (Warsaw: Spółdzielczy Instytut Badawczy, 1972), p. 60.

11. Jan Śliwa, "Ogólne problemy i postulaty dotyczące polityki cen konsumpcyjnych" [General Problems and Postulates Concerning Consumers' Market Price Policy], in *Problemy długofalowej polityki wyżywienia w gospodarce planowej* [Problems of Long-Term Nutrition Policy in a Planned Economy] (Warsaw: Spółdzielczy Instytut Badawczy, 1972), p. 206.

12. See *Gospodarka Planowa*, No. 7 (1973): 435; also Józef Okuniewski, "Rolnictwo w połowie planu pięcioletniego" [Agriculture in the Middle of the Five-Year Plan], *Gospodarka Planowa*, No. 11 (1973): 721–27.

13. *Gospodarka Planowa*, No. 7 (1973):435.

14. Ibid.

15. See Stanisław Grużewski, "Polski przemysł maszynowy i jego możliwości kooperacyjne" [Polish Engineering Industry and Its Cooperation Possibilities], *Handel Zagraniczny*, No. 3 (1973):88–90. For more details, see also United Nations, Economic Commission for Europe, *Analytical Report on Industrial Cooperation Among ECE Countries* (Geneva, 1973), pp. 63–65.

16. See Mieczysław Jagielski, "Udział w socjalistycznej integracji gospodarczej–drogą do rozwoju kraju i dobrobytu narodu" [Socialist Economic Integration–The Way to the Development of the Country and to the Welfare of the Nation], *Trybuna Ludu*, September 28, 1973.

17. See the speech of Prime Minister Piotr Jaroszewicz published in *I Krajowa Konferencja PZPR, 22–23 października 1973, Podstawowe dokumenty i materiały* [First National Conference of the PUWP, October 22-23, 1973, Basic Documents and Materials] (Warsaw: Książka i Wiedza, 1973), p. 97.

18. See the speech of Prime Minister Piotr Jaroszewicz (cited in note 17), p. 100.

19. See a press conference of Józef Pińkowski, First Vice Chairman of the Planning Commission, reported in *Gospodarka Planowa*, No. 5 (1973):289–94; and Józef Pajestka, "Doskonalenie gospodarowania w organizacjach wprowadzających nowe zasady systemu ekonomiczno-finansowego" [Improved Functioning in Organizations Introducing the Principles of a New Economic and Financial System], *Nowe Drogi*, No. 10 (1973):49–63.

20. See "Drugi etap prac Komisji Partyjno-Rządowej dla unowocześnienia systemu funkcjonowania gospodarki i państwa" [The Second Stage of Work of the Party-Government Commission on Modernizing the System of Functioning of the Economy and the State], the speech of Jan Szydiak, the Chairman of the Commission, reported in *Gospodarka Planowa*, No. 8 (1973):505–508.

21. See Andrzej M. Zawiślak, "Zasady kształtowania płac i premii w jednostkach inicjujących" [The Principles of Regulating Wages and Bonuses in Pilot Organizations], *Gospodarka Planowa*, No. 8 (1973):529–35; and Adam Lipowski, "Ceny w jednostkach inicjujących" [Prices in the Pilot Organizations], *Gospodarka Planowa*, No. 8 (1973):523–28.

22. See Mieczysław Jagielski, "Węzłowe problemy i kierunki perspekty-wicznego planu społeczno-gospodarczego rozwoju Polski" [Key Problems and Directions of the Perspective Plan for Socioeconomic Development of Poland], *Gospodarka Planowa,* No. 10 (1973):649–60.

23. See Lucjan Ciamage, "Rosnąca rola handlu i współpracy zagranicznej" [The Growing Role of Foreign Trade and Cooperation], *Nowe Drogi,* No. 3 (1973):74–85.

24. For a more detailed explanation of the characteristics of long-term planning approaches in the sixties, see K. Porwit, "Perspective Planning in Poland: Basic Issues and Experiences," United Nations, *Journal of Development Planning,* No. 3 (1971):17–59.

25. Among the studies and forecasts concerning a more distant future, the following have been published recently by the Polish Academy of Sciences Committee "Poland 2000": *Prognozy rozwoju demograficznego Polski* [Forecasts of Population Growth for Poland] (Wrocław: Ossolineum, 1971); *Prognozowanie potrzeb surowcowych* [Forecasting Demand for Raw Materials] (Wrocław: Ossolineum, 1971); *Prognozowanie sieci osadniczej* [Forecasting the Urban Settlement Network] (Wrocław: Ossolineum, 1971); *Prognozowanie rozwoju zatrudnienia i kształcenia w Polsce* [Forecasting Growth of Employment and Education in Poland] (Wrocław: Ossolineum, 1972); *Kształcenie dla przyszłości* [Education for the Future] (Wrocław: Ossolineum, 1972); *Człowiek i wartości—możliwości i granice przewidywania* [Man and Values—Possibilities and Frontiers of Forecasting] (Wrocław: Ossolineum, 1972).

26. For a more detailed review of the five-year plan for 1971–75 and its implementation, see the editorial in *Gospodarka Planowa,* No. 7 (1973).,

27. A comprehensive review of the social targets planned and implemented in 1971–73 has been given in the report of the Central Committee of the PUWP presented by First Secretary Edward Gierek at the First National Conference of the PUWP, October 22–23, 1973; see the publication cited in note 17.

28. Adam Andrzejewski, "Polityka mieszkaniowa i jej aspekty społeczne" [Housing Policy and its Social Aspects], in *Polityka Społeczna* [Social Policy], ed. Antoni Rajkiewicz (PWE–Państwowe Wydawnictwo Ekonomiczne, 1973), p. 246.

29. According to the estimates made by the Central Statistical Office, the per capita GNP of Poland calculated by the United Nations SNA method (in current market prices) amounted in 1970 to 1,200 U.S. dollars. See Leszek Zienkowski, "Dochód Narodowy Polski i krajów Europy Zachodniej" [National Income in Poland and in Western European Countries], *Gospodarka Planowa,* No. 6 (1973):382–85.

30. See the speech of Prime Minister Piotr Jaroszewicz cited in note 17.

31. Simultaneously, there is a strong shift towards investing in consumer goods industries, where the outlays in 1971–75 are expected to be 130 percent higher than in the previous five-year period, whereas the rise for producer goods industries is 45 percent. See Albin Płocica, "Polityka inwestycyjna w założeniach i realizacji" [Investment Policy—Its Foundations and Implementation], *Nowe Drogi,* No. 10 (1973):157–68.

32. This point was strongly emphasized and elaborated in Jan Szydlak, "O

nowoczesną, socjalistyczną Polskę" [For the Modern, Socialist Poland], *Nauka Polska*, No. 4 (1973):1–11.

33. This term was suggested and its implications elaborated in Józef Pajestka, "Dynamizm innowacyjny i sprzężenie nauki z gospodarką" [Innovational Dynamism and the Linkage of Science with the Economy], *Ekonomista*, No. 5 (1973):1021–37.

34. "Rok 1974 w liczbach" [The Year 1974 in Figures], *Zycie Gospodarcze*, No. 49 (1973):6.

35. See, e.g., Andrzej Bocian, "O wykorzystaniu modelu optymalizacyjnego w planie centralnym" [On the Use of an Optimizing Model in the Central Plan], *Ekonomista*, No. 5 (1971): 679–705; Andrzej Bocian and Józef Zajchowski, "Makroekonomiczne modele analiz strukturalnych" [Macroeconomic Models of Structural Analysis], *Ekonomista*, No. 6 (1972): 1015–1027; Andrzej Bocian and Józef Latoszek, "Zastosowanie metod matematycznych i elektronicznej techniki obliczeniowej w planowaniu na przykładzie SOMO" [Application of Mathematical Methods and Computerized Techniques—an Example of SOMO], Part 1, *Gospodarka Planowa*, 10 (1972): 607–12, and Part II, *Gospodarka Planowa*, No. 11 (1972): 678–81. (SOMO is an abbreviation for a Multiperiod Optimizing Model Computation System.)

36. See, e.g., *Model ekonometryczny gospodarki Polski Ludowej* [An Econometric Model of the Economy of People's Poland], ed. Zbigniew Pawłowski (Warsaw: PWN, 1968); Władysław Welfe, *A Medium-Term Econometric Model of the Polish Economy* (Instytut Ekonometrii i Statystyki Uniwersytetu Łódzkiego, Seria D. No. 2) (Łódz, 1973); Wojciech Maciejewski, Marian Opara, and Józef Zajchowski, "Ekonometryczny model gospodarki Polski: KP-1" [An Econometric Model for the Polish Economy: KP-1], *Gospodarka Planowa*, No. 8 (1973): 550–54; Wojciech Maciejewski and Józef Zajchowski, "Próba wykorzystania econometrycznego modelu gospodarki Polski do symulacji procesów wzrostu" [A Test of the Econometric Model of the Polish Economy to Simulate Growth Processes], *Gospodarka Planowa*, No. 9 (1973): 629–32.

37. *Rocznik Demograficzny 1973* [Demographic Yearbook 1973] (Warsaw: Główny Urząd Statystyczny, 1973), pp. 395–413.

38. Alfons Myśliński and Tadeusz Jaegerman, "Zastosowanie elektronicznej techniki obliczeniowej w pracach Komisji Planowania przy Radzie Ministrów" [The Use of Electronic Computers in the Planning Commission of the Council of Ministers], *Gospodarka Planowa*, No. 3 (1973): 192–94.

39. Andrzej Dąbkowski, "Projektowanie informatycznego systemu planowania centralnego" [Designing a Computerized Information System for Central Planning], *Gospodarka Planowa*, No. 7 (1973): 457–63.

Chapter Nine

Planning in Hungary

Tamás Morva

DEVELOPMENT OF A PLANNED ECONOMY

Some Basic Features of the Hungarian Economy

Hungary is, at present, on the way to becoming a highly industrialized country with a developed economic structure and up-to-date technology in most of its basic economic branches. In comparison with the economies of other nations, the Hungarian economy of the early seventies can be placed near the upper margin of the medium-development level. According to recent estimates, the per capita GDP in 1970 was around $1,600 per year,[1] about 34 percent of the level in the United States.

Economic growth in the last five-year period (1968–73) has been characterized by an average annual increase of 6 percent in the national income; gross industrial output rose by about the same percentage figure, while the average annual rate of growth of gross agricultural output reached a record level of 3.5 percent.[2] The results of the continuing prosperity in the Hungarian economy after the Second World War were evident. Beyond any doubt, the old Hungary with the still partly feudal social structure, mass poverty, and high unemployment level seems far in the past and a new society has been born.

Its present prosperity in contrast to the past can be easily seen if we compare some main features of the present economy with data of the period between the two world wars. In 1938, the last peacetime year, the national income per capita was about a quarter of the 1970 level (25–27 percent) and the annual rate of growth did not exceed 2 percent. Agriculture was still the leading branch of the economy and 48 percent of the arable land was occupied by large estates (more than 57.55 hectares), often remaining from feudal times and cultivated to a large extent by manual labor and primitive tools. A large part of the land was still in the ownership of the Catholic Church. The relatively low industrial development relied upon the dual conditions of low wages and undeveloped technology.

Investments were often made in machinery and equipment obtained from the developed Western European countries.

Economic growth after the Second World War was tightly and organically connected with a deep process of social transformation. The first step began early in 1945 with a land reform expropriating 35 percent of the arable land and giving the ownership to agricultural workers and poorer peasants and small-holders; altogether, 642,000 people benefited from the land reform. Further steps were a stabilization program, the introduction of a new currency, and the first three-year plan for the postwar reconstruction of the economy. These programs were supported by nationalization of the basic means of production. During the period 1946–49, the mines, banks, financial institutions, and industrial enterprises (excluding handicraft workshops) were successfully nation-alized. Nationalization, however, not only formed an institutional basis for a short period of reconstruction but also created a starting point for future development. The industrialization of the country, while rapidly increasing industrial output and its share in total output, also gradually modernized the fundamental technology in industry.

During the transition period, the economy had a double basis in nationalized industry and agricultural small-holdings. However, as early as 1948, the process of agricultural transformation had already begun with the collectivization of private farms by the establishment of agricultural production cooperatives. The collectivization of agriculture—following a regression in the middle of the fifties—was completed during the period 1959–61. Now 99 percent of the national income originates in the socialist sector of the economy, including agriculture.

The deep social changes which accompanied economic growth were also reflected in changes in the occupational structure of the population. The proportion employed in the main branches of the Hungarian economy are shown in table 9-1.

The number employed in industry more than doubled during the period, while in agriculture total employment fell by 40 percent. The share of agriculture is, however, still too high in our economy and will, gradually but permanently, decrease further in the future.

Table 9-1. Hungary: Shares of Major Branches in Total Employment, 1941 and 1970 (percentage)

Branch	1941	1970
Industry (including mining, manufacturing and construction)	23.4	43.8
Agriculture (including fishing and forestry)	50.4	26.2
Other branches	26.2	30.0
Total employment	100.0	100.0

The Development of National Planning

The postwar results of the Hungarian economy are closely linked to the development of national planning. The first three-year plan[a] guided the reconstruction of the economy; it repaired war damage and regained the prewar level of production, while exceeding former living standards of the population through a new distribution of the national income. The subsequent first five-year plan speeded up industrialization and the collectivization of agriculture.

The wide-ranging nationalization of the means of production not only was a precondition and a basis for national planning, but it also had a feedback effect creating a strong requirement for further government action. The need for establishing priorities and for nationwide coordination of branch production was a logical consequence of the nationalization. The distribution of nationalized resources and the distribution and redistribution of national income also required central decisions and guidelines.

The new situation called for new organizations. In 1947, the National Planning Office was established with the mandate to elaborate national plans and monitor their fulfillment. Later, specialized branch ministries came into being to control and manage nationalized sectors of the economy. Central guidelines assisted the newly established organizations and the management of nationalized enterprises to fulfill their new and complicated tasks.

In the development of national planning in Hungary we can distinguish four main phases:

1. 1947–53, in which the basis of the planned economy was laid down;

2. 1954–56, a period of improvement and correction in the system of national planning;

3. 1957–67, which brought the further extension and deepening of the role of central planning;

4. 1968 onwards, involving the introduction and realization of economic reform.

The first three phases together constitute a period of "extensive" growth. Beginning in 1968 a new orientation towards an "intensive" utilization of all resources of economic and social development has made higher and constantly improved economic efficiency a central economic policy aim.

[a]The list of medium-term plans in Hungary is as follows:
1. Three-year plan: 1947–49. (Started August 1, 1947 and fulfilled in two-and-a-half years by the end of 1949.)
2. First five-year plan: 1950–54.
3. Three-year plan: 1958–60.
4. Second five-year plan: 1961–65.
5. Third five-year plan: 1966–70.
6. Fourth five-year plan: 1971–75.
7. Fifth five-year plan: 1976–80. (In preparation.)
During the period 1955–57, the national economy was directed by annual plans only. The elaboration of a five-year plan for the years 1956–60 started several times, but because of political changes it could not be approved.

At the beginning of the first phase, the national plan was an economic policy tool without a detailed sectoral breakdown. It provided the main directives for the reconstruction of the economy and determined the main proportions in the distribution of resources, but it did not define the ways and means of implementation of the plan. Gradually, however, the emphasis was shifted to annual and even shorter-term plans in which a detailed sectoral elaboration of plan indicators was to be found. The authorities centralized more and more functions in the production and distribution of materials and goods. The difference between planning and operative management of industry disappeared in practice. Incentives in enterprises were directly connected with output plan targets and depended on the fulfillment and overfulfillment of output indictors.

All these changes in the methods of planning and management, when introduced, helped to accelerate the growth rate. But they also contributed, before long, to growing tension in the economy created by the overstrained industrialization targets. Because of these methods, planned proportions of the national economy were damaged, the fulfillment of the aims of the five-year plan was slowed down, and, in some respects, growth stopped. Compared with the speedy rate of growth of industry, agricultural output fluctuated strongly. A great dispersion was to be found in investment, losses and costs in production were high, and on the market there were often scarcities in basic goods and especially in agricultural products. Finally, in 1952, the living standard of the population decreased significantly.

During the first phase the foundations for the planned economy were laid down. The results, however, were overshadowed by the one-sidedness and deficiencies of the development of national planning. The economic policy aim of the next phase (1954–56) was to strengthen the planning of the main proportions of the national economy and to adjust inequalities in development. For that purpose some authority was decentralized: the role of branch ministries and local authorities was partially increased, and the circle of enterprise decisions was also broadened. The methods of national planning and the system of material incentives were also improved. In agriculture, important changes began as the obligatory delivery of products at fixed prices was gradually replaced by purchases of the surplus product at market prices and extension of the role of free market. The entire process, called at that time "the rationalization of national planning," also gave an initial push to discussions on principles and methods of national planning and plan implementation.

"Planned economy" was considered the opposite of "market economy," and it was strongly hoped that the former would harmonize economic growth in the long run. In practice, however, different economic policy aims were sometimes found contradictory and the full realization of plans encountered difficulties. The intention to use more detailed central planning and the increase in the number of physical indicators and balances could not solve the problems. On the contrary, the application of more comprehensive value indicators and decentralization clearly improved the implementation of basic plan targets. This was the first time in Hungary that discussions faced the problem of how to determine and regulate the relation of central planning and the market. But the discussions which aimed at improving the functioning of a planned economy later elicited proposals departing from it, and a number of economists lost their belief in the basic principles of a planned economy. These problems added heavily to the political crisis which occurred in 1956.

The new Party and government leadership drew conclusions from these developments and discussions in 1957. While the final objective of economic policy remained the building of a socialist society, and industrialization and the collectivization of agriculture were looked upon as the main instruments to achieve this aim, basic changes were carried out in the methods of national planning and management.

The rearrangement was based on the principle of maintaining the leading role of central planning and its directive nature. Medium-term planning was strengthened and annual plans were made on the basis of the well-established medium-term plan. The central role in the management of the economy was assigned to the annual plans, which were supported by a system of material incentives. Planning in value-terms developed, while the list of obligatory indicators in physical terms was radically diminished. The main responsibilities for the fulfillment of the national plan were given to branch ministries, and, in certain respects, to local councils. These authorities had some operational rights and independence in their own field of activity within the broader framework of planned indicators. At the enterprise level, instead of fixing the number of employees and the total sum of wages, a more flexible annual "average wage control"[b] system was introduced, and an end-of-year remuneration was paid to all employees up to a maximum of one month's salary depending on the annual increase of enterprise profits. In agriculture, the system of obligatory delivery of products at low fixed prices was abolished and replaced by annual contractual relations between the state organs, on the one hand, and cooperatives and private farmers, on the other.

This system of national planning and management contributed to the political and economic success in the post-1957 period but, in its actual functioning, the stimulating force of the system gradually decreased and several shortcomings came to light.

[b]In the "average wage control" system, ministries and other supervising authorities approved for the enterprises as obligatory plan indicators the annual average wage-level, rather than the total number of workers and employees and the total wage bill. This system gave some flexibility to enterprise managers, who could maneuver with the number of workers and employees and also with wages. However, it adversely affected the growth of labor productivity, because managers kept low-wage workers and employees even when they had no need for them and managers could not pay really high wages to reward exceedingly high performances. In the long run the result was a tendency toward equalization of earnings within each enterprise and a superfluously high employment level in industry as a whole.

In the first part of the sixties, Hungary experienced fluctuations of a somewhat cyclical nature in plan fulfillment, and repeatedly-appearing problems in investment activities and the foreign trade balance. Although the dispro-portion between industrial and agricultural development decreased as compared with the previous period, it was not yet eliminated. Similarly, the overall equilibrium in the market for both materials and consumer goods improved, but output of technically up-to-date producer goods and high-quality consumer goods often lagged behind the demand, and variety in the supply of materials and goods was still small. Technical progress was not accelerated as expected and the rate of growth of industrial productivity was relatively low. These problems could be attributed to the still too-centralized decisionmaking and to the limited responsibility, authority, and personal initiatives at the enterprise level.

Following the Party Directives, and under the leadership of the Party's central committee, a critical evaluation of the national planning and management system was organized in 1965. A large number of proposals were discussed and a program for change was elaborated, leading to the economic reform introduced in 1968.

Basic Principles of the Reform

The building of a socialist society entered into a new phrase: industrialization started to bear fruit; a new generation of workers, managers and intellectuals had grown up; in agriculture a few years had passed since the completion of collectivization and the greater part of the cooperatives had successfully started their activities. A turn towards intensive utilization of all resources and efficiency in all economic activities was needed more than ever.

The central idea of the economic reform [3] was to combine national planning and market relations on the basis of socialist ownership of the means of production. The question of how to regulate interrelations between central planning and the market was raised anew and new answers were elaborated. At this point, however, a few theoretical explanations are needed.

First, to avoid misunderstanding, we refer to the notion "on the basis of socialist ownership of the means of production," which thesis excluded a return to a private economy. The share of the private sector was at that time already marginal in our economy and no significant increase of this share was intended or carried out in the reform. The idea was to rearrange certain basic relations within the socialist sector.

Second, we exclude also the notion that the reform abandoned the basic ideas of national planning and management, although it incorporated some important changes in economics developed in the discussions of the last ten to fifteen years. "Planned economy" was treated as a certain unity of two different elements: central planning and management of the economy as a whole, on one side, and market relations among enterprises and other parts of the economy, on the other. Contraditions between these two elements have not been denied, but the feasibility of unity built on these controversial elements has been asserted.

National planning and the management of the economy based upon the plans determine consciously and over the long term the growth of the economy in planned economies. Overall development of a market economy is the spontaneous result of the play of market forces which depend nowadays not only on an enormous quantity of decisions taken by private firms and individuals but also on the activities of important organized actors of the economy such as state organs, trade unions, etc. There is no convergence between these two different economic systems—their basic difference rests upon the different ownership of the means of production—but certain common elements cannot and should not be denied.

Central planning and economic policy measures, which after World War II were generally applied in most of the developed market economies, illustrate that a certain kind of unification of these two contradictory elements can exist and function. The inclusion of the new elements improved the functioning of these economies but did not change their basic nature. In market economies central planning and state policy measures assist the functioning of the private economy in order to conciliate tensions and avoid larger fluctuations and recession.

In the case of planned economies the role of market relations is the main point at issue. Central decisions reflecting overall social interests should determine decisions taken at the branch, local, and enterprise levels. But there are many ways in which overall directives can be transmitted to the lower level. An oversimplified concept and a mechanical practice in the breakdown of national plan indicators into branch, local authority, and enterprise plan indicators caused many difficulties and losses in the development of planned economies in the past.

Experience has proved in all socialist countries that nationalization of the means of production and collectivization of private farms in agriculture do not abolish market relations in the economy. Money, prices, costs, finance, supply and demand not only are formal instruments of central management but they represent market dependencies. Market laws play an important role in the economy. More precisely, the influence of the market is not limited to distribution or relations between state and collective farms, or to private consumption, or to foreign trade. Rather, market relations have a significant effect within the state sector itself.[c]

Market relations based on socialist ownership of the means of production and the laws governing these relations need not conflict with socialist tendencies, nor do they themselves assist the development of a socialist economy. Past economy policy tended to limit market relations and abolish them as soon as possible. That intention resulted in an incomplete use of the means available to central planning and management, and also caused conflict and inefficiency.

---

[c]We refer, for example, to the discussion of whether means of production are market goods in the socialist economy. This theory has received general acceptance in recent years.

Reform principles in 1968 accepted for the long term the existence of market relations in socialism [4] and regulated the interconnections between planning and market relations according to the following principles:

1. National plans should determine economic growth in the economy as a whole and should enjoy primacy over market tendencies or, in other words, plans should guide and influence the development of the market.
2. As a precondition for the above thesis, planning should take into account market relations, in general not directly opposing market tendencies but guiding and influencing their development by means and methods which are in harmony with the nature of market relations.
3. Plans should give leeway for movements in the fulfillment of plans including feedback effects of market forces. Intervention should occur only where the national interest or basic allocations made by the plans are threatened.

The main consequences of the adoption of these principles fall within the field of plan implementation and methods of central management of the economy. The introduction of a regulator system taking into account market relations, instead of a direct disaggregation of plan targets to enterprises, was the most striking feature of the reform. It had, however, also important consequences in other fields.

The reform established new relations between central supervising authorities and enterprises. The apparatus of central authorities was rationalized and significantly decreased, while the responsibility and competence of local councils and mainly of enterprises were broadened. The role of material incentives increased, and profitability of enterprises was placed in the center of the system of incentives.

In various branches, first of all in agriculture, special reform measures were elaborated and applied, taking into account their particular features. The agricultural reform was based on a systematic and gradual increase in contractual state prices and the related rise in profitability. The autonomy and competence of cooperatives were broadened and strengthened.

Main Features of the Regulator System

Conception of planning. The adoption of the above principles had three main consequences for the conception of planning:

First, functions of national planning and enterprise planning were reformulated, separating enterprise from national planning and stimulating the development of their respective patterns.

Second, an interconnected system of national plans of different length was adopted, and a strong impetus was given to starting systematic work on the preparation of a long-term plan and to increasing the role of medium-term (five-year) plans in plan implementation. This gradual shift from annual plans to a greater rôle for five-year and long-term plans is also a characteristic feature of the reform. This change has had many repercussions.

Third, a new task was included among the functions of national planning: the coordination of basic effects and basic elements of the regulator system. Because of the more active role assigned to prices and financial means, their planning and coordination have also gained importance.

National plans form the basis for central management. It is an important function of the plans to transmit the economic policy aims from the overall social level to central management of the economy and, therefore, national plans are of a directive nature at this level. They are obligatory for the government and its agencies (ministries and similar authorities) in their economic activities. This principle has been maintained during the economic reform of 1968 but with fundamental changes in its interpretation and implementation.

Previously the compulsory character of central plans was extended to the plans of all economic units (enterprises, local councils, etc.). Enterprises received from their supervising authorities (ministries) annually and quarterly a smaller or greater number of so-called plan indicators, setting targets to be attained or limiting the use of one or another factor of production (output and export targets, the supply of certain materials, the average wage level, investment targets and financial resources, etc.). These plan indicators were derived by ministries from the national plan, and the attainment of the plan indicators either as minimum or as maximum targets was obligatory for enterprises and limited their activities to a greater or lesser extent.

One of the most important changes made by the economic reform of 1968 was the abolishment of the central fixing of enterprise plan indicators. Under the new system of economic management, ministries may not systematically give comprehensive plan targets to enterprises, and their direct intervention— according to the reform regulations—is limited to exceptional circumstances.[d] Instead the central management relies upon a system of economic regulators. Consequently, the new management is based on two principles: first, the obligatory nature of national plans at the governmental level and, second, respect for the autonomy of the enterprise. The managers of enterprises are assumed to be sufficiently competent and fully responsible for making the correct decisions.

Enterprise responsibility and authority. In consequence of nationalization, the main part[e] of the means of production has been put in the hands of the same

[d]Problems in this area will be mentioned in the evaluation of results and problems of further development in the "Conclusions" section below.

[e]An important part of the means of production is owned by cooperatives, and about 23 percent of the net national product was produced by the cooperatives in 1972. Cooperatives, however, have a special status. In this short description we deal only with problems of state-owned enterprises, especially industrial enterprises, and branch peculiarities are neglected.

owner: society as respresented by the state. This does not mean, however, that state-owned means of production could have been directed as a single technical-economic unit, without organizing a relatively large number of enterprises. The social division of labor; the extremely wide variety of products, technologies, machines and equipment; the historical background, size, and nature of investments; geographical distribution; the capabilities and costs of everyday organization and administration of work; and many other factors determine the enterprise structure of an economy. It is a very complex scientific problem to find a good (or even further an "optimal") structure, and this is far from being solved satisfactorily, either in theory or in practice. But the reform in Hungary made only minor corrections in the given structure. Instead, it took over the enterprise system resulting from the last general reorganization in 1962–63. The reform decentralized responsibility and authority to enterprises, despite awareness of the high degree of administrative concentration.

As state organs and state enterprises are considered basically to represent the same interests, it is a practical question to determine functions on different levels. Before the reform, rights of supervising authorities were not defined exactly and therefore they enjoyed a great freedom in their activities, whereas enterprises had a relatively limited "operational economic autonomy." The reform limited the role of supervising authorities to the following basic functions:

1. foundation, separation or integration, liquidation of enterprises, and definitions of their field of activity;
2. appointment and discharge of the leaders of enterprises and supervision of their activities; and
3. annual auditing and evaluation of enterprise activities.

These functions are carried out on behalf of the state by branch ministries in the case of larger enterprises of national importance, and by local councils in the case of smaller enterprises. Outside the above functions, state organs shape the economic regulator system which determines the basic orientation, economic possibilities, and limitations of enterprise activities. Continuous intervention and a take-over of decisions and responsibilities of enterprises were prohibited in the new regulations for supervising authorities. The right to intervene by direct instruction was maintained only for exceptional cases and situations.

The reform enlarged enterprise autonomy by different means:

1. in a legal sense, giving all rights to and placing all responsibilities on the director (manager)[f] of the enterprise—not only charging him with continuous

[f]The personal responsibility of the director (manager)—a basic principle of enterprise management in Hungary—was and still remains unchanged. Directors are assisted in their work, of course, by a group of managers but, in the end, decisions are, and should be, taken by directors personally.

implementation of the enterprise's plan and the organization of its work, but also entitling him to approve all enterprise plans and programs; and

2. in an economic sense, by decentralizing a large part of financial resources which make possible, in normal economic circumstances, not only the maintenance of the initial production level but also, to a certain extent, an extension of it.

According to the regulations, for a large expansion of production all enterprises can apply for bank credits or state loans. A bargaining process about credit terms has been established, and enterprises can relinquish an investment if they cannot accept the conditions of the bank credit or loan. In practice, however, the bargaining possibilities are limited as, generally, enterprise demand for investments is high and financial resources are limited. On the other hand, it is still correct to say that enterprises are not obligated to make one or another investment, so basic responsibility for investments does rest with them. In a few exceptional cases—in the establishment of new enterprises and in very large investments mentioned individually in national plans—central investment decisions are taken and enterprises are responsible only for the fulfillment of the programs. In the case of existing enterprises, these decisions are discussed with enterprise leaders in advance.

During the preparation of the reform a few suggestions were made to introduce a system of enterprise self-management in the economy. In Hungary self-management is the basic principle for the status of cooperatives, but state enterprises are supposed to be integral parts of the unified social property. These proposals, therefore, were refused both from a theoretical point of view and on the basis of the examination of practical experiences of self-management.

Price formation and regulation. The reform of prices had been prepared for a long period. Price formation in the fifties made large differences between the levels of producer and consumer prices. Consumer prices often differed greatly from total production and turnover costs, and as a result a large part of budget income came from the indirect turnover tax (e.g., in 1956, 53 percent of state revenues were from this source).[5] Also, the agricultural procurement price level was much below the retail price level.

The price reform of 1968 was based on the idea of unifying the price system both concerning price formation principles and also, as far as possible, in price levels. It was thought that a unified price-building system would exert the same stimulating effects on different enterprises, would put them under the control of equal circumstances, and would, therefore, both assist a clearer evaluation of costs and profitability at the central level and serve the development of market relations at the enterprise level.

New prices were introduced in industry and trade on January 1, 1968. In agriculture, their introduction started with certain changes in 1966 but successive steps were foreseen to achieve the goals completely. Preparatory calculations were carried out with a large price model as early as the middle of the sixties, and nearly one year before their introduction most price lists were discussed and gradually finalized. This process made it possible to put all preparatory calculations of the reform on the basis of new prices.

The basic function of prices was defined by reform principles so as to orient and stimulate producers and consumers in their economic decisions. The price system was meant to promote rational utilization of economic resources, the adaptation of production to demand, the spreading of up-to-date technologies and products, and the formation of an economical consumption pattern, as well as equilibrium between supply and demand.

In price-building, the following three main factors were taken into account at all levels:

1. costs of production and trade;
2. the influence of the market in expressing substitution effects and supply and demand relations: and
3. state preferences derived from the economic policy aims and the national plan.

In all phases of production and trade costs had to cover material inputs, wages and salaries, depreciation of fixed assets and centralized revenues of the state. The two main forms of centralized revenues were: a 5 percent uniform charge (like an interest rate) on all productive fixed and working capital and a total 25 percent charge on all wages and salaries. Above costs, prices had to make it possible for enterprises to achieve a certain amount of profit. State preferences, substitution effects, and supply and demand of different products were supposed to influence the profit rates of branches and mainly of different kinds of products.

The principles could be applied only with certain corrections in the different branches of the economy. Existing price relations, foreign trade prices, the given consumer price level and product-mix, and other factors influenced the determination of prices in the various branches, and many additional rules and changes were needed. The first approach was to keep the initial profitability level relatively low. In practice, however, profits included in the initial prices of the reform were 6.5 percent of the total value of assets in industry.[6]

The compromises and, mainly, the higher initial profitability decreased the stimulating force of the reform and within a short time caused high profitabilities and large differences to develop, often not directly related to the true economic performance of the enterprise. The changes in the price system proved to be of only limited help in improving central guidance of the economy and facilitating direct comparisons of results in different branches and enterprises.

Initial production prices were calculated with the condition that the overall consumer price level should be maintained and only small changes could be made in relative consumer prices. Price lists were elaborated as fully as previously in order to obtain initial calculated prices, but not all prices were issued, because the reform was also connected with new price regulations. Three basic forms of prices were introduced:

1. fixed prices;
2. officially regulated prices, including a wide range of different methods ranging from maximum prices, which functioned in practice nearly as fixed prices; through so-called guiding prices for a product-group, with more scope for declines in individual product prices; to the regulation of price-building methods, leaving enterprises to form individual prices on the basis of their own calculations;
3. free prices without central prescriptions, to be determined in contracts between enterprises, set for certain consumer goods by domestic trade enterprises, or developed in the free market.

Table 9–2 shows the relative importance of the different price categories in household expenditures, as planned for 1968.

In the sphere of production, the prices of raw materials and certain typical intermediate products were mostly fixed or maximum, while in other manufacturing industries the share of loosely regulated or free prices was very high, on the assumption that prices of materials, on the one hand, and consumer prices and related interests of trade enterprises, on the other, would impede a rapid general increase in producer prices.

The introduction of the price reform—as a part of the general preparations—was supported by preventive measures: state reserves and stocks of basic

Table 9-2. Hungary: Relative Importance of Different Price Categories in Household Expenditures (percentage of sales planned for 1968)

	Price category			
Product Group	Fixed	Maximum	Loosely regulated	Free
Foodstuffs	31	29	27	13
Clothing	–	21	54	25
Construction materials	20	70	–	10
Fuels	100	–	–	–
Miscellaneous industrial articles	7	50	22	21
Total retail sales	20	30	27	23

Source: Reform of the Economic Mechanism in Hungary, ed. István Friss (Budapest: Akadémiai Kiadó, 1969), p. 151.

materials and of most important consumer goods were increased; the balance between the purchasing power of the population and the supply of consumer goods was improved; and during the first two–three years the consumer price level did not increase more than the foreseen annual 1–2 percent. Later, however, the annual rate of increase rose somewhat, reaching 3.5 percent in 1973, but still remained relatively low.

The price reform, although it successfully supported the reform as a whole and brought improvements as compared to the past, could not completely fulfill the aims and hopes that were attached to it. An analysis of the cirumstances and reasons which caused the results in this field to fall behind expectations would, however, go far beyond the limits of this study.

Enterprise income regulations. The price system and enterprise income and other financial regulators are closely related. Prices should make it possible to self-finance production, not only on the previous level but also with some expansion of output. In the new system subsidies are not generally assumed.

Enterprise costs include important elements of budget revenues. A part of the depreciation of fixed assets is centralized; and the charge on productive assets and wage taxes and social insurance contributions are obligatory payments to the budget. At the same time, they orient enterprises to economize on different factors of production.

A central idea of the new system was that income regulations and material incentives should be based upon the interest of enterprises in the total sum of profit. In contrast to the 1957–68 period—when primarily the fulfillment of annual plan indicators oriented and measured the performance of enterprises, and the increase of profitability had a complementary role—in the reform, profit came to be the main guideline and measure of enterprise activity. The relation between annual plan indicators and profit changed. Previously, profitability was only one of the main indicators, the evolution which strongly depended on resources provided by central decisions and expressed by other plan indicators. In the broadened enterprise autonomy since 1968, the intention to increase profits has influenced enterprise activities strongly. As the total sum of profit depends directly on costs and the sale of commodities on the market, feedback effects of the market on economic development have manifested themselves to a much greater extent that before.

Profits earned by enterprises are taxed and their use is regulated by several central rules. These rules are important guarantees of national planning and management for balanced growth and they also influence significantly the interests of enterprises. Although stimulating both the enterprise as a whole and its workers and employees individually, the regulations have some inconvenient side-effects as well. Thus, these rules, though remaining stable in some basic elements, have undergone many modifications since 1968.

Profits of enterprises are divided into two main parts—allocations to the "development fund" and the "sharing fund"—according to the proportions between total assets and the wage bill, with the latter multiplied by a so-called wage multiplier ranging from 2 to 7 in the main branches of the economy, but generally taken as 3. The purpose of this division is to provide adequate funds for personal material incentives while taking into account the balance between the purchasing power of the population and the supply of consumer goods. The rules of distribution of enterprise profits into the two parts thus are determined in accordance with the proportions of accumulation and consumption in national income.

The part of the profit which is calculated in proportion to the *assets* is taxed linearly; generally, 60 percent should be paid to the budget. The remainder goes into the enterprise development fund, along with the portion of depreciation allowances retained by the enterprise. This fund is the source for enterprise investments and repayment of bank credits.

The second part of the profit, formed in proportion to a multiple of the *wage bill,* is taxed progressively. The tax rate is differentiated in bands and rises from 40 to 70 percent depending on the band proportion to the wage bill. Transfers from the sharing fund to the development fund are allowed, but the reverse change is prohibited. From the sharing fund, enterprises are entitled both to increase wages and to pay annual bonuses. The introduction of the sharing fund was the main stimulating force of the new incentive system, but the system was very sensitive to different rules regulating the use of the fund. Although wage increases above a certain level coming from the fund were again taxed progressively, the close link between profits and wage increases gave rise to unhealthy inequalities between enterprises. Low-profit enterprises could neither pay good bonuses nor increase wages, and their relative backwardness could only grow over time. Therefore, in recent years, although basic principles were maintained, the regulations were made more flexible.

Enterprises are also obliged to form a reserve fund related, according to central rules, to both the development and the sharing fund. The reserve fund provides security against risks and is regulated to level out annual profit fluctuations and their effects on funds.

THE CURRENT SYSTEM OF NATIONAL PLANNING

Planning Agencies

The organizational framework of central planning and the division of labor in central planning agencies have been determined by reform decisions and partly up-dated in the Act of National Economic Planning passed by the parliament in 1972.[7] The act also embodies the principles of national planning and was used in preparing this part of the chapter.

The directives of the long-term plan are discussed by the National Assembly, which approves its main features. The *five-year plan* is a legal act passed by the National Assembly on the basis of proposals submitted by the Council of Ministers (government), which subsequently informs the parliament from time to time of the progress of the plan. The approval of the *annual plans* is the prerogative of the Council of Ministers. But, together with the bill on the annual budget, usually in December, the government submits its report to the National Assembly on the progress of the on-going annual plan and informs the parliament of the main targets of the plan for the following year. It is part of the government's responsibility to take the decisions that ensure plan fulfillment.

National Planning Committee. The government is assisted in the realization of its economic functions by the National Planning Committee organized recently.[g] The Committee submits to the government plan proposals and proposals to ensure plan fulfillment, and it continuously observes and evaluates the realization of plan targets. It also takes a stand on other basic economic policy issues.

The National Planning Committee is led by a deputy prime minister who is also the Chairman of the National Planning Office. Members of the Committee are deputy prime ministers in charge of economic affairs, the Minister of Finance, the Minister of Foreign Trade, the Minister of Labor Affairs, and the First Deputy Chairman of the National Planning Office.

National Planning Office. The National Planning Committee is assisted in all its functions by the National Planning Office, which is the central organ of national planning. This Office directs and organizes the elaboration of national economic plans, the international coordination of plans in the Council for Mutual Economic Assistance (CMEA), and the coordination of the system of economic regulators. It continuously analyzes the development of the national economy and the realization of plan objectives, and initiates government measures if needed.

The elaboration of the conceptions and objectives for detailed planning work, a considerable part of plan computations, and the final coordination and formulation of the plan proposals are the main tasks of the National Planning Office. The methods to be applied in national economic planning are established by the Office, which is also responsible for continuous progress in planning methods.

The functional ministries. The so-called functional ministries (e.g., Ministry of

[g]The decision was taken on July 3, 1973. At the same time the previous Economic Committee of the government ceased its activity. The change is intended to strengthen central guidance at this high level. This tendency is expressed by the fusion of the chairmanship of the Planning Committee with that of the National Planning Office. It should be noted that in the Economic Committee all ministers charged with economic affairs were members but the new Planning Committee includes only a few of them.

Finance, Ministry of Labor Affairs) are responsible in a certain sense for the economic activities of the whole of the economy. They participate in national planning by preparing proposals for economic policy aims and for the regulators in the field of their responsibilities. They coordinate the proposals for the regulators with other ministries and after the government decision they are usually responsible for publishing the appropriate orders.

The branch ministries. The branch ministries (e.g., the Ministry of Metallurgy and Engineering, the Ministry of Food and Agriculture), which bear the responsibility for economic activities in their own branches, supervise enterprises and are connected also with national planning in many forms. They prepare analyses of the development of their branches and assist central plan preparation by technological and economic studies and proposals for policy aims concerning their branches. They also suggest, where necesssary, changes in the regulators concerning their branches and participate in the coordination of all these proposals. They assist in the international coordination of plans and organize the participation of the enterprises in this work. The realization of the plan targets in their branch is supported by economic policy measures, and the branch ministries promote the development of direct contacts between enterprises within the branch and between branches.

Plans of Different Time Horizons
The preparation of national plans is a complex task. National planning includes the following main elements:

1. *analysis* of past development, the present situation and the fulfillment of on-going plans;
2. *forecasts* based on past or recent tendencies which determine some of the external or internal conditions of future economic development;
3. *estimates* of the future course of certain flows (e.g., ongoing investment processes; the effects of economic regulators, prices, taxes; etc.) if economic policy intervention does not occur;
4. *determination* of social and economic *objectives* and of the main direction of development to be followed in the plan period, producing the so-called "plan conception" that serves as a basis for detailed planning and coordination;
5. *preparation* of partial alternative proposals and comprehensive *variants* regarding plan objectives and their implementation;
6. *continuous* and final *coordination* of plan proposals and variants with objectives, revision of partial solutions and their combination in such a way that they result in a coherent plan.

While in practice all the above elements are applied in different combinations, but in close relation to each other, a relatively clear distinction developed between plans of different time horizons. Experience has shown that all functions of national planning cannot be fulfilled by a single plan covering a definite time horizon. The basic functions of planning for different time horizons can be formulated as follows:

1. foresee the most important long-term tendencies and form long-term social and economic policy aims;
2. elaborate social and economic targets for a medium-term period, define tasks and means of national management, and determine the basic elements of the economic regulator system;
3. adjust current economic policy to the changing circumstances in harmony with long-term objectives.

Planning must take into consideration the great differences in the nature of different economic activities. Economic decisions should be made neither too early nor too late, but in accordance with particularities of each economic flow. Demographic forecasts and expected changes in the factors determining labor supply and demand often require a perspective of twenty–thirty years. Changes in social circumstances, education, and health services have an impact on long-term growth and, therefore, should be foreseen on such a long-term basis. The best utilization of natural resources is a similar problem. Investments in the energy sector and in production of some raw materials and semifinished products should be based on a fifteen–twenty year analysis. However, if we take the problems of structural changes in manufacturing industry, usually a medium-term horizon is sufficient to realize investment policies and to give enough flexibility for the accommodation of changes in domestic demand, in foreign markets, and in technology. Finally, if we look at equilibrium problems of the economy, current economic policy measures and annual corrections are still necessary.

Planning, however, not only should accommodate the differences in the nature of economic flows, but also must take into account the many interdependencies between economic flows and therefore must unify time horizons and methods in order to harmonize different parts and elements. The existing differentiated system of national planning and national plans developed under the influence of these factors.

Planning in Hungary is based on an interrelated system of national plans consisting of the following three types of plans:

1. long-term plan: looking ahead fifteen–twenty years with complementary projections in some fields for twenty-five–thirty years;
2. medium-term plan: the five-year plans as developed in practice with calculations for certain aspects up to ten years;
3. short-term plan: the annual plans that are also complemented by a perspective of two or three years.

The three types of plans, if correctly linked together, can create a harmonious system providing a stable basis while remaining flexible enough for changes needed during development.

The long-term plan affords a basis for the elaboration of the objectives of five-year and annual plans, but it is not practicable for long-term plans to contain details that can only be safely regulated for a shorter period. We must combine the long-term predictions with medium-term and short-term decisions and regulation. After the completion of a five-year period it is useful to extend the long-term plan for another five years. In this sense long-term planning may be considered a "continuous" activity that provides for every five-year plan a further ten-year perspective. This principle was first applied recently, when the time horizon of long-term planning was lengthened until 1990.

A different practice emerged in five-year planning. Experience proved that the annual "stretching" of five-year plans by a year is not workable because most of the advantages of the harmonization of different parts and elements would be lost and the two–three year time input expended on the preparation of a five-year plan impedes continuity. It seems practicable, however, in the third year of the plan period to evaluate results attained and, on this basis, to elaborate the main conceptions for the next five-year period. These objectives and data will provide an orientation to annual planning during the last two years of a five-year plan.

The long-term plan. The specific task of the long-term plan is to define a long-term economic policy orientation, to set a framework for five-year and annual planning, and to serve as a basis for decisions significantly influencing long-term social and economic growth.

After some previous experiments, long-term planning has been developed in Hungary following the economic reform of 1968. In the first phase work was aimed at preparing a long-term plan for the period 1971–85. Recently, after a decision by the Council for Mutual Economic Assistance (CMEA), the lengthening of the time horizon to 1990 has been decided.

We can approach the preparation of the long-term plan from two different angles: one is the examination of past economic trends and structural changes in order to define some progressive tendencies; the second is the exploration of future structures and changes in tendencies based on social, economic, and technical sciences. From this second approach might be derived the new demands and conditions which will characterize future development. A description of qualitative changes and an estimation of new structures are essential elements of long-term planning.

Special forms of organization are used in long-term planning. Committees have been formed with the participation of leading personalities from social, economic, and scientific institutions. The committees direct the work in economic ministries, scientific institutes, and social institutions. Proposals are put forward and variants are prepared for central coordination. The central committee for coordination is headed by the Chairman of the National Planning Office and committees are serviced by divisions of the same office. The National Planning Office bears the responsibility of coordinating suggestions and preparing unified variants for the economy as a whole.

Long-term plans are of quite a different nature from five-year or annual plans. They do not contain decisions and elements of the regulator system. A qualitative definition of objectives and tendencies has a greater part to play in these plans. But the economic policy orientation represented by long-term plans is extremely important, because it influences long-run economic growth and is a basis for the most important social and economic decisions which have permanent financial and material consequences.

Although an overall long-term plan has not yet been approved in Hungary, the theoretical requirements have been formulated. The long-term plan must deal with, and coordinate, the following groups of issues:

1. the rate of growth, the main proportions of the national economy and basic changes in social relations;
2. the long-term conceptions of the development of international economic relations;
3. the main directions of technological development and the growth of certain branches, such as the energy sector, transport, and communication;
4. changes in living standards and in circumstances of life;
5. conceptions of regional economic development.

In harmony with the long-term plan of the national economy, a plan is also under preparation which will determine the prospective direction of scientific research work.

The five-year plan. The reform principles have been fully applied for the first time in the preparation of the fourth five-year plan (1971–75). Therefore, we can introduce five-year plans by using as an example this plan enacted by the National Assembly on October 3, 1970.[8] Under the new system the basic instrument of national management is the medium-term plan. This principle is reflected in the comprehensive nature of the plan and in its relation to the economic regulator system.

A period of five years is short enough to permit a reasonable assessment of economic development and to set realistic tasks. Five-year plans therefore give the most complete definition of economic policy objectives. At the same time, it is a period long enough to ensure the necessary perspectives for the guidance of national management and enterprise planning. The stability of the system of economic regulators requires the major prescriptions of regulation to be valid for a certain length of time, ensuring thereby a stable environment for enterprises. This is why the system of regulators is so deeply involved in five-year plans. The fourth five-year plan consists of two main parts. In the first, economic policy objectives are defined, while in the second part the main characteristics of the system of economic regulators are determined.

The central economic policy aim of the fourth five-year plan is to increase the efficiency of economic activities in all fields. The growth rate, resource allocation, and planned proportions in the distribution of national income are all subject to this central aim.

The plan envisages a 5.5–6 percent average annual growth rate in national income, which is higher than the annual growth rate of the gross social product. This difference presumes a significant decrease in material inputs. The planned growth rate of the net product of industry is 7 percent per year. Another reason for the improvement in efficiency is the speeding up of productivity: 85 to 90 percent of the increment of the national income and 75 to 80 percent of industrial production growth are derived from the increase in productivity.

No change in proportions between accumulation and consumption within the national income is planned. The growth of output will be produced by a shift within the accumulation: In comparison with the preceding plan period, a smaller part of accumulation will go to the increase of inventories and a greater part will be used for fixed investments. Also, a higher share of investment is allocated to nonproductive branches—especially to housing and household services—than before.

The plan relies upon a more efficient use of fixed and working capital in the sphere of production. An important factor in increasing efficiency in Hungary has been and will be a more intensive participation of the country in the international division of labor. Thus, the average annual growth rate of foreign trade is planned higher than that of total output or national income.

The final economic policy aim of the plan is to attain a regular and relatively high rise in the living standards of the population, to improve living conditions and cultural facilities. Per capita real income of the population will increase at almost the same rate as the per earner national income. In addition, the plan envisages improvements in social benefits, a very high increase in state-financed residential construction, and the general introduction of the 44-hour work week.

When calculating improvements in efficiency, the plan takes into account the effects of the regulator system. On the basis of the two years of implementation of the new system, five-year planning could be evaluated and two main conclusions have been reached. First, interrelations between national plans and regulators should and could be improved, and, second, some provisional elements of the regulator system could be abolished, while basic principles could be applied more consistently. These ideas guided changes in the regulators.

The five-year plan also defined the sphere in which direct methods could be used, and the Act and a governmental decision settled the basic arrangements, which will now be described briefly.

The plan decided upon four so-called "central development programs." These programs, the complexity of which is a new striking feature in our planning, define development targets, investments in fixed and working capital, the main uses of products (e.g., private or industrial consumption, exports), financial resources and import cooperation if any, the time-schedule of realization, and related preferences and subsidies. The four fields where such decisions have been taken are: the development program of bus construction; the use of natural gas; the aluminum industry; and the development of domestic output and use of computers. These programs demonstrate the orientation of the plan to the development and use of modern techniques.

A second sphere of direct central decisions is investments. For a limited number of individual projects the plan contains actual decisions, whereas for other investments the plan only defines the aims and provides funds. Although in investments these central decisions are very important, most decisions on productive investments are instead decentralized. For example, in industry around two-thirds of envisaged investments will be decided by enterprises.

A separate chapter of the plan indicates the directions in technological development that enjoy priority and will be supported by credits or subsidies. Environmental problems, e.g., the reduction of air and water pollution, are also included under this heading.

The growth of household income and of living standards is closely connected with the increase in enterprise profits. But many corrections in relative income and wage structures are envisaged. The plan formed a special reserve fund for measures affecting living standards, and directives regulate the planned use of this fund.

Finally, central measures might be taken concerning domestic and foreign trade in certain products.

It is a basic principle, declared in the Act, that beyond the above mentioned decisions "the accomplishment of the different tasks determined by the plan should be promoted, in general, with the application of indirect economic regulation." [9]

The fourth five-year plan contains general policy directives concerning the development and application of economic regulators in the following fields: price policy, monetary and fiscal policy, credit policy, foreign trade regulation, wage regulation, and regional development. These policy directives of the plan are expounded in detail and applied to actual circumstances in orders [10] of the Council of Ministers or the individual ministries or agencies.

Decisions on the five-year plan and on changes in the system of economic regulators are taken on the basis of a detailed system of plan calculations. A great part of the analytical tables and plan indicators are published for the information of enterprises, economic authorities, and institutions. But no enterprise-by-enterprise or similarly detailed breakdown exists in this background information.

The annual plan. The annual plan is an important link between the five-year plan and current economic activity. The function of annual plans is to define the ways in which different conflicts between economic policy aims and everyday realization should be resolved.

Even in the best five-year plan it is impossible to foresee and harmonize economic flows in such depth that during the realization no conflict would arise and no deviations occur. In many cases, these problems can be resolved without intervention, and development can go forward uninterrupted. Experience, however, proved that conflicts do often arise causing major difficulties even on the macroeconomic level and that they impede the automatic return of the economy to normal growth as originally envisaged in the five-year plan.

Fluctuations in agricultural production and in branches using agricultural raw materials; changes in world markets and their effect on the domestic economy; delays in the realization of investment projects or, the reverse, over-investment; labor shortages or surpluses and relative differences in wages; and many other factors can cause tensions. It often happens that several of these factors combine to aggravate the problem. We must realize that the power of a five-year plan to anticipate economic development is limited in some respects.

To fulfill its functions, annual planning relies upon an overall analysis of the economic situation and of the realization of the ongoing annual plan. The examination of equilibrium and the exploration of possible fluctuations and tensions are of the greatest importance in this work. When preparing annual plans we often look ahead not only for one year but also for the following one to two years and elaborate a system of balances including input-output tables and coordinate expected economic flows in detail. This is a task of a complex nature.

Contrary to the practice before 1968, the overall analysis is needed only to check economic growth and to find where and by which methods we have to intervene. But in most cases there is no intervention, as basic elements of the economic regulator system cannot be changed every year.

The annual plan consists, like the five-year plan, also of two main parts: (1) economic policy aims and (2) decisions and amendments of the regulator system. Although the first part is very concise, it is comprehensive in nature, defining specific features of the economic policy applied to the given year and determining the ten to fifteen most important plan indicators which characterize development in the following year. The content of the second part changes every year depending on the situation and on the special needs for intervention. The list of investment projects to be started and to be finished, based on the decisions of the five-year plan, and domestic and foreign trade regulations are, however, generally included in this part. The annual plan also includes the annual credit policy directives of the National Bank and is prepared in close association with the annual budget.

Connections with enterprise plans. The fact that direct contacts between national and enterprise plans to determine enterprise plan indicators from above have been abolished does not mean that connections no longer exist.

National planning cannot exist without information from enterprises, and central planning is entitled to ask for calculations and proposals in the course of plan preparation. The information requirements of national planning may be divided into two groups:

1. information about the past development and present situation—data that serve for central calculations;
2. estimates and proposals regarding the future, which inform central planners of the intentions of enterprises and aid planners in working out possible solutions for certain problems.

The first type of information generally reaches planners through statistics. The demand for statistical information in a centrally planned economy is very high.

The second category of information is needed mainly in five-year planning but for specific problems such demands often arise also in annual planning. This work is organized directly by the National Planning Office.

By summarizing enterprise proposals regarding major comprehensive indicators of the entire national economy, we usually obtain less realistic forecasts than on the basis of central calculations and predictions, which can also evaluate interdependencies and foresee tendency changes earlier and in greater detail. Therefore, no complex enterprise plan proposals are asked and summarized.

Connections between national and enterprise plans should also exist after national plans are adopted. Enterprises are obliged to prepare medium-term and annual plans and to cooperate with each other in plan preparation by giving information to larger supplier and buyer enterprises. The plans of the enterprises should be in harmony with economic policy aims determined by national plans. But enterprises do not receive plan indicators from supervising authorities, nor is the form of enterprise plans centrally prescribed either. The plans of the enterprises are approved by the manager (director, general manager) or in cooperatives by the general assembly. The manager makes his decision after hearing the opinion of the workers of the enterprise. A series of informative meetings is organized together with trade unions, where general proposals as well as related workshop problems are discussed.

The organizations of central planning are obliged to inform enterprises at regular intervals of economic developments, results and problems in national plan fulfillment, and future plans. Following the enactment of the fourth five-year plan, all enterprises received detailed information on the content of the national plan to serve as a basis for their own planning. A similar but simplified procedure is applied in annual planning.

The Planning Process

The methods and the organization of national planning are under the influence of opposing factors.

On the one hand, interdependencies between the different sectors and different aspects of growth endow planning with a certain stability. On the other hand, changes in the domestic and the world economic situation and the ensuing alterations in economic policy aims, the accumulation of experience, and improvements in skill and training and new technical conditions (such as computers and other equipment at the planners' disposal) explain the continuous development in the methods and organization of planning. A given system and level of planning are therefore a result of all these effects.

During its development national planning in Hungary has become a more comprehensive system. However, we cannot explain this phenomenon in technical terms: product specification used in central planning and the number and breakdown of material balances are now less detailed than twenty years ago, and also the total number of staff actually decreased in certain years. But methods of planning for different time horizons or in different fields gradually became diversified. For instance, production planning in branches, planning of consumption levels and structures, domestic and foreign trade planning, collateral planning in constant and current prices, coordination in physical units and value figures, financial coordination, planning of price changes and of other regulators, have each developed their special methodology. The processes of combining traditional methods and mathematical models and of using computer techniques have also advanced significantly during the last few years.

A common feature of planning activities is that they integrate all the elements of analysis, forecasting, determination of policy aims and concrete targets, preparation of variants, and continuous coordination, as already mentioned above.

An iterative process is essential to the determination of the plan. At least two phases are defined in five-year and annual planning. In the first, we concentrate on the determination of the main social and economy policy aims and we produce guidelines for more detailed planning and coordination. In the second phase the plan is elaborated in detail and extensive coordination takes place. The second phase ends when plans are adopted by authorized social organs. In annual planning each of the phases requires two–three months; in five-year planning usually each phase takes at least one year but sometimes longer. In long-term planning the iterative approach and the need for more phases in order to elaborate the plan have also proved inevitable, but the system is not yet as well established as those for five-year or annual planning.

If we look into the technology of a phase of planning work, we can define three elements: (1) analysis, (2) planning of growth and structural changes, and (3) coordination. These are not phases following each other but rather are elements which are repeatedly and collaterally applied. Their separate treatment in this chapter is, therefore, somewhat arbitrary and intended only to clarify certain problems.

Analyses and forecasts. The preparation of plans begins with an analytical task. The length of the period to be analyzed depends on the time horizon of the plan under preparation. The background of the analysis for a long-term plan should be, as far as possible, a similarly long interval. Long-term planning in Hungary started with an analysis of growth and social and structural changes during the period 1950–68. Five-year planning is generally based on the analysis of the fulfillment of the previous five-year plan, which is partly an analysis of past development (including actual data of the first two–three years) and partly an estimate of the expected fulfillment of the plan in the concluding years. In annual planning, the last complete year and the expected fulfillment of the ongoing annual plan provide the two basic reference years.

This analytical work accompanies plan preparation until the end; from time to time the analyses are revised on the basis of new data which become available.

The analyses and the conclusions drawn from past development, as experience has often proved, are of a great influence on planned growth; sometimes they even have a determining role in decision making. A recent paper critically analyzed the strong correlation between the actual increase in national income and the planned rate of growth of the next five-year plan.[11] The data are presented in table 9–3, which shows that, with some leeway, planned rates of growth of national income followed the actual tendencies of the preceding period. The researcher therefore came to the conclusion that past analysis had in this case a stronger influence on plans than did the exploration of changing

Table 9–3. Hungary: Actual and Planned Average Annual Rates of Growth of National Income (percentage)

Period	Actual rate of the previous period[a]	Planned rate for this period
Second five-year plan, 1961–65	7.1	6.3
Third five-year plan, 1966–70	4.5	4.1
Fourth five-year plan, 1971–75	6.8	5.6

Note:
[a]For 1961–65, the actual rate for 1958–60; for 1966–70 and 1971–75, the fulfillment figures of the previous five-year plan period.

circumstances in the future. In the figures for national income this tendency is demonstrated relatively clearly. A deeper analysis could prove such an interrelation also in the development of many other indicators, but in other cases this tendency is generally not so significant because other factors often exert an overriding influence.

By a deeper analysis of future circumstances such simplifications can be avoided. We should reveal existing inefficiencies and inconsistencies, analyze problems and tensions, and examine their expected influence on future growth. In forecasts we should not only describe trends that are likely to continue, but also anticipate changes in tendencies. Economic growth has often demonstrated how evolution may be broken by smaller or greater changes in the tendencies. The future is never a simple repetition of the past, and planning should foresee significant changes. How far planning can meet these high requirements depends above all on the disposition of the society to accept changes and be critical of its own efforts and, furthermore, on the ability of planning to fulfill its duties.

One purpose of the analytical task is to select a set of social and economic policy aims for future development and to make a preliminary outline of the problems which should be elaborated in the planning period. The intention in the last five years has also been to combine analyses with forecasts that explicitly show the consequences of past trends for future development.

Forecasts contribute to better understanding of the past, to the exploration of existing inconsistencies and tensions, and they also often help to find possibilities and constraints of future development. However, the preparation of realistic forecasts is a very difficult problem.

According to Professor Tinbergen's definition: "By forecasts we mean an estimate of the future economic situation under the assumption that there will be no change in economic policy."[12] But it is often very difficult or even impossible to determine exactly what the assumption "no change in economic policy" really means and to distinguish the consequences of a given economic policy.[13] When the private sector prevails in an economy and state intervention is relatively rare and has a limited role, forecasting means to define the path of the ongoing movements in the economy. But when the public sector has a prevailing position and central management is a determining factor of growth, the distinction between planning and forecasting does not always have a clear meaning. For instance when, as previously in Hungary, central management had a wide sphere of direct activities and was based on short-term plans, separate forecasts—at least in short- and medium-term planning—had practically no meaning.

Forecasts as expressions of future movements have gained importance only since 1968, when central management has been based on medium-term plans, main rules have been determined for a longer period, and enterprises have been acting primarily under the influence of a system of economic regulators. Nevertheless, in practice the role of forecasts still remains limited. They are used with success only to forecast partial tendencies, to predict the future consequences of certain factors and individual measures. In overall planning, however, they have not been applied regularly.

The preparation of analyses and forecasts involves difficult methodological problems. Plan analyses examine simultaneously the tendencies of past development and the fulfillment of plans in previous periods. They usually include an estimate of the expected fulfillment for the remaining period of the ongoing plan. All these activities are carried out on the basis of the accumulated experience of economists. At the present stage, however, the statistical-analytical techniques used are generally simplified. As this field is especially suited for the application of more advanced mathematical-analytical methods, it is realistic to expect significant methodological developments not far in the future. This will in all probability contribute to a wider use of forecasts as well.

Planning of growth and structural changes. National planning in our concept is a systematic way to determine future development for the economy as a whole. Analyses and forecasts are necessary and important steps toward this goal, but the content of plans could never be determined if planning stopped at this stage. It should go forward: (1) to form a weighted and coordinated system of economic policy aims; (2) to plan the development of such comprehensive economic flows as production and employment, consumption and accumulation, developments in international economic relations; (3) to plan the growth of branches and to determine individual investment projects: (4) to plan regional development; and (5) to prepare targets for central decisions (where such decisions should be taken) and to plan regulators or changes in regulators that are needed to achieve planned results and to promote development.

The main role in development planning is still played by the experts' inventions and a gradual approach or, in other words, a trial and error process. Economic policy aims are quantified in a few macroeconomic aggregates, such as growth of national income, which serve as starting points for detailed planning in branches and in regions.

While analyses and forecasts can be prepared in all parts and at all levels of the economy simultaneously, planning of growth and structural changes generally begins from above, on the basis of central guidelines given to the branches. What they need most are the assumptions on growth rates of national income and consumption and some elements of investment and foreign trade policy. Usually a few figures are enough to give the first impetus to branch planning, which then becomes a self-generating process. Because of their interactions in the planning process, the intention of each branch to ensure adequate supplies and a market for its commodities stimulates the other branches to work out their own conceptions and to provide for the preconditions of their own development.

From time to time the progress achieved needs to be supervised. Results are summed up and checked by coordination departments of the National Planning Office and, if needed, further guidelines are given to rectify wrong estimates, change unrealistic proposals, and reveal and solve inconsistencies. In this work generally the same aggregates are collected as were given to branches at the beginning of the work. Growth of national income and consumption, total investments, total exports and imports, and the balance of foreign trade are the most frequently used indicators. But they are derived from detailed branch figures summarizing data of branch estimates and, therefore, their nature changes and they become "control" figures of the progress in planning. In this way, development planning and coordination join into a common flow. Sometimes new information on the progress of plan fulfillment, newly received statistical data and consequent modifications in the conclusions of the analyses, or changing foreign markets and other exogenous circumstances give a new impulse to planning.

Two factors now contribute more intensively than before to planning of growth and structural changes: international comparisons and examination of technical progress. The two approaches are closely related. Comparative analyses, particularly in a smaller country that is not highly developed technically, can explore ways to develop the industrial structure and to increase productivity, and can point to new products and new technologies which should be introduced. These analyses often aid demand forecasts, showing the main directions of progress in advanced countries. The same results can be achieved also by direct studies on technical progress and new technologies.

At this point difficult organizational problems should be solved. A wide circle of experts and scientists and also managers of industries must be involved in this phase of plan preparation. Before 1968 the branch five-year plan proposals and discussions of them between the National Planning Office and branch ministries constituted the main organizational framework, whereby the decisions on the more important technical proposals were made. These proposals were made and the meetings organized as a direct part of national planning when the enterprises' interest to receive maximum resources (for investment and other activities) was already dominating discussions and time was usually too limited. Therefore, in these proposals and meetings real experts played a minor role and real discussions were usually killed by administrative and tactical approaches.

A new approach to the problem was the suggestion to elaborate "conceptions of technological and economic development" for the more important technical proposals. The conceptions are not plan-proposals. Neither their time horizon nor their preparation is connected directly to the long-term or medium-term plan. They represent a sort of scientific analysis of the current situation of one or another industry, or of the production and consumption of a group of products, with alternative proposals for future development. The preparations of these conceptions is organized by branch ministries or, for those concerning complex problems, under the auspices of the National Commission for Technical

Progress. Their decisions, which are made after thorough discussions with the participation of scientists, managers and experts, are used as advice for long-term and five-year planning. However, the actual decisions are taken in the planning process in which production, investment and other basic indicators are coordinated with each other. This separation of the two tasks has solved many problems: the first discussion is free from the pressure which is always exerted by the scarcity of resources and time in plan preparation. Apparently a stock of such studies has already been developed that facilitates planning.

Coordination. Plan coordination is an ingredient of national planning. Wherever planning exists, we can find the task of coordination, but we also find that the greatest differences in the conceptions of planners are in this field.

In economies with a broad private sector, many tasks which are often attached to coordination are solved ex post by the market, and the role of coordination is thus more limited.

In socialist countries the requirement is a more detailed coordination. Interdependencies should be deliberately enforced between the branches' production and investments, between production and consumption, domestic and foreign trade relations, etc. This need for coordination in depth is a direct consequence of the fact that the prevailing part of the means of production is in state ownership. This is why the harmonization in advance of the basic economic relations within the plans is a precondition for the subsequent coordination of the decisions and economic regulators and, finally, for the smooth functioning of the market.[h]

Two general approaches are known to coordinate national plans. The first is characteristic of national planning as it is functioning today. The second method is expounded in studies suggesting the use of mathematical models for this task. Because the use of mathematical models in increasing rapidly, it is worthwhile to study both methods.

In practice planning starts with a set of economic policy aims and plan proposals, which usually are not easily balanced. For instance, demands for investment both to increase capacities and to accelerate technical progress generally overrun the available investment funds. The need for social improvements, housing construction, education, and health, together with demands to raise wages and salaries and other income for the active population also, as a rule, exceed possibilities. Under these circumstances, coordination decreases the number of proposals, by leaving out what is thought to be of secondary importance for the given period, and by reducing the degree to which different

---

[h]The coordination of basic economic relations in planning is a necessary instrument and a precondition of the realization of the primacy of plan against market. To the extent that harmonization on the level of the national economy as a whole is successful, the realization of the plan will go on undisturbed and balanced and the role of market will remain in shadow; but where and when inconsistencies in the plan are significant, disturbances will appear in the execution of the plan and elemental market forces will manifest their presence.

needs are satisfied. On the other hand, maximum efforts are made to accelerate development of scarce factors, for example, to improve the efficiency of exploitation of capacities of scarce products or to promote the rate of growth of exports.

In traditional planning a system of balances has been developed to reveal inconsistencies and solve the problems of coordination. The system of balances used in Hungary consists of the following types of primary balances:

1. material, or product balances (in the preparation of the fourth five-year plan their number was approximately 300);
2. manpower balances;
3. financial balances; and
4. the balance of foreign trade.

Each of the balances serves for coordination of resources and envisaged use of one or another factor of production. We synthesize the relations expressed in the primary balances and estimate the general equilibrium of the economy by means of the national balances, which include:

1. the balance of social product (gross output);
2. the balance of national income; and
3. the synthetic balance of manpower resources and use.

As a result of the developments during the last fifteen years, input-output tables and relevant mathematical methods of analysis are also regularly used in this synthetic work.

The system of balances aids coordination successfully, but the deficiencies of this system are significant.

Using this method we proceed from a larger group of proposals to a more limited circle step-by-step and, in this procedure, there is no equal criterion for measuring the proposals. What is from one point of view a worse proposal compared to another, and is omitted from later work, could be a better one if we could consider all suggestions at the same time, and with equal measures. When grading proposals according to a single efficiency criterion (in Hungarian planning, for a time, certain types of indicators were used, e.g., to rank investment proposals or export production), we receive a different list compared to the result of a balancing process in which the scarcity of different resources (and not efficiency) is the main criterion.

Another well-known deficiency of the method is the lack of simultaneous overall solutions. The whole procedure is directed to fighting inconsistencies and to the production of a complete plan proposal which satisfies constraints and economic policy aims within reasonable limits and in an acceptable combination.

This task usually needs the total time period given for the preparation of the plan.

Mathematical programming models could overcome these imperfections and provide for many overall variants ordered according to different objective functions, but here other difficulties arise. Such a model requires as data the results of nearly all the calculations prepared in the course of planning. In contrast, the current methods are very flexible: the proposals are often elaborated during the planning period and amended when conditions are gradually clarified. Another disadvantage of the applicable mathematical models is that coefficients should be linear because the dimensions of overall models at the present still exclude nonlinearity.

All these objections do not mean that linear programming models cannot be adequate for this task. In the preparation of the fourth five-year plan, after some previous experiments, a linear programming model has been applied closely linked to the traditional planning process.[14] The model received input data from an existing plan variant available three-quarters of a year before the final decision was taken on the plan (although it was not a fully acceptable and consistent variant). The constraints took into account all the main conditions of a consistent plan and the model produced complete plan variants ordered according to four objective functions.[i] However, mainly because of the poor computing facilities available at that time, only the computations of the ten branch submodels were ready in time. The solution of the overall model, which contained in a reduced form 1,782 variables and 1,626 constraints, was available a few months too late for practical use. However, the work resulted in important conclusions for the future.

It has been proved that traditional methods of planning can be combined with mathematical models successfully. This combination is needed, on the one hand, because the data input of the models comes largely from the existing planning system and, on the other hand, because harmonization and optimization can be improved significantly by mathematical models. The successful functioning of such a combined system depends on two main conditions: (1) on computing facilities, which have been improved during the last two years by the creation of an independent computer center for national planning; and (2) on improvements in input data handling. Only a chain of interrelated work can reduce the total input of time in the preparation and solution of the model. As these conditions are gradually improving, the application of mathematical models in the coordination of national plans will increase in the near future.

---

[i]The four objective functions were: (a) maximization of consumption above the minimum increase; (b) maximization of the surplus of foreign trade balance with the dollar area; (c) maximization of the surplus of foreign trade balance with the ruble area; and (d) maximization of the total of enterprise profits.

CONCLUSIONS

Accomplishments of Planning in Hungary

Postwar economic development in Hungary was tightly connected with the foundation of a planned economy. The reconstruction of the economy was directed by national plans, the level of output multiplied while the structure of production and consumption changed, and the living standard of the population improved significantly. Thus, during the first twenty-five years national planning produced good results, as shown in international comparisons, although the historical heritage was adverse and the country often had to face political difficulties and to compete with developed countries on the world market. The results were achieved by relying, first of all, on domestic resources, although development was also supported by the international economic cooperation of socialist countries within CMEA.

The planned economy, as it developed in Hungary, was especially appropriate to create new industries, to industrialize new regions, to help newly established collective farms, to start economic activities on a large scale and to introduce modern agrotechnics. A rather even and high rate of long-term growth was achieved, and experience was accumulated in regulating key proportions of the economy. The forms and methods of planning developed continuously, and solid foundations were laid down for future development.

As principal advantages of a planned economy, on the basis of Hungarian experience, we can emphasize two features:

1. A planned economy is an efficient system to unify national resources in order to realize common social aims.
2. A planned economy has all the means for continuous and harmonious growth and can avoid great fluctuations in economic development.

In our country national planning is a state function. The state, representing the society as a whole and as owner of the bulk of the means of production, is able to review future social needs and establish priorities. The system of plans with different time horizons and the related stepwise decisionmaking procedure are intended to solve this problem. The system of balances and models used in planning aims at the investigation of social needs, the clarification of their interrelations, and the determination of the degree of their urgency. The greatest problem, however, is not how to take into account the whole bundle of social needs and to weigh the social significance attached to them, but—when needs and existing tensions between needs and real possibilities are already known—how to determine and realize priorities. This task endows planning with a political nature. A precondition of the smooth functioning of the planning system is that basic decisions be taken on a political level in the Party leadership and by leading state organs.

We consider here as examples two basic problems: first, the degree of economic centralization of surplus product (the net residual of production and trade); and second, the determination of the proportion between consumption and accumulation in the use of national income.

A part of surplus product produced by enterprises generally should remain with those who produced it, while the other part is centralized and redistributed according to central economic policy aims. Naturally enough, enterprises and institutions fight for their own interests and want to keep and receive the highest possible share of resources. To give enterprises and institutions directives is therefore not a simple question of knowledge and of economic reasoning but in considerable measure a political task.

The first five-year plan was characterized by a very drastic centralization of resources in order to promote the development of heavy industry. In light industry there were branches where even a large part of depreciation allowances was not left with enterprises but was taken into central hands. Later the degree of centralization diminished and all branches got more possibilities to modernize their production from their own resources. The 1968 reform made an important step forward in the direction of further economic decentralization. A certain degree of centralization is, however, indispensable in the decision making and planning process.

A similar problem is the regulation of the distribution of national income between consumption and accumulation. Maintaining the already achieved per capita level of consumption determines the lower limit of this proportion, while using all of the increase in national income for consumption can be taken as an upper limit to the future share of consumption. The actual distribution is determined within these boundaries. On one pole, consumption represents the present and direct interests of the population, while on the other, accumulation serves future development.

The first five-year plan put a high preference on accumulation, trying to accelerate the rate of industrial growth to a maximum. Practice has shown, however, that when the growth of consumption is very limited, workers and peasants do not feel directly interested in production, and lower growth of productivity diminishes the overall rate of growth. Therefore, the highest rate of growth in the long run is produced not by the maximum possible share for accumulation, but by a good combination of increase in both consumption and accumulation. The shares of consumption and accumulation are again a basic policy decision, the execution of which should be enforced by state authority. Hungarian development has shown that good solutions—or long-term harmonization of interests which conflict in the short run—can be found and realized successfully, and in such cases the basic aims of national plans receive the support of the population.

Our experiences also show certain problems in the practical operation of a planned economy. In our history the potentials of the system were not fully exploited because of deficiencies in foresight and planning. In certain periods, resources and the possibilities for future growth were overestimated; these erroneous evaluations found their expression in overstrained output and investment plans and in an overdistribution of resources exceeding real possibilities. These periods were necessarily followed by unforeseen corrections and rearrangements carried out through annual plans. However, the amplitude of these deviations was not very significant—except during the first five-year plan period—and as experience accumulated it has decreased.

Another often mentioned problem was to find the best methods of plan implementation on the enterprise level. The first approach to this problem was very simplified: the plan was interpreted as the main instrument of its own implementation, and tasks of national plans were broken down to the enterprise level in an attempt to define exactly and in detail what enterprises should do. But rather soon the importance of enterprise autonomy and the great role of material incentives were recognized. Since the middle of the fifties adequate solutions to this problem were sought, and they were also among the basic goals of the economic reform in 1968.

Evaluation of the Reform and Its Future Development

The economic reform of 1968 envisaged deep changes in the national management system; a price reform and reforms in practically all main elements of the planning and financial systems were carried through. Although the changes were profound, due to the long and careful preparation the transition was smooth and the new instruments gradually showed their effects. The main results of the reform and current problems in its realization can be summed up as follows:

1. The reform has been followed by general improvement in the main indicators of economic performance and an acceleration in economic development. Both the per capita rate of growth of national income and the ratio of national income to gross output increased. The relative backwardness of agricultural growth was eliminated, and market equilibrium in all respects was strengthened. The rate of foreign trade turnover grew nearly twice as fast as the national income. During 1968–73 real per capita consumption of the population rose at an annual average rate of nearly 5 percent—more than one percentage point higher than the annual average of the previous seven years.[15]

2. The basic ideas of linking central planning with a broadened role for the market proved to be not only realistic but very advantageous, because feedback effects from the market helped accelerate growth and did not disturb to a great extent the planned development of the main proportions of the economy.

The organized study of long-term social and economic development began, and drafts for a long-term plan were prepared. The five-year plan became the central element of the planning system and now is the main link in the coordination of economic policy aims, concrete plan targets, and economic regulators. However, the harmony of plan targets and regulators was in practice imperfect.

The regulator system was established both to furnish relatively broad guides to orient enterprise activities and also to provide a common basis for evaluating their operations. The introduction of greater uniformity in price formation, charges on capital and labor factors, the use of profitability as the basic common yardstick of performance, and other related measures served these aims. However, already during the preparation of the reform many requirements expressed by regulators were loosened and too many exceptions and branch differentiations were introduced. Later the situation worsened further. Although further corrections were needed to make requirements more realistic for some enterprises, for a large number of enterprises high profitability was provided by the initial price level or by rapid improvement in other factors. The variability of the foreign and domestic market situation had also been underestimated. As a result of all these reasons, the role of annual plans and central intervention proved greater than foreseen.

3. Incomplete harmony between plan targets and regulators manifested itself most in the field of investments. Expenditure for central investment targets and also for enterprises' decentralized development funds exceeded the envisaged figures, and the share of accumulation in national income rose above the five-year plan goals. In these circumstances, with free price formation in construction and in machinery and equipment, the price level of investment goods rose rapidly. Although price movements reduced the real purchasing power of enterprise development funds and other fixed financial resources, price movements alone could not counteract imbalances and reestablish an equilibrium situation. Because of the significantly higher general level of enterprise profitability, the share of decentralized investment in total investment increased to a higher level than envisaged. In order to achieve central policy aims and finish ongoing investment projects, financial resources for central investments were often expanded. Thus, total investment grew also in real terms by extremely high rates (the peak figure in 1970 was nearly 17 percent).[16] Only central reallocation decisions could prevent further disequilibrium and return the economy in 1972–73 to the planned growth path.

4. Enterprises welcomed the reform and adapted to new requirements and circumstances rapidly. Production for market and sale became the first concern of enterprises; technical progress accelerated in many respects; direct cooperation between enterprises at home and abroad developed; the product-mix changed to meet demand better.

There were, however, also some drawbacks. The pressure of the market was not strong enough to press enterprises to decrease production and marketing costs significantly. Rather frequently smaller and medium-sized enterprises could adapt their activitiy to changing market relations better, and achieved a higher profitability, than some large industrial enterprises in different branches of heavy industry. The modernization of the technology and the product-mix of a few, but large and important, state enterprises needed and still needs special central attention.

5. The population actively participated in the preparation of the reform, and the importance of economizing and economic efficiency has been recognized generally. Being strongly interested in profitability, workers have helped solve enterprise problems, and their expectations and activity exerted a kind of pressure and control on enterprise management.

The reform fulfilled the population's expectations for improving living standards, but relatively large differences occurred in personal incomes of different strata of the population. Agricultural procurement prices continued to move upwards during the period: in the last five years their level increased by 23 percent [17] and the income of peasants grew at a higher rate than the income of industrial workers. Larger differences than before arose also within industry between branches or professions and between workers at different enterprises. As the increase of personal income depended on profitability and the dispersion of profitability became significant, after a few years unforeseen differences appeared in income levels.

Price-level movements also contributed to larger differences in growth of per capita family income. During the first three years after the reform, consumer price level changes remained limited and did not surpass the 1–2 percent annual average maximum determined by political decisions. However, consumer prices rose by an average of 2.9 percent in 1972 and 3.5 percent in 1973. Although these changes were envisaged in annual plans, and the annual increase in real income level was, respectively, 4.5 and 3.1 percent,[18] families were affected in a rather differentiated way and the population reacted unfavorably to successive increases in the price level. The central authorities decided to increase workers' personal income, and different measures were taken to limit the rate of subsequent price increases.

6. This summary evaluation of the reform is very positive. The planning and management system developed in harmony with new requirements and circumstances of our economy, the regulator system proved to be efficient, and future development of the management system and more concretely of regulators will be based on further application of the principles of the reform. However, certain problems must be solved and are now among the main concerns of economic policymakers and planners:

a. In the preparation of the next five-year plan, plan targets and regulators must be newly coordinated and changes in the regulator system elaborated.
b. The degree of decentralization in investment policy should be newly determined, with due regard to maintaining equilibrium.

c. Possible new regulation of wage increases is under consideration to secure more equitable relationships among industries and branches.
d. Evaluation of factors in price formation has been discussed for a long period, and a decrease in capital charges and an increase in labor input costs are generally considered desirable.
e. Price regulations should be revised to reduce differences in the operating conditions of enterprises with different proportions of output sold at fixed, regulated, and free prices.

These changes are being elaborated as a part of the preparations for the Fifth Five-Year Plan and some will be introduced in advance to facilitate a smooth transition to the next plan period.

NOTES

1. For background statistical data see (a) Hungary, Központi Statisztikai Hivatal (KSH) [Central Statistical Office] *Statisztikai Évkönyv 1970* [Statistical Yearbook 1970] (Budapest: KSH, 1971), and (b) *Statistical Pocket Book of Hungary 1970* (Budapest: Statistical Publishing House, 1970).
The 1970 GDP per head was 32,292 Ft., estimated to be equal to about $1,600.
2. 1968–73. Data of this period are to be found in *Statisztikai Évkönyv 1972* [Statistical Yearbook 1972] (Budapest: KSH, 1973). The last year's data are provisional estimates.
3. For a review of the Hungarian regulator system as introduced in 1968 and its application and improvements, see *Reform of the Economic Mechanism in Hungary,* ed. István Friss (Budapest: Akadémiai Kiadó, 1969), and *Reform of the Economic Mechanism in Hungary: Development 1968–1971,* ed. Ottó Gadó (Budapest: Akadémiai Kiadó, 1972).
4. The same approach was also demonstrated by the resolution of the Central Committee of the Communist Party of the Soviet Union (CPSU) in 1965. In his speech at the Plenary Meeting of the CPSU Central Committee, Leonid Brezhnev said: "In the course of building communism there continually arise many acute problems which require profound theoretical elaboration for their practical solution. Today, for instance, such questions come to the fore as socialist cost accounting, the use in planned economic management of profit, prices, credit, economic contracts, etc., elaboration of the theory of organization and management of socialist industry in the conditions of the current revolution in science and technology, the combination of centralized planning with economic independence of enterprises, etc." See *New Methods of Economic Management in the USSR: Plenary Meeting of the CPSU Central Committee, September 27–29, 1965* (Novosti Press Agency Publishing House, no place and date given).
5. See *Reform of the Economic Mechanism in Hungary,* ed. István Friss (cited in note 3), p. 136.
6. Ibid., p. 146.

7. Act VII, 1972. *Magyar Közlöny* [Hungarian Official Gazette] (Budapest), December 22, 1972.

8. Act II, 1970. *Magyar Közlöny* [Hungarian Official Gazette] (Budapest), October 1970.

9. Act II, 1970, para. 42 (2).

10. See *Reform of the Economic Mechanism in Hungary; Development 1968–1971*, ed. Ottó Gadó (cited in note 3).

11. See A. Stark, *Középtávú terveink teljesítésének néhány tapasztalata* [Experiences in the Fulfillment of Our Medium-Term Plans] (unpublished conference paper). See also by the same author, "Gazdasági előrelátásunk fejlődése" [Developments in Our Economic Foresight], *Közgazdasági Szemle* 20, 7–8 (July-August 1973): 785–802.

12. Jan Tinbergen, *Central Planning* (New Haven, Conn.: Yale University Press, 1964), p. 9.

13. Similar doubts are expressed also by Tinbergen, because he continues the above cited sentence as follows: "Clearly any forecast must always be based on a large number of assumptions, both about the operation of the economy and about the probable course of the so-called 'data' or external or exogenous variables. Everybody making a forecast chooses these assumptions as realistically as possible, but even so forecasts will, as a rule, not coincide with the actual course of events. There does not seem to be any reason, therefore, to make a distinction between forecasts and so-called projections." Ibid., p. 9.

14. The author of this chapter was the leader of the team that elaborated and solved the model. See the description of the model and the organization and the results of the first phase of work in T. Morva and G. Bager, "Principal Features of the Mathematical Model of the Fourth Five-Year Plan of Hungary and the Most Important Experiences" (United Nations Economic Commission for Europe, First Seminar on Mathematical Methods and Computer Techniques, Varna. Ref. No. ST/ECE/MATHECO/2. Geneva, 1972). The final results and evaluation of the model are summarized in the book *Népgazdásagi tervezés és programozás* [National Planning and Programming], ed. S. Ganczer (Budapest: Közgazdasági és Jogi Könyvkiadó, 1973).

15. The figures are 3.6 percent for 1961–67 and 4.9 percent for 1968–73. See Hungary, KSH, *Föbb népgazdasági folyamatok 1973* [Main Economic Flows 1973] (Budapest: KSH, 1974).

16. Hungary, KSH, *Statisztikai Évkönyv 1972* [Statistical Yearbook 1972].

17. *Föbb népgazdasági folyamatok 1973* [Main Economic Flows 1973].

18. Ibid.

Comments on
Krzysztof Porwit's and
Tamás Morva's
Chapters

Judith A. Thornton

The distinction between economic planning and management of the economy is not clearly drawn in the Eastern European economies, as the chapters of Tamás Morva and Krzysztof Porwit show. In the traditional Soviet model, economic planning was just the first step in central, administrative management of the economy. The annual plan played a key role in mobilizing resources toward centrally-set goals and in coordinating resource use to ensure some measure of consistency among centrally-set targets.

Planning and market principles were not viewed as alternative means for achieving the same economic coordination in the economy; rather, economic planning was the primary device for enforcing a distinctly different set of output structures and income distribution patterns on the economy than would have been feasible under arrangements that provided for voluntary decentralized market responses to government taxes and subsidies.[1]

Besides enforcing central priorities and coordinating resource flows, economic planning functioned to exercise property rights over the socialized assets of society: to create and maintain publicly owned assets, to control their use, and to establish financial arrangements that would centralize the income flows produced by publicly owned assets.[2] Where market signals were no longer functioning, economic planning arranged to do administratively all those things that are done automatically by a market system: to generate information, provide incentives, and impose constraints.

Economic reforms in Eastern Europe modified the traditional institutions of central planning and brought about changes in the role of planning. There were two main reform strategies for gaining greater flexibility and efficiency. One was administrative decentralization; the other marketization.[3] The chapters of Porwit and Morva allow us to compare these two strategies in the experience of Poland and Hungary. Polish reform presents an example of administrative decentralization designed to improve the functioning of central planning, while

Hungarian reform represents a move toward marketization designed to reduce the scope and role of central planning.

In Poland, the stress between planners' goals and consumers' desires for immediate gains in the standard of living was reduced by a program of consumerism. In production, the stress between directives and financial incentives was reduced by decreasing administrative intervention and the number of directives and by introducing improved financial indicators, most important of which was an interest charge on investment funds that had been allocated without charge previously. For a group of large pilot units, planners promised to abandon output directives altogether.[4]

Establishment of markets in Hungary brought about more substantial changes in the operating principles of that economy. Enterprises were freed of obligatory plan targets and were empowered to adjust outputs to market signals. Many prices were freed, particularly for consumer goods. A portion of enterprise profit was taxed into the budget, as before, but another portion remained with the firm for increase of wages, for managerial incentives, and for self-financed investment. In consequence, the structure of worker income began to show wide differentiation.

It would be misleading to describe either the Polish system or the Hungarian system as a stable model of reformed planning. Both are systems in transition. It would also be misleading to exaggerate the differences in the two systems. Both have evolved away from the rigid central planning of the early fifties. At this time, both are enjoying success in meeting the goals they hoped to achieve by reform. Poland's administratively decentralized planning system has market elements, and Hungary's market system is still under strict administrative control.

In Poland, both private agriculture and the large foreign trade sector introduce important market elements into planning. Direct interfirm contracts, a tradition of informal arrangements among firms, and strong bargaining between firms and their ministries all provide adjustment mechanisms outside of official administrative channels. Conversely, in Hungary, relaxation of controls turned repressed inflation into open inflation to which planners responded by price controls, by strengthened control over investment, and by a structure of taxes and subsidies that made enterprise profits unrelated to efficiency considerations.[5]

The two economies have similarities. Still, it will be useful to contrast dimensions on which they differ to see the implications for socialism after economic reform. The functions performed by economic planning may be grouped into (1) regulatory functions, (2) financial and fiscal functions, (3) property rights functions. In both Hungary and Poland, decentralization meant a decrease in the regulatory functions of planning together with a restructuring and, apparently, some increase in the fiscal and ownership functions exercised by the planning agencies. But the decrease in central regulation was significantly greater in Hungary than in Poland.

REGULATORY FUNCTIONS

Regulation of Supply

No change in planning is as significant as measures that free enterprises to adjust output supplies and materials demands in response to market signals. In Hungary, the new economic mechanism abolished the central fixing of enterprise plan targets except in special cases. The prices of goods constituting roughly half of retail trade turnover were classified as free or loosely regulated, although prices remained fixed for most raw materials and foodstuffs. With the reduction in operational control of the economy, the content of plans changed. The enterprise was required to report on past performance and to draw up a forecast of projected sales in consultation with its major customers and suppliers, but such projections were not binding on the firm. The operational part of the central plan consisted mainly of the annual investment program, taken from the medium-range plan, tax and budgetary forecasts and regulations, and credit directives for the National Bank. The major instruments of central control, then, were taxes and subsidies, credit regulation, centralized control of major investments, and partial price control.

In Poland, moves toward the market were much more hesitant. (If Hungarian reforms were described as "cautiously optimistic," then Polish reforms were "optimistically cautious.")[6] Some obligatory delivery targets were abandoned for agriculture, but four-fifths of industry was still guided by branch output targets and input normatives.

Some market flexibility was established with the designation of twenty-eight large enterprises or industrial associations as pilot units on January 1, 1973. For these large units, supplying some 20 percent of industrial output and later extended to cover 40 percent of industrial output, detailed branch administration was replaced by parametric controls. For these units, the branch ministry could specify total output targets; but the firms could plan their own assortment. Branch ceilings on the wage bill were replaced by a wage expansion formula that allowed wages to rise by a factor reflecting the growth of enterprise value added and a proportionality factor specified by the branch ministry. Allocations of foreign currency for purchase of machinery were to be based on economic, not administrative considerations, and allocations of investment to the firm would be made for the total value of approved projects and would not be doled out by the branch ministry in annual amounts.[7]

The Polish pilot units were large enough to enjoy bargaining power vis-à-vis their branch ministries, and they had improved financial incentives, but establishment of the large units increased the degree of both horizontal and vertical integration of industry. Interfirm transactions were transformed into intrafirm transfers, and formerly separate financial accounts were merged. (A similar consolidation had taken place earlier in Hungary.)

From the point of view of the consumer in both Poland and Hungary, allowing enterprises to respond to market, or at least to financial, incentives signaled a reduction in stress between planners' and consumers' tastes. Both countries began to show strong elements of consumerism, and, in Hungary, of consumer sovereignty.

Bargaining, Information, and the Branch Ministry

In Hungary, the rise of market relations brought about a reduction in the operational control of the branch ministries, although ministries still continued to select enterprise management and to retain general supervisory authority, including authority over large investments.[8] Where the firms were few in number and large, they could bypass their ministry and deal directly with the National Planning Office. In some respects, the branch ministries began to function as lobbies with the planning office on behalf of the firms in their industries.

In Poland, too, the establishment of pilot units out of former large enterprises and industrial associations appears to have been intended, in part, to reduce the operational control of the branch ministries and to increase enterprise autonomy. The procedure for drafting the annual plan was significantly altered. Formerly, the branch ministries submitted branch plans to the Planning Commission. The Planning Commission, in turn, combined branch plans and circulated detailed drafts back to the branch ministries and via them to the associations and enterprises to be revised and returned to the center. But the 1973 reforms directed that future plans were to be drawn up by the enterprises themselves in keeping with general guidelines received from their ministries and voivodship government councils.[9]

Scholarly descriptions of the planning process generally have the draft plan moving smoothly up and down the administrative hierarchy like a window-shade.[10] In fact, the process involves introduction of alternative plans and bargaining on several fronts. There is bargaining between the branch ministry and officials of the planning agency and the Ministry of Finance, on one front, and there is bargaining between the branch ministry and its subordinate associations and enterprises, on the other front.

Since, in this bargaining environment, the downward flow of directives, taxes, prices, and incentives from the planners to the firms is conditioned by the upward flow of information from firms to planners, the problem of distortion arises at each stage of the process. In a bargaining environment, a major planning function becomes the generation of hypothetical data to use in dealing with other administrative units. (In an interesting and realistic formal model of administrative planning, Michael Manove demonstrates that allocative planners may correct supply-demand imbalances with few adjustment steps, even in the absence of detailed knowledge of underlying technologies; but his model requires that information given and received be free of the bargaining distortions that affect so much of planning activity in Eastern Europe. [11])

The informational requirements of Polish planning remained larger than those of Hungarian planning, and decentralization had complicated, not improved the situation. (One source wrote, "Administrative methods have failed, parametrical methods have yet to be discovered."[12] And a Polish visitor to my campus complained, "We have left the period of the difficulties of planning and entered the period of the planning of difficulties.")

Mathematical Techniques

Although mathematical techniques provided the original impetus for intro-duction of efficiency considerations into the planned economies, the application of mathematical techniques to planning was, by and large, a tool of centralization in both countries. Proponents of mathematical planning elicited images of the Great Computer in Warsaw issuing a directive that read: "Produce 200,000 shoes. Half of them left shoes. Do not fold, mutilate, or bend."

Institutionally, the research organizations for mathematical planning are attached to central planning bodies—in Poland to the Planning Commission of the Council of Ministers and in Hungary to the Central Statistical Administra-tion. In both Poland and Hungary, the main activity of the research units was concentrated on the elaboration of classic input-output balances and on the modeling of specific policy problems, such as foreign trade or consumer demand policies, using the technique of linear programming.

The direct application of either input-output or linear programming to operational management of the economy was limited. In Poland, where coordination was still fostered administratively and where input-output could contribute to the balancing process, the formal models were organized on a commodity basis, while the functional ministerial organization was not. Industrial ministries were horizontally integrated over diverse outputs and vertically integrated to control various sources of supply.

In Hungary, both input-output and linear programming were used to provide "what if" projections of the consequences of certain policies or external events in much the same manner as these techniques were used to project the impact of a petroleum shortage on the U.S. economy in 1974. In addition, linear programming models provided the planners with measures of the marginal benefit of relaxing a particular constraint—a useful measure in the absence of the necessary prices.

There is some evidence that mathematical planning can be used, on occasion, to confront the planners with the true cost of certain policies or with the likely consequence of a decision, but there were also complaints that the planners used mathematical economists more often to justify than to test policy.

In my view, the quality of mathematical planning work in Hungary was higher than in the other Eastern European countries—in part because of a better data base.[13] But, even there, mathematical modeling was viewed by the government as a dispensable decoration, perhaps with some justification.

Was mathematical analysis important? On the one hand, its input into the planning process was small; on the other hand, the whole process of economic reform in Eastern Europe had been influenced by the reintroduction of opportunity-cost concepts via mathematical analysis.

Forecasting and Long-Term Plans

Planning is inherently concerned with forecasting and developing policy regarding the future, but given the rather limited ability of most published plans to anticipate future states, it is probably fortunate that traditional Soviet-type planning directed primary attention to immediate future periods. Future plans were derived from past performance by a method that might be called "status quo plus" planning. And past plans were revised to conform to subsequent performance by a method that can only be called "ex post" planning.

Hungarian economic reform shifted emphasis to medium-range planning. The Hungarian five-year plan contained both the central development programs and also the basic investment program. With economic reform, investment control became a primary planning device. The planning agency retained effective control over large investments and over the establishment of new plants or expansions requiring large imports. In addition, bank loans for investment were allocated at the discretion of the National Bank and the Investment Bank. These arrangements left centralized some of the same sorts of entrepreneurial and review functions that are likely to be concentrated in the central management of a large Western corporation.

In contrast to current planning, long-range planning tended to attract two groups: the political policymakers whose interests lie in setting future goals without having to confront the details of trade-offs, and the proponents of centralization who are concerned about shaping current macro-proportions in a manner consistent with long-range goals.

Morva's and Porwit's chapters imply a comfortable specialization between long-range and current planners in Poland and Hungary. But there is currently a major battle in the Soviet Union between the long-range planners and the so-called optimizers on the subject of the new fifteen-year plan. There is some evidence of the disagreeement in the discussions at a meeting on the long-range plan for the Soviet economy up to 1990 held by the USSR State Planning Commission in the fall of 1974.[14] At that meeting, Soviet scholars presented a proposal for long-range forecasting based on an Automated System of Plan Calculations. This Automated System would contain scientificallly substantiated normatives to be used in constructing mathematical models that would provide the basis for computer forecasting or modelling of future plans.

The scholars were not agreed on the relationship between forecasting and planning. According to Candidate Yu. A. Belik, "In some works, plans are replaced by forecasts, while in others they are confused with forecasts; in still others, the directive nature of the plan is replaced by an informational function. Certain authors call for the creation of a nationwide system of forecasting. They do this despite the fact that we have a well-structured state system of planning agencies!" [15]

The planning commission economists all seemed agreed on one thing: that the Automated System of Plan Calculation was inconsistent with what they called the "System for the Optimal Functioning of the Economy"—that is with the current optimizing models of the Central Economic-Mathematical Institute of the USSR Academy of Sciences. Since most of the mathematical economists in Eastern Europe analyze the efficiency of their own economies in terms of the models currently under attack, it seems likely that they will watch the Soviet debate with some concern.

FISCAL AND OWNERSHIP FUNCTIONS

Taxes and Credits

With public ownership of the non-human capital stock of society, the fiscal functions of the government and the ownership functions tend to merge. The workers earn wages and agricultural income which they spend on private consumption; the government owns the land and physical capital stock of society and manages prices and taxes so as to allocate to itself an amount that it directs to new investment, government administration, collective consumption, and transfer payments. The fiscal flows into the government budget might be viewed as tax flows, as centralization of the returns to publicly-owned assets, or as a mixture of both.

Price stability requires that the value of wages and farm incomes paid should equal the value of consumer goods produced at their retail prices. This restriction may be relaxed by private saving and private holding of assets. (In fact, both Poland and Hungary allow privately-owned houses and condominiums, which policy is not viewed as violating socialist ownership of the means of production, since housing is not considered to be part of the productive capital stock of society.)

If the production process allocated to labor a share of national income equal to its marginal productivity share, then the government could achieve fiscal balance either by restricting government expenditure to the residual—roughly, the returns to other factors of production—or by reducing labor's share to less than its marginal productivity share by taxing or by manipulating prices or wages.

In the traditional, centralized Soviety-type system, the government did not collect returns to social assets in the form of charges for land, natural resources, or capital. But it did allocate to the treasury a share of national income that approached half in some years by policies of low agricultural procurement prices, turnover taxes on consumer goods, and profits taxes on enterprise profits. Since the supply of consumer goods was restricted by central planning, the disparities between retail prices and marginal costs were substantial. With ineffective control over the wage bill of socialist firms, it was easier to raise output prices than to lower wages.[16]

Poland and Hungary made use of all the taxes just mentioned. And with decentralization they added new taxes and charges. One of the most significant changes in economic reform was the introduction of specific charges for capital on the firm. In Hungary, loans from the government were available for periods of up to ten years with interest rates differentiated among projects. Bank loans were available for six-year terms with interest charged at 5 percent before, and 7 percent after, completion of a project; or for three-year terms at 8 percent. These terms left excess demand for capital, but procedures for central allocation of investment gave further consideration to total profitability of the investment.[17]

In Poland, interest rates on government loans were also differentiated. The basic rate charged in the pilot firms was set at 8 percent, but terms of repayment could be deferred sometimes.[18]

Taxes on wages consisted of a social insurance charge on the base wage bill and also taxes on the portion of wages paid out of profits. Taxes on profits were differentiated according to the use of the profits. After payment of capital charges, firms in both countries had the right to set aside a certain portion of profits into a reserve fund which would be untaxed. The balance of profits could be divided between a development fund and a sharing fund. The development fund, together with that portion of the depreciation fund remaining in the firm, could be used for self-financed investment. The sharing fund could be used to expand wages and to pay management bonuses.

In Hungary, the government taxed the firm at a fixed 60 percent rate on its development fund and at rates varying between zero and 70 percent on expansion of the sharing fund. In fact, the tax rules differed depending on whether wage increases came from expansion of the wage bill or from the sharing fund.[19]

In Poland, the structure of wage and profits taxes was almost the same as in Hungary. There was a basic social insurance charge on the wage bill. The firm's development fund was taxed if it exceeded a given percentage of firm capital stock, and the fund for increasing wages was taxed at progressive rates ranging from 10 to 80 percent.

On net, the introduction of charges for capital and the expansion of bank loans repayable at positive interest rates provided the framework for a much more efficient exercise of ownership rights over capital stock. It presented the curious phenomenon of a socialist Treasury and National Bank acting as the supplier of investment capital to socialist firms and earning interest on the government loans, a development that was clearly in the market–socialist tradition. However, neither Poland nor Hungary went the next logical step to begin charging rent for agricultural land or natural resources. But such charges are so strongly implied by an efficient system that I would expect Hungary, at least, to introduce rental charges in the next few years.

In both countries, the share of turnover taxes was reduced, the share of profits taxes increased. This change shifted the tax burden away from agriculture and toward all consumers. And it also increased the liquidity of the firm.

Monopoly Elements

Many observers of Eastern Europe have raised the question of whether decentralization would generate monopoly results, since national markets are highly concentrated.[20] In Hungary, according to Balassa, some 40 percent of firms had no domestic competition, 48 percent had some, and only 12 percent had strong domestic competition.[21] Polish firms, too, tend to be horizontally integrated. With the conversion of industrial associations and expansion of pilot units planned to cover 40 percent of industry, Polish sectors look almost as concentrated as Hungarian industries.

I see the monopoly question somewhat differently. It seems to me that the issues raised by decentralization were: possible changes in the costs of enforcing existing monopoly, problems in the division of potential monopoly rents between the government and the enterprise, and, perhaps, changes in the margins on which monoply profits would be collected—rather than emergence of new monopoly power.

In the traditional centrally planned system, limitations on the output of consumer goods create what might be viewed as monopoly rents. And imposition of turnover taxes assures that the surplus will be centralized in the budget. In that system, the branch ministry is structured as a very efficient cartel. Once the desirable rate of output is determined, the industrial ministry allocates that output among enterprises. It controls materials allocations, wages, and investment. And it commissions new plants. Quite apart from the instructions given to firms, the ministry as a whole can increase its net rents by shifting production toward low-cost enterprises. (There would be an incentive to do this even in the case of an output-maximizing ministry, since it would have extra rents in its system to spend on the production of additional units of output whose costs exceeded their nominal prices.)

More work needs to be done on the maximizing behavior of a Soviet- or Polish-type branch ministry. At least in the consumer goods sectors, the amount of net rents earned in the sector is likely to be an important success indicator, since output-maximizing signals would put the whole pressure for securing central revenues on the resource constraints and enterprise prices imposed by the planners.

To the extent that decentralization in both Poland and Hungary increased the autonomy of the enterprise vis-à-vis the central ministry, the tight cartel structure of industry was slightly reduced. However, the shift from output to profit incentives would have created an incentive for firms to attempt to capture a portion of centralized profits from their operations. And there were obviously potential gains to both buyers and sellers if they could deal directly and evade government taxes altogether.

Much of the price rise in Hungary that was attributed to monopoly was merely a sympton of the repressed inflation that existed under central price control, leaving excess demand in numerous markets to be squeezed off by administrative allocation. Were the monopoly prices more costly to the economy that the former administrative allocations at controlled prices? Quite the contrary. To the extent that demanders spent real resources trying to get administrative allocations of goods that were worth more to them than their nominal prices under the lower price system, the higher prices after reform would eliminate the incentive for this kind of rent-dissipating activity. On the other hand, with several firms, the cost to them of enforcing cartel-like rules might well go up, since central planning appeared to be one of the least-cost ways of enforcing an industry cartel.

On net, it was true that both Poland and Hungary had concentration in industry that could generate monopoly pricing and profits. But such structures had always been inherent in ministry control. What was at issue was not whether monopoly pricing would occur, but how monopoly rents would be divided between firms and the central government. If they went to firms, then it was still not clear how they would be divided among workers, management, and the government as the nominal owner of capital.

PROPERTY RIGHTS FUNCTIONS

Exercise of Ownership

The problems of division of returns points up the whole problem of exercise of property rights over social assets under socialism. By ownership rights, I refer to the right to use or allocate among uses, to receive returns or benefits, to sell or transfer. And the benefits of ownership provide incentives to create and maintain assets. While the right to allocate resources among uses is partly delegated to firm managers in the decentralized system, the central planners still function as owners of the benefit streams.[22] Under the old-style central planning system, the efficiency costs of not making explicit charges for capital were high. In the absence of lobbying by ministries and firms, the planners might spend capital on low productivity uses. With lobbying, firms that enjoyed potentially high-productivity uses of capital had incentives to expend almost all of the potential rents to be gained from receiving an allocation of capital on real resources used in lobbying for such allocation.

Today, both Poland and Hungary provide capital charges, but they subsidize different industries by providing capital on differentiated terms. Such differentiation is likely to introduce distortion into factor proportions.

Failure by the central planners to charge for either agricultural land or natural resources provides incentives to decentralized users to substitute non-priced for priced inputs. If the central planners don't exercise ownership rights, then residual rights might accrue to the decentralized unit using the resources. But in the absence of capitalization of potential future revenues, decentralized units cannot profit from potential future revenues; they can only capture revenues from assets in the short run.

Profit-sharing arrangements between the enterprise employees and the state are intended to make managers more interested in the profitability of the state's assets. But, in the socialized context, such arrangements enforce the short-run bias just mentioned. In the absence of capital markets, the central planners have little information on the capitalized value of the firm and little basis on which to judge whether an increase in this year's profit is being earned at the expense of a large reduction in future profit.[23]

In fact, I think the problem of short-run bias is somewhat reduced by providing for the stable tenure of a management group in a single firm. This implicitly gives management some property rights in future returns of the firm.

The rights to create productive assets and to sell or transfer them are still largely centralized. In Poland, the establishment of new plants and allocation of large-scale investment are centrally determined. In Hungary, the extent of allocative control or veto power of the ministry over establishment of new plants and allocation of new investment has been a matter of some negotiation.

On net, decentralization resulted in the delegation of some of the allocative rights of ownership to decentralized managers. It increased the effective exercise of property rights in capital by the central planners. But it raised problems in the policing of property rights, and it left undecided who would get property rights to certain economic rents of the firm or whether, in the absence of effective ownership, such rents might be dissipated.

Income Differentiation

The question of capture of economic rents in enterprises was just one aspect of the issue of socialist income differentiation. Available data indicate that the range of relative wages by educational level is narrower in both Poland and Hungary than in the United States. A recent study by Marjory Searing finds a dispersion of wages going from 0.5 to 2.35 in the United States, of 0.931 to 1.511 in Hungary, and a range of 0.845 to 1.665 in Poland.[24] On the other hand, the structure of industry average wages in Eastern Europe is close to the structure in the West, and there is considerable evidence that, even under old-style planning, the competition of firms generated something like a marginal productivity wage structure.

So far, decentralization in Poland does not appear to have generated a large amount of wage differentiation, but in Hungary increased wage differentiation is occurring, particularly at management levels. In Hungary it is reasonable to expect that decentralized wage structures will approach marginal productivity structures so that wage disparities will reflect differences in human capital endowments. This raises the possibility of a considerable amount of inequality.

Income taxes are insignificant in both countries. Egalitarian measures take the form of subsidized provision of foodstuffs and a large role for collective consumption. Wage taxes that are levied are charged against enterprise wage bills, not the wages of individual workers. So there is presently no mechanism for a progressive income tax or any similar measure to reduce wage dispersion. Furthermore, to the extent that enterprise management begins to share in the economic rents of the enterprise, management incomes will have a non-labor component. (And without giving management a share of the benefits, it will be hard to induce risk-taking.) It seems to me that the income distribution effects of decentralization are likely to present the planners with unanticipated problems.

CONCLUDING REMARKS

Poland and Hungary represent two forms of decentralization that, at least in the short run, have been generally successful in yielding the results desired for their economies. The basic issue for both has been the desirable combination of plan and market, given the dual objectives of maintaining effective central control of economic policy and increasing the efficiency of producing units. It appears that, for these two countries, there are some trade-offs between these two goals.

Poland and Hungary differ in the extent to which economic units were freed to respond to market signals, with Hungary going much further toward market arrangements. The Hungarian case shows, however, that simply establishing market incentives does not necessarily result in efficient performance in economic units unless property rights in the firm's assets are fully exercised. The present socialist ownership arrangements are likely to provide for short-run and monopoly behavior and to generate income differentials that may reflect differential access to economic rents in the system.

To be successful, the decline in the regulatory functions of central planning will have to be accompanied by a substantial improvement in the fiscal and ownership functions of central planning.

NOTES

1. For an excellent discussion of this point, see Herbert S. Levine, "Pressure and Planning in the Soviet Economy," in *Industrialization in Two Systems: Essays in Honor of Alexander Gerschenkron,* ed. Henry Rosovsky (New York: John Wiley and Sons, Inc., 1966) pp. 266–85.

2. The Hungarian economist Márton Tardos has proposed separate organizations for exercising regulatory and ownership rights in socialist economies in "Problems of Economic Competition in Hungary" (mimeographed), translated by Tardos from a paper published in *Közgazdasági Szemle,* No. 7–8 (1972).

3. For purposes of discussion here, the crucial elements of a market allocation system will be the existence of market-clearing prices (except for

elements of tax or subsidy) and decentralized units that may adjust supply and demand offers freely in response to price and income signals. A planned system is one that constrains voluntary decentralized supply or demand responses of some economic units and substitutes administratively-determined signals and incentives for some market-determined ones. Decentralization of planning is accomplished by means of increased reliance on parameters for structuring pay-offs rather than reliance on detailed "addressed" instructions to individual actors. But, so long as the parameters differ from market signals, the system is still administrative.

J.M. Montias has presented a theoretical description of reform variants in "A Framework for Theoretical Analysis of Economic Reforms in Soviet-type Economies," in *Plan and Market: Economic Reform in Eastern Europe,* ed. Morris Bornstein (New Haven and London: Yale University Press, 1973), pp. 65–122.

4. Karol Szwarc, "One Year of the Pilot Units," *Polish Perspectives* 17, 7/8 (July/August 1974): 10–14.

5. Márton Tardos, "A Model of the Behavior of Central Agencies and Enterprises," *Acta Oeconomica* (Budapest), 4, 1 (January 1969): 19–35.

6. Leon Smolinski, "Planning Reforms in Poland," *Kyklos* 21, 3 (1968): 498–511.

7. Stanislaw Chelstowski, "New Steps to Efficiency," *Polish Perspectives* 16, 3 (March 1973):1–6; Szwarc, "One Year of the Pilot Units."

8. Bela Balassa, "The Firm in the New Economic Mechanism in Hungary," in *Plan and Market: Economic Reform in Eastern Europe,* ed. Morris Bornstein, pp. 347–73.

9. Chelstowski, "New Steps to Efficiency."

10. For good descriptions of the planning process, see Herbert S. Levine, "The Centralized Planning of Supply in Soviet Industry," U.S. Congress, Joint Economic Committee, *Comparisons of the United States and Soviet Economies* (Washington, D.C.: U.S. Government Printing Office, 1959), Part I, pp. 151–76; J.M. Montias, "Planning with Material Balances in Soviet-type Economies," *American Economic Review* 49, 5 (December 1959):963–85; and, for a formal model, Michael Manove, "A Model of Soviet-type Economic Planning," *American Economic Review* 61, 3 (June 1971), Part 1: 390–406.

11. Manove, "A Model of Soviet-type Economic Planning."

12. Edward Lipinski, "Thoughts About the Future," *Polish Perspectives* 16, 4 (April 1973): 8.

13. For example, see L. Halabuk, "Otsenka i struktura vtoroi ekono-metricheskoi modeli Vengrii" [Estimation and Structure of the Second Econometric Model of Hungary], *Ekonomika i matematicheskie metody,* No. 1 (1972): 28–43.

14. This discussion is reproduced in *Planovoe khoziaistvo,* No. 10 (1973): 152–57, and abstracted in the *Current Digest of the Soviet Press* 25, 47 (December 19, 1973): 1–4.

15. Translation from the *Current Digest* abstract of the discussion.

16. In fact, a recent model shows that, in certain cases, monopoly pricing of

consumer goods can yield the planners a greater surplus than monopsony pricing of inputs. Judith Thornton and Donn L. Leber, "On the Maximizing Behavior of a Monopoly Planner," *Economics of Planning* 10, 3 (1970): 159–69.

17. Balassa, "The Firm in the New Economic Mechanism in Hungary," pp. 361–63.

18. Szwarc, "One Year of the Pilot Units," p. 13.

19. Balassa, "The Firm in the New Economic Mechanism in Hungary," p. 353.

20. For example, Tardos, "Problems of Economic Competition in Hungary," p. 35.

21. Balassa, "The Firm in the New Economic Mechanism for Hungary," p. 357.

22. A discussion of these aspects of property rights is presented in Judith Thornton, "Resources and Property Rights in the Soviet Union," in *Soviet Resource Management and the Environment,* ed. W.A. Douglas Jackson (New York: Praeger, forthcoming).

23. This point is developed by Márton Tardos in "Problems of the Reform of the Economic Mechanism in Hungary" (Working Paper; Budapest: Institute for Economic and Market Research, 1973).

24. Marjory E. Searing, "Education and Economic Growth: the Postwar Experience in Hungary and Poland," in U.S. Congress, Joint Economic Committee, *Reorientation and Commercial Relations of the Economies of Eastern Europe* (Washington, D.C.: U.S. Government Printing Office, 1974), pp. 491, 495.

Index

aggregation: and interdependencies, 132; possibilities, 238; and production, 129
agriculture: and central planning, 242; and collectivization, 272
Augustinovics, M.: in Bornstein, 17
autonomy: concept of, in Augustinovics, 127

bargaining: and interest groups, 11; Polish pilot units, 313; and strategic planning in Korbonski, 63
Belik, Yu. A., 316
bureaucracy, 57; and limited information, 111

centralization: government interference, 90; of surplus product, 304
CFDT (Confederation Française Democratique du Travail), 168
CFTC (Confederation Française des Travailleurs Chrétiens), 168
CGT (Confederation Générale du Travail), 167
China: agricultural system, 55; Mao, 57
CMEA (Council for Mutual Economic Assistance), 289
CNPF (Conseil National du Patronat Français), 167
communism: government systems and market, 54; as used by Lindblom, 28
competition: and cartels in Japan, 213, 214; in France's Sixth Plan, 173
consistency: concept of, 77
consumption: and accumulation, 304; and "fixed" points, 131; and resources in Radner, 96; and social welfare goals, 249; and state valuation function, 100

convergence: and approximate iteration, 134; uncertainty and planning, 94
corporations: management and growth, 223; multinational and cooperation, 244; planning, methodology in Korbonski, 64; planning strategy, 48; private firms in Japan, 202
Czechoslovakia, 123

decentralization: autonomy and cartel structure, 319; economy and activity levels, 97; and equilibrium, 307; and flexible decisionmaking, 15; in Hungary and Poland, reviewed by Thornton, 312; information flow, 107; in Lindblom, 30; Plan implementation in France, 165; and planning process in Bornstein, 7; Portes on Radner, 121; and social interaction, 58
decisionmaking: and certainty-equivalent problem, 104, 105; and communist planners, 54; decentralization, 180; government intervention in France, 165; hierarchic authority structure in Poland, 240; information and policy, 97; iterative, 135; and industrial policies, 208; and optimal allocation, 94; and perspective studies, 77; and plan coordination, 147; and planning process, in Bornstein, 7; role of, in Hook, 91
deGaulle, Charles, 155, 156
D'Estaing, Valéry Giscard, 159
democracy: as conceived by Lindblom, 29; and Komiya view of economic institutions, 205; and strategic planning, 47
Durkheim, E., 38

EEC (European Economic Community):

goals, 252, 253; investment, 318, 319;
central planning, 262; concept of microstructure, 239; short-term plans, 254, 255;
trends, 19
policy: aim of five-year plan in Hungary,
290; central planning and management
in Hungary, 277; certainty-equivalent,
106; central planning and international
projects, 243; France's Fifth Plan, 157;
Japan's plan targets, 196; —making in
China and USSR, 56; —making in Lindblom, 23; optimal and price system, 101;
optimal and state valuation function,
100; and optimization models, 112; vs.
plan in Bornstein, 2; planning machinery
in France, 166, 617; planned shipbuilding,
216; and preference guided society, 31;
regional in Kirschen, 185; as sequence of
decision functions, 97; social interaction
and civil liberties, 36; wages, 35
politics: democratic and market quality, 49;
inclusion in plan coordination, 147;
leadership and elite, 38; nature of
and decisionmaking, 132; participation in
Lindblom, 29; and strategic planning, 46
PPBS (planning-program-budgeting System),
47; French version, 162
price: flexibility and probabilistic forecast,
103; formation and regulation in Hungary,
281–283; in France's Fifth Plan, 159; as
information signals, 108; projections and
sector analysis in France, 161; signals and
allocation decisions, 109
problem-solving: and social organization, 32
production: and activity analysis model, 96;
additive consistency approach, 129; capacity and excessive competition, 214;
expansion and regulation, 281; "fixed"
points, 131; multinational corporation,
175, 179; and price reform in Hungary,
283; and price signalling procedure, 108;
and resource allocation, 54
profits: enterprise and growth, 292; and
enterprise income regulation, 285
property rights, 320
protectionism: agricultural, in Japan, 197
public services, 80

rate of interest: and shadow prices, 102
reform: evaluation in Hungary, 305, 306
REGINA, 162
regionalization: defined by Hook, 84
resource allocation: as definition of economics, 57; and efficiency, 43; and
equilibrium price problems, 108; flexibility, 11; and growth, 81; by market
system determination, 30; Portes on

Radner, 119; primary balances, 301; and
uncertainty in Radner, 94

Sartori, G., 61
Schultze, Charles, 47
Searling, M., 321
shadow prices, 98; calculation, 104; and
optimal policy, 102; Portes on Radner,
120; theory of, 101
Shonfield, Andrew, 159
Simon, H.A.: in Lindblom, 26; in Portes,
123; in Radner, 95
social change: in Lindblom, 25
social disequilibrium: in Trzeciakowski, 233
social indicator, 80
social interaction: components, 39; conciliation in France, 168; Dernberger on
Komiya, 230; in East and West, 19; and
corporate interpretation and strategy, 51;
and preference guided society, 30; as
problem-solving device, 10; and problem-
solving strategy, 35; and strategic planning,
45
social objectives: France's Fourth Plan,
156; households and socialized sectors in
Poland, 240; inclusion in plan corrdina-
tion, 147; interdependency and consistency, 135; Kirschen on Franch Plans,
187; reform in Hungary, 307; and
taxes, 318; —welfare function and policy,
98
social organization: concept of elite in
Lindblom, 27; methodology, 40
specialization: and regions, 251
Ståhl, I. and Ysander, B.C., 76
STAR, 162
state valuation function: concept of, 99,
100; Portes on Radner, 120
strategy: corporate and goal identification,
50; five-year assessment, 76; French Plan
implementation, 164; and interdependencies, 136
Sweden: disaggregation, 83; nature of
target-setting, 91; productivity, 81

Tanaka, K., 197, 226
taxes: Hungary and Poland, 317, 318;
and income redistribution, 85
technology: information processing and
planning strategy, 113; innovation, 239;
and international comparisons, 299; and
market systems, 54; of planning, 256,
257
Theil, H., 106
time horizon: and convergence problems,
98; defined by Bornstein, 12; and five-
year planning limitation, 77; French

About the Contributors

Morris Bornstein is Professor of Economics at the University of Michigan, where he has also served as Director of the Comparative Economics Program and of the Center for Russian and East European Studies. He received his Ph.D. in Economics at the University of Michigan in 1952 and was an economist for several U.S. government agencies before joining the University of Michigan faculty in 1958. He has also held visiting research appointments at the Russian Research Center, Harvard University, and the Hoover Institution, Stanford University. His books include *The Soviet Economy* (with Daniel R. Fusfeld; fourth edition, Irwin, 1974); *Comparative Economic Systems* (third edition, Irwin, 1974; and Italian and Spanish translations); and *Plan and Market; Economic Reform in Eastern Europe* (Yale University Press, 1973). He has contributed chapters to a number of collective volumes, including *Comparisons of the United States and Soviet Economies* (U.S. Congress, Joint Economic Committee; U.S. Government Printing Office, 1959); *National Security: Political, Military, and Economic Strategies in the Decade Ahead* (ed. David M. Abshire and Richard V. Allen; Praeger, 1963); *New Directions in the Soviet Economy* (U.S. Congress, Joint Economic Committee; U.S. Government Printing Office, 1966); *Disarmament and World Economic Interdependence* (ed. Emile Benoit; Columbia University Press, 1967); *Comparison of Economic Systems: Theoretical and Methodological Approaches* (ed. Alexander Eckstein; University of California Press, 1971); and *Soviet Economic Statistics* (ed. Vladimir G. Treml and John P. Hardt; Duke University Press, 1972). His articles have appeared in the *American Economic Review, Quarterly Journal of Economics, Review of Economics and Statistics, Soviet Studies,* and other journals.

Mária Augustinovics is head of the Division of Mathematical Methods in the Long-Term Planning Department of the Hungarian National Planning Office. Her research fields include mathematical modeling of the economy, input-output matrices, money flows, and foreign trade. Her articles have been published in the

major Hungarian economic journals, the proceedings of several international
conferences on input-output techniques, research studies of the United Nations
Economic Commission for Europe, and *Economics of Planning* and other
Western European economic journals.

Robert F. Dernberger, Professor of Economics at the University of Michigan,
is an authority on the Chinese economy. His articles have appeared in *Asian
Survey* and other journals, and he has contributed chapters to a number of joint
volumes, including *Economic Nationalism in Old and New States* (ed. Harry
Johnson; University of Chicago Press, 1967); *International Trade and Central
Planning* (ed. Alan A. Brown and Egon Neuberger; University of California Press,
1968); *China Trade Prospects and United States Policy* (ed. Alexander Eckstein;
Praeger, 1971); and *China's Modern Economy in Historical Perspective* (ed.
Dwight Perkins; Stanford University Press, 1975).

Erik Höök is Director of the Secretariat for Economic Planning in the
Swedish Ministry of Finance and has represented Sweden at meetings of the
Organization for Economic Cooperation and Development, the United Nations
Economic Commission for Europe, and other regional and international
agencies. He is the author of many government reports and played a major role
in the preparation of *The Swedish Economy 1971–1975 and the General
Outlook up to 1990* (Swedish Government Publishing House, 1971).

E.S. Kirschen is a Professor and Director of the Department of Applied
Economics at the Free University of Brussels. He has written widely on
comparative economic policies, European integration, and international trade.
Among his publications are *Economic Policy in Our Time* (3 vols.; Rand
McNally, 1964); *Financial Integration in Western Europe* (with Henry Simon
Bloch and William Bruce Bassett; Columbia University Press, 1969); *Megistos: A
World Income and Trade Model for 1975* (with C. Duprez; North-Holland,1970);
and *Economic Policies Compared, West and East* (North-Holland, Vol. 1, 1974;
Vol. 2, 1975).

Ryutaro Komiya is Professor of Economics at the University of Tokyo. In
addition to many publications in Japanese, his research has appeared in *Postwar
Economic Growth in Japan* (University of California Press, 1966); *Foreign Tax
Policies and Economic Growth* (National Bureau of Economic Research, 1966);
Direct Foreign Investment in Asia and the Pacific (ed. Peter Drysdale; Australian
National University Press, 1972); and *Toward a New World Trade Policy* (ed.
C. Fred Bergsten; D.C. Heath and Co., 1975).

Andrzej Korbonski, Professor of Political Science at the University of
California, Los Angeles, is an authority on the politics and international relations
of Eastern Europe. He is the author of *Politics of Socialist Agriculture in Poland,
1945–1960* (Columbia University Press, 1965); contributions to collective
volumes, including *International Political Communities* (Doubleday, 1966),
Soviet and East European Agriculture (ed. J.F. Karcz; University of California
Press, 1967), and *Regional Integration* (ed. Leon Lindberg and Stuart Schein-

gold; Harvard University Press, 1971); and articles in *Slavic Review, Problems of Communism, Comparative Politics,* and other journals.

Charles E. Lindblom is Professor of Economics and Political Science and Director of the Institution for Social and Policy Studies at Yale University. His research has emphasized social decisionmaking processes. especially those affecting economic policy. His principal publications include *Unions and Capitalism* (Yale University Press, 1949); *Politics, Economics and Welfare* (with Robert A. Dahl; Harper, 1953); *A Strategy of Decision: Policy Evaluation as a Social Process* (with David Braybrooke; Free Press, 1963); *The Intelligence of Democracy; Decision Making Through Mutual Adjustment* (Free Press, 1965); and *The Policy-Making Process* (Prentice-Hall, 1968).

Michael Manove is Professor of Economics at Boston University. His articles on the theory of economic planning in centrally administered economies have appeared in the *American Economic Review, Econometrica,* and *Review of Economic Studies.*

Tamás Morva is Director of the Research Institute of the Hungarian National Planning Office. At the time his contribution to this volume was written, he was Deputy Director of the Projections and Programming Division of the United Nations Economic Commission for Europe. His research on the theory and practice of economic planning in Hungary has appeared in leading Hungarian journals and in United Nations studies.

Richard Portes is Professor of Economics at Birkbeck College, University of London. His articles on enterprise management and labor markets under central planning and on economic reform in Hungary have been published in the *Review of Economic Studies, Oxford Economic Papers, American Economic Review,* and *Soviet Studies.* He is coeditor (with Michael Kaser) of *Planning and Market Relations* (Macmillan, 1971).

Krzysztof Porwit is Director of the Research Institute of the Polish Planning Commission and a Professor at the Central School of Planning and Statistics in Warsaw. He has written widely on various facets of the theory and practice of economic planning. In addition to many studies in Polish, he is the author of *Central Planning: Evaluation of Variants* (Pergamon Press, 1966); "Perspective Planning in Poland: Basic Issues and Experiences," *Journal of Development Planning* (1971); and "Techniques of Interregional Plan Formulation in Poland," in *Issues in Regional Planning* (ed. David M. Dunham and Jos. G.M. Hilhorst; Mouton, 1971).

Roy Radner is Professor of Economics and Statistics at the University of California, Berkeley, and a leading contributor to the literature on mathematical planning models and decision theory. His publications include *Optimal Replacement Policy* (with D.W. Jorgenson and J.J. McCall; North-Holland, 1967); *Economic Theory of Teams* (with Jakob Marschak; Yale University Press, 1972); *Decision and Organization* (coeditor with C.B. McGuire; North-Holland, 1972); and articles in *Econometrica, Review of Economic Studies, Journal of Economic*

Theory, International Economic Review, Management Science, and other journals.

Claude Seibel is Chief of the Economic and Statistical Information Service of the French National Ministry of Education. At the time he prepared his chapter in this volume, he was Chief of the Programming Division of the French National Institute of Statistics and Economic Studies, where he played a major role in developing models integrating the physical and financial aspects of French national plans. Among his publications are *La planification française en pratique,* (coauthor under the collective pseudonym Atreize; Editions ouvrières, 1971); and *Le Modèle FIFI* (with Michel Aglietta and Raymond Courbis; Collections de l'INSEE, 1973).

Per Sevaldson is Senior Research Officer at the Norwegian Central Bureau of Statistics, where he has worked on the development of economic planning models for Norway. In addition to his publications in Norwegian, his studies include "An Interindustry Model of Production and Consumption for Economic Planning in Norway," in *Income and Wealth,* Series X (International Association for Research in Income and Wealth; Bowes & Bowes, 1964), and contributions to *Macro-Economic Models for Planning and Policy-Making* (United Nations Economic Commission for Europe, 1967); and *Planning and Markets: Modern Trends in Various Economic Systems* (ed. John T. Dunlop and Nikolay P. Fedorenko; McGraw-Hill, 1969).

Judith A. Thornton, Professor of Economics at the University of Washington, is the author of a number of studies on Soviet economic growth and factor productivity, and on planning models for centrally administered economies. Her articles have appeared in the *American Economic Review, Journal of Political Economy, Journal of Economic History, Economics of Planning,* and *Slavic Review.*

Witold Trzeciakowski is Deputy Director of the Research Institute of the Polish Ministry of Foreign Trade, where his research has emphasized theoretical and empirical analysis of the use of optimization methods in planning foreign trade. In addition to many studies published in Polish, he has contributed to *Economic Planning in Europe* (United Nations Economic Commission for Europe, 1965), *Multi-Level Planning and Decision-Making* (United Nations Economic Commission for Europe, 1970), *Jahrbuch der Wirtschaft Osteuropas/ Yearbook of East European Economics, Regional Science Association Papers,* and *Revue de l'Est.*